Praise for

The Re-Set Process: Trauma-Informed Behavior Strategies

The Re-Set Process provides a clear and concise how-to guide for teachers and administrators seeking trauma-sensitive, practical ways to work with students demonstrating challenging behaviors. Dyane brings her extensive real-life experiences and expertise to this resource, sharing her highly effective strategies with educators, mental health professionals, parents, and others seeking to implement proactive methods to positively impact the lives of children.

—Jill Koser, Ph.D., Director of Curriculum and Instruction
School District of the City of York, PA

If you care at all about kids in classrooms, you'll want to know more about The Re-Set Process and how it can help with even the most challenging students. Authors Carrere and Kinder have created a powerful model based on trauma-informed practices that should be on every educators' bookshelf.

—Pamela McCartney, M.S., School Psychologist, Assistant Executive Director
Lancaster-Lebanon Intermediate Unit, PA

The Re-Set Process provides the tools that teachers are constantly seeking to move from behaviour management to learner engagement and resilience. Proactive and reactive templates mindfully guide teachers' responses. The programme integrates rather than adds to the teacher's day and can be used in an individual classroom or an entire school. Target audiences mentioned are teachers, school administrators and professional development coordinators, but this text is a significant breakthrough for teacher trainers working in colleges and universities around the world supporting the development of the next generation of teachers.

—Ross Bernay, Ed.D., Deputy Head of School
Auckland University of Technology, University of Auckland, New Zealand

With this text, educators can quickly implement meaningful and impactful strategies by the end of each chapter! Congruent with Dyane's approach to coaching school teams, the processes and recommendations outlined in *The Re-Set Process: Trauma-Informed Behavior Strategies* are based on lived interactions and experiences from Dyane's deep background in positive and proactive behavior support. Wynne's mindfulness lens enhances this work even further. As a school and district leader, I have utilized many of the strategies outlined in this book with a high degree of student success.

—Josiah Keene, PhD., Assistant Superintendent
Annville-Cleona School District, PA

Underlying many deficits in academic learning and prosocial school behavior is a lack of ability to self-regulate, which is foundational for progress in academics, in friendships, and overall, in school and life. Self-regulation is best taught and practiced through healthy relationship-building. The Re-Set Process offers a step-by-step behavioral guide to give students this essential tool of self-regulation, leading to success in school and beyond. I love this work.

—Lark Eshelman, Ph.D., M.S., M.L.S., Educator, Author, School Psychologist
Eshleman Mental Health Consulting, Mt Joy, PA

The Re-Set Process: Trauma Informed Behavior Strategies is one of the most comprehensive approaches to teaching a struggling student the skills for self-management. This will not only change his/her behavior but decrease the disruptions in the classroom environment, maximizing learning for all students.

—Melinda Wells, M.S., School Principal
Martin Luther King Jr. Elementary School, School District of Lancaster, PA

Implementing The Re-Set Process and associated practices have been game-changers for many of our students with trauma. Because of that success, implementation is expanding throughout our district. This book provides extensive classroom and school-friendly strategies that have proven to de-escalate and re-regulate students while maintaining an environment that maximizes learning. Dyane's consultations have moved us forward by providing strategies that balance the needs of students with the needs of staff and now this book makes her process and knowledge available to a much wider audience.

—**Angela Marley, M.Ed.,** School Principal
Denver Elementary School, Cocalico School District, PA

The Re-Set Process has changed our school into a place where our highly reactive students feel more academically successful and positive about school. It gives them a chance to use adults as advocates, practice self-reliance, and feel happy about the school environment as a supportive place to learn.

—**Florence B. Krane, Ph.D.,** School Principal
Price Elementary School, School District of Lancaster, PA

The Re-Set Process

The Re-Set Process
Trauma-Informed Behavior Strategies

by

Dyane Lewis Carrere, M.Ed.
Dyane Carrere Consulting, LLC
Southampton, MA

with

Wynne Kinder, M.Ed.
Wellness Works in Schools
Wrightsville, PA

Baltimore • London • Sydney

Paul H. Brookes Publishing Co.
Post Office Box 10624
Baltimore, Maryland 21285-0624
USA

www.brookespublishing.com

Typeset by Progressive Publishing Services, Inc., York, Pennsylvania.
Manufactured in the United States of America by Sheridan Books, Inc., Chelsea, Michigan.

The individuals described in this book are composites or real people whose situations are masked and are based on the authors' experiences. In all instances, names and identifying details have been changed to protect confidentiality.

The information provided in this book is in no way meant to substitute for a mental health practitioner's advice or expert opinion. Readers should consult a mental health professional, school counselor, or school psychologist for more information. This book is sold without warranties of any kind, express or implied, and the publisher and authors disclaim any liability, loss, or damage caused by the contents of this book.

Library of Congress Cataloging-in-Publication Data

Names: Carrere, Dyane Lewis, author. | Kinder, Wynne, author.
Title: The re-set process: trauma-informed behavior strategies /
    by Dyane Lewis Carrere with Wynne Kinder.
Description: Baltimore: Paul H. Brookes Publishing Co., [2020] |
    Includes bibliographical references and index.
Identifiers: LCCN 2020017062 (print) | LCCN 2020017063 (ebook) |
    ISBN 9781681254197 (paperback) | ISBN 9781681254203 (epub) |
    ISBN 9781681254210 (pdf)
Subjects: LCSH: Behavior modification. | School psychology. | Psychic
    trauma in children. | Child psychology. | Classroom environment.
Classification: LCC LB1060.2 .C365 2021 (print) | LCC LB1060.2 (ebook) |
    DDC 370.15/28—dc23
LC record available at https://lccn.loc.gov/2020017062
LC ebook record available at https://lccn.loc.gov/2020017063

British Library Cataloguing in Publication data are available from the British Library.

2024   2023   2022   2021   2020

10   9   8   7   6   5   4   3   2   1

Contents

About the Online Companion Materials

The Re-Set Process: Trauma-Informed Behavior Strategies offers online companion materials to supplement and expand the knowledge and strategies provided in this text. All purchasers of the book may access, download, and print these resources, which are divided into three sections that correspond to their location in the print book.

Resources in the print book that are available for download have a ⬇ listed in the Table of Contents. A complete list of resources that are available online—including blank templates that do not appear in the print book—appears below. The resources are as follows:

Book Study Guide (online only)

Section I

    Section I Resources   Glossary

Section II

    Re-Set Process: Proactive Forms (Figure 3.2)

    Re-Set Process: Reactive Forms (Figure 3.3)

    At-a-Glance: Proactive Whole-Class Re-Set (Figure 4.2)

    At-a-Glance: Proactive Student-Choice Re-Set (Figure 4.3)

    At-a-Glance: Proactive Individual Re-Set (Figure 4.4)

    At-a-Glance: Proactive Re-Set Room (Figure 4.5)

    At-a-Glance: Reactive In-Class Re-Set (Figure 5.1)

    At-a-Glance: Reactive Alternate Classroom Re-Set (Figure 5.2)

    At-a-Glance: Reactive Hallway Re-Set (Figure 5.3)

    At-a-Glance: Reactive Re-Set Room (Figure 5.4)

    Processing Plan for Primary Students (blank template of Figure 6.1)

    Processing Plan for Intermediate Students (blank template of Figure 6.2)

    Agenda for Re-Set Room Meetings (Figure 7.1)

    Section II Resources   Appendix A: Re-Set Activities Organized by Step

                           Appendix B: Scripts for Regulating Activities

                           Appendix C: Fiddle Objects and Marble Maze Directions

Section III

    Help Flip Sign (blank template of Figure 8.1)

    Basic Regulation Plan (blank template of Figure 9.5)

    Intermediate Regulation Plan (blank template, online only)

    Advanced Regulation Plan (blank template, online only)

    HELPS Self-Care Plan (Figure 11.1)

Section III Resources   Appendix A: Team Collaboration Survey

Appendix B: Seating Positions

Appendix C: Spotlight Strategies: Simple Ways to Create Predictability

Appendix D: Spotlight Strategies: Simple Ways to Protect Emotional Safety

Appendix E: Spotlight Strategies: Simple Ways for Nurturing Adult-to-Student Relationships

Appendix F: Spotlight Strategies: Simple Ways for Nurturing Student-to-Student Relationships

Appendix G: Cooperative Learning Structures

Appendix H: Modulation Exercises

Appendix I: Behavior Management Systems: Risk Assessment

Appendix J: Ticket and Pocket System

Appendix K: Playing Card Reinforcement System: Delivering Specific Positive Feedback to Students

To access the materials that come with this book

1. Go to the Brookes Publishing Download Hub: https://downloads.brookespublishing.com

2. Register to create an account or log in with an existing account.

3. Filter or search for the book title *The Re-Set Process: Trauma-Informed Behavior Strategies.*

About the Authors

Dyane Lewis Carrere, M.Ed., Author and Educational Consultant, Trauma Informed School Practices,Owner, Dyane Carrere Consulting, LLC, Southampton, MA 01073

Spanning more than 40 years, Dyane's career in education has taken many forms—teacher, administrator, adjunct faculty member, consultant, and staff developer. Throughout this time, her work has concentrated on supporting students whose struggles have placed them at the fringes of school success.

Dyane has worked in preschool through secondary settings, as well as with families and service agencies, focusing on developing compassionate, creative, effective behavior supports. She has both taught and been a guest speaker at the college level, bringing her lens on behavior to pre-service educators and Masters-level educators.

During the last 15 years of her career, Dyane has focused on supporting schools in understanding trauma and developing practices that support students with trauma histories. She has shared this work with others through local, state, and national forums.

Dyane believes that the educators and students whom she has had the opportunity to learn from and with have been the greatest gifts of her professional life. They have profoundly informed her work through their insights, their intentions, their feedback, and their stories.

Wynne Kinder, M.Ed., Educator and Author, Wellness Works in Schools, Wrightsville, PA 17368

Wynne's teaching career spans 30 years in public and private schools and includes 15 years of bringing mindfulness and trauma-informed strategies into regular, special, and alternative education classrooms (K–12). Her teaching, curricula, and program, Wellness Works in Schools, has reached thousands of teachers and their students. Wynne's training and teaching tools address and integrate mindful awareness, attention, self-care, re-regulation, trauma in the classroom, healthy connections, social emotional skills, and behavior guidance. She teaches two graduate courses at Eastern Mennonite University: Trauma, Restoration, & Resilience in Educational Environments and Self-Care for Teachers.

Foreword

The Re-Set Process: Trauma Informed Behavior Strategies

Nineteen years ago, my husband and I found our son in a Bulgarian orphanage when he was 3 years old. That meeting set me on a journey that has profoundly shaped my life. While going through the long process of bringing my son home, I was working as an assistant principal in an elementary school and, prior to that, as a special education teacher in Grades 2–12. In these roles I was continuously presented with students who were struggling and for whom typical strategies were ineffective. And so, my personal journey to understand and support my son and my professional life supporting students became inextricably woven together. In the ensuing years, I earned my doctorate in developmental trauma in schools, conducted research, and wrote books on trauma-informed practices in schools.

As my child grew and moved through school and my career shifted to directing special education, the need for trauma-informed approaches became even more evident. My work in the field led me to the realization that children who have experienced early childhood trauma need unique care and support in our schools—support that has its roots in traumatology theory, which had not yet found its way into practice.

Imagine that our schools are simple ecosystems. Some organisms thrive in such ecosystems: The environment suits their needs, yet others do not. Their needs are not the same. We now know that schools can no longer function as simple ecosystems: They must be broader and more complex so that students with an ever-widening set of needs are able to thrive alongside their peers. As it happens, a trauma-informed approach (i.e., a more complex ecosystem) supports a vastly larger group of students.

Transitioning to a trauma-informed approach requires a paradigm shift—a new way of seeing and understanding students. As the authors of this book note, a trauma-informed approach requires a trauma-informed lens. Educators must be compassionate and curious. Rather than asking *What's wrong with you?* they wonder *What's happened to you?* They must assume that student misbehavior is an issue of *cannot* rather than *will not*. These changes allow adults to help children with developmental trauma improve how their brains function and strengthen their attachments. Fortunately, The Re-Set Process provides many of the tools needed to guide educators in making this much-needed shift.

I had the opportunity to review the manuscript for *The Re-Set Process: Trauma-Informed Behavior Strategies* during its development. Its message immediately resonated with my own understanding of the needs of students with trauma, and the intersection of my work with Dyane and Wynne's work was evident. Applying a trauma-informed lens to the world of behavior has been an essential focus for me as a special education administrator guiding trauma-informed behavior assessment and intervention. This book does exactly that. After reading the manuscript, I invited the authors to present at the Attachment and Trauma Network's annual conference in Atlanta in 2020. It was obvious from both the sold out registration for Dyane's two sessions and the feedback afterwards that the concept of the Re-Set Process resonated with practitioners. The process offers much-needed direction for those seeking practical, specific guidance regarding challenging behavior.

I'm happy to write that traumatology research has finally made its way into mainstream educational practice. There are now many books that address the impact of trauma on child development, trauma-informed classroom strategies, and creating trauma-sensitive schools. There are no books, however, written to expressly explain the shift from traditional behavior approaches to a trauma-informed behavior response. Until now! *The Re-Set Process* provides cohesive, clear, and detailed guidance on a process that will significantly change the interaction patterns between students with trauma histories and their educators. The authors teach readers about trauma as well as the process itself. Importantly, the Re-Set Process is uniquely designed to heal the impact of trauma rather than simply seeking to extinguish problematic behaviors. It provides key strategies for social–emotional learning (SEL) and can be a companion to any existing SEL programs.

As both a parent of a child with trauma and an educator, I love that regulation considerations are paired with attachment considerations without one being more important than the other—something that is essential as we seek to be truly trauma-informed educators. Readers will find that this resource is rich with specific examples of language and activities that support educators in meeting these two critical needs.

I have no doubt that readers will find that the Re-Set Process contains both familiar and unique methodologies. What's magical is the way the elements are organized and explained. On a very practical level and as a school administrator, I value that every step of the process is presented with an eye towards implementation. Intervention can truly be a seamless team effort—many adults will be empowered to provide the necessary guidance (both regulatory and relational) that students need. The accompanying Study Guide is an excellent, reflective resource that I myself will use with school teams in implementing the Re-Set Process.

It is clear that the importance of this work has been magnified by the times in which it is being published. The COVID-19 pandemic and ensuing quarantines, as well as the critical calls for racial justice, have invited to us to look deeper inside ourselves, to better understand who we are and who we want to be, and how to improve our support for all students in our circle of influence. The process and practices in this book are designed to foster a culture of compassion, inclusion, competence, and hope.

Please remember to take care of yourself while doing this important work (hint: see Chapter 11 for self-care strategies). With your own oxygen masks on, you'll be empowered to create schools and classrooms where all of our children feel at home and learn the skills they need to become healthy, well-adjusted adults.

Melissa W. Sadin, Ed.D., M.A.T., M.Ed.

School Board Member and Director of Special Education, Somerville Public School District, Somerville, NJ

Executive Director, Ducks and Lions: Trauma Sensitive Resources, www.traumasensitive.com

Program Director, Attachment & Trauma Network, North Dartmouth, MA

Preface

For me, new practices often are born of experience with a child. Once my mind is tilted off its axis by that experience, I am compelled to dive into research, which then informs the design of supports. The origins of the Re-Set Process are in one such experience 15 years ago.

The student I was observing responded to his teacher's directive to *take a time-out* by rolling around on the floor, crawling to the time-out chair, and then proceeding to kick anything within the stretch of his legs. He sprawled in the chair, his limbs at odd angles, toes tightly pointed, hands in fists, head banging against the nearby wall. His physicality was accompanied by moans, mumbled curses, and self-deprecating statements. His face was contorted, reflecting anger, sorrow, and embarrassment. After a solid 30 minutes, he fell quiet and was invited to rejoin the class. All I could think was, *There has got to be a better option for students and their teachers.*

My readings had led me to see the connection between behavior and the presence of high levels of adrenaline in the body and cortisol in the brain. Change the chemicals and change the behavior? I asked his teacher, *What about switching from a time-out chair to a time-out square— a defined space in which the student could move while regaining self-control?* Being able to move could burn off those action chemicals in a more constructive and healthy way. After all, that was what the boy's body was doing, in its own way! I suggested a few ideas for activities to try once the student was in the square. A week later, I received an encouraging email that said, "It's working!" Students settled more quickly when given the option of the time-out square. This dedicated teacher, armed with a bit of information and a suggestion for a slight shift in practice, had implemented the very first—albeit simple—version of the Re-Set Process.

I dove deeper into the neuroscience of trauma. I wondered what else we could learn from research about how to support children who struggle. Specifically, how does the body—and the brain—go from highly agitated to settled? What facilitates that process? How do we develop calming pathways in a student's brain? How does the experience of trauma shape a child's physiological and psychological systems, and what does that mean for our practices? The steps in the Re-Set Process began to emerge.

As I talked with colleagues about this concept, there was intrigue around what it could mean for the most troubled students. A thoughtful middle school educator asked, *What if we could do this instead of sending students to the office or to a disciplinary space? What if we could get them back in class faster and ready to learn again sooner?* And the Re-Set Room was born. Initially, we called it the PRIDE room: Physical exercise, Rest and re-regulate, Intellectual activity, Develop a plan, and Exit. The school selected and sent higher-need students there when they manifested significant difficulties in the classroom. Students responded well to the process and we began to see both expected and unexpected positive outcomes.

Many questions emerged, and answers were found as my research continued both in the laboratory—our PRIDE room—and in the pages of books by experts such as Dr. Bruce Perry, Robin Karr-Morse, and Dr. Bessel van der Kolk. As an increasing number of schools began to set up spaces like the PRIDE room, we learned more through the implementation process. Together with in-the-field partners, I began to develop a proactive version of the room to prevent challenging behavior from occurring, and further refined the reactive forms of the process to better handle challenging behavior in the moment.

I then noticed that some elementary students who were escalated needed a brief amount of time to feel safe prior to being asked to engage in physical activity, which is Step 1. So, I added Cocoon, or Step 0. (*Note*: We now know that this option might be needed by students of any age.) I refined the process based on feedback, I added activities, and I developed more guidance regarding the structure—all in response to the trends I observed as the process was implemented. The phrase rooted in science and grown through practical experience emerged to describe the evolution of the process.

The buzz around the Re-Set Process increased because of its successes with some of the most fragile and challenging students. Teachers began to ask how they might adopt the concepts and apply them to situations that arose in their classrooms. School counselors explored their roles as they related to the process, and administrators asked how they might be able to apply the process when they intervened with escalated students. The vision of a Re-Set continuum grew, and I developed materials to be referenced by implementers.

The next step forward occurred when I was presenting on the fight or flight response and the process of helping settle a dysregulated system at a professional conference. A woman raised her hand and began to share her thoughts about the freeze response. I immediately thought, *I need to get to know her!* That woman was Wynne.

We had read much the same research, worked with many of the same schools, saw the same needs in students, but we had two different points of entry and two different sets of experiences with supporting educators and their students. Her work in schools bringing mindfulness into classrooms was broad—all ages and needs—and unique—an eclectic mix of awareness, attention, and personal skills. We began to intentionally connect to discuss how our work could be integrated.

Meanwhile, the educators with whom I was working began to ask that I write this book so they would have a go-to reference upon my retirement from public education. I knew that if I were to undertake such a project, I would want to collaborate with Wynne. It had become clear to me that the field of mindfulness, as practiced in the school setting by Wynne and her program Wellness Works in Schools, could positively contribute to the structure of the room and to the continuum at large. Wynne's understanding of nervous system activation within dysregulation had enhanced my own, and I wanted to continue to explore that.

My partnership with Wynne brought enhancements to the Re-Set Process such as the mirroring strategy for students who were in freeze. As the author of FLOW, Think About It, and Maximo content for GoNoodle (online movement and mindfulness-based videos), Wynne gave educators a set of go-to resources that we incorporated into the list of whole-class Re-Set activities.

Beyond her influence on elements of the Re-Set Process itself, Wynne kept me tuned in to the concept of self-care, which is reflected not only in the first and final chapter but throughout the text. She helped me consider how the state of an educator's nervous system could affect their ability to guide a child through the Re-Set Process and how implementation of the process might impact an educator's own resilience.

So, here we are now, where the Re-Set Process is both a specific process and a way of thinking, and we invite you into our journey.

With warmest regards,
Dyane

Acknowledgments

From Dyane

With endless appreciation of . . .

My husband, Stephen, and my children, Marissa, Emily, and Tyrek, for their unwavering support of the myriad manifestations of my concern for children with trauma, among which has been the writing of this book. Your constant love and belief in me were foundational to this undertaking. You are my grounding, my joy, my respite, my balance, my heart.

My beloved grandchildren, Oliver, Louisa, and Sylvie, who inspire me to work all the harder for every child's right to feel safe, loved, and empowered.

My parents, Ann and James Lewis, who taught me to stand in alliance with marginalized people. You haven't just talked about doing the right thing, you have genuinely demonstrated it since my first memories of childhood. My understanding of unconditional love began in your arms.

My siblings, Howard, Brian, and Jennifer, for a lifetime of encouragement, love, and wisdom and, now, your ongoing consultation and support through this writing process. Jenny, your perspective as an introspective, dedicated educator was a phenomenal contribution.

The many student-centered educators from across my career; you are all treasures, and you have enriched me beyond words. I am both humbled and inspired by the work you have done day in and day out on behalf of the children in your schools.

My colleague and friend, Wynne, without whom I would not have had the confidence to go forward with this project. I am so grateful for the unique lenses and wisdom you brought to these materials and for your personal reminders to pause. You are a gift in my life.

From Wynne

Gratitude to the educators I encounter daily, who support the most vulnerable among us with their genuine compassion, enduring patience, and authentic hope. They return each morning to ensure connection with their students or increasingly to re-establish a relationship broken the day before. Their work is heart-wrenching, heart-filling, and oh so hard. I honor them with my efforts, support, and tools.

I also acknowledge the bolstering of encouragement my family and friends provide as I juggle the variety of paths my work takes.

And Dyane, what a ride this has been. Your wisdom, determination, and remarkable legacy have been my pleasure to witness.

From Dyane and Wynne

In gratitude to . . .

This work's early implementors, readers, from-the-field writers, and manuscript reviewers. You each have shaped and informed this work, bringing it toward greater clarity. It has been an honor to learn with and from you, to witness how you have taken these ideas and made them happen in the field, and to consider your feedback on this developing manuscript: Judy Averill, Ross Bernay, Aly Boyd, Jill Craig, Michelle DeEmilio, Lark Eshelman, Jennifer Frasher, Jenna Ginder, Jayne Hain, Lucinda Harnish, Nikole Hollins-Sims, Anne Katona-Linn, Jill Koser, Steve Lauer, Lindsey Longo, Kathy Lutz, Rosemarie Mann, Angela Marley, Shaun McDonald. Kelly Melanson, Joe Morales Jr., Brittany Moyer, Clare Reich, Stephanie Renninger-Reiser, Melissa Sadin, Beth Shaughnessy, Ken Travis, Lucille Wakefield, Jamie Walton, Denice Weaver, Denise Young, and our anonymous reviewers.

Dr. Bruce Perry for his body of work, extraordinary inspiration, and the gracious sharing of his neurosequential model image for inclusion in this book.

Chris Dimond and Michael Kooman for allowing us to include a portion of the phenomenally poignant lyrics from their song, *Lost in the Waves*. Its rich, textured reflection on a childhood tragedy provides the perfect introduction to the book and linked almost magically with the wave analogy that we had used from the first days of the writing of this book.

Carol Kuntz for her beautiful painting that graces the cover of the book and Erin Geoghegan whose amazing cover layout visually conveys the concepts of both trauma and the Re-Set Process.

Our Managing Editor, Melissa Solarz Flanigan, whose enthusiasm for the manuscript from the very beginning and phenomenally dedicated editorial work brought this book to fruition. Thanks also to Hudson Perigo, Mary Beth Winkler, and the entire Brookes team.

To the children who carry unimaginable burdens and to the educators who seek to meet their needs and nurture their resilience

Section I

Defining and Understanding Trauma

The waves etch out a pattern
Long after they're gone.
The lines that they trace, they quickly erase,
But something's still lingering on.

Lost in the waves.
I am lost in the waves.
No one but me and the silent black sea;
I am lost in the waves.

—Michael Kooman and Christopher Dimond, 2011

 **Section I Online Companion Materials**

Glossary

Chapter 1

Trauma Foundations

The day starts at 8:40 a.m. with grab-and-go breakfasts in the classroom, the inevitable cereal sloshing onto desks, plus two sticky juice spills, requiring full binder, desk, and floor wipe-downs. Today's special is Guidance, which is held in the classroom. Although it is my designated planning time, the time is spent redirecting behaviors and helping the novice school counselor, all while trying to check homework folders. One of my most challenging students refuses to follow directions, despite ultimatums from the counselor. Yelling, the student charges from the classroom, ignoring my suggestion that he retreat to the designated chill zone. I follow him to the time-out room and confer briefly with the interventionist; we agree that I should contact the parent. This, unfortunately, escalates the student's verbal tirade.

Back in the classroom, I go over directions and pass out a math assessment. Already, the need for reading assistance with the assessment is frustrating several students. Someone with high anxiety starts to bang his hands on his desk and lament, "I will never be done with this test!" The special education teacher arrives to provide support for identified students. I glance at the clock: it's 10:30 a.m. I am not only off schedule, I am tired.

My student returns from the time-out room, momentarily contrite, but it's his third trip in two days—clearly this is not working, but it's the only choice I have. We have been teaming about him since September and have yet to find a behavior plan that works consistently, and which doesn't escalate his behavior. He even struggles with positive supports.

I visually check on my English language learner (ELL) student, whose mother had tearfully told me through a translator that her daughter had been assaulted. I worry about this student because I know she goes to testify in court soon. Not surprisingly, she's picking at her paper but not writing. I am momentarily grateful that this was not one of those days when my administrator pops in for a walk-through evaluation. Then I wish she would, because I wish that she could witness firsthand all that I am juggling. We close out the written portion of the test and take a breath. We are all in need of a break.

I'm a seasoned teacher with more than 30 years of experience. I hold multiple degrees and I regularly engage in training opportunities. My teacher toolkit is heavily stocked, and I strive to match my experience and training with a depth of caring, spending a great deal of time building community in the classroom and with families. Despite all of this, I find that the strategies I have learned are ineffective with many of my students with trauma histories. I know I need a new approach, but I don't know where to start.

THE BIG PICTURE

Think of trauma-related student behavior as a wave in the ocean. Most of us would agree that the crash and roar of water breaking against the shoreline grabs our attention the most. It is noisy, full of churning energy, and quite capable of knocking us off our feet. It pulls, pushes, and tugs on us in ways that demand our immediate and intense focus. We worry about the undertow dragging us away from where we stand.

If we look out past the white caps, though, we can see the origins of the wave, though we are not as aware of it in that form or of its potential. Once we catch our breath from our struggles at the shoreline, we must shift our focus to the larger forces that created the wave, which formed and gathered momentum long before it crashed on the shoreline. In our schools, we need to deal with the urgent moments—the crash at the shoreline—but we also need to be able to understand the broader dynamics at work—the out-at-sea needs—and address them proactively.

Each intervening collective, whether an individual educator or a school's entire staff, must assess the unique needs of its students, as well as the needs of the supporting adults, and find the balance between reacting and preventing. Only when the needs of both are met can staff provide robust and cohesive behavior supports. A well-rounded set of tools allows us to successfully navigate the turbulent times at the shore and the rolling swells out at sea that are the challenging behaviors of our children with trauma.

The Layout of the Book

This book is designed to be a reflective guide to trauma-informed behavioral practices. As is depicted in Figure 1.1, it is rooted in scientific research and has grown in the sunlight of practical experience in classrooms and schools. The materials are divided into three sections that include resources directly related to the content of each section. These resources include a glossary of terms, expanded information, samples, directions for creating tools, and more.

In Section I, we lay the foundation for all that follows. We explain our carefully considered use of language and terminology and place behavior in a trauma-informed context. We also connect our approach to trauma-informed behavior supports with other practices that you may already have in your educational setting, including mindfulness, Positive Behavior Interventions and Supports (PBIS), Responsive Classroom Approaches, and restorative practices. We also share our five core principles of trauma-informed behavioral practice.

Section I also examines the most educationally relevant concepts regarding childhood trauma. We define **trauma**, examine its potential etiology, and identify some of its manifestations in the lives of the children we seek to support. We share what neuroscience tells us about the physiological impacts of childhood trauma—including dysregulation—and then consider the psychological impacts—including attachment and trust.

In Section II, we explain the Re-Set Process, a trauma-informed practice that profoundly influences what happens at both the shoreline of student behavior and out at sea. This process is a scientifically sound, educator-friendly methodology we developed based on our extensive experiences working with students of trauma. The Re-Set Process has been refined

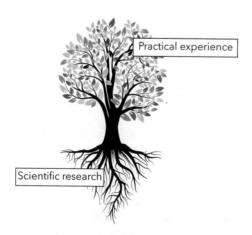

Figure 1.1. The phrase *rooted in science and grown through practical experience* emerged to describe the evolution of the Re-Set Process.

through nearly a decade of implementation practice and through the input of a multitude of educators, including school counselors, classroom teachers, special educators, principals, psychologists, occupational therapists, physical therapists, speech and language pathologists, paraprofessionals, and the students themselves.

We begin by providing an overview of the process, and then thoroughly examine the proactive and reactive forms of Re-Set. We also provide the information needed to implement the various Re-Set Process structures in your classroom or school. We devote a chapter specifically to the Re-Set Room, where the most intense proactive and reactive forms of the Re-Set Process occur. It is important to note that, although it is preferable that the Re-Set Process be embedded throughout the practices of a school, many educators have used some form of it successfully within their own smaller sphere of influence. This section closes with a chapter about implementing the Re-Set Process and addresses questions that many readers are likely asking themselves—namely, where to start and what steps to take.

Section III discusses related proactive strategies such as creating predictability, protecting emotional safety, nurturing relationships, and building regulation skills. These are the "out-at-sea" strategies. In the vernacular of a multi-tiered system of support (MTSS), these are the underpinnings of a trauma-informed Tier 1 approach. (A Tier 1 approach is universally supportive and targets all students.) Ultimately, it is Tier 1 strategies that make the biggest systems-level impact if we attend to them in an integrated and collaborative manner. Many of these strategies fall within the purview of individual teachers for use within their classrooms, even if a building as a whole is not focusing on being trauma-informed.

Section III also examines common behavior management strategies that are incompatible within a trauma-informed approach. We discuss how to make language that is related to reinforcement and redirection more trauma-informed and empowering for the student. We consider the risk factors that are associated with many familiar classroom systems and other behavioral practices, and then offer alternatives that are sensitive to the vulnerability of students with trauma histories and that build connection with others and self-confidence in the student.

Our final chapter focuses on educator self-care and is followed by an appendix, which provides a set of guided questions for use in a book study group or a professional learning community (PLC).

Our Carefully Chosen Language

We have found that the language we use in this work is incredibly important, and we have thought carefully about how we reference trauma, particularly in the educational context. We deliberately use the label *trauma-informed behavior practices* in discussing our body of work. We have found that other ways of talking about trauma (trauma-informed care and trauma-sensitive approaches) sometimes inadvertently communicate to educators that they are expected to be therapists. Terms such as trauma-informed interventions may connote that there is a need to wait for trauma to show up before intervening, which is not the case with the Re-Set Process.

Of course, these terms are widely used in the field, and there are many powerful understandings, strategies, and resources that appear in conjunction with them. For the purposes of this text, we have chosen the term trauma-informed behavior practices in order to speak as directly and intentionally as possible to our audience of educators about what they can do, day in and day out. We want it to be abundantly clear: We are not asking teachers, administrators, paraprofessionals, and support personnel to become therapists. We are asking them to engage in a set of practices that fit their education and training and their roles and responsibilities, as well as their school contexts. We want to convey that trauma-informed behavior practices are both proactive and reactive in nature and account for the complexities inherent in the bodies and minds of students with trauma histories.

You may notice that we often address the reader as a classroom educator, sharing strategies that are specific to the classroom environment. The Re-Set Process is bigger than the classroom, however. On a more macro level, administrators, professional developers, and other school leaders who are reading this book will gain critical knowledge and encounter tools for planning and implementing the Re-Set Process and related trauma-informed practices. Whatever your position or sphere of influence, this book will provide you with a new lens and new strategies for supporting all students, including those with a history of trauma.

As you read about children with trauma histories, we invite you to think deeply about the difference between how they may present on the outside and how they actually feel on the inside. Sometimes their behavior misleads adults, causing us to believe that they are tough and should be handled firmly when, in fact, their behavior may be a protective shell designed to contain the pain they have experienced. Children may curse, throw things, reject, bluster, and say things such as *I don't care* or *I hate you*. In these moments, we ask you to pause and consider that children with a history of trauma are vulnerable, and their growth may be uneven and tenuous. Our hope is that you are compassionate in interpreting challenging behavior and thoughtful in your decision-making. Students with trauma histories are some of the strongest, bravest children we have encountered and simultaneously the most fragile. It is our responsibility as educators to handle them with care.

Student and teacher names in the case studies are fictitious. All identifying information—including which one of us was involved—is either not provided or has been changed to protect privacy. Some case studies are reflective of several situations that were highly similar and that have been amalgamated into one story. Notes From the Field were written by practitioners from urban, suburban, and rural schools and are identified only by role and level.

Finally, we consciously made the decision that, for the most part, so that the material would read more cohesively, the book would reflect us as collaborative authors rather than be a set of separate experiences and thoughts. To accomplish this, we have chosen to use the third-person *we* throughout the book.

Understanding Behavior Through a Trauma-Informed Lens

It seems like we cannot open an educational journal, a list of podcasts, or a series of social media group postings without seeing the word *trauma*. The word is bantered about in casual conversations, and it is seriously examined in more professional venues. We use it colloquially (*oh, my gosh, I was so traumatized by . . .*) and precisely (*this student has experienced significant trauma as a result of . . .*). Like many concepts of human behavior, educators come to the notion of trauma through myriad entry points, and they react to it with a wide variety of responses based on their support, skills, experience, and education.

In order to be effective in anything we do to support our students with trauma histories, the very first thing we must do is recognize that this wave is a different kind of wave—a rip tide, if you will. We need a new lens through which to view behavior, and we need to have confidence that, once we *apply that lens*, we are in a better position to do better. We cannot simply go with our gut, our habits, our defaults.

To continue our analogy, we need to proactively understand the dynamics and conditions of rip tides long before they reach the shore. Reactively, we need to recognize signs that a rip tide exists and have strategies for the time when we are caught up in one. We need to let go of strategies that may have worked in other conditions but that will not work in these conditions, such as trying to swim directly back to shore when caught in an actual rip tide. We need to rely on the research of what works in these conditions and use those strategies even if they feel temporarily uncomfortable, such as when one floats or swims parallel to the shore for a period of time when being pulled out to sea by a rip tide.

What does this mean in behavioral practices? First, we need to accept that the behavioral methods we have known and implemented may not fully position us to design intervention that is compassionate, effective, and efficient for students with significant trauma histories. We need to consider that some familiar behavioral practices may be insufficient or counter-productive and even ethically questionable when used with students with trauma histories. Once we accept that trauma calls for new ways of thinking, we are poised for success because we are open to new approaches.

Now, if that leads to you feeling overwhelmed, let us assure you of several things:

- The most critical intervention for all behavioral change is a positive, nurturing relationship between student and adult—this still stands true.

- Effective instructional techniques still matter.

- Strategies developed for students of trauma tend to also support students without significant social, emotional, and/or behavioral needs.

- Many of your practices may need only to be adjusted or refined rather than completely abandoned.

To know what to hold on to, what to alter, and what to leave behind in order to design effective behavioral support, the behaviors of students with trauma need to be seen through that new lens. Seeing through a trauma-informed lens allows us to:

- Reframe behaviors that have perplexed us, annoyed us, alienated us, frustrated us, and angered us as manifestations of a student's trauma—as part of what happened to them, not something they are choosing to do to us—thereby developing a deeper compassion for our students who challenge us.

- Understand that our gut reactions to behavior may make the situation worse.

- Accept that behavioral interventions that work for many of the students we teach may simply *not* work for children of trauma.

A trauma-informed lens allows us to envision different kinds of strategies and practices—ones that move beyond simply controlling or containing behaviors to addressing the neuro-logical and attachment needs of these students. If we merely implement something different without changing our mindset about the origins and underlying needs of behavior, we may subtly defeat our own dedicated efforts. New understandings lead to critical nuances in our interventions, which result in greater success for our students and for us.

How does trauma-informed behavioral practice fit with everything else that is going on in your school district—the academic curricula, the standards, the new classroom mate-rials, ever-changing technology expectations, testing, social and emotional instruction, and more? Here is the really good news: As we already shared, much of what you already are doing probably addresses trauma and may lay the groundwork or provide the structure for supporting students affected by trauma. Practices that match the needs of students with trauma histories already exist in the context of many other school approaches, although they might be a bit fragmented or too low in intensity. The thing is, with a trauma-informed lens in place, a school, or an individual educator can determine valuable practices that are already occurring and enrich those practices in an intelligent, focused manner. As edu-cators consider where they invest their energies, it is also important to consider what we mentioned briefly already—that most trauma-informed practices make a difference to a sig-nificantly broader group of students than those with trauma. When undertaken with inten-tion and collaboratively, these practices can create a culture that supports students with a host of needs—students who are tired, who may be experiencing temporary stress, who are perfectionists, who struggle with anxiety or depression, or who have autism—just to name a few. The bottom line is that a culture that is rich in relationship and understanding is a culture that is good for all students.

Are you thinking, *Great, one more thing on my already full plate*? Rest assured, you do not need a place in your schedule for trauma-informed practices time. These practices are integrated into your relationships, your instruction, your interactions, your transitions, and your environments. It is about applying that new lens to the whole of what is done throughout schools, including classrooms, hallways, special classes, student services offices, classroom meetings, parent-teacher conferences, playgrounds, school buses, and extracurricular events. The lens and resultant approaches are fully mobile and can be flexibly integrated into the life of the classroom and school.

Applying a Trauma-Informed Lens to Your Practices

In Section III, we examine classroom culture and give you a chance to reflect upon your practices. When you apply a trauma-informed lens to what you do as an individual educator, you are invited to reflect on your personal practices. During your reflections, you may find that what you are already doing works well for students with trauma histories. We describe these reflections as *Affirmations*. You may also find yourself making thoughtful adjustments based on your new knowledge, which we describe as *Attic Treasures*, *Refinements*, and *Careful Considerations*.

Affirmations   There are many things you are doing day in and day out that are very effective practices for students with trauma histories. We are guessing you will have many affirmations, such as the following example:

The routine students follow upon entering my classroom that I introduced to them at the beginning of the year/semester instills predictability and a sense of comfort that allows for more successful academic and behavioral performance.

Attic Treasures   As you reflect on new learnings regarding trauma, you may realize that you did things in the past that are a good fit and reinstitute them into your teaching practice. An example of an attic treasure is:

I used to take time at the beginning of each school year to do getting-to-know-you activities with my students. We did a different one as part of the class throughout the first 5 days of school. As the academic intensity ramped up, I found myself eliminating these. As I learned more about the importance of making connections and feeling emotionally safe, I reinstituted this practice. I felt confident in doing this because I also had come to understand that this wasn't fluff or just something nice to do—it was important because students with better connections tend to function better behaviorally. I realized that I would be able to make up the time because, ultimately, I would spend less time in redirections and conflict disputes.

Refinements   There may be some things that almost work but that need some adjusting in order to really fit students with trauma. Often educators find that these minor tweaks result in major impact. An example of a refinement is:

Most of my students are energized by the competition of review games. Knowing that competition can shut down students with trauma, I made a change to the way that teams compete.

Previously, teams earned points by answering questions correctly—the goal was for one team to beat the other. Now I create four teams that huddle together to generate answers. The scores from all four teams add up to a total classroom score. Once the class reaches a certain number of points, they all earn a 10-minute social time. With this new practice, I get the needed review in and my students work together to be productive—win–win!

Careful Considerations   Certain strategies may best be set aside until the timing is more appropriate. As you reflect on learnings about trauma, you may find yourself becoming more selective in the strategies you employ at certain times of the year. We all adjust to the students we have in front of us each year, but awareness of student stress and trauma may lead us to be more deliberate as we select what we will do to fit our current student group. An example of a careful consideration is:

I often use the cooperative group structure of four students teaming together right from the beginning of the school year. When you're an individual in a group of four, it takes fairly sophisticated social skills to navigate relationships with three other people at one time. Students of trauma, in particular, may struggle with this, so I hold off on the quad-grouping and use partners only until I get a better sense of how students are functioning together.

CONNECTED EDUCATIONAL PRACTICES

Many schools systemically support practices and initiatives that are trauma-informed, specifically mindfulness in schools, PBIS, Responsive Classroom, and restorative practices. It is no surprise that these current, research-based practices are promising for children of trauma— they were developed and assessed for their effectiveness in the context of today's student population. We want to specifically acknowledge the powerful role that these practices have in supporting students with trauma histories.

Mindfulness in Schools

Based on long-time success in broader fields like health care, mental health, stress management, human resources, business, sports, and law, mindfulness emerged as a field within education around 2001. In some contexts, the practice of mindfulness intersects with spiritual practice. That is *not* the case in the educational practice of mindfulness. As is true in many other settings, mindfulness approaches in schools are purely secular in nature.

Within the countless applications and implementations, mindfulness as a practice or as an outcome has been defined in many ways. One definition might be paying attention to the present moment with openness and compassion. Another is single-tasking. Yet another is what emerges when we attend to the present moment in a particular way. Most approaches include purposeful, mindful practices that train attention to select, direct, and sustain focus. A trauma-informed approach to mindfulness in schools includes choice (how and how much to engage), flexible expression of practice, routine check-ins to ensure individual comfort, and opportunity for reflection.

Repeated present-moment awareness for people of all ages can be simple and challenging at the same time. Consistent mindful practices in the classroom can lead to changes in self-awareness, self-care, emotion regulation, concentration, and mental flexibility, which can then lead to improved self-regulation in the classroom and beyond. Mindfulness has been proven to strengthen the working memory portion of the brain, mitigating some of the impact of trauma. Mindfulness practices can be still, active, individualized, synchronized, loud, quiet, calm, or energized. Mindful movement is becoming more and more useful in reaching and engaging populations with diverse needs and across a wide range of ages.

Mindfulness and the practices that are inspired by it may have a similar foundation and intention, but they can look very different from one classroom to another and from one day to another. Definitions and expressions can take many turns depending on the teacher, the group of students and the needs of each classroom. When we try them out and make the practices our own—as the adults leading it—mindfulness can become a powerful personal habit and an invaluable gift that we give our students, no matter what their histories.

Foundations of mindful awareness and invitations to engage in mindful practices have been woven throughout this book. Whether labeled or implied, there are threads of mindfulness within the foundation of the Re-Set Process and these will be explored along the way. Specific resources to enhance and expand your understanding of its possible role in your setting are provided at the end of some sections.

Positive Behavior Interventions and Supports

According to the U.S. Department of Education technical assistance centers (National Technical Assistance Center on Positive Behavioral Interventions and Supports [PBIS], n.d.), PBIS is a framework for supporting students in schools. Structures, strategies, and assessments are organized across three tiers of intensity. Tier 1 is universal practices designed to support all students, Tier 2 is targeted supports for groups of students who are non-responders to universal practices, and Tier 3 is intensive interventions that are designed to support the needs of an individual who has not responded to the supports of the previous two tiers. In the PBIS framework, the concept of intensity reflects increasing levels of supports—people, time, and individualization—in order to meet the needs of students.

Broadly, PBIS is designed to help schools and agencies become more effective and efficient while also enhancing equity for student with disabilities, students of color, and other marginalized populations within those systems. PBIS targets all students (PBIS, n.d.) and, by creating a positive environment, aims to improve students' academic and social/behavioral functioning. As such, PBIS is poised to provide a sound framework in which trauma-informed practices may occur if care is taken to align the goals of both fields.

PBIS frameworks includes

- The use of evidence-based, respectful, non-punitive, prevention-oriented behavior practices

- A focus on skill teaching and reteaching as necessary

- The availability of a continuum of supports that meet the needs of all students

- Data-based decision-making

- Ongoing assessment of students' needs as individuals and as subgroups

- Family and community involvement

- Involvement and cohesion across all adults in the school, and even across the district (PBIS, n.d.)

Within that framework, there is a fair amount of space for local implementation considerations, with guidance provided by trainers associated with PBIS. This flexibility is the opening for making PBIS highly trauma-informed.

Two of the original driving developers and researchers behind PBIS were Dr. Rob Horner from the University of Oregon and Dr. George Sugai from the University of Connecticut.

For close to thirty years, Dr. Horner has been guiding and studying school behavior practices that shift school culture toward more productive, successful environments for all students. When speaking about PBIS, Dr. Horner often shares the four characteristics of behaviorally successful schools—they are "predictable, consistent, positive and safe" (Horner, 2011, 2015).

Interestingly, Dr. Bruce Perry, a medical doctor who focuses on child and adolescent psychiatry, identifies the same needs when considering what it takes to support a developing child. In summary notes from a lecture describing trauma-informed practices—available through his website—Perry states that, "If [a child's] world is safe, predictable, and characterized by relationally and cognitively enriched opportunities, the child can grow to be self-regulating, thoughtful, and a productive member of family, community, and society" (Perry, 2005, para 3).

Clearly, from the perspective of leaders in these two fields, the broad goals of PBIS and those of trauma-informed practices are aligned. If a school system embraces a PBIS approach and operationalizes it with fidelity, that system is positioned to provide critical support to students with trauma histories. Some of the specific practices that align with the needs of students with trauma-histories are as follows:

- Clearly defined positive expectations (predictability)

- Explicit instruction in expectations (nothing is assumed, what is expected is taught)

- Consistent language across adults (focused language, consistency)

- Positive, concrete reinforcement of expected behaviors (recognition of successes that helps student see self as positive)

- Visual display of expectations (appeals to an easier way to process—visual input)

- Non-classroom areas are monitored (safety, opportunities for positive noticing, relationship-building)

- Classroom-managed behaviors are defined (expectations are clear and consistent, increasing predictablity)

- Office-managed behaviors are defined (consistency, creating emotionally and physically safe environments for all, decreases the likelihood that students of trauma will be over-sent to the office)

- Data-based decision making (decreases the likelihood that students of trauma will be over-identified or disproportionately receive consequences)

- Tiered supports (opportunities for increased coaching/instruction, additional reinforcement opportunities, engagement of community supports as behaviorally indicated)

- Family involvement (consistency, opportunities to support the whole child) (PBIS, n.d.)

From the universal design methods such as core expectations (Tier 1) to the methodologies and supports provided at the small group level (Tier 2) and to the intensive, individualized level (Tier 3), there are myriad ways that the needs of students with trauma may be addressed. Because PBIS is a framework and not a limited set of practices, it can easily be the perfect structure in which to house and organize school supports related to trauma. Wisconsin State Superintendent Tony Evers, in the publication *Using Positive Behavioral Interventions & Supports (PBIS) to Incorporate Trauma-Sensitive Practices into Schools*, makes this explicit connection between the structure and practices of PBIS and the needs of students with trauma-histories (Evers, 2016).

Notes From the Field

Trauma is an important consideration as schools build out their tiered behavioral frameworks in order to be responsive to individual student needs. We can no longer approach behavior with a one-size-fits-all model, particularly as we seek to provide equitable disciplinary practices. The backgrounds of students cannot be ignored. PBIS calls us to reframe problematic behaviors and consider them as indicators of needs, perhaps some of which might be related to childhood trauma.

Educational Consultant, School Psychologist, Co-Statewide Lead, Behavior Initiative

Responsive Classroom Approaches

The practices of the Northeast Foundation for Children Responsive Classroom model began in a small, private lab school and quickly expanded into the much larger forum of Washington, D.C., public schools. Since then, the Responsive Classroom model has been implemented widely across the United States in rural, suburban, and urban public school settings. Responsive Classroom practices have been developed both for elementary and middle school settings— Grades Kindergarten to 8 (K–8) (Responsive Classroom, n.d.).

From the outset, Responsive Classroom, an evidence-based approach to education, sought to integrate academic and social/emotional goals. This allowed students to develop their social/emotional skills in the context of learning and, conversely, how to learn in the context of relationships. Based on a set of developmentally driven practices that include Morning Meeting, Logical Consequences, Small Things Time-Out, Guided Discovery, and Procedures and Rules, the model has focused on making learning a joyful, relational experience (Charney, 1992).

Responsive Classroom's approach to behavioral issues has always been that behavior, like academics, is something to be explicitly taught. This developmental orientation translates to understanding the individual's needs, which is core to trauma-informed practices. Responsive Classroom also focuses intently on emotional safety and maintaining predictable, consistent routines with supports. Once again, the alignment with the goals for serving children of trauma well is clear: safe, nurturing, predictable, and consistent (Responsive Classroom, n.d.).

The Responsive Classroom approach moves beyond simply having similar goals. Brain-based understandings support Responsive Classroom structures, making the approach an excellent fit for students with trauma. The approach emphasizes the importance of teacher modeling—both for behavior and academic inquiry purposes—and providing time for children to think for themselves rather than rushing to simply follow through on adult directives. It also encourages the use of visual supports, laughter, and fun. The Responsive Classroom model emphasizes the importance of classroom rites and rituals and articulates the need for respectful interactions, even at the most difficult times.

With just a quick look at Responsive Classroom's Morning Meeting structure, it is abundantly clear how synchronous this approach is with the needs of students with trauma. Here are some of the components of a Morning Meeting and their benefits to students with trauma histories:

- Routine use of Morning Meeting (predictability, consistency)

- Ordered structure within Morning Meeting (predictability, consistency)

- The act of gathering in a circle (connection opportunity)

- Use of specific signals within Morning Meeting (predictability, consistency)

- Greeting—smile (dopamine release), positive touch (dopamine release and building tolerance to touch), name (connection, experience of name being a positive thing), laughter (dopamine release), the greeting itself (serve and return opportunity)

- Sharing—connection opportunity, positive social interaction (dopamine release), listening/speaking opportunity (serve and return practice)

- Group activity—smile (dopamine), laughter (dopamine), movement (burn off stress chemicals), incidental touch (building tolerance to touch, decreasing hyperreaction to touch stimuli), games themselves may offer additional opportunities (modulation, serve and return practice), opportunity to be trusted with materials and social interactions

- Morning message—settling opportunity, guided shift from social to academic thinking (modulation), expectations for day (predictability)

- Option to pass or to do adapted version of greeting, sharing (emotional safety)

- Teacher language—encourages reflection through guided questioning (personal agency)

Responsive Classroom focuses extensively on nurturing the caring, guiding adult tone that is critical in implementing any trauma-informed practice. It also emphasizes developing a student's internal voice—the ability to develop one's own guiding moral center, to have confidence in one's abilities, and to self-reflect on one's choices. As a child-centered, development-centered, strategy-specific approach, it provides a sound structure for any adult who is looking to support students of trauma.

Restorative Practices

Restorative practices, like Responsive Classroom, is a relationship-based approach to interactions between adults and students and between students and students. Like PBIS, it is a framework to nurture positive student behavior and to handle—in a meaningful way—issues with misbehavior. Also, like PBIS, it emphasizes proactive over reactive measures, looks to teach new sets of behaviors to students, and involves the whole school community.

Some of the guiding principles of restorative practices that are found in almost every school's implementation guide includes the encouragement of personal reflection, accountability for one's behavior, and healing for both adults and students. Based on the structure of a restorative justice approach, these practices have been adapted for the school setting. The approach seeks to develop positive relationships among students through community-building meetings and then, again, much like Responsive Classroom's problem-solving model, seeks to address interaction issues within a supportive peer circle as appropriate (Center for Restorative Process, n.d.).

This model works well in tandem with PBIS and similarly supports the concept of enhanced student voice that the PBIS framework promotes. Like PBIS, it offers levels of support of increasing intensity that fit well within PBIS's three-tiered framework.

According to the San Francisco Unified School District Restorative Practices Resource Packet, the benefits of restorative practices approaches in the school setting include

- A safer, more caring environment

- A more effective teaching and learning environment

- A greater commitment by everyone to take the time to listen to one another

- A reduction in bullying and other interpersonal conflicts

- A greater awareness of the importance of connectedness to young people—the need to belong and feel valued by peers and significant adults

- Greater emphasis on responses to inappropriate behavior that seek to reconnect and not to further disconnect young people

- Reductions in fixed term and permanent suspensions and expulsions

- A greater confidence in the staff team to deal with challenging situations (Student, Family, and Community Support, n.d.)

Again, we see the common threads of safety and positivity reflected in the benefits noted in the preceding list. When done with fidelity, restorative practice supports the development of teacher skills and related teacher language, and it addresses the relationship-building opportunities among students—all of which are foundational for supporting students with trauma histories. Because of its emphasis on student voice and reflective thought, restorative practices directly support the development of agency, which is a profound need for many students with trauma histories. Finally, its focus on healing over blaming is extremely aligned with trauma-informed approaches.

Some districts we've worked with have found that using the Responsive Classroom model for the elementary years and the restorative practices model for the secondary years creates a cohesive approach by using language and concepts that make sense to educators at those two different levels.

Our review of these four connected practices has been superficial, and yet, it clearly illuminates some specific ways in which these broad approaches fit with trauma-informed practices. As you become more trauma-informed, we have no doubt that you will see many more connections for yourself.

CORE PRINCIPLES OF TRAUMA-INFORMED BEHAVIORAL PRACTICE

When I was a boy and I would see scary things in the news, my mother would say to me, "Look for the helpers. You will always find people who are helping."

—Fred Rogers (2003, p. 187)

Before we can move forward with any discussion of intervention and change, as the helpers—implementers, guides, coaches—we need to orient to the core principles that guide trauma-informed school practices. Like the North Star, these five principles help us chart our course and continually provide direction as we go. As a reader, they should help you understand the practices that we discuss in this manual more profoundly and support you as a practitioner in the field when you are faced with uncharted territory.

Principle 1: Develop a Trauma-Informed Lens

Trauma-informed teaching begins with recognizing our universal needs through a caring, nonjudgmental lens and recognizing that all people involved—including ourselves—are affected by trauma. This lens does not require that we know or learn the initial cause, the long-term source, or the personal details behind anyone's wounding—just that we know and feel that these elements possibly exist. We always assume that trauma is present in the room and we, therefore, recognize behavioral issues as a manifestation of that trauma.

This sort of lens also involves thoughtfully, openly, and proactively examining what we do including our behavioral practices, interactions, word use, and modeling of self-regulation. Developing this lens enables us as professionals to empathize with students, avoid triggering behaviors, and create a safe learning space.

Principle 2: Establish Safety in All Environments and Interactions

Safety is not about metal detectors, double-locking doors, or armed guards. Those are security measures. Security is provided by external factors that enhance physical protection, limit accessibility, and lessen threats. Ironically, some of our efforts to make our schools more secure can actually make some students feel less safe and more anxious, increasing the need to focus on developing a comprehensive sense of safety for all students.

What is safety? Safety stems from an inner sense of stability, efficacy, and trust in oneself and trust in others. Safety grows within a person, a family, a peer group, or a classroom. It develops when we learn through repeated experience to trust the information we detect through our own senses. With that learned ability and awareness, we come to trust our own instincts and act through our personal choices. We feel safer when we practice self-care, which eventually shifts to demonstrating care within the many social groups to which we belong.

Safety is a preventative measure. It addresses the causes that can lead to the need for security within a community. Inner safety can lead to outer expressions of empathy, healthier social interactions, and healing. These, in turn, lead to inclusion and collaboration which then lead to real changes in students, groups, and schools. Bullying is reduced. Isolation and the resulting depression can be lessened. Competition can become a healthy motivator instead of a harmful divider. Marginalization and incidents of violence become less prevalent. Hearts, minds, and behaviors shift as safety and other core issues are addressed.

Teachers need tools and support to create this type of safe learning environment—one built on a culture of trust. Daily, teachers can model safe behavior by pausing to notice the moment, attending to one thing at a time, recognizing their role in setting the tone, adjusting to diverse and often adverse situations, openly caring for others, thinking carefully about the words they use, knowing when they need their own time-out, addressing bullying consistently, and speaking directly about safety as non-negotiable in their classrooms.

Research shows that social and emotional skills around safety can be taught, learned, and practiced in our schools. Teachers are uniquely equipped to meet students where they are and to guide them toward new skills. Explicitly taught curriculum can lead students to notice what they need, encourage them to speak up, and support them to create safety for themselves and their peers. Structures such as community/class meetings can invite student voices forward and encourage children of any age to act as more powerful forces in creating a physically and emotionally safer environment.

Although our goals should be to establish this broad sense of safety for all students, we can establish a sense of safety within the space of a single interaction with one student. Our body language, voice tone, words, expressions, and how we prioritize safe expectations can be powerful components for creating safety for each student at every moment.

Principle 3: Read Your Students

As we have acknowledged, language is powerful, especially the words we use in a classroom. For some students, we need to be even more cognizant of the words we use and what they may trigger. Some words that seem innocuous may need to be replaced because they can be triggering to students who have been victimized.

Consider these commonly used words: deep, spread, and bend. We integrate them into instructions almost every day. *Take a few deep breaths and then begin your test. When you write your answers, spread out your digits so I can read your numbers. Clean-up time—bend over and pick up any scraps of paper under your desk.* In a trauma-informed classroom or counseling office, the educator would be aware of the possibility of reactivating trauma and may deliberately change their language using safer words instead. *Breathe out all the way a few times and then begin your test. When you write your answers, put space between your digits so I can read your numbers. Clean-up time—look and reach below your desk to pick up any scraps of paper.* We also see some students triggered by having their names called or by certain behaviorally related words like *No!* or *Stop!* We may want to consider how we can replace those words and practices at the times that it makes sense to do so.

Of course, we cannot eliminate all triggering words from our vocabulary, but if we notice the words that routinely escalate a student, we can develop verbal habits that reduce triggering. We can practice using alternative words. We can deliberately call the student by their name paired with a genuine compliment—which begins to make their name a positive rather than a negative. We can give directives that tell what to do rather than what not to do. The point of this principle is not to have us hesitate every time we open our mouths to talk with our students. It is more about taking the time to tune in to how our language may be affecting our students and adjust accordingly.

We also need to tune in to the fact that some students may be triggered by nonverbal actions in the classroom—by something in our body language or our movements, or by the physical positions we ask them to assume. We have experienced students who would panic when approached quickly and others who would escalate if we crossed our arms while in conversation. Again, the point of this principle is not to have us feel frozen in place for fear of moving in the wrong way. Rather, it is an invitation to pay attention to how movement and positioning impact our students.

On a personal level, we have learned to recognize our own signs of dysregulation—and so have our family members! Wynne's son learned at a young age that when mom's right ear turns red, it is in his best interest to pause, back away, and engage later. He knew that mom needed some cool-down space and, if he continued to push, question, or challenge, his wishes would not be met with the empathy and understanding he hoped for. Wynne's sign of dysregulation—her right ear turning red—is a physical and visual cue. As awkward as it seemed at first, she liked being aware of this simple but consistent early-warning signal. It has helped her and her son navigate the frequent parent–child power struggles with some grace. Upon noticing the ear, Wynne's son might choose to wait until later to engage. Or, if Wynne felt the heat rise, she might ask for a moment before responding.

Noticing early indicators of needs is a two-pronged principle. When supporting our students, it means reading early signals that indicate rising dysregulation before problem behaviors are demonstrated. The better we know students, the more we can jump in and intervene, and the earlier we do that, the more likely we are to reach a positive outcome. Ideally, by really knowing the student, we can anticipate the situations and conditions that tend to lead to rising dysregulation and make a change even before those early signs emerge in full force. Chapters 2 and 9 provide more information about dysregulation.

On the adult side of things, noticing early indicators of needs also means reading ourselves. What are our early signs that we are being knocked off-kilter? What can we do to intervene with ourselves? How do we take care of ourselves amid caring for classrooms full of students? While we certainly cannot walk out of our classroom when the needs of our students are overwhelming us, we can do things to keep ourselves better regulated all along the way. We will take a look at this a bit more in Principle 5.

Principle 4: Invite Student Choice

Choice is a set of opportunities within a framework of limits and guidelines. Bring choice back into the daily lives of students—all students, not only those living with the choiceless moments of trauma and the dysregulation that follows. Choice does not mean removing structures, ignoring rules, or lowering standards. Even minimal choice-making ensures that when options can be provided, students get to reclaim the power they lost, maybe even long ago.

You might wonder, if students get to choose for themselves—won't chaos follow? What if they do not do what we want them to do? Great questions! Let's clarify what we mean in the following scenario: The class sits in chairs during a sleepy, midmorning work time. Is there an opportunity for choice? Absolutely. First, we take time to sense our own experience, mindfully. Then, we model that awareness, followed by choice, and encourage our students to do the same. *I am sitting here feeling drowsy and need to stand for a few minutes. Notice how you feel. Stay in your seat or stand behind it to feel more awake. It's up to you.* Students participate by noticing and choosing for themselves. That is what we mean by the principle of inviting choice.

Classrooms are filled with even simpler opportunities for choice: how to sit at circle time, which book to read, what color crayon or pen to use, where to settle for solo work, which topic to examine for a research paper, or which mindful practice to try when agitated. Other settings in school provide opportunities for choice also: where to sit in the library, when to ask to see the school counselor, who to talk to in the hallway during passing time. Triggering is minimized when we encourage individual choice in moments both big and small.

For children who have experienced choiceless moments, healthy, age-appropriate choice is a critical part of healing. This principle is about providing a balance of both structure and opportunity as appropriate to the age and needs of our students.

Principle 5: Respect and Nurture Yourself

Parker Palmer asserts in *The Courage to Teach* that "we teach who we are" (Palmer, 1997, p. 1). This means that the nervous system you bring to the classroom impacts your ability to connect with your students. Because secondhand stress is real and transferable, we are responsible for caring for ourselves first, and then bringing our best selves to our relationships and our work. Ancient wisdom tells us that an empty pitcher cannot fill another.

This principle is about knowing what fulfills you, and then taking the time and care to access those things. Remember: Self-care is not selfish—it is strengthening. Self-care is what sustains us in caring for our students. This wisdom comes in the form of the safety message we hear on airplanes at the beginning of a flight: Be sure to secure on your own oxygen mask before tending to the needs of others. These ideas are not new, yet, as educators, we continue to struggle with putting them into action.

When thinking about self-care, we also need to consider what can a school system do to provide supports for adults—otherwise known as "community care." One of the most effective behavior plans for an extremely traumatized, intensely acting-out student that we ever developed was one that gave that child's teacher a 15-minute break part way through the morning. We had the student spend those 15 minutes with the school counselor, which gave the teacher a break from what they described as walking on eggshells for the first two hours of the day. That 15 minutes served the student well and occurred during a time when the teacher also needed it—win-win. Chapter 11 examines these topics of self-care and community-care and will provide you with an opportunity to reflect on your own plan.

We hope that when you finish exploring the strategies shared within this book, you will feel

Honored and affirmed: We hope that you close this book with a more acute understanding of how much we honor the work that educators do every day and how skilled you already are before even reading this book. Your knowledge and skills make a difference to the children in your circle of influence. Celebrate that.

Energized and equipped: Of course, we hope that you will have learned some strategies that will make a difference in your practice. We want you and the students whose lives you touch to be even more successful. We also hope that you will have new insights and strategies at the ready and be well equipped to move forward.

Compelled and confident: You might think, *Compelled? Confident?* Yes and yes! Compelled to collaborate—to gather ideas from others and to confidently share yours. Compelled to learn other ways to think about trauma and to confidently share these with others. We are acutely aware that collaboration has brought us some of the best practices of our careers and, in turn, has given us the opportunity to share the best of what we know. This work is too hard, too complex, too exceedingly important to do alone or without confidence in your abilities. Be of brave heart!

Regardless of your personal entry point into this content, and whether you are reading this book as part of your own personal/professional growth or as part of a system that is collaboratively searching for answers to complex challenges, we welcome you on this journey. But before you dive in, we also invite you to pause—to remember who this is all about. Whether you are standing at the riotous shore or sailing miles out on the rolling sea, always keep your eyes and heart on the students with trauma histories who, without your informed and compassionate work, might be lost in the waves.

A Closing Note to Readers

The topic of trauma is a difficult one for all of us. Whether you have personally experienced significant trauma or have borne witness to the trauma of others, trauma leaves its mark. As you read and interact with the materials that follow, please monitor its impact on you. As you begin this book in earnest, please remember that you can pause at any time. When you notice irritation or hesitation, pause, fold the page corner or slip in a bookmark, take a moment, and return when you wish. Consider the following mindfulness practice when you experience your own feelings of dysregulation:

Sense You Are Here

Settle in your chair, with your feet solid on the floor.
Hands rest in your lap. Eyes gaze forward or closed.
Detect the sensations in your body that indicate that you are here, in this moment.
Sense that you are here, right here, right now.
Feet, seat, back, hands. Shoulders go down. Body is still. Sense you are here.
If you notice that you are tense in your body, take another, more significant moment to care for yourself.
Try something just for you—go for a walk, pet your dog, grab a cup of coffee or tea, stretch, twist, yawn.
The key?
Notice what you need. Do that. Return when you are ready.

Chapter 2

Trauma in the Room

We were almost 2 months into the school year and dark-eyed, sweet Scott had yet to display any behaviors that led me to believe that he belonged in my Emotional Support classroom. Sure, he was a bit of an active child, but what 5-five-year-old boy isn't? He seemed to need reassurances and wanted to lean up against me frequently, but wasn't that normal for a young child? I was a relatively new teacher to Emotional Support and to teaching in general, so I worried I was missing something. I also worried that he had landed here more as a result of his social history than his actual manifestations of that history.

This was what I knew: Scott had been sexually abused in his biological home and had been put into the foster care system by 18 months of age. I imagined that some naive preschool educator had struggled with his activity and neediness and reacted poorly, thereby exacerbating the problems. His records included diagnoses of oppositional defiant disorder (ODD) and pervasive developmental disorder (PDD); one specialist had identified him as having autism. All I knew was that this little boy seemed to be doing pretty well in my classroom.

And then, he wasn't. It was a beautiful mid-October morning when Scott flew out of his seat from where he was working with my paraprofessional, screaming a scream that I had never heard from any child. He raced to me and I opened my arms to comfort him and he began clawing violently at my face while making this high-pitched, feral sound. It took over an hour to settle him down, but then he fell asleep as I rocked him.

I called our educational team together, but we could not figure out what had triggered the event and were relieved when days went by without another issue. But then it happened again and, after some time passed, again. We reconvened to try to determine the function of the behavior, to consider what might have shifted. Allergies? Foods? Medication changes? Changes in the foster home? We could find nothing.

Shortly thereafter, Scott was assigned a new case manager, and we invited her to the table, hoping that fresh eyes might see something we missed. Instead, she casually dropped a completely new piece of information into our discussion. "Well, you know about the cayenne-pepper juice in his first foster home, right?" We had not known. We hadn't even known that he had been in more than one foster home.

It turned out that after being removed from his biological home where he had been sexually assaulted, Scott was moved to a foster home where, when he fussed, he was given a drink with cayenne pepper juice in it. Somehow—I have no idea how—this was discovered, and he was removed from that home and placed in the loving foster family that I knew.

Armed with this new information, we began putting the puzzle pieces together. Our classroom was down the hall from the cafeteria, and we considered the potential impact of the smell of food. . . . That was it! Whenever there was something peppery being prepared in the cafeteria and the weather was such that the hot air was blowing down the hallway and into our classroom, Scott reacted. He fought against the viscerally remembered pain and fought me, the person in charge, as though I was his abuser from whom he could not escape.

As educators, we are tasked with creating healthy connections, consistent guidance, and safe places to help children grow and thrive. But challenges abound and resistance happens.

For a student with a history of trauma, a single word or a seemingly neutral gesture can **trigger** shutdowns and confrontations that then bring about hurtful behaviors and loss of connection. Some students react to events, emotions, and challenges by either acting up or shutting down. Learning stops for that student and often for others.

When dealing with struggling human beings, we need to assume that there is trauma in their past, whether recent or distant, and respond based on that belief. We may never know if this assumption is accurate, but we do know that it is essential. When we act in ways that are responsive to trauma, we are showing our wisdom. In a world made better by universal design (think about curb cuts originally designed for people who use wheelchairs for their mobility), we can choose responses that are sure to do no student harm, will be helpful to students who have not experienced trauma but who have behavioral needs, and will be critical to students with trauma histories. When we function as if trauma is always in the room, we serve *all* our students well.

TRAUMA DEFINED

When we ask lay people to define **trauma**, their responses are usually something similar to *when something really bad has happened* or *a terrible accident*. Most responses tend to implicate a single event and focus on the action that occurred, giving little or no weight to any concepts related to the nature of the person who was affected by the action. These definitions are a starting point and are important to listen to because they tell us where people's understanding is on the topic.

We turn to professional organizations and the medical field for their comprehensive definitions from the field of practice:

- The U.S. Department of Health and Human Services Substance Abuse and Mental Health Services Administration (SAMHSA) describes trauma as something that is "physically or emotionally harmful or life-threatening with lasting adverse effects on the individual's functioning and mental, physical, social, emotional, or spiritual well-being" (SAMHSA, 2017, para. 2).

- In her 2015 TED Talk discussing the original Adverse Childhood Experiences (ACEs) study that was conducted by Felitti et al. in 1998, Nadine Burke Harris defined childhood trauma as "threats that are so severe or pervasive that they literally get under our skin and change our physiology" (Burke Harris, 2015).

- Bruce Perry, in a 2016 interview for *The Sun Magazine*, stated, "I define trauma as an experience, or pattern of experiences, that impairs the proper functioning of the person's stress-response system, making it more reactive or sensitive" (Supin, 2016, para. 8).

Ask us for an educators' definition of trauma and we will say that it is an event or a collection of experiences that overwhelm a person's inner resources and impact a person's ability to regulate, trust, and function at their full potential. But, ultimately, to define trauma in any manner is itself limiting. All trauma is subjective, experienced uniquely by the individual. We can take it apart, analyze it, label it, and hopefully, get better and better at supporting children who have experienced it. Still, when regarding the experience of trauma itself, mere words are insufficient to cover all that trauma is, does, and can do.

Traumatic events may be buffered by supports and other **mitigating factors**. Always, trauma is a visceral experience as opposed to a cognitive one, which is why words cannot capture it in its totality. Trauma lives in the body and is remembered in the emotional brain. It is outside of time, and re-experiencing feels contemporaneous rather than a thing of memory. Past may become present in a heartbeat, disorienting the individual from what all others around them are experiencing.

Childhood trauma is unique from **adult trauma** because it occurs 1) in the context of a smaller experience base (fewer years on the planet), 2) in the context of the affected person being highly dependent on others for both physical and emotional safety, and 3) in the context of the ongoing development of a child's body and brain.

What causes childhood trauma? Trauma is the result of **acute stressors** and/or **chronic stressors**. A single experience that results in acute, **toxic stress** often is referred to as **event trauma**. Event traumas might originate from experiences such as: a serious car accident, a home fire, the loss of a significant person, hospitalization/illness requiring intrusive medical procedures, home invasion, a single experience of assault (physical, sexual), or natural disaster.

> *Trauma devastatingly disrupts the ordinary linearity and unity of our experience of time, our sense of stretching along from the past to an open future.*
>
> —Robert D. Stolorow (2012, para. 2)

Although event traumas can certainly cause shock waves throughout the child's physical, social, and emotional systems and can impact behavior, they typically do not have as profound an effect as chronic stressors. Some event traumas do have a cascading effect: they begin as an event but that event triggers subsequent events that may lead to more chronic **stress** on top of the original event. For example, a home fire may result in financial stressors that result in multiple moves, changes in caregivers, change in school, and other disruptions. When this cascading impact occurs and, if there are insufficient mitigating factors, that event trauma may become chronic trauma.

The terms **chronic childhood trauma**, **childhood complex trauma**, and **pervasive developmental trauma** all refer to a collection of toxic experiences that occur during a person's childhood or adolescence. We will use the term pervasive trauma in this text. This type of trauma occurs when, during the course of development, there is a high-frequency assault on the child's sense of emotional and/or physical safety with an insufficient counterbalance of mitigating factors. This may be a result of chronic stressors alone or chronic stressors punctuated by acute event stressors. Pervasive trauma may originate from experiences such as emotional abuse, physical abuse, sexual abuse, emotional neglect, physical neglect, witnessing violence toward or abuse of another family member, household substance abuse, household mental illness, parental separation or divorce, an incarcerated household member, deployment of a household member, a serious illness of a significant person in a child's life, ongoing hospitalization/health issues of self, bullying (by another child or an adult), witnessing chronic violence outside the home, ongoing discrimination, such as racism or sexism, homelessness, living in a war zone or refugee camp, or chronic low socio-economic status/poverty.

It should be noted that, although being part of a family of lower socio-economic status does not necessarily result in pervasive trauma, poverty puts so many aspects of life in a state of instability (e.g., food, housing, clothing, heat) that it is highly associated with chronic stress and pervasive trauma. It is that *instability* that may take its toll on a child's developing systems. Regardless, it would be erroneous to assume that many or all children living in poverty are traumatized; we still need to consider each situation individually.

What types of behaviors may be exhibited by children with trauma histories, either acute or chronic? Many align with behaviors associated with other diagnoses but may, in fact, be manifestations of a child's trauma history. In schools, we may witness behaviors such as hyperactivity, aggression (verbal and/or physical), hyperarousal/jumpiness, hypervigilance, lack of connection with others, hyper-connection, lack of focus, impaired memory, uneven performance, overreacting to stimuli, irritability, defiance, bristling to touch, intense desire to be hugged, constant need for reassurance, inappropriate emotions for situation, hoarding, self-injury, drug and/or alcohol abuse and/or high-risk activities, avoidance behaviors (e.g., certain people, places, activities), absenteeism, and out-of-the-blue reactions. Although trauma certainly is a psychological phenomenon, it is also significantly a physical phenomenon and this list of manifestations reflects that duality. At the core of the physical phenomenon is significant neurological change, which then affects the functioning of everything else—physiological, emotional, social, and cognitive functioning. In children with pervasive trauma, the behaviors we deal with every day in our schools are not necessarily directly related to the *specific memories* of the trauma(s), but by the dysregulated emotions they trigger.

When this impact is understood, we realize that traditional therapy is far from the only answer in supporting people with trauma histories. When trauma was previously understood purely as a psychological experience, interventions fell within the professional purview of therapists. Educators' jobs were to be *sensitive* to the trauma a child may have experienced. Our updated and enhanced understanding of trauma as a neurological, psychological and experiential event, positions us as educators in a much more active interventionist role. We are called to use the tools of our profession to address the **underlying needs** of our students.

As educators seeking to make a difference in the lives of children with trauma histories, we have two significant entry points: 1) address **dysregulation**, and 2) develop a **trusting relationship**. The nitty-gritty of accomplishing those two goals, however, rests in skills that we can manifest daily as quality educators and in opportunities that can be part of every school day. We need to be able to teach regulation and we need to be able to connect with students. If anyone is uniquely poised to do this work well, it is us.

STRESS AND ITS RELATIONSHIP TO TRAUMA

We must consider brain science and psychology when navigating trauma. To understand the changes in the brain that accompany trauma, we first need to begin by examining what happens in the brain and body when it is stressed.

Types of Stress and Impact

It is important to note that **stress** and trauma lie on a continuum. There is **productive stress** (also called *eustress*), such as the stress that gets us energized for a competitive run or gives us the extra energy to study for an exam. This productive stress provides the extra oomph to get over a hurdle and when we do, we expend the associated stress hormones. All is well.

There are times, however, when we experience **intolerable stress** and we are not able to tackle the source of the stress. We feel as if we have no control. If there are a low number of these experiences and they are not extremely intense in nature, we can tolerate this level of stress. It may have some short-term impact but, generally, we are able to move forward.

When stress overwhelms our systems because of its intensity or chronic nature, we have turned a corner and have reached the other end of the continuum. We experience toxic stress or trauma. This continuum is reflected in Figure 2.1.

Figure 2.1.   Stress and trauma lie on a continuum. Productive stress occurs when the body and brain are able to respond to increased demands. Toxic stress occurs when demands or experiences severely compromise an individual's ability to respond effectively, which in turn negatively affects his or her physiological and psychological well-being.

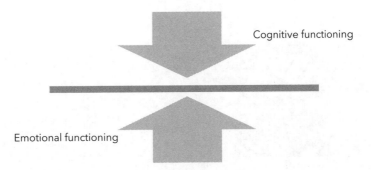

Figure 2.2. When emotion and cognition are integrated together to support healthy functioning, we experience a state of balance and well-being.

Well-Being and Balance

The human brain experiences emotions and cognition simultaneously. Typically, the brain functions in relative balance. When these two ways of interpreting life—emotion and cognition—are integrated together to support healthy functioning, we experience a state of well-being as depicted in Figure 2.2.

Stress tips us toward more emotional functioning. We deploy our brain's emotional regions for a specific purpose—to encode a memory, to deal with something that is challenging, to alert our safety systems—all while still being able to think rationally. After the stress has passed, we quickly return to a cognitive-emotional balance and experience a state of homeostasis. When we do this routinely, our lives as a whole are characterized by balance. Figure 2.3 shows this imbalance and then the return to balance during stressful experiences that are tolerable.

Intolerable Stress and Thinking Imbalance

Under intolerable stress, however, the balance shifts dramatically enough that we are not able to function in our typical way. Intolerable stress elicits an imbalanced response of emotional and cognitive functioning. The emotional center of our brain, the **amygdala**, becomes more active and **cortisol** floods the brain. We react more reflexively (Sylwester, 1995). We become significantly more emotional in our choices. Simultaneously, there is decreased activity in the cognitive regions of our brain. We struggle with retrieving known information, with new learning and even with discriminating between salient and non-salient information. This significant shift is shown in Figure 2.4.

Depending on the intensity of the stress, we may only be able to retrieve the procedural, well-practiced types of memory and there are times when even that is lost. An intensely

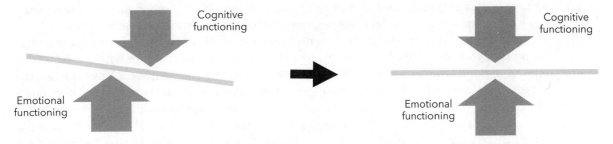

Figure 2.3. Stress tips us toward more emotional functioning. In healthy conditions, we quickly return to a balanced state of emotional and cognitive functioning after the stress has passed.

Figure 2.4. Intolerable stress creates a significantly imbalanced response between emotional and cognitive functioning. Choices are much more emotional and reflexive, and cognitive activity markedly decreases.

stressed person *may* be capable of driving the familiar route home but cannot navigate a detour in the route, which is a less rote cognitive task. Under much higher levels of stress, an individual may even become disoriented driving that familiar route as the stress chemicals flooding their brain begin to compromise **procedural knowledge**.

It is important to recognize that, at times of high threat, this shift away from the thinking regions of the brain is absolutely *functional and adaptive*. We do not want to be distracted by a whole assortment of thoughts, we need to pay attention to the threat and take protective action—fast!

Sensory Changes

Other brain changes accompany this brain shift from cognitive-emotional balance to emotionally dominated. Some are immediate and readily observable. Some changes, those that are the result of **cumulative stress**, are a bit more cloaked except to the trauma-trained eye.

Immediate Impact   Our vision center becomes more active. Our pupils dilate and we *tune into the visual information available to us*. Educators have often reported to us that they notice a student's eyes going dark when they are getting upset; what they are reading is pupil dilation—a visual stress response. Not only do the eyes dilate to take more information in, but in fact, the region in the visual cortex that registers images when they first enter the brain, Brodmann's area 19, becomes very active (van der Kolk, 2014). Our visual centers also become selectively attuned to visual stimuli. This selective attunement is reflected in the work of Dr. Beatrice de Gelder, et al. of Massachusetts General Hospital in Boston who found that aroused visual centers are more tuned into the body language of others experiencing fear than they are tuned into the fearful facial expressions of others (Tamiettoa, Castelli, Vighetti, Perozzo, Geminiani, Weiskrantz, & de Gelder, 2009). In situations of high stress/threat, our brain becomes highly efficient at reading certain key factors and avoids tuning in to the totality of the outside world. In the case of reading fear, we focus on body language because it is more quickly assessed and easier to see and interpret, in 360 degrees, than facial expressions are (O'Neil, 2004).

As vision dominates, our language centers recede, resulting in changes in both receptive and expressive language abilities. Have you ever found yourself stressed and what you hear from someone talking sounds closer to *blah-blah-blah* than to any real sentence? Have you noticed that when you are under stress you may request that someone repeat themselves or slow down their speech? Those experiences reflect the change in your receptive abilities. Expressively, you may have found that in a stressful social situation, you use more monosyllabic words than you would otherwise. For our students, this drop in receptive and expressive language may result in them not understanding what we are asking of them and/or thought-stuttering—giving us simple verbal responses over and over that are not connected to our actual question or comment.

The other changes brought about by stress happen throughout our bodies. While cortisol is flooding our brains and making changes there, **adrenaline** is coursing through our bodies. This companion response allows us to engage in the action that our brain is demanding. Our body is mobilized for that fight *or* flight response by elevating heart rate and increasing respirations so that we can send oxygen to our extremities. Less important functions, such as digestion in the stomach, dial back, allowing for a diversion of energy so we can take action, whether it is pushing away an attacker or swerving the car out of the path of an oncoming vehicle.

Again, being able to take action in such situations is extremely adaptive—the brain and body work in a coordinated fashion in an attempt to ensure our safety. In most situations when we experience a threat, our brains are quick to sense it, our bodies become chemically prepared for it, we take some sort of action and then, once safe, our bodies return to a state of homeostasis/calm and our brains do the same. We again become able to engage in **reflectivity** (Sylwester, 1995).

Understanding this process and knowing that, for some of our students, it can be triggered by events that we personally do not recognize as threatening allows us to both notice student reactions and intervene earlier and more effectively. We invite you to pause and think about what you can expect of a student when their thinking brain is less available. Consider how the reduced ability to process and generate language might change how you interact with a student. What might you see in their interactions with you? Reflect on which of your interventions exacerbate the fight or flight response and which take that energy and use it in a positive and reregulating way.

We also invite you to consider how challenging students impact *your* ability to think clearly, see accurately, hear well, and stay physically calm. How will you take care of yourself, deal with the stress that is flowing through your own body and brain? What is your self-care plan? How might your educational community support you? We will continually circle back to these concepts and considerations throughout this book. Process this information for yourself and then talk with your colleagues as you find answers that fit.

Cumulative Impact

Unfortunately, the same biological systems that save us in many circumstances also can turn against us under other conditions. If we cannot respond by fighting or taking flight, freezing becomes our only available response. In situations where we can take sufficient action, the cortisol in our brain is used up/burnt off. When we can only somewhat take action or when we freeze, cortisol remains in the brain, causing damage.

In fact, anytime we cannot react in a manner that completely burns off our brain's stress chemicals, the cortisol remains and compromises portions of the brain—in particular, the prefrontal cortex and the **hippocampus**, which is the portion of our brain that moves short-term memory into long-term memory. According to Daniel Goleman (2005), in the hippocampus, the damage takes the form of reducing the number of neurons added in those structures, as well as increasing the number of neurons lost. Research has shown that adults who spent most of their lives in the high-stress conditions of poverty have 20% smaller working memories and the size of their hippocampi are observably smaller when imaged (Hall, 2009). It is important to note that although this impact is quite concerning, it is now known that, when the hippocampus is no longer under siege by stress chemicals, it can regenerate, particularly during childhood (University of California, San Francisco, 2018).

The prefrontal cortex, our executive functioning portion of the brain, is also vulnerable to the neurotoxic effect of cortisol (Lupien, McEwen, Gunnar, & Heim, 2009). A compromised prefrontal cortex means that our ability to plan, organize, conceptualize time, initiate tasks, delay gratification, and avoid impulses are all at risk for being underdeveloped, making us less skillful in resourcing those abilities which may result in learning challenges. Knowing this, is it any surprise that our traumatized students struggle academically as well as with organization and relationships?

There is a toll caused by stress chemicals on the body as well. When stress chemicals (adrenalin and others) remain, they keep our blood pressure high, interfere with healthy digestion, stop the regeneration of cells in our skin, and cause other compromises to our physical well-being.

PERVASIVE TRAUMA

In conditions of pervasive trauma, stress is chronic, and the carryover of stress chemicals happens time and time again. The negative impact is cumulative to both brain and body systems. In addition, the brain becomes shaped for future interactions based on the negative interactions of the past. In other words, our brains become hard-wired to *not* return to the balance we discussed earlier.

Chronic System Activation

Nadine Burke Harris (2015) in her TED Talk speaks to this process through the analogy of a bear confrontation in the woods. It is adaptive to be hyper-alert to that bear and therefore, the process is protective. She cautions, however, that a system that is activated night after night by the bear being in the home is one that develops health issues and one that may develop behaviors that become maladaptive in non-dangerous situations. A system built under chronic stress is wired differently, and it takes less and less to trigger the full stress response. The **allostatic load**—cumulative stress hormones—and the changes in the brain predispose the individual to this kind of chronic, high-level reaction.

> *I do not know how to describe the sound of a world crashing. Maybe there is no sound, just a great emptiness, an enveloping sorrow, a creeping nothingness that coils itself around you like a stiff wire.*
>
> —Charles Blow (2015, p. 67)

Remember that remaining cortisol doing its damage to important cognitive regions? Well, its prolonged presence does benefit one part—the amygdala (Lupien, et al., 2009). With repeated threats—real or imagined—the amygdala becomes more and more robust, more quickly sending out the warning signals, which further predisposes the person to hyper-arousing—including at nonthreatening situations. This smoke-detector of the brain goes off with less and less smoke in the air (van der Kolk, 2014). A frequently activated amygdala shifts the balance of what we remember toward **implicit memories** and away from the hippocampus' explicit/conscious memories—resulting in behavioral triggers. Many times, the visceral nature of these triggers (think of the peppery smell in Scott's story) makes them indiscernible to observers.

This helps to explain the student who is constantly reporting in an agitated manner that *So-and-so is looking at me!* or who seems unduly distressed by a change in schedule or the introduction of new academic material. In situations of toxic stress, the stress reaction that was designed to keep us safe from harm becomes part of the cycle of ongoing hurt.

Poor Sleep Hygiene

Students experiencing toxic levels of stress also are at increased risk of experiencing other conditions that exacerbate their experience of stress. Lack of healthy sleep is a powerful multiplier of stress-related issues and, conversely, stress is a source of many sleep issues—a chicken and egg conundrum. The neurochemicals present in the brain and in the body as a result of stress prevent settling and interfere with healthy sleep cycles (National Sleep Foundation, "Trauma and Sleep," n.d.). Issues including difficulty falling asleep and staying asleep and dream/nightmare problems create poor sleep and, over time, may create poor sleep habits. Poor sleep causes daytime fatigue, a more vulnerable emotional state, and lack of cognitive focus, which all tend to contribute to higher levels of stress. It is a cycle that is challenging to change and requires us to consider all the elements related to healthy sleep hygiene—quantity, quality, and consistency.

We often think of sleep in terms of quantity. *Did the student get enough sleep?* The National Sleep Foundation, based on rigorous research, recommends the following quantity of sleep by age category (National Sleep Foundation, "How Much Sleep Do We Really Deed?" n.d.)

- Preschoolers (3–5): 10–13 hours

- School-age children (6–13): 9–11 hours

- Teenagers (14–17): 8–10 hours

- Younger adults (18–25): 7–9 hours

- Adults (26–64): 7–9 hours

Unfortunately, most children and adults do not get the right quantity of sleep. Quantity, however, is just one part of the healthy sleep equation, it also needs the companion components of quality and consistency. What does quality mean? It means undisrupted sleep, which allows for sleep phases where the brain heals then synthesizes the information that was acquired during the day, making the information more retrievable. By the way, disruption does not have to be something that wakes you fully; it can be something as mild as the cell phone on your nightstand vibrating with an incoming email that does not wake you up but pulls you out of your deep sleep phase. For children, it can be noises from a nearby room or from the street, the activity of a sibling who shares a room, or, as in the adult example, technology (Bronson & Merryman, 2009).

Consistency means the same time for going to sleep and the same time for waking up. The brain does best with routine and studies have shown that sleep shifting (i.e., getting to bed later but still sleeping the same length of time as usual) for even *just an hour over a couple of days* can have ramifications for the ability to learn and behave (Bronson & Merryman, 2009). If you have ever observed the meltdown behavior of children on vacation, you probably have glimpsed the result of sleep shifting.

If we think of sleep as analogous to oxygen (Vedantam, 2018), we begin to understand that you cannot stock up on sleep, and you cannot make up for lost sleep by sleeping longer the next night. To do our best, we need it routinely, purely, and in sufficient amounts. Good sleep hygiene results in a more efficient prefrontal cortex, that all-important executive-functioning portion of the brain. Good sleep translates to a better regulated, organized, focused individual allowing us to be efficient thinkers and more socially and emotionally successful beings. Compromised sleep means a compromised ability to initiate tasks, maintain attention to tasks, control impulses, predict outcomes, and other related skills (Bronson & Merryman, 2009).

Even after one bad night of sleep, many of us will feel like we are operating in a dark fog; we feel dull and cranky. Part of this is related to our inability to smoothly retrieve information in general but another part is related to the orderly process in which the brain synthesizes. Our brain gives preference (early synthesis) to the amygdala and lower preference to the hippocampus (later synthesis). The amygdala processes negative memories and the hippocampus processes neutral and positive memories. Putting those two facts together explains our day of crankiness after a bad night of sleep and, more broadly, why people who are quality sleep deprived feel more depressed—a sleep-deprived brain is one that remembers the bad elements of one's life more easily than the good (Bronson & Merryman, 2009). Now, let's think about our students who are coming from high-stress environments. By definition, they experience more of the negative that the world has to offer and then, without proper sleep, they remember all that bad stuff more easily and lose track of any good stuff that occurred. Is it any wonder that children coming from chronic trauma express feelings of sadness, negativity, anxiety, and worthlessness?

You may be reading this and thinking, *Why talk about our students' sleep hygiene when it is beyond our control as educators?* You are right, it is beyond your control—for your students. It is more under your control for you. (Remember that self-care thing?) Many adults have poor sleep hygiene, and improving their habits makes them more optimistic, quick-thinking, and able to handle their daily stressors.

There are elements related to your students' sleep that are under your influence. First, we share this information so there is an understanding of the roots of some of the behaviors you may witness because that invites compassion and helps to stop us from taking unpleasant moments personally. We also share it because, knowing that our students may remember negative events more readily, we can intentionally build more positive experiences and make them more memorable in other ways. One simple way to do this is to provide a couple of minutes each day for students to add to a list in a success journal and then read over their list (a success journal is simply a list of simple, good things one did such as *I remembered to take my jacket home, I shared my markers, I did a couple of long exhalations before I responded, I picked up the trash next to my desk.*) We share it because the ability to notice when students are struggling with being tired will allow us to embed activities that may help students regulate-up/awaken. It is foundational knowledge that some educators have respectfully and tactfully discussed with families, and it has proven helpful to those families and their children. Finally, we share it because sometimes sleep in the form of a quality nap during the school day has become a part of a few of our students' behavior plans.

REGULATION

What is **self-regulation**? Siegel (2013) defines self-regulation as the ability to maintain a balance between the accelerator (energizing components) and the brakes (calming components) of the emotional system. Williams and Lewin (2014) write that self-regulation is what enables individuals to manage their emotions and direct their attention, thinking, and actions to meet adaptive goals. Rather simply, Stosny (2011), says, "Behaviorally, self-regulation is the ability to act in your long-term best interest." We think of self-regulation as the ability to manage one's physical movement, attention, and emotions in order to function successfully in the greater social environment.

Physical regulation is about the ability to control body movements, including vocalizations—how big/small, fast/slow, hard/soft, and loud/quiet the body is being. It is about the balance between calmness and alertness. When we are physically regulated, our activity level fluctuates to match the context and we deploy the correct motor response (gross motor, fine motor, rate of breathing) for the context. It is what allows us to cheer at a baseball game and then sit back down and focus quietly on the batter, to settle into work after a period of exercise, to fall asleep at the end of an action-packed day.

Attention (mental control), as in the skills of focus, awareness, and concentration, is affected by somatic (body) settling. As the body modulates down, the vagus nerve sends a message up to the brain that we are safe—ready and able to shift to a state of rest, maintain focus, as well as check in on and tune in to less survival-oriented systems. When we can regulate our attention, we are able to select the important things to pay attention to and we are able to tune out less important stimuli. We are more successful at persisting with a task and at paying attention to the behaviors of others for a longer period in order to understand them—their feelings and needs.

Severely abused children show confused emotions. Their affect is off. They may laugh at scary moments or cry when surprised. They grew up ad-libbing parts in a play they never understood.

— Tobin (1991, p. 16)

Emotional regulation is also about matching the outside context. When regulated, we emotionally react to events with the appropriate intensity and we move from a high emotional state to a calmer, less intense state. We are tuned into our emotions (i.e., emotionally aware). We know what they are, why we are feeling them, and how we are demonstrating them. Our emotions fit the context because we not only have an array of emotions we can show, we are able to display those emotions at different intensities. Further, healthy emotional regulation also means that we understand the emotions of others—what they are and why they are feeling them. It is this understanding that allows us to adjust our behaviors accordingly. This is the ability to have empathy. When we become highly upset with someone but then shift to calm after a genuine apology, we are emotionally regulating. This ability allows us to be sad in response to another's loss, it allows us to contain our laughter in a solemn environment even if we just witnessed something genuinely funny within that situation. Just like physical regulation sets the stage for healthy attention, emotional regulation sets the stage for healthy social interactions. When we are emotionally regulated, we easily read the social context and adjust our voice volume or the content of what we are saying. We can tune into the emotional states of others, we can express our disagreements using reasonable language and we can incorporate others' thoughts into our thinking.

Dysregulation is the opposite experience. The *match* between the outside world and the interior world of the student are out of sync. Students may experience physical dysregulation, emotional dysregulation, and/or cognitive dysregulation. What does that look like? How do children end up in a state of dysregulation?

Some children may be dysregulated by temporary conditions—too little sleep, shifted sleep, too much screen time, rapid developmental growth, and/or transient stressors. Students with trauma histories are more likely to experience dysregulated states that are frequent and significant. To consider dysregulation as it relates specifically to trauma, let's begin with the work of Dr. Bruce Perry (Perry, B., & Szalavitz, M., 2006) and his neurosequential model as seen in Figure 2.5. Perry uses his neurosequential model to understand, map, and treat the impact of early experiences of trauma. Intervention, according to this model, first addresses more foundational neurological development needs by engaging the child in somatosensory activities that help develop his or her ability to regulate. Later, after the child is able to self-regulate, intervention moves on to cognitive processes.

We know that children's brains that have been built through patterned, predictable, calm life experiences are ones that develop in an organized manner from the bottom level up to the highest cognitive levels. These children are highly likely to be regulated individuals. This happens because their lives, in Abraham Maslow's terminology (1943), are ones in which their basic physiological and emotional safety needs are met. They experience low amounts of startling, so their blood pressure, breathing, and heart rate do not rise precipitously or often. When they cry, they are soothed, which helps them develop calming pathways in their brain and provides the opportunity for them to learn how to self-soothe, thanks to the model of their involved, caring adult. They are eased into sleep and are calmed as they awaken from sleep. They experience healthy satiation—they become only a bit hungry, and then they are fed; they

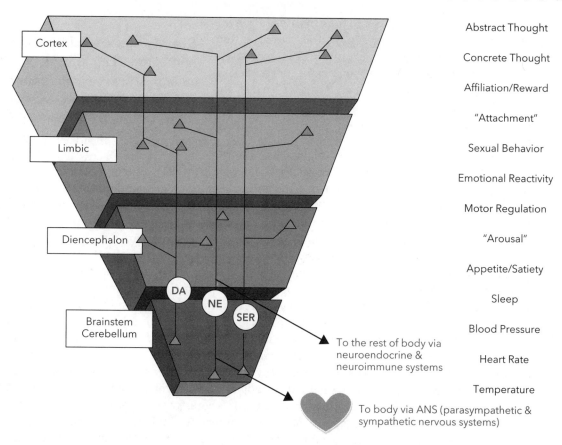

Figure 2.5. Perry's neurosequential model. *Source:* Perry, B. D. (2019).

become slightly uncomfortable from a wet diaper, and they are relieved of that discomfort. When they signal they have a need, it is almost always attended to within a reasonable time frame. These experiences allow their neurological systems to develop in what Dr. Perry calls a coordinated, cohesive manner (2014). These children are neurologically regulated, so their physical, emotional, social, and cognitive systems are more easily resourced and function more smoothly and completely. As a result, these children are able to act in their own long-term best interest.

Conversely, Dr. Perry (2006) has found that children whose neurological systems have been built under the conditions of chronic stress (and without sufficient mitigating factors) are organized more chaotically. Children who experience trauma at a very young age may have their most basic needs compromised. Loud noises, rough handling, frequent changes in care- givers and other experiences can result in quickly rising heart rates and rapid increases in blood pressure causing those systems to be less stable. If children's lives do not provide pat- terned and predictable self-settling/sleep routines and or feeding routines, their midbrains are not regulated, and those children will struggle with learning how to self-settle. This lack of ability to self-settle has consequences for motor regulation, eating, emotional regulation, and all that is farther up on the triangle. These children certainly can connect with others and do higher-level thinking, but it is more difficult for them to do so. Nothing comes as easily to them. Think about that elementary student who cannot calm down after coming in from the playground, or the middle school student who is bouncing off the walls after PE class. Those students cannot self-settle or regulate themselves easily as they move from one activity to another.

The bottom line is that when children are *not* lovingly held, rocked, fed, and soothed in a predictable, consistent manner, and when they are frequently exposed to startling, they do not form an *integrated* neurological system, and that has myriad implications. Those implications include insufficient *tuning up*, lack of self-calming pathways in the brain, areas of the brain that are sidelined, and struggles with attunement and attachment (Perry, 2005).

Insufficient Tuning Up

A system that is not integrated may be not fully tuned up neurologically, which means the child does not sense the world accurately. In fact, research has shown that children with developmental trauma have brains that do not light up—activate—when the child touches objects in the same ways that brains of children without trauma do. They literally do not perceive the physical world the same way (van der Kolk, 2014).

In schools, we see manifestations of these insufficiently tuned-up systems when students have food all over their faces without being aware of it or when they touch others with too much force or when they cannot turn the pages of a book efficiently. To enhance understanding of this lack of tuning up, we often reflect with our colleagues about what we see in the elderly population whose systems are in the process of neurologically tuning down, and whose symptoms are highly similar—lack of awareness of food on the face or in their teeth, for example, and difficulty with fine motor tasks, such as buttoning or page-turning. When we recognize the neurological element to some of these behaviors, we can come to understand that it may not be a behavioral choice and that it may be the result of a neurological system that is not functioning at the optimal level. Think about what that might mean for how we respond to a student who is touching peers too hard or who is falling behind after we have given directions? The following case study shows the power of considering an insufficiently tuned-up neurological system as the reason for behavioral struggles.

SAMI

Sami was referred to her school's behavior team due to her lack of focus, disruption to other students, tantrum behavior, disorganization, and chronic out-of-seat behavior. After the teacher attempted several reward systems and then punishment systems that failed to work, I was called in to observe and make recommendations.

I noticed that Sami struggled to put away papers in the proper folder and frequently ended up shoving them into her desk. When she needed to get a paper to bring to small group, she would not be able to find it in the time frame provided by the transition period, and she would then come late to small group without the required material.

Once she was behind, she tended to give up and would bother her peers in the group or leave the group to wander the classroom. If she stayed, when asked to turn to a page in a text, she rarely got to the page before the activity commenced. Once on the correct page, she was able to turn pages one at a time to keep up with the group.

In general, anytime she had to find a paper in the tornado ruins of her desk, she would not succeed, and she often had to begin tasks over despite her protestations that she had done most of the work already. Sometimes those protests were followed by crying and then slumping in her chair, refusing to do anything being asked of her.

The gift of being an outside observer is that your only task is to watch that individual student. I was able to observe that every time she wasn't complying or wasn't focused, it began with her not being able to handle fine motor tasks associated with handling papers. My hypothesis was that her neurological system may not have been fully tuned up and that she needed support in handling papers and book pages.

Of course, there also were other complications—she did have focus issues—but given that there could be a physical explanation for the origin of her downward spiral of behavior, her teacher put into place these interventions:

- Provided student with finger cones (soft thimbles to help with page turning).

- Connected student with a peer buddy to help with keeping materials and desk organized.

- Periodically used student's book as the model of which page to be on for the group or whole class (teacher turned to correct page and held it up for others to see), which put her on the right page from the start.

These interventions made a difference. She still was not always focused but she often started tasks with the group and her participation increased significantly while the wayward behaviors decreased.

Lack of Self-Calming Pathways

Here is a little experiment. Take a water bottle and shake it up. Now set it down on the counter. How fast does it return to its original settled status? How comfortable are you with opening the cap right away? Now take a soda bottle and shake it for the same length of time and set it down on the counter next to the water bottle. How comfortable are you with opening *its* cap? Do you have any concerns about the mess that may follow if you do? Students with trauma histories are much more like the soda bottle than the water bottle. When life interacts with them, they grow dysregulated and require a longer period of time than many other students do to settle down or there may be some sort of behavioral mess. When children's brain architectures have been built under toxic conditions, they do not develop the self-calming pathways that automatically allow them to settle like the water in the water bottle does. This impacts life on a daily basis and it also leaves their brains even more vulnerable to future stressors. Infants who are routinely comforted develop strategies for self-comforting and then they become school-age children who have socially appropriate ways to comfort themselves.

Infants who have many experiences of modulation (e.g., a parent singing and then humming and then barely audibly whispering) learn to move from a more active state to a calmer state (i.e., the development of calming pathways). These children become students who can navigate the shift from PE class to taking a test, from the social busyness of the cafeteria to the quiet of the computer lab. Without those experiences provided to them, children cannot simply create those methods for themselves because all brains develop in a use-dependent manner. For those students to learn to settle and to modulate their activity, they need to be provided with specific methods, given opportunities to practice, receive coaching as they practice, and be positively recognized for their efforts. They are students who need much more than the simplified cue of *time to settle down*. They require explicit instruction in self-soothing and modulation (see Chapter 9).

Sidelined Areas of the Brain

Chronic stress leads to the sidelining of some portions of the brain, which means that those parts do not develop robustly and are not as easily accessed as other parts. It is, again, that use-dependent way our brains are built—any part of the brain that is not exercised is not as easily accessed and its talents are less available.

Among the parts of the brain that are sidelined are the posterior cingulate—which helps a child be aware of their body in space—and the dorsolateral prefrontal cortex, which, along with the thalamus, allows the child to make sense of time and sequence and to remember events as a cohesive story. The cluster of the medial prefrontal cortex, anterior cingulate, parietal cortex, and insula and posterior cingulate—self-sensing parts of the brain and where we hold our self-awareness—also are not as wired-in (van der Kolk, 2014). This compromises a child's ability to make decisions, set priorities, and have a sense of agency in the world. As we shared earlier, the hippocampus of a child who has experienced toxic stress is likely to be smaller so working memory capacity may be decreased—a reality that can lead to additional new stressors associated with learning and social relationships. Again, it is not that a child who has had significant, unmitigated stress cannot be successful in the world—it is just substantially more difficult to do so.

We see many behaviors that are related to these sidelined brain areas. Think of students who lean against the wall as they walk down the hallway, students who fool around and then quickly try to finish their work to no avail, students who chronically answer almost any question with *I don't know* or a shrug, and students who cannot seem to follow a simple set of directions that most other children their age can follow. There may be many reasons for these behaviors, but a trauma-informed behavioral perspective asks two questions first, *Could it be related to how trauma has shaped their brain? How can I build in supports so they can do better?*

ATTUNEMENT AND ATTACHMENT

Attunement is the ability to be aware of and responsive to one another, to tune into each other, to read another person's signals. There is a reciprocity to attunement. So, what do we mean by **attachment**? In our context, attachment is when a child feels safe and secure in the presence of an adult and trusts that the adult will protect them. When a child and adult are attached, they both find pleasure and benefit in the relationship. Attachment is the foundation for all other forms of relationship that develop between a child and an adult. In healthy conditions, regulation allows for attunement, and attunement promotes attachment, which then further supports regulation as seen in Figure 2.6 that follows.

Children who have experienced pervasive trauma may have had limited or erratic experiences with one or more pieces of this sequence prior to interacting with their educators. Even children who have been attuned to others and who may have attachment with others may be dysregulated enough that they cannot attune and attach in school. Children who are uncomfortable in their own skins (dysregulated) cannot devote energy to being aware and responsive to others. They are not routinely calm enough to look into the eyes of a caregiver, to interact verbally or non-verbally in a responsive pattern, or to be responsive to the caring ovations an adult may make toward them. Without being able to tune in to adults, children cannot sense the safety and security a caring adult has to offer. In other words, without regulation, it is extremely hard for the child to attach to others.

Figure 2.6. In healthy conditions, regulation allows for attunement and attunement promotes attachment, which then further supports regulation.

Children who are difficult to soothe, who startle easily, and who cannot efficiently do many of the things that are being asked of them are children who do not naturally invite others to tune into them either. A dysregulated child does not tend to be reinforcing for any caregiver. Instead, they are prickly, which drives caregivers to turn away from them and toward other children who are more responsive to their efforts. Without regulation, it is challenging for others to attach to the child.

Good attachment does not inoculate a child against later misfortune, but it does get the child off on the right foot.

—James Garbarino (1999, p. 39)

Without regulation, the *serve and return* interactions that create a bond of trust between a child and a caregiver are disrupted and the access to social learning and social comfort is lost. It is vital that a child who is highly dysregulated be guided into regulation so attunement and, ultimately, attachment can occur between the adult and the child and, eventually, between the child and his or her peers.

For children with trauma histories, unaddressed dysregulation and the resultant lack of attunement will continue to drive away adults unless those adults are trauma-informed and determined to stay connected. That attunement foundation must start with the adult whether that adult begins the connection or responds to the hidden bid for connection within the dysregulated child's behaviors. What is a hidden bid for connection? It is the child's best attempt to make a connection with others and often it comes in the form of what is referred to as challenging behavior. The bid says *I need you* or *I am interested in you* or *I like you* but in a way that requires translation. Think about students you know who hang around you constantly complaining or those students who catch your eye and then do something belligerent. Are you able to see those as bids for connection? Undoubtedly, that requires an adult to see the student through a trauma-informed lens, to have the ability to translate the student's communication and continue the work of supporting the student to regulate and connect.

Becoming a regulated individual opens the door for attunement and then attachment and then even more. In their book *Reclaiming Youth at Risk*, authors Brendtro, Brokenleg, and Van Bockern state that "research indicates that children who are securely attached to significant adults become more curious, self-directed and empathic. In a very real sense attachment fosters achievement, autonomy, and altruism" (2009, p. 75). McClelland, Ponitz, Messersmith, and Tominey (2010), in their chapter for the handbook *Self-Regulation: The Integration of Cognition and Emotion*, also express this greater reach of self-regulation and identify it as affecting motivation and future thinking, as well as life satisfaction and improved mental health as depicted in Figure 2.7. Clearly, the payoff is significant, but the work is hard. Being gently relentless is key.

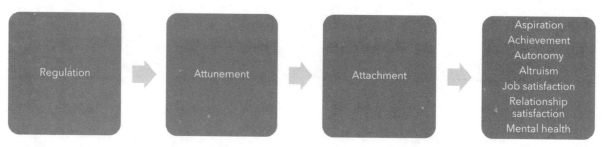

Figure 2.7.   Becoming a regulated individual opens the door for attunement, then attachment, and then so much more.

JAVIER

When I first met Javier, he was 14 and about as prickly as a child that age could be. He would take nothing, absolutely nothing from me, not so much as a pencil or a small compliment. Every day when I greeted him, he scoffed, refusing to make eye contact. I remember making the decision that I would be relentlessly caring and that gave me the energy to joyfully greet him every day, to continue to offer help as he struggled on schoolwork—despite his turned back and mumbled curses. It took several months but eventually, he asked, "You plan to keep this up?" with his mouth in a slight curl. I responded quietly, "What do you think?" He looked up through his bangs and nodded.

Our relationship moved forward from there . . . tiny steps forward and, periodically, several large steps back. Once open to my academic coaching, Javier began to do very well in his classes and that seemed to give more momentum to the development of trust between us. By the end of the school year, we had a close teacher-student relationship, complete with inside jokes and honest conversations. I was elated; perseverance and optimism had prevailed! Javier would be moving up to high school and I was pretty convinced he would be successful there both academically and behaviorally. The last day of school, Javier came into my classroom hiding behind his bangs again, his back turned toward me. I quietly bent to check in on him and he growled that he was going to kill himself that summer and suggested that I should kill myself as well. I was taken aback, did what I should do when such things are said, tried to connect with him, but was rebuffed again. He spent some time in the school counselor's office and then, at the end of the day, he picked up his coat and left without another word to me.

A couple of years later my landline rang. "Hi, it's me, Javier." I immediately knew who it was and tried to not let the relief I felt surge through my saying of his name back to him; it felt tidal in my chest and I was afraid it would wash him off the line. He continued, "I hope you don't mind; I found your number and I wanted to call to let you know that I'm okay and I'm sorry for what I said." We talked for close to an hour and he shared about his therapy, the distance he had come, his plans for the future. When he thanked me at the end, I responded that it was me who needed to thank him for the gift he had given me with his call.

I think of Javier all the time, and that is not hyperbole. I think of him whenever a student rejects me and I could take it to heart—but I don't. I think of him every time I hear a teacher say that they don't know whether they have made an appreciable difference with a student. Javier has allowed me to say to them with great confidence, "You may very well have, but you might never know."

Trust in Adults

The ability to trust is a significant casualty of trauma, and it has myriad cascading effects. If a child experiences life without an adult present who can provide for their basic needs, who can comfort them, and who can protect them from harm, the child comes to believe that such a connection will never happen. This lack of trust is likely to extend beyond the caregiver to other adults, including you, the student's educator.

Even if an adult did their best to support a child, their inability to adequately perform those caretaking behaviors may result in the child having an internal sense of skepticism toward adults. Families living in economically stressed situations are vulnerable to this—the adults may be doing all they can, but the child still perceives that they cannot trust their parents to ensure their basic physical and emotional needs will be met. This may never be articulated in language or even perceived in the conscious mind, yet it may exist in the child's subconscious.

Certainly, children who have experienced trauma at the hands of an adult have great reason to not trust. When that adult, someone who the child looked to for a sense of safety, was a *source* of their pain, the ability to trust *any* adult, even a very caring adult, is at great risk. Abusive and/or neglectful parenting sets the stage for a child to struggle mightily with any trust in connection and that plays out in copious ways including chronic opposition, sabotage of relational gains, and avoidance of healthy interdependence. Dr. Kenneth Ginsburg, a Philadelphia pediatrician who has specialized in supporting teens of trauma writes in his book, *Reaching Teens,* "Immature human beings are helpless for a longer period of their lives than any other species. This dependency has necessitated an extensive attachment system between adults and offspring that results in devastating deficiencies whenever that young person fails to receive this kind of protection" (Ginsburg, & Kinsman, 2014, p. 42).

Relationship building is an endurance event. Those who seek quick and dramatic changes in a child should recognize that patterns laid down over a lifetime may be slow to change.

—Brendtro, Brokenleg, & Van Bockern (2009, p. 81)

Children who cannot trust adults are both *emotionally exhausted* (imagine having no one you can trust?) and *emotionally exhausting* to the people who are seeking to support them. They may be highly disrespectful when they long to be respected by others, they test limits when they desperately need guidance, they reject when they need relationship desperately, they aggress when they ache for comfort, they sabotage when their deep desire is to be trusted.

Children who do not trust adults require adults who are steadfast. They also require adults who know how to build relationship slowly, micro-step by micro-step. Hardest of all perhaps, is that they require adults who can endure rejection after it seemed like trust was established. This tendency for a child with trauma to pull away after having allowed a relationship to grow is to be expected and, somehow, in expecting it, it becomes more tolerable, less of a jolt to the adult's psyche.

Trust in Self

When you are a child and cannot trust adults, who do you trust? Many children seem to think that they are the only one they can trust; they become the boss of themselves—seeking control over things large and small. They are described as oppositional, defiant, unmanageable, argumentative. In reality, they are just trying to manage the best they can, to know where the edges of their lives are. They are all surface bluster disguised as confidence. That facade is a dreadfully heavy task for younger children and is still a draining one for adolescents.

When their energy is low, these very same children who want to control everything may make no decisions for themselves, not unlike the dogs in Seligman's learned helplessness study who simply endured electronic shock, making no effort to escape it (Ackerman, 2019). Seligman et al., found that when dogs were routinely exposed to pain or discomfort with no control over escaping it, they no longer attempted to escape, even when they could. Other studies that followed found the same results in humans: once a person learns that they will experience discomfort over which they have no control, they stop trying to escape that discomfort. Seligman proposed that the repeated experiences of pain without the ability to control it results in emotional, cognitive, and motivational deficits. Combine this with what we know about the lack of activity in the self-sensing part of the brain for children of trauma as discussed earlier, and this extreme passivity is no surprise. The child has learned that his or her actions are not of consequence in the world. Agency, the trust in oneself, may become Oz's wizard (Metro-Goldwyn-Mayer, 1939)—all smoke, mirrors, and mechanical thunder, while the child stands behind the curtain shaking.

Trust in Peers

Trust issues extend beyond developing trust in adults. We know that children who come from social and emotional environments that are healthy and that support the soul and body long for and enjoy peer relationships. That desire for peer connection tends to increase across their school years. What happens to peer relationships when trauma is shaping relationships in a child's life? It's no surprise that those relationships are likely to be tumultuous or tenuous. They are defined by a mindset of scarcity because trauma, by its very nature, is a condition of scarcity. In the child's mind, adult protection and nurturing was insufficient and/or unpredictable. Peers, therefore, are likely to be perceived as competition for all-too-scarce resources such as adult time, adult assistance, loving attention, sufficient food, and soothing. At best, peer relationships with children the same age may tend toward being more transactional; a peer may be a means to an end—a tool for having needs met rather than a relationship of value in and of itself.

Valuing peer relationships becomes another thing to be taught to these students, and that teaching can happen through the day-in and day-out experiences at school. Just like the development of an adult–child relationship, these peer relationships will need to be constructed by caring educators. Think about how this knowledge informs us! It asks us to pay attention to how we use—or should not use—competition in the classroom, and it demands that we intentionally build student-to-student relationships so that our children of trauma can discover the deep value of these vital social relationships.

It also means we need to be sensitive to what may happen when one of our students decides to trust us. Why is this so critical? Think of yourself as a life preserver. When a student who has experienced trauma finally has taken that risky step of trusting in you, connecting with you, allowing you to help them, it is as if they have been drowning and they have finally decided that it is *you* who can help them keep their head above water. They finally can take a full breath and then another and relax their body just a bit. The feeling is unfamiliar but incomprehensively wonderful to them. But then, suddenly there is another student who is swimming up for you to be their life preserver as well (or perhaps only to ask you a question about a math problem). Panic sets in and two things might happen. Your relationship with the student of trauma may temporarily suffer (the student with trauma decides they are back on their own and they desert the safety of your relationship) or they get territorial and metaphorically (hopefully) kick away the second student who was swimming up to you.

We can plan for this moment by simultaneously nurturing our relationship with the student *and* nurturing student-to-student connections. It does not mean that they will not experience some degree of panic, but it increases the chances that it will be less dramatic and less enduring. One of the things a traumatized student learns in a trauma-informed classroom is that they can be valued in the context of many other students being valued—that the worry about scarcity is unnecessary. That takes time and experiences. And then more time and more experiences. Gently relentless.

Trust in Chaos

So, if you are a child of trauma who does not trust adults, struggles with trusting your peers, and you cannot always trust yourself, what can you trust? We believe that children of trauma come to trust chaos—it becomes the *easy button* of their life. If they cannot be sure they can be academically successful, they push the easy button of disruption; if they cannot be sure a relationship will be positive, they push the easy button of rejection. What does chaos/negativity get these children, then? Predictability. *I can predict the outcome of an academic task if I refuse to engage in it; I can predict how a relationship will be if I am unlovable.*

Predictability is one of the great needs of human beings. Think about how comforted you are by checking your calendar, by knowing what is on the agenda, by hearing in advance who might be at a party you are going to attend. For people with a great deal of predictability in their lives, surprise is often experienced as delightful. For people for whom little has been predictable, surprise is likely to be yet another unpleasant jolt to the system. If one's life has been characterized by lack of choice and control, predictability settles the tumult, especially if it is something you controlled. A child of trauma often will default to chaos they control rather than dare to hope in the unknown.

For some children with trauma chaos may offer more than predictability—it may, in fact, feel comfortable. We've heard students say, *I like things this way, I like crazy*. How can that be comfortable? A chaotic experience may get them to the chemically familiar state of high stress hormones flooding their bodies and brains.

Understanding these two chaos-related concepts is profoundly important for they lead us to a rich bounty of interventions. Some of those interventions will instill positive predictability in the lives of children of trauma and others will help them to become somatically familiar with a calmer emotional state—a new chemical norm that can be cocreated with them.

CONVERSATIONS ABOUT STRESS

Children who have experienced trauma—that choiceless experience—heal more fully by working *with* their supporters. It is essential that, for a substantial part of this journey, they are in partnership with us. This does not mean that we should be talking with them about their trauma—this is not the role of most educators. Rather, it means we should be engaging them in conversations related to their physiological status and their self and world views. Our job then becomes helping them design effective ways of changing their status and finding new ways for them to imagine their lives and to interpret the larger world.

We have found that using the word *stress* rather than trauma when talking with students is better—it keeps us in our educator-lane and helps some students to feel less awkward or defensive. With younger children, we can offer simple, individualized lessons focused on concrete experiences such as what they notice about their own bodies and what they find makes them feel calmer. With older students, we can offer lessons about coping with stress at the whole-class level, in targeted small groups, or individually.

One of the ways we have explained stress as it relates to thinking is through the following analogy:

Thinking requires the passing of a message from one brain cell to another in a certain pattern, kind of like passing a baton in a relay race. In your brain, though, we have to move the message through liquid—like a relay race in a pool. When all is well and we are not feeling stressed, we swim that message through the water—it takes a little bit of effort, but the message gets there reasonably easily. When stress chemicals begin to flood our brain, we have to swim that message through jelly, which, as you can imagine, takes more effort, but it is still do-able. When we are very stressed, it is like swimming that message through peanut butter and it is almost impossible for us to think clearly and quickly. When we do activities to reduce our stress (we provide age-appropriate examples), we can turn that peanut butter to jelly and that jelly to water so we can think well.

Sometimes, we have older students consider times when something was on the tip of their tongue, where they could somewhat talk about it, but they could not find the exact words they wanted. We share this as a jelly experience—not a serious inability to think, but a compromised one. This allows us, then, to talk about peanut butter experiences, where he or she cannot begin to find the right words at all.

Although that analogy may seem silly, kids get it. It provides simple, non-judgmental language for them to share their status with us, and for us to communicate with them about what we are thinking. When we have common understandings and shared language, communication about dysregulation and related useful strategies becomes easier. We will discuss dysregulation and strategies more in Chapter 9.

Of course, all conversations about stress need to happen in the context of a caring relationship. Being present with our students, seeing their strengths, understanding their struggles, celebrating their effort and their success, and presenting ongoing opportunities for growth are all a part of the nest of a connected, positive relationship that allows us to explore what stresses a student and how he or she can respond.

FINAL NOTE

We've been told that, although fascinating, some of the science of trauma feels a bit difficult to process and the weight of the work can feel overwhelming. As we move into application, the science should begin to make more sense. Allow yourself to move back and forth between science and application and we have no doubt that you will find comfort with it over time. Do what you can each day and, remember, even the smallest acts matter.

Glossary

acute stressor   A condition or demand that occurs within a short time frame that causes an individual to have a physiological and psychological reaction. Being involved in a car accident, taking a college entrance exam, and having an argument with a significant other are examples of acute stressors. An acute stressor is a single event and time-limited.

adrenaline   A hormone produced in the adrenal glands that is released into the body as a response to some type of stressor. Released adrenaline creates a shift in the physiological system of the individual, such as increased blood flow and breath rate—it prepares the body to take action in response to the stressor. This hormone is related to preparing the body for fight or flight. Also called *epinephrine*.

adult trauma   An event or a collection of experiences that occur during adulthood (18 years and older) that overwhelms an individual's inner resources and that impacts their ability to regulate, trust, and function at their full potential.

allostatic load/cumulative stress   The toll on the body and brain caused by the continual presence of stress chemicals that increases the likelihood an individual will respond more intensely to new stressors.

amygdala   A structure of the brain's limbic system that receives information from all the senses as well as from the visceral systems—body systems, such as digestive system, heart, and so forth—and which directs the brain and body's responses to stress. The amygdala is essential in encoding emotional information, including both positive/pleasurable and negative memory.

attachment   The deep bond or emotional connection of one human being to another that endures across time.

attunement   A healthy, well-matched reaction to another person's needs, whether emotional or physiological. Healthy attunement is characterized by an ongoing set of appropriate reactions to the needs of another.

childhood complex trauma/childhood trauma/chronic childhood trauma/pervasive developmental trauma   A collection of experiences that overwhelms a child's inner resources and that has a significant impact on the child's physiological and psychological development. The impact of the experiences is so significant that the child's ability to regulate, trust, and function at their full potential is affected and diminished. This form of trauma compromises a child's sense of self, safety, and security. The terms are often used interchangeably.

chronic stressors   Life events that occur repeatedly and that, over time, cause the body and brain to launch into the stress response over and over again, diminishing the threshold for recovery.

cortisol   A hormone connected with the stress response, although it is also involved in non-stress functioning such as paying attention and metabolism. High levels of cortisol remaining in the brain can negatively impact learning and thinking.

dopamine   A neurotransmitter (brain chemical) released in the brain that is associated with pleasure and positive feelings. It's presence improves mood, attention, memory, regulation, and motivation. Is also associated with motor control. Interacts with the pleasure centers of the brain.

dysregulation   A mismatch between the states of the physiological, emotional, and/or cognitive systems in an individual and the demands of the external environment in which the individual is seeking to function.

event trauma   A single experience that is so significant that it overwhelms an individual's ability to effectively respond and leaves a lasting impact on the individual's physiological and emotional systems. Event traumas often can result in the development of a trigger—a significant, subconscious response to a stimulus that is related to the original event.

hippocampus   A structure of the brain that is directly involved in learning. It is where working memory (short-term memory) occurs and is critical in moving information into long-term memory.

implicit memory   The portion of an individual's memory that does not need to be consciously recalled. Implicit memory is highly related to habits and skills that are developed and then manifested with ease. Examples include riding a bike, driving a familiar route, and brushing one's teeth.

intolerable stress   When stress overwhelms an individual's ability to respond effectively to a demand or set of demands.

mitigating factors   Internal characteristics and/or supports available to the individual at the time of a high-stress experience that could otherwise result in trauma. These factors may reduce the impact of these experiences or may entirely prevent them from becoming traumatic.

preconscious memories   Thoughts, stories, experiences, and images from childhood that are not in immediate awareness but that may be brought back with concentrated thought or through a sensory or visceral trigger.

procedural knowledge   The information an individual uses in the performance of a task without conscious awareness. Examples include typing without looking at a keyboard, pouring milk into a glass, and even routine social exchanges. Directly related to implicit memory.

productive stress   When the body and brain experience a successful, healthy reaction to increased tension or demand. With productive stress, the stressful reaction—changes in physiology and emotional state—allows the individual to accomplish a goal and, in the process, the associated chemicals are expended. Also called *eustress*.

reflectivity   The ability of an individual to think before acting.

self-regulation   The ability to manage one's physical movement, attention, and emotions in order to function successfully in a greater social environment.

stress   The body's physiological and emotional reaction to a stimulus or set of stimuli. It is sometimes described as tension in reaction to a demand.

toxic stress   Demands and/or experiences that severely compromise or incapacitate an individual's ability to respond effectively and as a result, negatively impacts their physiological and psychological well-being. The origins of toxic stress can be strong acute experiences (e.g., a rape), prolonged experiences (e.g., ongoing neglect), and/or prolonged, unmitigated burdens (e.g., food insecurity).

trauma   An event or a collection of experiences that overwhelms an individual's inner resources and impacts their ability to regulate, trust, and function at their full potential.

trigger   A sensory/visceral stimulus or set of sensory/visceral stimuli that suddenly evokes the memory of a stressful/traumatic condition—emotionally and physiologically returning the individual to the place and/or time of the initial trauma.

trusting relationship   A relationship that provides attunement to a child's needs and is characterized by being nurturing, consistent, predictable, and safe.

underlying needs   Needs that are the root causes of an individual's observable behaviors—something that causes a behavior to be manifested. These needs are best conceptualized as they relate to Maslow's hierarchy (physiological needs, safety needs, love/belonging needs, esteem needs, and self-actualization needs) and are directly related to a human's ability to survive and thrive.

universal design (educational context)   A method of approaching the education of children in which strategies that are selected for implementation are good for all—not just for specific cohorts of children. Elements may be essential for some students but also are helpful for others. Strategy selection is both effective and efficient.

Section II

The Re-Set Process

Section II describes the Re-Set Process, the Re-Set Room, and implementation considerations for classroom teachers, school leaders, and others.

 **Section II Online Companion Materials**

Re-Set Process: Proactive Forms (Figure 3.2)
Re-Set Process: Reactive Forms (Figure 3.3)
At-a-Glance: Proactive Whole-Class Re-Set (Figure 4.2)
At-a-Glance: Proactive Student-Choice Re-Set (Figure 4.3)
At-a-Glance: Proactive Individual Re-Set (Figure 4.4)
At-a-Glance: Proactive Re-Set Room (Figure 4.5)
At-a-Glance: Reactive In-Class Re-Set (Figure 5.1)
At-a-Glance: Reactive Alternate Classroom Re-Set (Figure 5.2)
At-a-Glance: Reactive Hallway Re-Set (Figure 5.3)
At-a-Glance: Reactive Re-Set Room (Figure 5.4)
Processing Plan for Primary Students (blank template of Figure 6.1)
Processing Plan for Intermediate Students (blank template of Figure 6.2)
Agenda for Re-Set Room Meetings (Figure 7.1)
Section II Resources   Appendix A: Re-Set Activities Organized by Step
                                 Appendix B : Scripts for Regulating Activities
                                 Appendix C: Fiddle Objects and Marble Maze Directions

Chapter 3

The Re-Set Process Overview

For students on the edge, schools can become islands of stability or arenas for battle.

—John Seita & Larry K. Brendtro (2005, p. 14)

LEAH

Six-year-old Leah was a kindergartner in Ms. Kimura's classroom. Initially, Leah was able to follow class routines for the first hour of the day, even though at times she manifested mildly destructive behaviors, such as shredding the edges of papers, chewing at her clothing, and breaking crayons. After the first hour, she would wander away from her learning center, disrupt other students, or get into materials that did not belong to her. When that pattern became clear, her teacher decided to try a special movement break. The teacher would turn on a GoNoodle video, thinking that might help Leah burn off some of her energy. Leah initially resisted participating, but after she was involved, she quickly became wildly out of control, knocking into her classmates and becoming excessively loud. When the break was over, the other students settled back into their centers. Meanwhile, Leah threw herself onto the floor in a full-blown tantrum. Ms. Kimura felt defeated and regretted trying the movement break, which had backfired.

DEVON

Devon, a wiry fourth-grader, was registered at the school earlier in the day, his third school that year, and it was only early December. Mr. King had noticed that Devon seemed quite jittery when he first arrived, so he spent more time than he usually did with a new student to help Devon settle in while the rest of the class worked on their research projects. Later that morning, Devon got up and began knocking materials off the counters and bookcases in the classroom. As Mr. King approached to intervene, Devon promptly began tossing materials with more vigor, now appearing to aim them toward his classmates. Mr. King spoke in a quiet tone to Devon, offering to have Devon come with him to get a drink and find out how he could help, but Mr. King's offers were met with curses. When Devon made a dash for the classroom door, Mr. King blocked it and called the office. Devon was kicking the wall when the crisis team arrived to escort him from the classroom.

JUSTINE

Midway through the school year, Justine, a seventh-grader who typically performed at a B– to C+ level, suddenly refused to engage in many of her classroom tasks and would become defiant when pushed to work. Her teachers were aware that her parents had gone through an acrimonious divorce and that her grandmother had just passed away after a long battle with cancer.

The seventh-grade student support team, after gaining permission from her parents, talked with Justine and presented a plan for a lower level of academic demands for a few weeks while Justine adjusted to the loss of her grandmother and began working with a grief therapist. There were fewer battles during this time, and the team was hopeful that the counseling was being effective. At the end of the agreed-upon period, demands were systematically increased, and Justine's defiance also increased.

The team met again and decided that Justine needed to be dealt with more firmly. They felt that more structure and firmness would create a sense of security and consistency for her—a natural next step in helping her return to her normal. The plan was that Justine would be quietly and privately redirected twice, and then, if she did not respond, she would relocate with her work to another team member's room for a time-out. After 10 minutes, if she had done a reasonable amount of work, she would be allowed to return to her classroom. If classes changed while Justine was away from the group, she was to turn in her work to the partner teacher, and then move to her next class. Justine initially agreed to this process, but the first time she was sent to a partner teacher, Justine sat picking at her split ends and doing no work. When the partner teacher approached her, Justine walked out of class and left the school campus.

THE MISSING PIECE

One or more of these cases might feel familiar to you, regardless of the ages, names, and genders of the students. In each case, educators used behavior techniques that had worked with other students in similar situations. In each of these cases, the educators cared deeply about students who were manifesting very concerning behaviors. The professionals who were supporting the students found themselves searching for something, anything, that would turn things around for the student, but they felt stumped. Perhaps you have been there: well-informed, caring, and well-intentioned, but frustrated and at a loss?

The students who inspired these scenarios had at least one thing in common that prevented their educators' best efforts from making the needed difference. What was that common element? They were students whose nervous systems were chronically dysregulated due to trauma. What was missing in each intervention was an effective strategy for dealing with that dysregulation.

The Re-Set Process is designed specifically to support dysregulated children. It has proven successful time and again with children like those in our case studies. The process is not a panacea, but a complementary practice that often sets the stage for other support strategies to take hold.

Through the Re-Set Process, a dysregulated person progresses *from* a state where emotions and survival instincts are ruling the brain *to* a state of restored balance—a balance of healthy emotional and cognitive functioning. The process meets the student where he or she is, and then moves the student, step by step, toward his or her own more regulated state. From that more regulated state, the student is poised to engage in a learning task, to talk through a difficulty, to understand someone else's perspective, and so much more. The foundation is always regulation. As Perry (2005) informs us, we first must be regulated, then we are able to relate, and then we regain our ability to reason.

Other processes may eventually bring an unsettled, dysregulated student to calm. The Re-Set Process brings a dysregulated student to calm in a shorter time frame, within the context of the school, while teaching the student a step-by-step method to re-regulate themselves in the future. So, what is the key to the Re-Set Process? It is a compassionate, effective, and efficient process. Re-setting follows a set of prescribed steps that are composed of thoughtful, accessible, flexible, and safe activities. The process is designed to offer choice to children whose lives have all too often been choiceless, to offer predictability to children whose lives have been chaotic, and to communicate acceptance and expectations, all in tandem. At its most intensive, Re-Set also provides systematic opportunities to connect with caring adults who coach the student through the process, building relationship every step of the way.

The Re-Set Process approach to behavioral challenges is not simply about changing the behavior of the student or decreasing disruptions to the classroom environment, although those certainly are both worthy goals. The Re-Set Process does those things, but it also is designed to teach the struggling student valuable skills for self-management—skills that he or she needs to be successful in school and beyond. It is a nonpunitive, relational approach that is structured for consistency.

Dysregulation is not uniform and, depending on the student, it might manifest either internally or externally. External behaviors are by nature easier to spot. Most of our work in establishing the Re-Set Process in schools has been in response to students whose dysregulation results in unsettled, agitated, active behaviors. Some students of trauma experience dysregulation that is more of a shutting down or closing in. Unfortunately for these students, their associated behaviors do not issue the same loud call for help that the more externalizing, unsettled behaviors do, so their needs may not be identified or addressed as quickly. In the chapters that follow, we will share adaptations to the process for these students so that these children, too, can benefit from Re-Set.

THE RE-SET PROCESS: NAME, GOALS, LOCATION, AND STRUCTURE

We now will explain several important elements of the Re-Set Process, including the name, primary goals, foundational concepts (referred to as *Rails* and discussed in this chapter), proactive and reactive forms of the process, and core steps.

The Name: Why the Re-Set Process?

Why not use restart? Why not refresh or reboot, or simply regulate? The word, *re-set,* which means to set again, has a neutral connotation. It is simple enough for even young children to understand. It allows for accountability without being an emotionally charged word. The word *restart* can mean to go backward, perhaps even all the way back to where one started. The word *refresh* feels too lightweight, and the word *reboot* clears all away—it means to turn off and then turn on again. The word *regulate* is a bit of a mouthful, although that was the word we used until we settled on the word *re-set,* which meets the student where he or she is and helps him or her move forward, to try again. And, frankly, it is a nice, short word that communicates exactly what we need communicated.

We also selected the word *process* intentionally, inspired by nature's processes, which unfold in a systematic and predictable manner. The Re-Set Process explicitly guides the involved student through the gradual, natural, healthy phenomena of regulation and attachment. It is designed to teach those processes to students through experience until it is internalized.

Goals: Individuals and Groups

Our goals for the Re-Set Process fall into two categories: individuals and groups.

These are goals for individuals:

1. To bring a student from a dysregulated state to a regulated one so that thinking can happen, both for the student who is the focus, and for nearby students

2. To build a student's understanding of and experience with safety, trust, and choice, which affords opportunities for healing connection and attachment between student and supportive adults

3. To teach a student's brain how to self-calm through practicing a consistent process

4. To allow other supportive interventions to be more successful because they are occurring in the context of a brain that is better prepared to show what it knows and better able to learn new things

These are goals for groups:

1. To bring a group of students from a mildly dysregulated state to a more regulated one, so thinking and learning can happen

2. To provide opportunities for students to see one another engage in regulation, to make regulating a common experience and demystify it

3. To provide adults with an opportunity to regulate during the school day by participating in the activity with their students

4. To use resources in an efficient manner by supporting multiple mildly dysregulated students at one time

Structure: The Two Rails of Re-Set

The concepts of regulation and attachment are at the heart of the Re-Set Process. We refer to these concepts as *Rails*, as seen in Figure 3.1, and we describe each in detail.

Rail 1: Regulation   Regulation is the ability to manage one's physical movement, attention, and emotions in order to function successfully. As we discuss at length in Chapter 2, being able to regulate is the foundation of being able to calm down, focus, concentrate, engage, attune, and attach, as well as to achieve, empathize, be curious, have autonomy, and act in an altruistic way. We also make the connection between dysregulation and behaviors that create distance

Figure 3.1.   The two rails of the Re-Set Process: regulation and attachment.

between the student and others, and which prevent the student from learning. Practicing and teaching regulation skills is the essential first rail of the process.

The Re-Set Process is based on critical understandings from the fields of neuroscience and psychology about the needs of students with trauma. The activities of each step of the process, described later in this chapter, walk the scientifically informed fine line of *not fun, but not punitive either* while meeting the regulation needs that drive the behavior of concern. It is important for any coach, whether a teacher, caregiver, parent, school counselor, paraprofessional, school psychologist, or any other adult implementer, to understand that the activities for each step have been carefully selected and should be followed as described.

Rail 2: Attachment   When a child feels safe and secure in the presence of an adult and trusts that the adult will protect them, the child has a secure attachment. An attached relationship is mutually positive. The type of adult-to-student interaction that is associated with each step has intentionally been selected to systematically connect the student with a caring adult, seeking to meet the attachment needs of the student. By using a prescribed process that allows a student to know what to expect of the adult (the coach), we build predictability into the process. Our goal is to build trust through repeated experiences with an adult who is caring, listening, present, safe, and kind.

Through the direct involvement of a caring adult, the Re-Set Process provides students with positive relationship-building experiences. These may include an adult listening to them, an adult providing them with limited choice, an adult engaging with them, an adult directing them, and an adult guiding them. This variety of experiences and the order in which they occur is not random. Rather, it considers the student's needs for safety, choice, and predictability while shifting the adult from a more directive and/or parallel role to an interactive role (mirroring serve and return processes) to a coaching role, at which point the student is empowered to think for him- or herself.

Although the process provides an opportunity for the student to attach to an adult, the process also holds as one of its goals the reciprocal sense of positivity between adult and student. The coach is in a position to genuinely experience the student growing, and this success fosters the adult's attachment to the student. From an attached position, the coach is better able to advocate for the student in the larger school setting.

These are the two rails of the Re-Set Process: regulation and attachment. Both are essential if the student is to move forward in his or her social and emotional growth.

Notes From the Field

When utilizing the Re-Set Room with students, what was perhaps most profound to me was the power of the relationship in the process. Whether I had just met the student or had known them for several years, the importance of genuine interest and concern for the student's difficulties often were pivotal factors in the student's success with re-regulation. Along with the critical importance of structure and consistency, the relationship investment is significant. We always need to remember that the coach may be providing the connection and care that the child truly needs that day.

Elementary School Counselor

Location: Defining the Most Intensive Location: The Re-Set Room

The Re-Set Process may take place in one of several locations, which can include classrooms, hallways, and a separate space called a Re-Set Room. We will first turn our attention to this separate space and how it functions and then examine other options of locations. The Re-Set Room is an established area *beyond the classroom* that is intentionally created as a space to provide safety, to teach regulation, and, when necessary, to provide an alternative to traditional send-away types of responses to challenging behaviors. Both the process and the space are designed to guide students from feeling out of control in their bodies and with their behaviors to a calmer, more rational state of mind and body. Students do all this in the context of a relationship whose nature is established by the involvement of a caring, supportive, trusting adult. This form of the Re-Set Process is designed to support the most challenging students in the school whose behaviors are the most troubling. Any student who requires the Re-Set Room for reactive purposes should also be scheduled into it proactively.

The Re-Set Room is composed of carefully selected activities and guidelines for practice in order to meet both the regulation and attachment needs of students—the two Rails. Improvisation of any sort needs to fit the guidelines or the value of the process is diminished. As noted, students who require the Re-Set Room for reactive purposes should be scheduled into it proactively as well.

A Coached Process

The Re-Set Room and some other forms of the Re-Set Process require a coach who has been trained in the specific steps of the process and who has ongoing opportunities to reflect on the process with other trained personnel. The use of the term coach is very intentional. The adult in this role provides safety, critical information, guidance, modeling, encouragement, and some game plans for the student to move forward behaviorally. The coach also needs to be keenly aware of when to step back and allow the student to have choice and take responsibility. Like any sports coach, the adult in this process is *fully* present, focused on the person who is being coached, and focused on keeping everyone safe while maintaining an eye on the goals of the process. We will discuss the ways schools have deployed staff to fill the position of coach later in Chapter 6 and in the discussion of staff training in Chapter 7.

An Instructional Environment

Are we not allowing students to get access to a break by engaging in negative behavior? This question will probably pop into your head almost every step of the way in this process . . . it is how we have been trained to think about behavior.

Here is how what we are doing is different:

- We are meeting a student's needs in a structured, purposeful way while following an established agenda. It is not play, and we do not approach it in a playful way. To borrow the orientation of educators from the Northeast Foundation for Children Responsive Classroom (Charney, 1992), we are being firm but friendly. Our tone is to be guiding, respectful, and calm, and to reflect our sense of empathy. If you are one of the many people who wonder what empathy is about, check out an enlightening video by Brené Brown, located at https://www.youtube.com /watch?v=1Evwgu369Jw theRSAorg (2013). Finding this tonal place may be a journey for you, and that is okay . . . be gentle with yourself. You will find it with reflection and practice.

- We are teaching. This structure is about *explicitly* teaching healthy, socially acceptable regulation processes to a student who does not have sufficient methods or who has only inappropriate ones. It is no different than taking the time to teach phonics; we are explicitly teaching all the components of a process that will lead to regulation fluency in the student's future.

- We are keeping data to learn more about the behavior so we can proactively support the student. Implementation of this process can be part of a comprehensive behavior assessment approach. A student being routinely dysregulated during a specific activity is a good indicator that something about that activity (i.e., academic content, instructional technique, social demand) is triggering this response. We can examine these factors and others that will help us generate strong hypotheses regarding function. Additional interventions might then be added to holistically approach the dysregulation issue.

Focused on Self-Regulation Skills

The Re-Set Room is a place where students learn the process of self-regulation. Whether it is being used proactively (scheduled) or reactively (in response to a behavior), a student will be guided to become aware of what his or her body feels like and what his or her thoughts are when he or she is dysregulated. The student will be exposed to different materials and strategies to use, and he or she will be coached to develop plans for using these tools in real-life contexts. Self-awareness, self-regulation, and self-advocacy are all intended outcomes when this room is being used proactively or reactively.

A Place to Experience and Practice Connection

Throughout the process of the Re-Set Room, the adult is making steps toward social attachment. We are moving from being present through parallel interaction and ultimately to caring, problem-solving supportive interaction. We are engaging the student in the dance of attunement and attachment beginning with the simplest of steps. Each time the student experiences these different forms of human interaction, it is a practice. As the relationship with the coach evolves, real (as opposed to structured) connection may emerge. Just as the room is a place to learn to regulate, the coach in the room is a relationship through which a student learns to attach and trust.

The retreat into isolation can sometimes feel more controllable than being flooded with a sense of needing another person for comfort and connection.

—Dan Siegel (2012, p. 385)

Reliance on Data

The room's use needs to be monitored by collecting critical data and analyzing that data *on a routine basis*. What kinds of data related to the Re-Set Room should be collected? Certainly date, time, and student name for each use of the room, at a minimum should be collected. Although data such as day of the week and the grade level of the student can be determined through collecting basic data, often it is helpful to simply have a field for each of these items, for efficiency.

The data allows for a more macro-level assessment of the space's functioning—to determine whether this intervention is being used in the building, who is using it, and what times tend to be high-use and low-use. In addition, the data can help determine whether personnel commitment is matched to the need level of the building. It can support an administrator's recommendation to the central office or school board members for hiring a designated coach rather than pulling in other people who work in the building to coach, in addition to their other responsibilities. It also can support a recommendation of complementary job responsibilities to be allocated to a coach who has some open time in his or her schedule.

Other data points, such as how the room was selected as an intervention (e.g., administrative action, scheduled) and notes about specific details of activities used will help educators take a more micro-level look at how the room is working (or not working) for individual students. The data may drive decisions about other supports that the student needs.

We found that most schools used an Excel spreadsheet for data collection because it allowed for simple aggregation and disaggregation of the data. Other schools were happy with an old-fashioned binder and paper recording. Our recommendation is for each team to use the data collection format that works for them because, as we all know, data is only good if it is entered properly and then routinely analyzed.

Re-Set Room Data Excel Worksheet Categories

1. Date

2. Student

3. Grade level

4. Arrival time

5. Departure time

6. Total minutes

7. Proactive or reactive (P or R)

8. Notes (may include specific activities student has used)

Part of a Comprehensive Support System

As much as we would love to be able to say that the Re-Set Room is a miracle intervention, of course, we cannot. It is *not* a panacea, but it *is* a new process that has been making a difference for many students, and it can help educators design new types of individual action plans or behavior support plans. It does not in any way exclude the use of *some* of our traditional practices and, in fact, there are many companion practices (both proactive and reactive), some of which will be discussed in the chapters that follow.

Just as a Re-Set Room is part of a comprehensive approach to supporting an individual student, the Re-Set Room is part of a comprehensive set of school supports. It needs to live in the context of all the other behavioral approaches in the building and relate to those practices and data fields.

Students should access the Re-Set Room as a result of a clearly delineated procedure. It is critical that any time that a student spends away from the learning environment is used effectively and efficiently.

Proactively, use of the room should be defined in an informal action plan or, for other students, in a formalized behavior plan. It should be part of a comprehensive set of interventions that support the student. Reactively, a student's involvement also may be part of an established plan, or it may be a crisis intervention. If it is the result of a crisis response to escalating behavior, an administrative team decision should be made (i.e., someone from the administrative team or building leadership team, in consultation with the student's teacher, makes the determination of referral to the room). Without this filter of administrative referral, there is a high risk of the room becoming an easy go-to for students who are being problematic in classrooms. If this room becomes overloaded, it cannot serve its core purposes. Including the reactive use of the Re-Set Room as one option in the array of administrative responses on a discipline flow chart (as is often a part of PBIS plans) would communicate how it is to be accessed and reduce chances of misuse.

Generally, if a student has been referred to the Re-Set Room as a crisis response more than once in a month, it should be a documented intervention in the student's action plan or behavior plan. We have said it before, but we cannot emphasize it enough—if a student participates in the room reactively, he or she should be scheduled into it proactively.

Data from the use of the Re-Set Room should be considered with all the other data being collected about student behavior. Care should be taken that students whose behaviors are being flagged through discipline referrals are being considered for some form of the Re-Set Process, and perhaps the Re-Set Room itself.

Notes From the Field

I have used the Re-Set Process in my school counseling room with multiple students. I have found myself recommending it at our student support team meetings and have taught my teacher colleagues about them. We are now meeting together to make a Re-Set Room that will provide all the different kinds of brain-based time-outs.

Elementary School Counselor

What the Re-Set Room Is *Not*

In education, we have used send-away structures of all kinds for decades. There is some common ground between these previous practices and the Re-Set Room so a cursory look at this concept may leave you thinking that you have done this before, just with a different name. The Re-Set Room, despite some of its common ground with other practices, is radically different. If we are going to establish it with fidelity, we need to examine those differences so that we do not find ourselves morphing the Re-Set Room into something we knew before—that drift back into prior practices. We will differentiate....

Not a Punishment Space   As you look at the steps of the Re-Set Room, you will see that it is characterized by a very different tone than any punishment space such as traditional time-outs or being sent to the office. Its purpose is not to segregate a child from others. It is not designed to ignore, shame, or embarrass. It is not a place of harshness or anger. It is, at its core, a place of safety, connection, healing, and learning.

That said, the student *is* removed from his or her peers for a period of time and we acknowledge the benefit of that for the student, his or her peers, and his or her teachers. When a student's behavior has been significantly disruptive in the classroom, it is a good thing to allow the class a chance to settle back down. We can increase the sense of safety of all children by providing that settling opportunity *and* by doing it in a way that is not shaming or harsh to the child who is leaving the room for a period of time. If we understand that as human beings we feel only as safe as the least safe among us in any given context, we can see that even when other students feel relieved to have a disruptive peer away from the class for a period of time, the way in which that happens directly affects all students' greater sense of safety.

In this reactive implementation of the Re-Set Room, the movement to the space does follow behaviors of concern and would be considered a consequence using behavioral sciences' definition of that word. In casual vernacular, the word consequence has come to be associated with pain. Can you hear the warning of pain in statements like, *There will be a consequence for your behavior, young woman!?* In our society, there is an all-too-common—and frankly, dangerous and erroneous—belief that to get someone to change, you must subject them to hurt or pain. In some primal ways, pain does teach us (e.g., you touch a hot stove coil and you get burnt and, yes, you probably will not touch that glowing red coil again), but in more complex human-to-human interactions, we know that there are many more effective and humane ways to teach something a child needs to learn. Understanding trauma also helps us recognize that some children are *driven to touch that glowing red coil*, regardless of the pain and that we need to find ways to address the underlying need in order to eliminate that drive. The Re-Set Room provides a break in a series of behaviors and can be a logical consequence response to behaviors of concern. It is a respectful, caring, supportive structure that is designed to have a child feel safe, to meet a physiological need, to nurture and maintain connection with adults and peers, and to teach new skills.

Not a Place to Deliver Disciplinary Consequences   Sometimes the seriousness of a student's behavior that got them sent to the Re-Set Room to re-regulate does need to be followed by a school disciplinary action, according to school procedures. If this is absolutely necessary, this disciplinary consequence needs to be identified and/or served in an *alternate* location. For example, if a student has aggressed against another student and caused an injury and school policy/procedures require a phone call home and a one-day in-school suspension, both the act of making the call home and informing the student of the suspension should occur outside of the Re-Set Room (probably most appropriately in the school office).

In addition, the adult who identifies disciplinary consequences should not be the adult who has been the coach. Does this mean that a school principal can never act as a coach? School principals can certainly be coaches—just not in the same event *if at all possible*. To be realistic though, life in schools is complicated, and there may be times that the school principal who was just acting as the coach also needs to be involved in issuing disciplinary consequences. In these cases, a different space is what is being banked upon to create the needed separation between the Re-Set Process and the disciplinary event. Separation of the Re-Set Room process and other, more emotionally provocative disciplinary processes is critical.

Not a Padded Room   In some schools, students who have shown intensely out-of-control behavior have been taken to an alternate space in which they were allowed to *burn off their aggression*. Many times, these rooms have been padded to prevent a student from hurting themselves. The adults remained outside of the room, looking in through a window, or in the room with a padded barrier between them and the student. *This is the antithesis of the Re-Set Room.* We now know that there is no such thing as burning off aggression. Being aggressive only teaches being aggressive, and what appears as resolution really is just exhaustion (Bushman, Baumeister, & Stack, 1999).

The padded room (inadvertently) sanctions aggression; the Re-Set Room systematically prevents aggression and teaches healthy alternatives to aggressive behaviors. A padded room communicates to the student that being out-of-control is part of who he or she is; the Re-Set Room communicates that the student is valued and capable of gaining more and more control of his- or herself. The padded room allows for movement that is random and without pattern; the Re-Set Room maximizes predictable, patterned movement. The padded room tells a student that he or she is on his or her own when he or she is in his or her most troubled state; the Re-Set Room deliberately connects the student with an adult who can guide the student when he or she feels most hurt and intent on hurting. The only common ground between these two approaches is that they both ultimately seek to control a student's out-of-control behavior. Even in that common zone, there is a stark difference; a padded room seeks to control the outcome of a student's behavior from without by providing protective walls, whereas a Re-Set Room protects the student from within by nurturing him or her to become self-controlled.

Not a Play Space   Because some of the items that may be used in the Re-Set Room can also be used in playful or fun ways (e.g., trampoline, putty, coloring sheets, kettlebells) some people may mistakenly think this is a place where students are having fun or goofing off. It is important to know that in the Re-Set Room, the same materials that may be used for play are being used in a specifically guided way—they are *tools*, not *toys*. Think about a classroom: There are many instructional materials that can be used as tools or as toys. We guide students in how to use the materials at specific times. It would be a mistake to assume that because the Re-Set Room is not punitive that what happens there is playful. There also are many instructional activities that are not playful, but which certainly are not punishing. A good Re-Set Room and process strives for that same engaged instructional sweet spot of not play and not punishment.

Not a Sensory Space   Sensory rooms are used to meet specific needs of students whose neurological and physiological systems are out of balance. In this way, a sensory room has common ground with the Re-Set Room. In fact, many of the materials that are found in a sensory room are ones that could be found in the Re-Set Room as well. However, there are a few key differences that separate these two interventions.

First, some materials and equipment (e.g., a Sit-and-Spin) that might appear in a sensory room would be inappropriate for use in this space and for meeting the needs of students with trauma histories. The materials and activities that are selected for Re-Set Rooms are chosen specifically to meet the unique needs of students with pervasive trauma or high levels of toxic stress. Second, the Re-Set Room is composed of a series of steps that are designed based on science to regulate the systems of dysregulated students; it is not open-ended sensory experience. Finally, the Re-Set space has language that is defined for each of the steps. That language may or may not overlap with language commonly heard in a sensory room. The language in a Re-Set Room is essential for laying the foundation for connection, which is not a stated goal of a sensory space.

Not a Simple Calming Space/Chill-Out Space   In the field of trauma-informed school practices, recently there has been a great move toward establishing calming corners in classrooms and calming spaces in schools. Most of these spaces have not been described or defined at length, so there is extensive room for implementers to interpret the objective and design of a calming space. However, the essential intent of a calming space is to provide an area where a student can go when he or she is feeling the effects of his or her trauma, somewhere where he or she can feel safer.

Although the Re-Set Room has the exact same intention, it is a more structured process, so we would like to differentiate it from the more general concept of a calming space. Although our goal is the same (to allow a student to calm and, therefore function better and feel better), this structure is designed to get a student back into class as *efficiently* as possible so that learning is not compromised.

We feel strongly that meeting a student's needs and then moving the student back into a learning state allows him or her to more quickly access another major way that he or she will heal from the effect of trauma . . . to develop skills and experience success. We also want to make sure that we are not inadvertently sending the message to the student that he or she is unable to handle any of the challenges of learning; we want to help him or her see that, although he or she may briefly need a respite from that challenge, he or she is quite capable of handling academic challenges a great deal of the time. Although calming spaces are proving to be very effective, the Re-Set structure is designed to also be *effective in a more efficient manner*. That said, we are not discounting the use of calming spaces altogether. For some students, some of the time, in some settings, there may be a benefit to those therapeutic calming centers. We offer the Re-Set space as an option to consider that offers a quicker return to learning and decreases the likelihood of students learning to escape to calm spaces rather than wrestle with any learning challenges. We also worry that sometimes unstructured calming spaces may lead to a student just sitting with his or her trauma and becoming more emotionally lost. As with all practices, care needs to be taken regarding which practice is used when, by whom, with whom, for how long, and for what purposes.

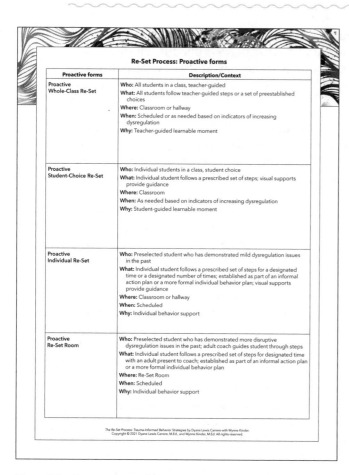

Re-Set Process: Proactive forms

Proactive forms	Description/Context
Proactive Whole-Class Re-Set	**Who:** All students in a class, teacher-guided **What:** All students follow teacher-guided steps or a set of preestablished choices **Where:** Classroom or hallway **When:** Scheduled or as needed based on indicators of increasing dysregulation **Why:** Teacher-guided learnable moment
Proactive Student-Choice Re-Set	**Who:** Individual students in a class, student choice **What:** Individual student follows a prescribed set of steps; visual supports provide guidance **Where:** Classroom **When:** As needed based on indicators of increasing dysregulation **Why:** Student-guided learnable moment
Proactive Individual Re-Set	**Who:** Preselected student who has demonstrated mild dysregulation issues in the past **What:** Individual student follows a prescribed set of steps for a designated time or a designated number of times; established as part of an informal action plan or a more formal individual behavior plan; visual supports provide guidance **Where:** Classroom or hallway **When:** Scheduled **Why:** Individual behavior support
Proactive Re-Set Room	**Who:** Preselected student who has demonstrated more disruptive dysregulation issues in the past; adult coach guides student through steps **What:** Individual student follows a prescribed set of steps for designated time with an adult present to coach; established as part of an informal action plan or a more formal individual behavior plan **Where:** Re-Set Room **When:** Scheduled **Why:** Individual behavior support

Figure 3.2. Proactive forms of the Re-Set Process teach self-regulation skills when the cognitive brain is most available to learn.

Not a Counseling Space The common ground between these two concepts is that both are designed to be therapeutic in nature. By therapeutic, we mean that they both are a form of treatment that is intended to have a positive effect on our students' brains and bodies. But, again, there are distinct differences. The Re-Set Room, unlike many forms of counseling, actually encourages *less* language to be used throughout most of the process and, specifically, the language of emotion is almost nonexistent. This expectation often is quite challenging for many school counselors when they support this room because they are trained in talking with students, particularly about emotions. Talking about emotions is their default, and they will need to very consciously override this approach when they are supporting a student in the Re-Set Room. The choice of language that is used is quite intentional, as will be explained later.

This space is *not* designed to replace counseling but, rather, to serve as a complement to counseling. One of our unexpected discoveries in conducting the Re-Set Room process is that students who went through the process were better prepared to speak even more candidly with counselors, which allowed the students to access supports that otherwise might have gone untapped. A student who indicates a readiness to talk should be quickly referred to the appropriate support after he or she completes the last step of the room. This maintains the Re-Set Room for its intended use and gets the student connected with the right people to support him or her.

As you learn more about the Re-Set Process and its associated forms in the chapters that follow, you will better understand how to implement it in a variety of locations in addition to the Re-Set Room itself.

Structure: Forms of the Re-Set Process

The Re-Set Process can be a proactive or reactive practice. There are four proactive forms and four reactive forms. The forms are described next, and they are summarized in Figure 3.2 and Figure 3.3.

Proactive Forms Proactive forms of the Re-Set Process are less intensive and teach self-regulation skills when the cognitive brain is most available to learn. These are the proactive forms of Re-Set:

1. **Proactive Whole-Class Re-Set** takes place at a prescribed time in the classroom. All students follow teacher-guided steps or pre-established choices. The entire class benefits from this proactive measure by learning self-regulation skills and strategies.

2. **Proactive Student-Choice Re-Set** also takes place in the classroom, but it is not scheduled ahead of time. Rather, a student elects to follow a prescribed set of steps if the student is experiencing increasing but still mild dysregulation. The student and teacher must first learn to recognize the signs that indicate dysregulation. Based on this information—either self-identified by the student or with the teacher's help—the student elects to engage in Re-Set in order to reregulate and then rejoin the class. This proactive measure allows a student the opportunity to apply self-regulation skills and strategies before he or she loses control.

3. **Proactive Individual Re-Set** takes place in the classroom and is designed for a student who has been preselected based on mild dysregulation challenges in the past. An individual student follows a prescribed set of steps at a designated time. This proactive measure is scheduled ahead of time and is implemented as part of either an informal action plan or a more formal individual behavior plan.

Re-Set Process: Reactive forms

Reactive forms	Description/Context
Reactive In-Class Re-Set	**Who:** Student demonstrating mildly disruptive behavior **What:** Teacher quietly directs individual student to the designated Re-Set Space in the classroom; student proceeds through the established steps **Where:** Designated location in the classroom **When/Why:** Student behavior is mildly disruptive and has been unresponsive to repeated redirects. Student behavior is increasing in intensity but still not tipping into serious concerns.
Reactive Alternate Classroom Re-Set (aka Buddy Teacher Re-Set)	**Who:** Student demonstrating mildly disruptive behavior **What:** Student moves to a new location and proceeds through the established steps **Where:** In a buddy teacher's classroom, in a predetermined, structured space **When/Why:** Student behavior is mildly disruptive in nature and has been unresponsive to repeated redirects. Student behavior is increasing in intensity but still not tipping into serious concerns. Teacher determines that the classroom environment may be triggering the increase in behavior intensity.
Reactive Hallway Re-Set	**Who:** Student demonstrating mildly disruptive behavior; adult/coach **What:** A supporting adult comes to the classroom and accompanies the student to the hallway. In the new location, the student proceeds through the established steps and is guided by the coach. **Where:** Hallway **When/Why:** Student behavior is significantly disruptive or has been nonresponsive to in-classroom and/or buddy teacher forms of Re-Set
Reactive Re-Set Room	**Who:** Student determined by administrative team and/or established behavior plan; adult/coach **What:** Adult coaches the student through all established steps in the Re-Set Room; Most intense and most restrictive form of the Re-Set Process **Where:** Re-Set Room **When/Why:** Student behavior is significantly disruptive and is persisting despite attempts at other Re-Set Process options. Student behavior is endangering or destructive.

Figure 3.3. Reactive forms of the Re-Set Process address problematic behavior as it is occurring.

4. **Proactive Re-Set Room** is the only proactive measure that takes place in the Re-Set Room and with a dedicated coach. This scheduled option is for a preselected student who has demonstrated more disruptive dysregulation issues in the past. The student follows a prescribed set of steps working with an adult coach. This proactive measure is established as part of either an informal action plan or a more formal individual behavior plan.

Reactive Forms   Reactive forms of the Re-Set Process address problematic behavior as it is occurring. By definition, these forms of Re-Set occur in the moment and therefore are not scheduled. Building relationships while simultaneously teaching regulation skills is critical in the more intensive forms.

These are the four reactive forms of Re-Set:

1. **Reactive In-Class Re-Set** is for a student who is demonstrating mildly disruptive behavior that has not been responsive to redirects. Student behavior is increasing in intensity but still is not tipping into serious concerns. In such instances, the teacher quietly directs the individual student to the designated Re-Set space in the classroom. The student then proceeds through the established steps. The teacher should touch base with the student after he or she has engaged in the Re-Set Process—affirming the student's engagement in the process and providing the needed personal connection.

2. **Reactive Alternate Classroom Re-Set** (also called **Buddy Teacher Re-Set**) is similar to Option 1, but it takes place in another teacher's classroom. Like Option 1, student behavior is mildly disruptive, has been unresponsive to repeated redirects, and is increasing in intensity but still is not tipping into serious concerns. The main difference is that the teacher determines that the classroom environment may be triggering the increase in behavioral intensity. Therefore, the student moves to the new, predetermined classroom and proceeds through the established steps. As with Reactive In-Class Re-Set, it is important that the student's teacher connect positively after the student's engagement in the process.

3. **Reactive Hallway Re-Set** is appropriate for times when student behavior is significantly disruptive or has been nonresponsive to in-classroom or alternate classroom forms of Re-Set. A supporting adult (coach) comes to the classroom and accompanies the student to the hallway. The student proceeds through the established steps and is guided by the coach.

4. **Reactive Re-Set Room** occurs when a preselected student's behavior is significantly disruptive, is persisting despite attempts at other Re-Set Process options, or is endangering or destructive. In such cases, the student has been selected for the Re-Set Room by the administrative team or as part of an established behavior plan. In the Re-Set Room, an adult coaches the student through all the established steps. This is the most intense form of the Re-Set Process.

Figure 3.3 describes the four reactive forms of Re-Set. All proactive and reactive forms include a prescribed set of steps and a corresponding location and context. Every form is based on the same core concepts, but each is implemented by using specific methodologies that are appropriate to the intensity level of that form. Chapters 4–6 discuss proactive and reactive forms in more detail.

Structure: Core Steps in the Re-Set Process

There are four core steps to the Re-Set Process (as seen in Figure 3.4), plus one additional step and an additional intervention that may be used under certain conditions. Forms of the process that are less intense may blend some steps as is described in the chapters that follow. To begin, we introduce each step and its general purpose and offer guidelines for direct adult involvement when applicable.

Step 1: Move Your Body   Step 1 is designed to burn off in the most efficient way possible the stress chemicals (e.g., cortisol and adrenaline) that are flooding a dysregulated student's brain and body. Many of the activities simultaneously introduce calming chemicals into the student's system through pressure into the major joints and through the use of pattern and rhythm. At Step 1, students often are simply focused on the intensity of the activity—a very somatic focus, and that is fine. Students are introduced to counting or a pattern of movement. Focusing on the adult is not a goal at this point. The amount of choice provided to the student at Step 1 is dependent upon the specific form of Re-Set and the student's unique needs.

Figure 3.4.   The four core steps of the Re-Set Process.

At this step, we also are intentionally expelling those stress chemicals rapidly so they do not have time to damage the student's brain and body systems. As the body begins to feel calmer, the cognitive portions of the brain become more available. The level of dysregulation and stress the student is experiencing affects how quickly the student can return to a thinking state. For students who are mildly dysregulated or mildly stressed, this step may be very short, and it may be composed of a few effective movements; other students may require a greater number of movements/more time in gross motor activity. Step 1 is just part of the process of modulating from high arousal to lower arousal. Predictability and choice are the ways that we create a sense of safety in Step 1 if an adult is not involved to establish those elements.

Adult Involvement   In forms of Re-Set where an adult is directly involved, the adult is to provide gentle guidance to the student and make on-the-spot decisions about the amount of choice that is provided to the student. The adult may guide the student by making recommendations, providing visual cues or options, and by counting to keep the student engaged in the activity in a manner that is patterned or rhythmic. The adult also may participate in the movements or in a version of the movement with the student.

Interaction should reflect warmth and involve simplified language. It also may involve synchronous movements or synchronicity between a student's movements and an adult's voice. The adult's body language should be relaxed and inclined toward the student. If the student seems to need more space, the adult should respect that but still stay in tune with the student through nonthreatening eye contact, brief verbal interactions, and positive facial expressions. The adult should focus on sending nonverbal messages: *I am present for you. I care about you. You will be okay.* Talk should be minimal. Safety is enhanced through the adult's tone and body language, in addition to the elements of predictability (the structure of the step) and choice (the options that are provided to the student for activities).

Step 2: Modulate Down   Step 2 is designed to continue the settling process by both burning additional stress chemicals and introducing additional calming chemicals into the body and brain. The activities are designed to move the student from highly active gross motor activities to more refined gross motor movements or fine motor activities. Depending on the level of dysregulation initially experienced by the student, he or she may move on to breathing exercises. These activities not only continue to burn off toxic chemicals, they teach the student *how* to modulate down and provide the student with the opportunity to explore tools and activities for future use in the classroom and other school settings when he or she begins to notice signs of dysregulation. If large motor activities are still being used in this step, they need to be shifted from fast to slow, big to small, less precise to more precise. This step should be concluded with some simple fine motor or breathing activity because these are the most portable ones for use in many school settings. As the student engages in Step 2, he or she tends to become more aware of his or her own bodies and the outside world. Predictability and choice continue to create a sense of safety.

Adult Involvement   In forms of Re-Set in which an adult is directly involved, Step 2 has the adult engage by using a posture and attitude that are very similar to those used in Step 1. Choice is an important part of Step 2 and is generally more successful as the student's cognitive brain is now more online. The adult may join with the student in doing the activity, offer suggestions, ask guiding questions that help the student notice things about how tools or techniques are working for him or her, but still should be very cautious about talking too much. This is *not* a time for bombarding a student with an adult opinion, suggestions, or discussion of what happened prior to engaging in the Re-Set Process. Step 2 is about tuning in quietly through parallel activity, about showing interest in the student and what he or she is doing and providing guidance as requested or needed. Listening is key; allow the student to take the lead as much as possible. Specific examples of language are provided in Chapter 6.

The nature of the activities does allow for closer adult proximity, and adult posture should be one of interest in the student and of warmth. It is best if the adult is still positioned across from the student so that each can see what the other is doing. The same nonverbal messages that are used in Step 1 should continue, along with some verbal messages of guidance and affirmation. Language should still be kept to a minimum. The adult's behavior enhances a sense of safety.

Step 3: Activate Thinking

Step 3 is designed to directly reactivate the cognitive portions of the brain and to keep it activated through tasks that are familiar and emotionally nonthreatening. Tasks are to be at the student's mastery level and should be based on student choice. This step prepares the student's brain for the higher level of thinking that is required in Step 4. Think of this as priming the engine for thinking.

Adult Involvement   In forms of Re-Set in which an adult is directly involved, Step 3 marks a shift in the balance between adult-directed activity and student-directed activity. The student is still operating within a framework, but choice is incredibly essential because it is part of communicating trust in the student's judgment. As a student's thinking brain returns, the opportunity for choice itself can be an intellectual activity. Adults can make suggestions, but it is recommended that there be choice among those suggestions. This is part of helping the student feel safe and trusted.

Some activities at this step are orchestrated serve and return activities in which attunement continues to be practiced. It is important to shift who leads in these activities and to allow the student to take greater responsibility at times. This conveys trust and allows for the experience to be truly reciprocal.

Step 4: Make a Plan

Step 4 may have many different goals depending on a whole host of variables. In some forms, it may simply be to have the student use his or her engaged cognitive brain to plan for a return to learning. Other times, the planning may be about which tool or tools to use when the student is feeling dysregulated. Step 4 may be a forum for problem-solving and figuring out restitution. All forms involve some sort of planning, either in the mind or on paper.

We have found that at this stage, many students long to atone out of their genuine feelings to reconnect. Many times, students will take the lead in doing this. Sometimes, as the student's supporting adult, the coach must make sure that the restitution is not an overcorrection that is driven by feelings of being bad. This is where the adult helps the restitution be in balance with the hurt that occurred.

At this step, we have found that students often knew the right thing to do during the events that precipitated use of the Re-Set Room, but they were too dysregulated to access that knowledge. Therefore, our focus is not on making a better choice; rather, it is about taking care of regulation needs, which will automatically lead to demonstration of the students' skills. If this is the case, the adult might guide the student to reflect on early signs of dysregulation so they can proactively reregulate next time.

Ultimately, the outcome of this step will be highly related to the form of Re-Set that is being used and whether or not an adult is coaching the student. Relevant details will be shared within those specific forms as they are discussed in the chapters that follow. Although each form may have unique goals, all forms have at least one global end goal that is the same—to return the student to the learning environment better regulated, ready to learn and to interact more successfully.

Adult Involvement   In forms of Re-Set where an adult is directly involved, Step 4 is the coaching phase. The coach's ability to ask good questions and to listen carefully to the student's responses is paramount. The coach provides guidance, active listening, effective questioning, and, sometimes, even challenges to the student's thinking.

Collaboration is expected, but the student's voice must not be overwhelmed by the adult's voice, thoughts, or emotions. The adult in this step should be seated next to the student, to convey, *I am your partner.* The adult's role is to question, encourage, and be optimistic. These characteristics help with attachment—they communicate to the student *I have your back* and *I believe in you,* and they serve to remind the adult of his or her belief and trust in the student, in the child's innate goodness and value.

Structure: An Additional Step and Intervention

The most intense reactive forms of Re-Set sometimes are enhanced by the introduction of an additional step, Step 0: Cocoon, as seen in Figure 3.5. We have also found that at times, some situations require an intervention prior to the beginning of the process, which we include here as mirroring intervention (also seen in Figure 3.5). These two elements are not necessary when students are mildly or moderately dysregulated, but they may be a very salient part of intervention with a highly escalated student. These elements require an adult who can be solely focused on the student and are to be used only with the most intensive forms of Re-Set.

Step 0: Cocoon Step 0 is an optional step that may be used when a student's state indicates that it would be a useful way in which to begin this process. Step 0 is a moment for the student to feel safe prior to or when first moved to a new space in or beyond the setting where he or she was highly dysregulated. What indicates that a student might need this step? If a student is not able to respond to even simple adult requests, he or she may have entered a freeze state from which he or she needs to have a profound sense of safety in order to emerge. Some students may have engaged in flight before the freeze, and they may have already selected a place to cocoon. In that case, we should consider joining the student in that area. If the student has made it to the Re-Set space, he or she may still need to spend a couple minutes in that new space to acclimate before engaging in the process. The more escalated the behavior, the more likely this step will be necessary.

The name Step 0 (zero) fits perfectly because the number 0 cues the intervening adult to remember that talking should be virtually nonexistent, body language should be neutral, movements should be slow and calm, and expectations of the student should be limited to simply remaining in the space.

Our first interaction in Step 0 should be to offer a comfort item (perhaps a weighted blanket or lap pad, or a water bottle or cool cloth for a child who appears overheated). If we can make

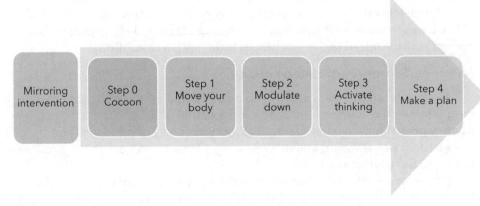

Figure 3.5. Additional step and intervention of the Re-Set Process.

this offering by using gestures alone, that is for the best. This gesture is one of kindness, one designed to nonverbally say, *I want you to feel safe. I want you to be comfortable.*

One of the hardest things for many of us in education is to not talk or to talk minimally, so wrapping our heads around the importance of this very low level of interaction is critical. A student who is feeling highly dysregulated feels very unsafe. The student's hearing and language processing are barely functioning. His or her system is on high alert. Everything we do at Step 0 needs to send a message of safety, including not irritating his or her system by language that is incomprehensible to them in his or her current state.

The adult should tell the child that he or she will set a timer, which signals when the adult will check back in with the child. Adults can do this with minimal language and with the visual cue of the timer. Our favorite timer for the purpose of cocoon is a sand timer and setting it is done by simply turning it over. Typically, the adult will use a 2-minute timer and leave it where the student can see it. Because some children have negative associations with timers (timers may have been used as a threat—*do this before the timer rings, or else*), it is very important to consider whether using a timer will be a trigger. If necessary, eliminate the use of the timer until it can be processed with the student when he or she is calm and instead simply approach him or her again in about 2 minutes. If a child has experienced cocoon before, we do not need to use any verbalization when we show the timer; we can simply set the timer and put it where the student can see it. We like to accompany the placing of the timer with a gentle smile and head nod to communicate, *This is your time. I won't invade it.* When we process the use of the timer with a student after the fact, we can actually articulate that sentiment. Another way to communicate this point is by offering the student a choice in sand timers, perhaps between a 1-minute and a 2-minute timer.

During those minutes, the adult is not in close proximity to the student, but the adult should remain within eyesight of the student. Adults should use care to express relaxed body language and should gaze at something else (a personally chosen foil is a piece of paper with something written on it). The goal is to not loom over the child or make the child feel that he or she is being watched or contained. The adult should think of themselves as a guardian of the child's safety. Nonverbals should all communicate, *I care about you. I will keep you safe. You are entitled to your space so you can feel safe.*

When the timer is done, we should approach the child to check whether he or she is ready to move to Step 1. The tone for this should be warm, friendly, and quiet. If the student indicates, verbally or through behavior, that he or she is not ready the timer is set again for 2 minutes. Re-setting the timer should be accompanied by a simple verbalization that conveys, *You are welcome to have more time if you would like.* At the end of that second period, the approach should be, *Let's try one thing from Step 1. What would you like to choose?* Offering visuals or actual items that depict choices is recommended. It is extremely rare for a student to not feel safe enough to move on at this point. If a student is not able to engage at this point, we would recommend the mirroring/sensory focus intervention that follows.

Mirroring/Sensory Focus Intervention

When we entered, Danny was wiggling and rolling on the tile floor at the far end of the long first-grade classroom. His class, on the carpet at the other end, was engaged in a math lesson with its teacher. Danny was instead noisily twisting and flopping. The teaching assistant was standing above him saying, "Time to go back to the group. Get up. Let's go." But Danny continued.

The administrator who was with me chose to sit on a chair nearby. Having never met Danny, I gave him space but gradually mirrored his position on the floor. For the moment he had settled into a coiled position on his side, knees bent, face turned down. I did too.

I kept my comments minimal: short, quiet, and simple. I noticed that he had a band-aid on his knee. "Big band-aid," I whispered as I pointed. I showed him a minor scratch on my hand and said, "I need one too." He was slightly interested.

I just laid there on the floor with him. After a few moments, he pointed to my scratch and said, "Yes, you need one." He reached down and started to pull at the one on his own knee and said, "Here." I declined, as graciously as possible.

I showed him that I was okay, and that I could open and close my hands. "They still work. Can yours open and close too?" He showed me.

"Reach up and keep going," I said to him. We both sat up to reach, then got to our feet to reach higher. With hands still opening and closing, we reached, stretched, and then floated arms down to pause.

"I have to show you something!" he said as he walked directly to his desk and I took a seat at a nearby table. He returned with a small can of colorful putty, and said, "Let's use this. Squeeze this, it helps." I curiously opened and closed my hands as he placed a small piece of putty onto one of my palms. He split the remaining putty between his two hands and did the same. Squeeze and release. Squeeze and release. I made sure I showed him how I slowly opened and relaxed my hand. I accompanied the relaxation with a long breath out.

Students who are so highly dysregulated *and* acting out so that they do not or cannot respond to the traditional cocoon option often benefit from the adult engaging in a mirroring/sensory focus intervention. The fully dysregulated child feels isolated, disconnected, and, often, misunderstood. We need to be careful that we are not courted by his or her behavior into talking *at* him or her, trying to reason with him or her, or using gestures that dysregulate the student further.

We tend to come upon these students after they have acted out against other people or objects in the classroom or fled the space (their desk, the learning center, or even the classroom). The student is not hiding, which may lead us to think that he or she should be able to move. Often, these children are moving, making sounds, or even talking or yelling, but if we pay attention, we will see that what they are doing is repetitive, locked-in behavior—it's a frozen pattern of behavior rather than the frozen (still) body we might have seen in some students. Freeze in humans can be different than the freeze we see in animals, which might be the eponymous deer-in-the-headlights freezing. We will explain.

Freeze mode in the nervous system is not a choice; it is an involuntary mobilization of survival energy that is fight and flight modes combined. In fact, freeze is a doubly powerful state that might be more difficult for the child to come out of than fight mode or flight mode alone. The way we engage a frozen nervous system requires understanding and patience. We need to understand that the rational/language center in the brain is completely offline, so words are irrelevant. Safety feels unattainable for the student. Connecting and helping a child in this state may take time and a willingness to attend to nuance—the form and space his or her body is in, the rate his or her breathing has taken, and the place his or her eyes have focused on.

When we mirror another's body form, without speaking a word, we project, *I am here with you. I can wait until you feel safe. I honor what you need right now.* Mirroring begins with us reflecting the student, and then it intentionally evolves to inviting the student to reflect us. It is establishing connection at the most primitive level, which is where a student's brain is functioning when he or she is in this deep freeze state. By engaging in mirroring, we are attuning to them before asking them, even in the simplest ways, to attune to us.

Mirroring certainly is not always necessary for a dysregulated student, but it has emerged as a useful tool prior to Step 0 for the group of students who demonstrate locked-in behavior or who are in what we consider a deep freeze state.

Notes From the Field

Using the Re-Set Process, I've been able to help many children with trauma. From the child who is angry after an intense game of gaga ball at recess to the child whose world is filled with abuse and neglect, this process has changed how I work with children.

Before learning about Re-Set, I didn't understand the ways that trauma affected the brains of children. Some of the strategies that I've used in the past had been unsuccessful because I was attempting to process situations with children who were too stuck in dysregulation to delve into the details and emotions of their situation. This process allows me to transition children back to the classroom, ready to learn, more effectively and quickly than any other process I've tried. Using the Re-Set Process, students can take control of the situation they are involved in and feel empowered to solve their problems.

This process has been so successful at my school that we have developed an area in every classroom that includes a set of flip cards that detail the Re-Set Process steps as one of our Tier 1 classroom interventions. Using this process, students spend more time in the classroom, and the Re-Set Process has become the way we teach students to cope with frustrating situations that they encounter academically, socially, and emotionally.

Elementary School Counselor

THE RE-SET PROCESS: CASE STUDY APPLICATIONS

This chapter describes many aspects of the Re-Set Process, including its goals and structure. Although important variations exist between the proactive and reactive forms, the end goal is the same: improved outcomes for students and teachers through increased sensitivity to and awareness of trauma-based dysregulation.

What would the Re-Set Process look like for our three students from the opening of this chapter? Leah, our kindergartner, with her signs of mild dysregulation first thing in the morning, would be served well by engaging in the Proactive Individual Re-Set as an opening to her day—whether in the classroom, in the hallway, or in a Re-Set Room. Given her age, we would lean toward the location being the Re-Set Room to help her learn the process through the coaching she would receive. Her teacher, Ms. Kimura, might want to rethink her movement break a bit by shifting it to one that intentionally regulates students down—otherwise known as Proactive Whole Class Re-Set. This form, placed a bit later in the morning, perhaps after a period of focused activity, would provide everyone with a regulation opportunity, and it would give Leah a second round of regulation and modulation fairly early in her day.

Devon, as an older child with a higher level of dysregulation and more concerning behaviors, would lead us to recommend Proactive Re-Set Room first thing in the day. We also would recommend this form because, as a student who is new to the building, Devon would benefit from the direct, caring, guided connection with a school adult. This relationship could support him in feeling safe and trusting of other school adults, as well. Devon might also be the kind of kiddo who would request Proactive Student Choice Re-Set times after he has several experiences with the Re-Set Room and understands the process. Time in the Re-Set Room could help Devon develop his plan for regulation that he could use in the classroom. The Reactive Re-Set Room may be necessary if serious behavior still occurs in the classroom while Devon is learning to respond to the proactive forms.

Justine, our seventh grader who was dealing with high levels of stress in her living situation, and dealing with the loss of her grandmother, may simply need access to Proactive Student-Choice Re-Set when she senses she needs it. If Justine is unaware of her early signs of dysregulation, she may require a reactive or scheduled form. As an older student, learning to regulate probably would be something she would want to do in a setting other than the class-room (whether hers or a buddy teacher's) so we would recommend Proactive Individual Re-Set in the hallway, Proactive Re-Set Room, and, if necessary, Reactive Hallway Re-Set supported by an adult. Involving Justine in making the decision regarding which proactive forms she would access would increase her investment in the process.

Ultimately, Re-Set is as much a way of thinking as it is a process. As you learn about and implement the specifics of the various forms of Re-Set, we hope you will begin to experience Re-Set as more than a structured collection of activities in specific settings. We hope that it will become a way of being with your students and even yourself.

Chapter 4

The Re-Set Process: Proactive Forms

ROBERT

It was the end of the first week of school when Robert joined his new first-grade class. His mother reported that he had not been feeling well, so she hadn't started him on the first day. She feared that he might not do as well if he was "a bit under the weather." His mother also brought records from his previous school, a private one, which indicated that he was on or above his grade level in both reading and math. Mother proudly reported that he had the vocabulary of a third-grader, so he would have no trouble joining the class late.

For the first 15 minutes, Robert sat next to his teacher, Ms. Linder, on the carpet. For the next hour, he darted around the classroom ignoring his teacher's and classmates' attempts to direct and redirect him to the appropriate place. Ms. Linder was pleased that his classmates invited him to join them rather than complaining about his behavior, but she was frustrated that even their kind overtures were ineffective. She decided to let him explore, feeling like he might settle down once he had a sense of the classroom. "Robert, once you've checked things out, please just join us or find your seat." She gestured toward his spot, pointing to the name sign on the table.

He still had not settled down by lunch, so she thought it would be best if she ate with the class. Robert moved with her through the line, sat next to her, ate a couple of bites, and then jumped up and ran from the cafeteria. He agreeably returned with her when she caught up with him, but he made a few more attempts to leave before lunch was over. The afternoon was much like the morning.

Over the next weeks, cafeteria aides noticed that Robert frequently covered his ears during lunch. They also reported that he continued to make attempts at escaping. He was offered headphones and remained in the cafeteria most of the time in the weeks that followed.

Classroom behavior showed some improvement as he learned the routines and after a high-frequency reward system was put in place—although his active wandering still proved to be disruptive to his learning and the learning of his peers.

EARLY INTERVENTION

If you have lived through or witnessed a student displaying chronically disruptive behaviors, you might not have initially thought, *Gee, I need to get proactive here!* The stress and urgency that are created by these kinds of events seem to beg for immediate reaction instead.

Other than reactively ensuring safety, Robert's teacher fought that urge and used a combination of positive reinforcement (e.g., tokens that could be turned in for small prizes) and antecedent strategies (e.g., introducing headphones in order to meet his needs). The teacher's efforts paid off—somewhat. The level of dysregulation Robert experienced still was fairly significant. His educational team found themselves developing a series of plans that would work for a period of time but then become less and less effective for him—an experience that is not unfamiliar to many educators.

Robert is the type of student who may well benefit from engaging in a form of the proactive Re-Set Process. As part of his plan, it could be considered an antecedent strategy—to decrease the likelihood of a problematic behavior occurring—or a replacement skill strategy—to replace the problem behavior with regulation skills. Which form of the Re-Set Process Robert should follow would depend on an assortment of variables that are unique to his classroom and to him. We would tend to start with Proactive Re-Set Room for Robert first thing in the morning, if that option is available in the school. It would settle him early in the school day, and it could help establish a key adult relationship for him. If such a space is not available, we would recommend an individual Re-Set in the classroom or hallway on a scheduled basis. This process would need to be taught to Robert. Involving an adult, as is done in the Reactive Hallway Re-Set form, in this scheduled time makes sense until he is able to engage in the process on his own.

The Teachable Moment and Behavior

Do you know the term *teachable moment?* It is an excellent idea for academic opportunities, but it is highly questionable when applied to behavior. Perhaps the intention never was to apply this concept to significant behavior issues but, time and again, we have observed it being suggested and tried—often with little or no effect.

As we learn more about the science of behavioral learning, we understand the faults with an approach that is based on the teachable moment idea. We will take apart that concept word by word. *Teachable.* We now know that when a student exhibits challenging behaviors, the student's cognitive brain is not very accessible, which means that the student is not very teachable. The student's brain is not laying down new learning pathways, and it may not even be able to retrieve some known information. *Moment.* We also know that new, sophisticated emotional learning is *not* created in haphazard moments; rather, it is the result of planning for introduction, scaffolding, practice, reinforcement, and generalization. So, what do we do instead?

The Learnable Moment and Behavior

Contrary to the teachable moment concept, the Re-Set Process is designed to teach the skills of self-regulation at a time when the cognitive brain is most available to learn, and to do so in structured ways so that the brain is most likely to learn the skills to fluency. It is a process where the student, regardless of age, is guided to discover the strategies that are most effective for him or her personally. Re-Set teaches a student to replace his or her less successful skill set with appropriate and effective skills.

The Re-Set Process intentionally creates the calming neural pathways (i.e., the brain's default setting that triggers a set of self-calming behaviors whenever stressed) in a student's brain through structured practice. To accomplish this goal, one must follow the process and not skip steps. With practice, the chronology becomes the student's natural default over time—it teaches the student how to *ride a regulation bike.* We want to get to that *muscle memory* state, where a series of complicated decisions occurs without needing to intensely think through details. These practices become guided opportunities for students to recognize where they carry stress and tension in their own bodies and to explore tools that are helpful in self-regulating. Think about healthy ways that you regulate. Do you twist a rubber band, doodle, play with an earring, stretch your neck in a couple different directions, breathe in and out slowly, close your eyes for a moment, go for a walk, shoot hoops? Do you find yourself doing some of these things without a conscious thought about needing to calm yourself down? This is what the Re-Set Process is designed to accomplish with your students.

PROACTIVE FORMS

The first two proactive forms of the Re-Set Process are as follows (see Table 4.1):

1. Proactive Whole-Class Re-Set takes place at a prescribed time in the classroom or in response to signs of increasing dysregulation. All students follow teacher-guided steps or preestablished choices.

2. Proactive Student-Choice Re-Set takes place as needed in the classroom when a student elects to follow a prescribed set of steps if they are experiencing increasing dysregulation.

     The first form, Proactive Whole-Class Re-Set, is designed to resettle the entire class. Proactive Student-Choice Re-Set is used by specific students when they are noticing low-level unsettled behavior in themselves. What is the difference between unsettled behavior and problematic behavior? Unsettled behavior does not interfere with learning in any significant way, whereas problematic behavior *noticeably* interferes with the student's own learning and with learning for others. Where these behaviors fall in a continuum is indicated in Figure 4.1. Unsettled behaviors are things such as repeatedly stretching in one's chair in a way that causes materials to drop or the student to fall out of the chair, dropping a pencil over and over as an excuse to get up and retrieve it, lightly drumming or tapping on the desk instead of working, looking out the window briefly but often, talking to a peer, or thumbing through the pages in a book absentmindedly.

Table 4.1. Re-Set Process: Proactive forms

Proactive forms of the Re-Set Process teach self-regulation skills when the cognitive brain is most available to learn.

Proactive forms	Description/Context
Proactive Whole-Class Re-Set	**Who:** All students in a class, teacher-guided **What:** All students follow teacher-guided steps or a set of preestablished choices **Where:** Classroom or hallway **When:** Scheduled or as needed based on indicators of increasing dysregulation **Why:** Teacher-guided learnable moment
Proactive Student-Choice Re-Set	**Who:** Individual students in a class, student choice **What:** Individual student follows a prescribed set of steps; visual supports provide guidance **Where:** Classroom **When:** As needed based on indicators of increasing dysregulation **Why:** Student-guided learnable moment
Proactive Individual Re-Set	**Who:** Preselected student who has demonstrated mild dysregulation issues in the past **What:** Individual student follows a prescribed set of steps for a designated time or a designated number of times; established as part of an informal action plan or a more formal individual behavior plan; visual supports provide guidance **Where:** Classroom or hallway **When:** Scheduled **Why:** Individual behavior support
Proactive Re-Set Room	**Who:** Preselected student who has demonstrated more disruptive dysregulation issues in the past; adult coach guides student through steps **What:** Individual student follows a prescribed set of steps for a designated time with an adult present to coach; established as part of an informal action plan or a more formal individual behavior plan **Where:** Re-Set Room **When:** Scheduled **Why:** Individual behavior support

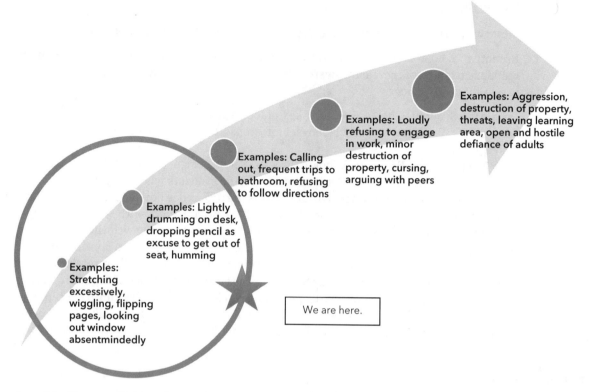

Figure 4.1.   The range of behavior, from mildly unsettled to very problematic.

Problematic behaviors are behaviors such as repeatedly getting out of one's seat and wandering in a way that greatly distracts others, frequently calling out about things that are unrelated to the classroom topic, fiddling inside a desk for an extended period of time so that no work occurs, or arguing with a classmate. Of course, any behaviors that create an ongoing, significant disruption to the class, which are clearly defiant, or which create safety issues would be considered problematic.

Some educators consider any low-level behavior that does not respond to several redirects to be problematic. Proactive forms of the Re-Set Process offer a solution in these cases. Instead of engaging in several redirects, teachers can use the Proactive Whole-Class Re-Set or Proactive Student-Choice Re-Set early on as a way to prevent unsettled from becoming problematic. This is true for an individual student, a group of students, or an entire class.

The remaining two forms of proactive Re-Set are not based on a student's demonstration of concerning behavior (see Table 4.1).

3. Proactive Individual Re-Set is a scheduled in-class opportunity for a preselected student to follow a prescribed set of steps for a designated amount of time.

4. Proactive Re-Set Room is a scheduled option for a preselected student to go the Re-Set Room and follow a prescribed set of steps with an adult coach.

These two forms are part of the student's schedule—just as they would go to the nurse to get medications at a set time of day. Access is unconditional. Having this in the student's schedule is the result of a teacher or behavior team studying the pattern of the student's disruptive behaviors and deciding on this intervention. The timing of the intervention is critical. Teachers and other decision-makers should consider when these dysregulated behaviors were typically exhibited and schedule Proactive Re-Set times accordingly. The goal is to give students a predictable opportunity to re-regulate before dysregulation occurs.

Guidance of some form is always provided during any Re-Set Process. That guidance may be an adult leading or modeling the process in real time, or a set of visual steps, for example, on cards or a poster that guides the student after a previous orientation by the adult. The steps are to be followed consistently in order to create those self-regulating pathways in the brain, to teach the brain how to default to healthy methods of resetting. It is intentionally structured based upon neuroscience and is not an open-ended break in the learning process.

You will notice slight differences in the types of activities being recommended for the steps depending on the form of the Re-Set Process being described. These variables match the unique conditions of each form. This may be where you adapt to fit your individual situation. For example, we do not have jumping jacks as an option for Step 1 for the Proactive Student-Choice Reset because a student jumping in the back of the room could distract peers. However, if your designated space for this form of the process is in the hallway, you might choose to add that as an option because it would not distract. To help support you making the process fit your situation, you will find descriptions of all these activities with clarifying details provided in the resources at the end of this section.

Proactive Whole-Class Reset

Who: Whole classroom of students or a small group of students who are working together

What: Teacher-guided Re-Set with the whole class

Where: In the classroom or in a hallway

When: Scheduled. It may be a routine part of the schedule or done on an as-needed basis. Consider the times that a class as a whole wrestles with staying in their seats and being focused on learning. For some classes, it may be first thing in the morning due to riding on buses (which we affectionately call *dysregulation containers* thanks to the acoustics, the crowdedness, the social dynamics, and the bumpiness of the road). For others, it may be after lunch or after PE class, or during guidance lessons, which may present some emotional challenges. And of course, many of us have found ourselves facing a classful of dysregulated students the day before a long vacation.

After observation data is gathered, intervention time can be scheduled shortly before the period of concern. That data does not have to be extensive; it may simply be paying more attention to patterns of behavior in the classroom. If you do not have a scheduled time, you may simply want to assess your class for its restlessness, find a logical time for an instructional break, and then insert a Proactive Whole-Class Re-Set.

Implementation Considerations   You may be thinking, *I already handle this kind of restlessness with my brain breaks. Why should I do something different?* The answer is that you may not need to do anything different—*if* your current strategy, such as a brain break, is working for *all* your students. If, however, there are one or more students who finish a brain break and still cannot settle down, you may want to consider making the shift to the Proactive Whole-Class Re-Set Process. This shift actually is rather minor because you already have determined the time when movement is needed, and you have probably engaged your students in a type of Move Your Body (Step 1) activity.

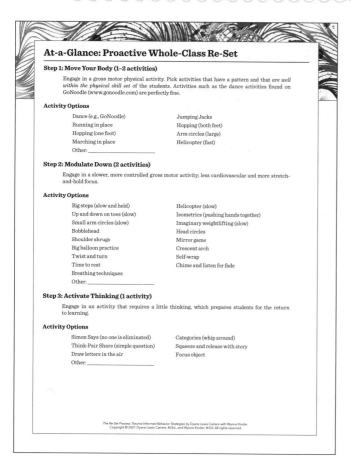

At-a-Glance: Proactive Whole-Class Re-Set

Step 1: Move Your Body (1–2 activities)

Engage in a gross motor physical activity. Pick activities that have a pattern and that *are well within the physical skill set* of the students. Activities such as the dance activities found on GoNoodle (www.gonoodle.com) are perfectly fine.

Activity Options

Dance (e.g., GoNoodle)	Jumping Jacks
Running in place	Hopping (both feet)
Hopping (one foot)	Arm circles (large)
Marching in place	Helicopter (fast)
Other: _____	

Step 2: Modulate Down (2 activities)

Engage in a slower, more controlled gross motor activity; less cardiovascular and more stretch-and-hold focus.

Activity Options

Big steps (slow and held)	Helicopter (slow)
Up and down on toes (slow)	Isometrics (pushing hands together)
Small arm circles (slow)	Imaginary weightlifting (slow)
Bobblehead	Head circles
Shoulder shrugs	Mirror game
Big balloon practice	Crescent arch
Twist and turn	Self-wrap
Time to rest	Chime and listen for fade
Breathing techniques	
Other: _____	

Step 3: Activate Thinking (1 activity)

Engage in an activity that requires a little thinking, which prepares students for the return to learning.

Activity Options

Simon Says (no one is eliminated)	Categories (whip around)
Think-Pair Share (simple question)	Squeeze and release with story
Draw letters in the air	Focus object
Other: _____	

Figure 4.2.   At-a-Glance: Proactive Whole-Class Re-Set.

There are some important differences between typical brain breaks, however, and our defined process. Our process is different in the following ways:

- It deliberately guides students to modulate down from higher activity to lower activity.

- It makes sure that more than 50% of the time is spent in calming activities versus activating ones. If you are a GoNoodle.com user, you may need to fade out one of the busier activities like dance after 2 minutes and then shift to one of the calming activities for the remaining 3 minutes of your brain break, and then wrap up with a few good breaths.

- It ends with a simple thinking activity that provides a transition back to learning.

There also are important overlaps with brain breaks and the Re-Set Process. Just like brain breaks, this process achieves the following objectives:

- It provides a way to frame learning—a stop and a start to instruction—increasing the retrievability of the information that is being learned.

- It gets the blood flowing, making oxygen more available to the brain allowing for improved functioning.

It is better to have more frequent, short experiences with this form of Re-Set than fewer longer ones. By working with students to settle themselves very early in the dysregulation process, they settle more easily, so the process can be shorter. Providing a 30-second Whole-Class Re-Set during which the students run for 10 seconds, stretch slowly for 10 seconds, and breathe for 10 seconds is an example of a short experience that can happen frequently.

Some schools have been instituting a movement path in their hallways during specified transition times. How to make these paths more Re-Set-structured is discussed in detail in Chapter 9.

It is important to note that engaging in a proactive form of the Re-Set Process does not harm any student who does not need it. Those students whose systems are highly regulated benefit from having peers who are more regulated. In addition, these students benefit from the instructional breaks for memory and increased oxygen in the brain for focus. Figure 4.2 shows the quick reference At-a-Glance Chart for Whole Class Re-Set.

Proactive Student-Choice Re-Set

Who: Individual student

What: Student engages in a series of steps, each which offer a few choices of activities. No adult is directly involved—rather, the process is guided by visuals. The time in this space should take no more than 2–4 minutes.

Where: In the classroom or just outside of the classroom, in a hallway

When: As with other proactive forms of the Re-Set Process, this form is designed to settle a slightly dysregulated student to allow him or her to be a more productive learner. It can be implemented because either a student or an educator noticed small indicators of increasing dysregulation. It is *not* the result of the exhibition of a problematic behavior, but rather of *unsettled* behavior.

Implementation Considerations Some schools have used a laminated folder with pictures for each step and a check-off box. Others have used a series of pictures on the wall and have had the student mark his or her progression through the steps by moving a visual from one hook-and-loop dot to the next until the process is completed.

When the space is located in a hallway, some schools have used a flip book that a student carries with him or her and flips as he or she completes each step, or the teacher has posted the steps on the wall, and the student moves a clip as he or she progresses. No matter what the materials are, the critical element is having a visual way for a student to know how to move through the sequence. Of course, like any practice that requires independent functioning, students should be taught the process in advance, and they should be provided with direct adult guidance, if necessary. It is very important that only the materials that are directly related to the activities be stored in this space. If there is a concern regarding material management, consider including the activities that minimize or eliminate the use of materials.

Because there has been no problematic behavior or high escalation, the proactive forms of the Re-Set Process do not have a Step 0 or Cocoon. There also is no need to make a formal return to learning plan, so all individualized forms only have *Do a class scan: Where should you be? What should you be doing?* at Step 4, which supports a smooth re-entry into the learning activity. Figure 4.3 shows the At-a-Glance chart for Proactive Student-Choice Re-Set.

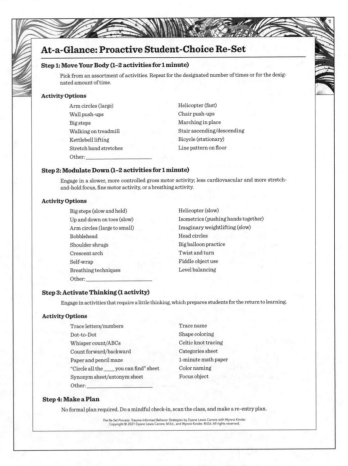

Figure 4.3. At-a-Glance: Proactive Student-Choice Re-Set.

Proactive Individual Re-Set

Who: Individual student. The process is established as part of an informal or formal plan for a student who has manifested relatively *mild but chronic* dysregulation issues in the past.

What: This form is the same as the previous one, with the exception that it is scheduled based on an individual student's history of unsettled behaviors.

Where: In the classroom or in a hallway

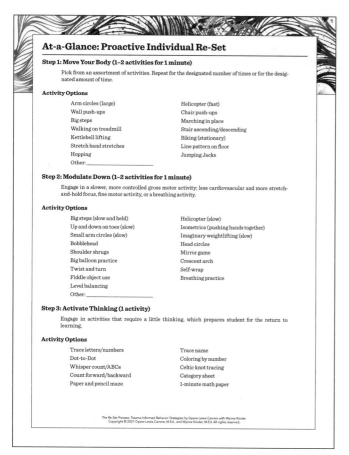

Figure 4.4. At-a-Glance: Proactive Individual Re-Set.

When: The schedule is established based on data collected on an individual student.

Implementation Considerations   When examining data that reflects when a student is most likely to become unfocused or unsettled, consider a time frame of about 15 minutes before those behaviors tend to occur; schedule the Re-Set Process then. Many times, educators use a combination of the schedule of the learning activities and that idea of a 15 minutes-ahead window to determine the best time for the student to be scheduled for the proactive Re-Set space. See Figure 4.4 for the At-a-Glance chart for Proactive Individual Re-Set.

Proactive Re-Set Room

Who: Individual student as an established part of an action plan that is either informal or formal. The targeted student has manifested more disruptive dysregulation issues in the past and probably has experienced a reactive form of the Re-Set Process in response to those more significant behaviors.

What: A preselected student goes to the Re-Set Room and is coached by an adult through a series of steps.

Where: In a designated space in the school beyond the classroom—often a specific room (see Chapter 6 for guidelines).

When: This form of the Re-Set Process is a scheduled use based on data regarding the student's prior history of disruptive behaviors related to dysregulation issues. Although use is related to previous serious behavior events, it is *not* the result of a current problematic behavior.

Implementation Considerations   This form of Re-Set, although proactive in nature, is based on a history of significant issues. Frequently, students who are using this proactive form for the first time are also still having times when a reactive version of the Re-Set Process is used for them. Our intent, of course, is to have the student become stronger in his or her regulation abilities so that the reactive form is no longer necessary. The reality is that this often takes time.

As a result, though a proactive process, this form of Re-Set is much more structured, and the steps are individualized so that the process mirrors how it is being used reactively with that student. More detailed information about the Re-Set Room is in Chapter 6.

This form requires a coach to assure both consistent practice and student reflection. Students with this intensity of behavior also need to have the opportunity to build connection with a caring adult—their coach. Over time, the coach may fade his or her supports (i.e., decrease scaffolding) but observation and feedback are still critical, as are relational components. When a student is able to move through the steps with very little guidance from the coach, it is a cue that the student has made critical growth and is ready to have his or her proactive Re-Set Process be one that happens in the classroom or hallway on a scheduled basis.

Factors to Consider

Cohesion of Practice   If, with a coach, the student has developed a plan for regulating, it should be used during this process. For example, if a certain fiddle object or calming routine has been found to be effective, practicing with that object or routine during this time is critical. Likewise, if a self-talk script was developed that guides a student's inner dialogue during a high-stress time, that script should be reviewed during Step 4. A brief explanation of self-talk scripts is found in the resources at the end of this section.

Unconditional Part of the Student's Schedule   Proactive use of the Re-Set Room is something that has to happen in accordance with a plan. This good mental hygiene practice is just like access to food—it should not be made conditional. Certainly, sometimes there may be situations that can affect the exact timing of when the student accesses the Re-Set Room (e.g., weather delays, special school events) but every effort should be made to hold to the intent of the planned time. The scheduled time should not become something that shifts a great deal to avoid creating more dysregulation for an already dysregulated student. In fact, sometimes, the very things that might result in the temptation to cancel the Re-Set Room are things that make its use even more critical. Often, those events increase the sense of chaos and destabilization that Re-Set addresses (e.g., delay in start of day, absence of a teacher).

Reactive Re-Set Room Use Does Not Eliminate Proactive Use   A student who engages in behavior that results in using the Re-Set Room reactively should still have access to use of it proactively as per the schedule. It should not be viewed as, *They already had that time earlier, so we are canceling the regularly scheduled time.* Now, obviously, if a student is scheduled to participate in a proactive Re-Set Room process at 10:30 a.m. and at 10:25 a.m. he or she has a serious behavioral issue, you run the reactive process. You may, however, want to reschedule a proactive practice later that day, if feasible. We have worked in schools long enough to know that sometimes the theoretical has to yield to the practical, but we would urge you as practitioners to seek to meet the intent of this process and to be as transparent as possible with your students when changes have to be made.

Proactive Re-Set Is Not Taking a Break   This process is not about having a student leave the classroom and just chill for a period of time—which is how it varies from other methods, like sending a student on an errand. Although chilling-out may be enjoyable and even somewhat helpful in settling a student, it is not necessarily an efficient way to settle, and it may create some other issues, such as escape-related behaviors.

Scheduling Process   There are two ways to schedule this proactive form. The one that a school selects often is based on availability of staff who can coach.

   1. Student Data-Based Scheduling   Look at what that student's data has told you about his or her specific dysregulation patterns. If a student falls apart by 10:00 a.m., schedule his or her Re-Set time by 9:45 a.m.—the key is to get ahead of the need to be reactive. Look for early signs of dysregulation—fumbling in desk, dropping pencil repeatedly, drumming, emerging calling out, talking with peers at inappropriate times.

   This is the sweet spot for scheduling the proactive time for many reasons: the student has not yet practiced—again—a highly problematic behavior, his or her peers have not witnessed or been affected by a negative situation, the student's teacher is not exhausted by a significantly

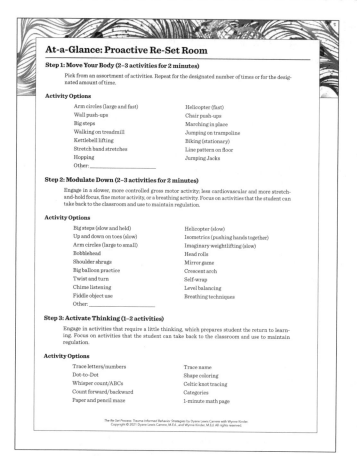

Figure 4.5. At-a-Glance: Proactive Re-Set Room.

challenging incident, *and* the student is coming to the space at a time when most of the efforts and time in the Re-Set Room can be focused on practicing ways to re-regulate.

2. Logical Times of the Day Sometimes, schools have people available to coach the Re-Set Room only at certain times of the day. By looking at typical (rather than student-specific) high-stress times, you can deploy your limited resources at the most useful times, creating a schedule based on *generalized likely needs* rather than individual ones.

We know these patterns. Young students may need to be scheduled to participate in the Re-Set Room process at the beginning of the day, as well as before or after times where there is a lot of stimulation (e.g., before or after visits to the cafeteria, specials, or recess). Older students tend to be okay first thing in the school day, but then need an opportunity to regulate just prior to midday, such as before heading to the intense social demands of lunchtime. They may also need an end-of-the-day opportunity before they head to the bus and the overstimulation (e.g., loud noise, bumpy ride) and unsupervised social interactions that are inherent in being in a small space with sixty other adolescents.

Why invest in an end-of-day regulation process? Those last precious minutes of the school day may seem like the wrong time to schedule a time. We have almost made it through the day, and it may seem unnecessary (and also difficult) to schedule a student for another practice of regulation before he or she leaves the school. Our minds are ready to get the students out the door so we can turn to lesson planning, setting up labs, getting to committee meetings, and all the other many end-of-day tasks that come with being an educator.

Here is why . . . If we send a student home, to the bus, or to whatever place follows school, we are sending a more regulated person into those environments, which increases the likelihood that he or she will be more successful in those environments. The student will get better feedback, have better relationships, feel better about him- or herself, which all are valuable outcomes. But there is another somewhat hidden bonus to an end-of-the-day Re-Set and that is this. Students with trauma often return to a space at the same regulation level as when they left it. If a student leaves your classroom highly dysregulated, more often than not, that is the *marker* for how he or she returns. For a child with high levels of **allostatic load** (carryover stress chemicals) whose emotional brain is in overdrive, what happened last in a specific space remains *big* in his or her mind.

By providing those students with the opportunity to regulate *before* they leave your classroom or the school building, how they last felt in school was settled, and returning to your class cues them to return to that settled state. There is a positive association with school—that sense of calmness in the body and mind and the individualized connection with an adult, and that is a good thing. Figure 4.5 provides you with an At-a-Glance chart for the Proactive Re-Set Room form.

As we mentioned in Chapter 3, a smaller proportion of students manifests dysregulation by internalizing and retreating—think of the freeze effect. Their behavior may not gain adult attention as quickly and, therefore, may not be attended to as often—particularly in a proactive manner. Consider your students who may be under-engaged and under-stimulated. What behaviors might you see that would be considered mild in nature? We would consider distractibility/daydreaming, being slow to respond to directives, and lack of social engagement all to be signs that a student needs to regulate up. For these students, the Re-Set Process would reverse Steps 1 and 2—beginning with fine motor and breathing activities, and then moving to the gross motor activities. Steps 3 and 4 would remain the same.

Next, in Chapter 5, we discuss the reactive forms of the Re-Set Process.

The Re-Set Process: Reactive Forms

Behavior is the language of children who have lost their voice.
—Purvis, Cross, & Lyons (2007, p. 12)

JONATHAN

Jonathan entered his sixth-grade classroom with what Mr. Foster, his teacher, described as a chip on his shoulder. He was scowling, kicking at the legs of desks, and bumping into chairs as he made his way to the coat closet. When two other students rushed up to their teacher, reporting that Jonathan had shoved them in the hallway on the way in from the bus, he yelled over their voices, "Liars! Liars!" Then, Jonathan threw his backpack at the doorway, just missing another student.

Having been trained in de-escalation techniques, Mr. Foster paused, took a breath, and cued the other students to take their seats. Then he quietly checked in with Jonathan. In a whisper, he asked Jonathan whether there was anything he could do to help him, to which Jonathan responded, "Leave me alone," and walked away before slamming his notebook on the desk. Mr. Foster kept an eye on Jonathan but gave him space and engaged with other students.

Moments later, Jonathan jumped up, flipped his chair, and proceeded to yell at his teacher, "You hate me! I know it! That's why I always get in trouble!" When Mr. Foster slowly approached him and quietly picked up the chair, Jonathan backed away and ran out the door. Mr. Foster contacted the office and they notified the crisis team, who prevented Jonathan from leaving the building. The crisis team physically escorted Jonathan to the front office, where he kicked chairs and yelled at visitors (parents, other students, and volunteers who were checking in) to stop looking at him, until the principal, coming from another escalated situation that was occurring in the building, arrived on the scene.

The reactive forms of the Re-Set Process are designed to address problematic behavior as it is occurring by addressing the dysregulation students are experiencing. Not all behavior stems from a student having a highly dysregulated neurological system, *but* nearly all behavior occurs in the context of dysregulated stress (i.e., dysregulation caused by high levels of stress chemicals flooding the brain and body). In other words, even if trauma-related dysregulation is not the cause of the challenging behavior, dysregulation of some sort almost always drives the behavior. As adults, we know we are more likely to snap at our spouses, eat poorly, and avoid work tasks when we are dysregulated, and this is true despite the boatloads of resources, knowledge, and success stories in our histories. Think about your own behavioral struggles during childhood or even now. Did they happen when your thinking brain was in balance with your emotional brain, or did they happen when you were stressed or out of balance? Perhaps some of your behaviors were very deliberate but, just as is true for students in your classroom, many were probably not meant to be as intense as they were. As Ross Greene (2008), author of *The Explosive Child* and *Lost at School* reminds us, "Kids do well if they can" (p. 53).

The Re-Set Process is about getting back to balance so students can do well. It is also about nurturing regulation skills through intentional, structured practice in order for students to do well on a routine basis. Our ultimate goal is to help students develop regulation skills that drastically reduce their exhibition of challenging behavior in the future while simultaneously nurturing connections between students and caring educators.

How does this Re-Set Process compare with other traditional reactive approaches like time-out, sending a student to the office, or suspending a student? Many reactive strategies are designed to stop the behavior or at least shift it to a setting where its impact is lowered. The Re-Set Process is designed to do that as well. Traditional reactive strategies seek to hold students accountable for their behavior and the Re-Set Process is designed to lay the foundation for that also. The Re-Set Process, however, has two additional, massively critical goals: the development of new skills and the improvement of adult-student relationships—the two Rails of regulation and attachment we described earlier. This learning and relational context is what allows a *genuine* sense of accountability to be developed. This approach calms a student faster, returns them to learning more quickly, and decreases the likelihood of reoccurrence of the problem behavior that day and beyond.

There are some important differences between traditional time-out and our defined process. Our process:

- Begins with gross motor activity as opposed to requiring that a child sit in a chair. We call this *the shift from a time-out chair to a time-out square.*

- Moves students through a process that guides them to modulate their behavior rather than expecting it to stop simply because they have been sent the message that their behavior is unacceptable

- Focuses on healing dysregulation rather than punishing a student for it

There remain overlaps between traditional time-out and reactive Re-Set Forms. As is true for traditional time-out, these forms:

- Provides a break in the cycle of behavior

- Are intended to guide a student in his or her return to learning after a brief period of time away from the activities of the classroom. That said, in our approach, guidance is delivered in a more explicit, empowering and relational manner than in most time-out methodologies.

Notes From the Field

I have found that I am teaching self-regulation strategies in almost all my individual and small-group counseling sessions. It seems that no matter what the presenting issue is for coming to my room, big feelings creep into the conversation. Self-regulation strategies help the student return to a calm state, from where the student can face his or her problem with more clarity.

Elementary School Counselor

REACTIVE FORMS

The goals of all Re-Set Processes are to heal a dysregulated system, build connection, and develop a healthy internal voice. These goals are more quickly attained when a student's behavior can be addressed through a proactive form of Re-Set, but they are also the focus of all reactive forms of the process—with the understanding that this healing may require much more time and patience.

Our case study student, Jonathan, is typical of students we have worked with. His teacher employed many correct strategies, but Jonathan's dysregulated status did not allow those strategies to make enough of a difference to prevent escalated behavior. In essence, his dysregulation formed a shield against the teacher's intentions and compassion. Once again, we are reminded of Bruce Perry's (2018) sequence—regulate, relate, and then reason. Re-set is rooted in regulation.

It is critical to note that the Re-Set Process is *not* designed to shame a student or to force compliance. We know that shame is a toxin to the human spirit and that it drives away human connection. Compliance occurs only in the presence of a governing force and not otherwise. The Re-Set Process is about healing and developing self-control and self-efficacy.

There are four different forms of the reactive Re-Set Process. They are defined by the intensity of student need and the associated amount of support required for the student to move through the process. Your decision about which form is appropriate for your students is based on the student's behavioral intensity. Table 5.1 should help bring some clarity and continuity to

Table 5.1. Re-Set Process: Reactive forms

Reactive forms of the Re-Set Process address problematic behavior as it is occurring.

Reactive forms	Description/Context
Reactive In-Class Re-Set	**Who:** Student demonstrating mildly disruptive behavior **What:** Teacher quietly directs individual student to the designated Re-Set space in the classroom; student proceeds through the established steps **Where:** Designated location in the classroom **When/Why:** Student behavior is mildly disruptive and has been unresponsive to repeated redirects. Student behavior is increasing in intensity but still not tipping into serious concerns.
Reactive Alternate Classroom Re-Set **(aka Buddy Teacher Re-Set)**	**Who:** Student demonstrating mildly disruptive behavior **What:** Student moves to a new location and proceeds through the established steps **Where:** In a buddy teacher's classroom, in a predetermined, structured space **When/Why:** Student behavior is mildly disruptive in nature and has been unresponsive to repeated redirects. Student behavior is increasing in intensity but still not tipping into serious concerns. Teacher determines that the classroom environment may be triggering the increase in intensity.
Reactive Hallway Re-Set	**Who:** Student demonstrating mildly disruptive behavior; adult/coach **What:** A supporting adult comes to the classroom and accompanies the student out to the hallway. In the new location, the student proceeds through the established steps and is guided by the coach. **Where:** Hallway **When/Why:** Student behavior is significantly disruptive or has been non-responsive to In-Classroom and/or Buddy Teacher Re-Set forms.
Reactive Re-Set Room	**Who:** Student identified by administrative team and/or with this component in behavior plan; adult/coach **What:** Adult coaches the student through all established steps in the Re-Set Room. This is the most intense form of the Re-Set Process. **Where:** Re-Set Room **When/Why:** Student behavior is significantly disruptive and is persisting despite attempts at other Re-Set Process options. Student behavior is endangering or destructive.

your decision-making. Always, your understanding of your student and the bigger context in which the behavior is occurring may lead you to lean a different direction than the chart would suggest. This is where professional judgment is so critical, where having that North Star set of principles from Chapter 1 will help to guide you.

Although it is not included in the reactive forms chart, the Re-Set Process also can be applied to groups of students who have been dysregulated by the behavior of a student who is seriously acting out. This situation is examined at the end of this chapter.

Reactive In-Class Re-Set

Who: Individual student

What: When a student is exhibiting the designated intensity of behavior, the teacher quietly directs him or her to the Re-Set space in the classroom. It is helpful if there is a simple phrase for that direction so that it is a fairly private communication. The student then proceeds through the established steps. At each step, a student may choose from an assortment of available activities to help his or her body feel settled. A longer-term goal of the process is that the student finds a combination of activities that works best for him or her. Younger elementary students may need more of a prescribed set of activities during each step— *Do these two things, 10 times each, in this order*—while older elementary students and middle schoolers may do better with a menu—*Choose one from column A and one from column B.*

Where: In the classroom, at a designated, designed location

When: When an educator notices a student experiencing increasing dysregulation (e.g., jiggling legs, breaking pencil tip, dropping items, losing place in work) or disruptive behaviors (e.g., calling out, out of seat, refusal to participate in learning activity, bothering peers) that are unresponsive to repeated redirects, this reactive form of Re-Set should be selected. Typically, it will be noticed that the student's behaviors are increasing in intensity yet still are not at a level where they are seriously destructive or dangerous.

Implementation Considerations   Because students may have had prior experiences with traditional time-out, it is very important to make this area look and feel different. It is also critical that the process is taught so that students understand why they are engaging in certain activities. The more that students understand the rationale, the greater the chance they will be able to make healthy decisions for themselves. Explicitly taught rationale leads to choices and eventually an intrinsic ability to self-manage.

1. Establish a location in the classroom for the Re-Set space. This should be an area where, at a minimum, the student can be on his or her feet, stretching out his or her arms. Some teachers have found that their students do better if this area is out of the line of sight of other students, so they provide a way to screen the area. Sometimes that is not logistically feasible, so positioning the space as privately as possible is recommended. Some teachers have established the location just outside their classroom door, particularly if their door offers an alcove area.

2. Consider what you will call the space if you choose not to call it the Re-Set space. Avoid names similar to time-out—because of prior connotations—and chill spot (connotes doing nothing). Think carefully of what the title communicates and make sure that it aligns with the intention of the process (to regulate and return to learning).

3. Create visuals for each step in the process. The visuals need to be well-developed and specific enough to guide the student through the process without adult assistance.

4. Gather materials that are needed for each of the steps and organize them in the space—perhaps in numbered bins. This includes anything you are adding to the environment, such as taped lines on the floor or handprints on the wall to guide movement.

5. Set up the space.

6. Decide how you will direct students to the space (e.g., visual cues, a quiet verbal cue), exactly what you expect them to do when they are there, and how you would like them to return (e.g., after they give a signal and you cue them, upon your cue, on their own when they have completed the steps).

7. Explicitly teach a lesson or two with the whole class about how and when the space will be used. Have the class practice with you the use of signals, the steps, the associated materials, and the method of return. Be sure to repeatedly state that this is not a punishment or a time to play. Rather, it is a time to Re-Set and settle so they can focus better on learning. Obviously, the use of language that is appropriate to your grade level is important. This initial orientation to the process is critical because this is not a coached approach—it is designed to occur while the teacher continues to work with the rest of the class.

Be prepared that some students may want to do something just so they get to experience the space. One way to prevent the use of negative behavior as an entry point is to also use the space proactively. We have found that the majority of students will be curious and want to explore it but then will use it only when they genuinely need it.

Periodically reorient students to the process. In the meantime, remember to positively and privately acknowledge students who use the process appropriately. If at all possible, meet with students who use the process more than once to discuss what strategies they are finding helpful and to explore how the students might use those strategies *before* they show behaviors of concern. Remind them of how to access those strategies while working at their seat or by using the Re-Set space proactively.

It has been helpful to have a student who is a frequent user of the reactive Re-Set Process (in any form) meet with a school counselor or school psychologist (or other involved professional) to discuss the student's toolbox of strategies and signs of dysregulation. These discussions and reflection times are essential to developing students who can authentically self-check and self-regulate. Development of a regulation plan is essential if the behavior is to be decreased. We provide some examples of regulation plans in the resources at the end of this section.

We have noticed that, in the life of a classroom, sometimes these spaces become gathering spots for other materials. It is *very* important to keep this area clear of things that are not materials that are directly related to the process. A space that is cluttered with other materials will not support the process and may invite play, which will then reinforce the problematic behavior. Remember, too, that messy environments contribute to dysregulation. The more organized and simpler these spaces are, the better they will support the process. This may require some ongoing monitoring (a new classroom job, perhaps?).

Some educators express concern that the Re-Set space may be too much fun for students. If this is your concern, remember to use activities only from the recommended list to be sure that the process walks that not play/not punishment line. Sometimes, when people improvise, the process may tip toward fun and compromise the process (e.g., using mini-basketball hoop throws as a Step 1 activity—*not* a good idea). We do want to acknowledge, however, that some of the ideas we have received from others who improvised are now some of our very favorites (e.g., lifting kettlebells to a count as a great Step 1 activity for middle schoolers). So, improvise, but please do so with *extreme* care.

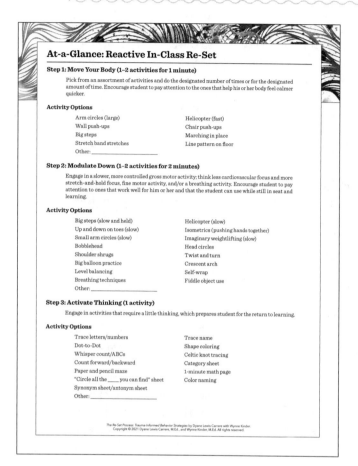

Figure 5.1. At-a-Glance: Reactive In-Class Re-Set.

Others worry that a student may engage in problematic behavior in order to gain access to the downtime of Re-Set. If this is your concern, there are two things you will want to consider. First, if a child is escaping from the classroom demands, what changes might be needed to reduce the need to escape? Second, what is really happening during the Re-Set Process? Re-set should not ever feel like downtime if it is implemented properly. See Figure 5.1 for the At-a-Glance chart for Reactive In-Class Re-Set Process.

Reactive Alternate Classroom Re-Set (aka Buddy Teacher Re-Set)

Who: Individual student

What: When a student exhibits the designated intensity of behavior and the educator judges that the behavior is being maintained or even increased by remaining in the current classroom setting, re-setting may occur in a buddy teacher classroom. It is helpful if there is a simple phrase for that relocation so that the direction is quick and private.

When in the new location, the student is to proceed through the established steps. At each step, a student can choose from an assortment of available activities to help his or her body feel settled. A longer-term goal of the process is that the student will find a combination of activities that work for him or her. Younger elementary students may need more of a prescribed set of activities at each step (e.g., do these two things, 10 times each, and in this order), and older elementary students and middle school students may do better with a menu (e.g., choose one from column A and one from column B).

Where: In the buddy teacher's classroom, at a predetermined, structured space.

When: When an educator notices a student experiencing increasing dysregulation (e.g., jiggling legs, breaking pencil tip, dropping items, losing place in work) or disruptive behaviors (e.g., calling out, out of seat, refusal to participate in learning activity, bothering peers) that are unresponsive to repeated redirects, this reactive form of Re-Set may be selected. Typically, it will be noticed that the student's behaviors are increasing in intensity, but they still are not at a level where he or she is seriously destructive or dangerous. *The buddy teacher form of the Re-Set space should be used when there is something about the current environment that seems to be triggering the behavior and maintaining or increasing its manifestation.*

Implementation Considerations   When sending a student to a buddy teacher, it is important that the behavior being shown is not significantly disrupting, destructive, or endangering to safety. Nothing will damage a collegial relationship faster than sending a student who is emotionally or physically destroying your classroom over to theirs to do the same.

As with all forms of the Re-Set Process, it is important that the behavioral manifestation match the intervention. Sending a student who is quite out of control to another classroom will not put him or her into a situation he or she is going to get the help needed to regulate. Students who are more significantly out of control need to go where they are coached through the process of regulating. It is not doing them or anyone else a favor if they are given a shot at a less intensive intervention when their behavior requires greater supports. Remember that the form of Re-Set that is being used must be determined by the intensity of behavior, and all forms of Re-Set are supportive and instructional in nature.

There is always a debate with buddy teacher structures as to grade-level placement. Should a buddy teacher be the same grade level? Should he or she be a level up or a level down? Educators are rightfully concerned about how a student may feel if he or she is in a buddy teacher's room where same-age peers are, particularly during the upper elementary years. If the buddy teacher is also using the Re-Set Process, this concern can be set aside because students will be familiar with it and not perceive the space to be a *You're in big trouble, buster* space. They will have been introduced to it as a space to regain regulation, and it will carry less emotional baggage with its use. There are many factors that go into deciding who a good buddy teacher is: easy physical access from one class to another, the physical space in a room, how students might feel in that particular room. As is true for everything we do, we should make the best initial decision we can, and then pay attention to how our decisions affect our students—and adjust them, as necessary. See Figure 5.2 for the At-a-Glance chart for Reactive Alternate Classroom Re-Set (aka Buddy Teacher Re-Set).

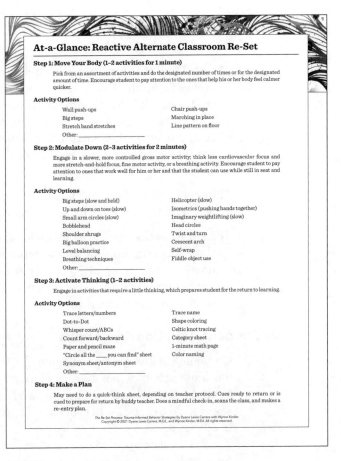

Figure 5.2. At-a-Glance: Reactive Alternate Classroom Re-Set.

Notes From the Field

One of my schools uses buddy teachers as a re-regulation space for students who have become slightly escalated. To ensure consistency in how these spaces are utilized, the dean of students developed a set of visuals for every classroom to indicate appropriate student behavior while visiting the buddy teacher space. Included in these visuals were a variety of seating options that calm the neurological systems of dysregulated students. This was critical because some of these seating options otherwise might have been disallowed by some teachers.

Elementary Intervention Specialist

Reactive Hallway Re-Set

Who: Individual student

What: This is the first *directly* coached reactive form of the Re-Set Process. A supporting adult comes to the classroom and accompanies the student out to the hallway. The tone of the supporting adult is to be calm and kind.

Once in the new location, the student then proceeds through the established steps fully guided by the coach. The number of activities at each step and/or the duration of those activities is determined by the coach's assessment of how regulated the student is or is not becoming.

Where: In the hallway (*Note*: It also may be an office, conference space, or another nearby space that is functioning as a *temporary* Re-Set space.)

When: A teacher observes behavior that is significantly disruptive—running around room, throwing relatively harmless items, screaming at peers or adults, or milder behaviors that have not been responsive to other less-intense interventions—and feels that the student needs to leave the classroom in order for his or her needs to be met and for the classroom at large to regain its footing.

Implementation Considerations

Obviously, hallways can be some of the most dysregulating spaces in schools, especially at a middle school when classes change. Use of the hallway for the Re-Set Process requires timing—not during class change—and/or finding safe spaces in hallways and related common areas to go to in order to process all the steps. It is important to think about these conditions in advance.

Hallways do provide an excellent environment for the movement required in Step 1. Going for a walk, at an even pace, can meet the regulation needs being addressed in Step 1. Going for a walk also can create a form of privacy that is not available in a classroom setting.

This form pays particular attention to the second rail of the Re-Set Process—attachment. Students with this level of behavioral concerns often have significant trust issues and may not have any adult in the school with whom they feel a secure attachment. The adult who supports them in this process may very well be the experiential model of adult-student attachment for the student. Toward this end, it is critical that the adult who appears at a classroom door to accompany the student presents as a helper or a coach—*not* as a traditional disciplinarian. This can be a challenge when that person also functions as a disciplinarian in the school. (Many assistant principals find themselves in these dual roles.)

The tone of the adult supporter as he or she greets the student is all-important. Carefully chosen and gentle language is most effective. Some things the coach can say that serves this intention well are *Hey, let's take a walk and work together,* or *I hear you could use a break to regulate, let's take a few minutes,* or *Show me which way you would like us to walk.* The words are casual, and the tone is friendly. Choice is inserted as appropriate.

Because attunement and attachment also are to be addressed in this particular form of Re-Set, consideration should be given to body language and body position throughout the steps. Walking next to or standing across from the student during Steps 1, 2, and 3 are both appropriate—with proximity being as close as is comfortable for both parties. A litmus test for this is asking yourself, *Would someone who is observing the adult and student think that they were having a positive conversation together?* During Step 4, it is important for the coach to be next to the student or in a lean-in type of posture that a caring coach would assume during a confidential conversation with an athlete right before an event.

Although we identified the space for this form of Re-Set as the hallway, implementers have found that it sometimes makes sense to do Step 4 in an office or setting where the adult can sit down next to the student, which supports the ability to assume a coaching posture. The goal is to send the message *I am with you, supporting you, helping you be successful*, as well as *We are looking at this issue together, from the same point of view.*

Because we want the student to be aware of and connect with the steps of the Re-Set Process as part of learning how to self-settle, it is important that the supporting adult have visual tools with them—tools that provide visual anchors that are referenced as the adult and the child move through the process. Remember, Re-Set has several goals, two of which are to regulate the student *at the time* and to teach the student how to regulate *over time*. In order to teach, we need to reference the steps. Some educators bring along a small ring of cards that they can flip to reference the process and the choices of activities in each step. Others have found that students who tend to behave at this level of concern have individual Re-Set plans that the adult can grab and bring with them to reference as he or she works with the student. Copies of individual Re-Set plans should be maintained in offices of people likely to be called to support the student, and in the student's classroom or homeroom.

When a student has left a classroom to engage in a Re-Set Process, returning to that same classroom is very important. However, in some schools, where classes change, returning to the classroom may not be logistically possible. If that is the case, it is important to find some way to reconnect that student with the adult whose class he or she left. We are not suggesting that the return is to make an apology—although restitution may be designed into the plan. The return is to reconnect, to let the teacher know that the student has practiced his or her regulation strategies, and that he or she is back in balance. Sometimes, it may be best that the student shares a plan for next time or thanks the teacher for connecting him or her with the coach, or perhaps the student may advocate for something he or she needs in the classroom context (e.g., one student who we worked with was able to ask for a change of assigned seat because another student's banter was very provocative for him). This is about more than restitution or self-advocacy; it is about healing the relationship between the adult and child. It is about having the child re-enter that classroom the next time feeling emotionally safe because there are no concerns related to a previous event hanging over his or her head.

When a student has left a room due to his or her behavior, the question about makeup work often comes up. Care should be taken to not use work as a punishment, and yet, making up work helps keep a student progressing academically. When considering this issue, ask yourself, *How important is it that this particular work be completed?* If making up work is important, it needs to be scheduled and supported.

We would encourage anyone in the role of supporting a student in this hallway Re-Set Process to carefully read Chapter 6. It provides much more detail for adults who are coaching students through a Re-Set Process, and it may answer any lingering questions. See Figure 5.3 for the At-a-Glance chart for Reactive Hallway Re-Set.

Reactive Re-Set Room

Who: Individual student as determined by an administrative team or as part of an established plan for that student

What: This is the most intense form of the Re-Set Process and requires coaching through all the established steps. The number of activities at each step and the duration of those activities is determined by the coach's assessment of how regulated the student is or is not becoming.

Where: In the Re-Set Room

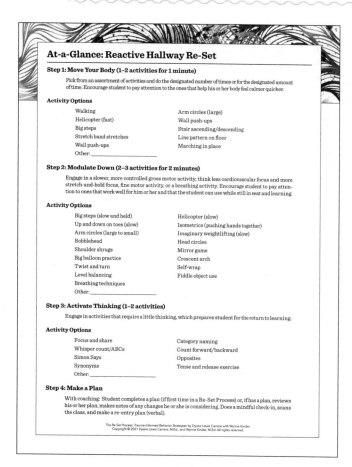

When: A teacher observes behavior that is significantly disruptive or destructive/aggressive in nature—running around room, throwing relatively harmless items, screaming at peers or adults, or milder behaviors that have not been responsive to other less intense interventions—and refers the student to administration for participation in the Re-Set Room Process.

Implementation Considerations Please see Chapter 6 for very specific guidance about implementation of the Reactive Re-Set Room. See Figure 5.4 that follows for the At-a-Glance Reactive Re-Set Room chart.

Figure 5.3. At-a-Glance: Reactive Hallway Re-Set.

MRS. NELSON'S RE-SET PROCESS

Elise Nelson developed an in-class form of the Re-Set Process, but she found that some of her students needed more support than the visuals alone provided. If she had a paraprofessional in her room and a student who was having difficulty engaging in the process without direct guidance, she would provide direct support. When she was able to do so, her engagement with the student usually had the desired effect. Most of the time, however, she was busy working with a small group or instructing the entire class, so her direct involvement in the Re-Set Process wasn't possible. She decided to train her paraprofessional to support students if the schedule allowed. This, too, made a difference for students who struggled. She also noticed a positive difference in how this support person interacted with students outside of the process.

At the same time, Elise began campaigning for her school to develop a Re-Set Room. The immediate response was that there was no space available, and it was unclear as to the feasibility of staff coverage. (Note: Consideration of these factors in the future was offered by her administrator.)

A colleague asked Elise whether the process worked for her students, and she explained, "It works very well for some students, but not when children are really explosive."

Elise found herself using a less intense form of the Re-Set Process for students with very intense behaviors. As a result, she did not see the kind of overall improvement she had hoped for. When able to do so, she created her own version of the Re-Set Room within her classroom, which did help a couple of her challenging students—but only some of the time.

The Right Kind of Hose: Intensity Matters

Elise was doing what we call trying to put out a house fire with a garden hose. She did not have the right tool to work with some of her students, but she was using the one she had. Sometimes, all we have is a garden hose. As educators, we give it our best shot, and maybe we will sometimes succeed. It is important, however, to understand that we need the right tool for the job and that we should not judge the garden hose for not doing the fire hose's job. Some students need more intense forms of the Re-Set Process to show the desired improvement. We cannot blame them or the process for lack of change if we do not have those other forms available.

Hopefully, though, as we get to know our students and recognize the subtler signs of dysregulation, we can use less intense, more proactive forms—preventing the fire in the first place. We know, though, that some students arrive at our classroom doors with needs a'blazing, and therefore, it is best if we have more fitting and intense options at the ready.

The Reactive Re-Set Process for Students Who Need Tuning In

As we consider students who may be significantly under-engaged and who need support tuning in to the world around them, we would change the order of the Re-Set Process steps. This change would be specifically for students who are very locked down or consistently disconnected as evidenced by behaviors, such as failing to respond to conversation, hiding away, or presenting as if lost in another place.

For these students, we are likely to need to begin the Re-Set Process by engaging in the mirroring strategy. Then, we can move to Step 2 (fine motor and breathing), then Step 1 (gross motor), and finally to Steps 3 and 4. When we do this, we are meeting students where they are, and then systematically moving them to being more attuned to the world, more awake. Be aware that students who present this way may require a longer amount of time in the steps than students who externalize.

Middle School Caveat

Although the forms are presented in order from least intensive to most intensive, we do want to note that, for middle school settings, we almost always find our start point to be the Reactive Hallway Re-Set Process. The ability to regulate in the presence of peers in the classroom or in a buddy teacher's classroom is difficult when one of adolescents' big developmental concerns is their place in a world of peers.

We have witnessed highly dysregulated students who will engage in very immature, out-of-control behaviors in front of their peers, but who will be completely embarrassed by going through a series of settling behaviors in front of those same peers. Perhaps it is because those out-of-control behaviors occur in the context of such great dysregulation, whereas settling

At-a-Glance: Reactive Re-Set Room

Step 1: Move Your Body (determined by coach and student)

Pick from an assortment of activities and do the designated number of times or for the designated amount of time. Encourage student to pay attention to the ones that help his or her body feel calmer quicker.

Activity Options

Arm circles (large)	Helicopter (fast)
Wall push-ups	Chair push-ups
Big steps	Marching in place
Walking on treadmill	Jumping on trampoline
Kettlebell lifting	Bicycle (stationary)
Stretch band stretches	Line pattern on floor
Hopping	Jumping Jacks
Other: _____	

Step 2: Modulate Down (determined by coach and student)

Engage in a slower, more controlled gross motor activity; think less cardiovascular focus and more stretch-and-hold focus, fine motor activity, or a breathing activity. Encourage student to pay attention to ones that work well for him or her and that the student can use while still in seat and learning when back in classroom.

Activity Options

Big steps (slow and held)	Helicopter (slow)
Up and down on toes (slow)	Isometrics (pushing hands together)
Small arm circles (slow)	Imaginary weightlifting (slow)
Bobblehead	Head circles
Shoulder shrugs	Mirror game
Big balloon practice	Crescent arch
Twist and turn	Self-wrap
Coloring pairs	Chime and listen for fade
Fiddle object use	Breathing techniques
Level balancing	Squeeze and release script
Other: _____	

Step 3: Activate Thinking (1–2 activities)

Engage in activities that require a little thinking, which prepares student for the return to learning.

Activity Options

Trace letters/numbers	Trace name
Dot-to-Dot	Shaded coloring
Whisper count/ABCs	Celtic knot tracing
Count forward/backward	Categories

Figure 5.4. At-a-Glance: Reactive Re-Set Room (see Chapter 6).

activities occur as the student moves into a more self-aware, regulated state. Whatever the reason is for this disparity, to honor this developmental need, we have found that taking the Re-Set Process out of the public eye is often critical for this age group.

RE-SET FOR THE REST (OF US)

We know that a dysregulated student can be very dysregulating for us as adults, and certainly for that student's peers. How do we help a class heal after a difficult event? How do we help them stay in relationships with a peer who is frightening, hurtful, or distancing?

After a child who has exhibited dangerous behavior has left or been removed from your classroom, implement the following steps.

Take Care of Yourselves as a Community

Kelley Harrell (n.d.) on her web site has the banner, "We don't heal in isolation, but in community," and we wholeheartedly agree. Going through the Re-Set Process as a community can be one way to encourage that healing.

Set the Stage

Identify what happened as *stressful*. It is the elephant in the room that sometimes we are uncomfortable addressing, but we can talk about it in a respectful, kind way. Sample script: *Whew, this has been a difficult afternoon. I am so glad that _____ will have people helping her, I care about her a lot. I also care about every one of you and myself. Let's take a couple minutes to settle ourselves so we can feel okay and so our thinking brains can be strong.* Then, move through the relevant steps of the Re-Set Process together.

Step 1: Move Your Body   Select activities that have the added bonus of pattern, weight, or pressure on the large joints of the body—these features increase **dopamine.**

Announce to students, *Let's get our bodies settled by doing these activities carefully together.* Count to keep the group together in the movements. Research cited in *Science Daily* from the California Institute of Technology shows that doing movements together increases a sense of bonding (Yun, Watanabe, & Shimojo, 2012). Emphasize doing the movements with accuracy not speed.

Do *not* use a dance party–type music as your gross motor activity. Although this is fine in a proactive situation, we do not want to use anything that is more dysregulating for students who probably are already heavily dysregulated. We also do not want to confuse students by inadvertently sending the message that we are celebrating that one of their peers has left the class.

Try: Big steps, jumping jacks, marching, chair push-ups, large arm circles, helicopter twists. Do this type of movement for 2–3 minutes.

Step 2: Modulate Down   Select activities that require more control and focus to accomplish. Begin with gross motor and move to fine motor or breathing. Students begin out of their seats, but during this step, have them move back to their seats.

Announce, *Now we will help our bodies become calmer and our brains more focused.*

Try: Up and down on toes, movement routine, slow arm circles, mirror game, chime—listen to fade, trace a Celtic knot, tense and release, shaded coloring, breathing technique. Do this type of movement for 2–3 minutes.

Step 3: Activate Thinking   Select activities using skills that all students have mastered, and do them as a community (e.g., think quietly and then gather responses around the circle, or use another sequential method). Allow for repeats and passes to keep emotionally safe.

Announce, *Let's really warm up our brains and work together to do this.*

Try: Simple questions (favorite animals, foods, colors), count around the circle (skip counting), say a word that starts with the letter _____. Do one or two of these activities, depending on how long they take.

Step 4: Make a Plan   This is where your role as emotional leader and coach is so critical. Depending on what you expect about the student's return and your student's ages, as well as other variables, make a plan for:

- Talk about ways to help that student feel comfortable when he or she returns—emphasize the value of that student to all of you as a community.

- Describe ways every student can take care of his or her own body if he or she feels stress at other times.

- Remind the students of the sources of support that are available to all of them.

Obviously, if this issue is chronic, you may choose not to go through Step 4 every time, but you will want to do it periodically. We are most stressed when we feel that there is nothing we can do about our situation. This conversation empowers you and your other students to take action, to see what it is that they can do and need to do. It also helps heal the relationship between the student who is struggling and his or her peers.

An interesting aside: A student who has previously been removed or had to leave may be present for this processing when another student is removed or has to leave. When that student experiences firsthand the caring and concern present in the room and then participates in the self-care group Re-Set activities, he or she can better understand that he or she was not villainized. The student can understand that he or she did affect how his or her peers felt, but that it was a sense of caring that prevailed.

Next, Chapter 6 applies the steps in the process to the Re-Set Room in greater detail.

Chapter 6

The Re-Set Room

After all, when a stone is dropped into a pond,
the water continues quivering even after the stone has sunk to the bottom.
—A. Golden (1999, p. 265)

The experience of trauma ripples out from a child's life and those ripples may appear as serious behavior challenges. L. Tobin (1991, p. 10) cautions us that often these children "are distinguished by their regrettable ability to elicit from others exactly the opposite of what they really need." The Re-Set Room provides us a way to respond to the genuine needs of these students with more significant behavior concerns. We began our examination of the Re-Set Room in Chapter 3 where we explored what it was and what it was not and then we placed it as a practice in context with other proactive and reactive forms in Chapter 5. In this chapter, we provide additional specific implementation guidance. Regardless of which Re-Set Process forms you first implement, we recommend that you read this chapter because it reflects the heart and soul of the Re-Set Process and provides many detailed considerations.

INTRODUCING THE ROOM

The Re-Set Room generally should be introduced to students on an as-needed basis. If students who pass by the room question its purpose, it is totally appropriate to say that it is one of the places in the school that is designed to help some students refocus their thinking—being brief and matter-of-fact about it. We do not want it to be a dark mystery, nor do we want to advertise it.

If a student has been sent to the room based on an administrative team decision (e.g., crisis response, administration was contacted for support) and the student has had no prior exposure, *briefly* explaining the general purpose as the child enters is the most verbiage that should be used before the student moves through Steps 0–3 (e.g., *This is a space to help calm your body and help you focus.*). In Step 4, when the thinking brain is available again, the student should have the process explained to them, perhaps including the student's immediate experience (e.g., *You might have noticed that after Step 1, your body felt less shaky and you were able to breathe better.*).

In cases where the student has not been involved with the room as a crisis response, but the room is being recommended for use on a scheduled basis, the student should be taught about the room prior to his or her first experience. Walking the student through each step, explaining its activity options and its purpose, should be done.

Schools that have special education classes that support students with social or emotional challenges have found that an orientation to the room for the whole class makes sense. Based on their prior experiences, some of these students may assume that this space is like a padded room or a punishment space. It is critical that the students be introduced to it during a positive time, with a full explanation and the opportunity for practice, so that they understand the difference between the Re-Set Room and prior experiences. Depending on how frequently the room is used, teaching regulation lessons or mindfulness strategies in this space with students from special education classrooms also would make a lot of sense because it reinforces the concept that the space as a learning environment.

APPLYING STEPS IN THE RE-SET ROOM: COMMON QUESTIONS

There are four or five steps that are to be followed in a specific order in the Re-Set Room. You are already familiar with these steps because they occur in other forms of Re-Set. In order for the desired effects to be achieved, the steps are to be followed in the established order. The only step that may ever be skipped is Step 0—otherwise, the entire process is to be followed, both during a scheduled, proactive use or in a reactive use of the Room. The process can be individualized by using the various activities that are available at each step and in the amount of time spent at each step, but *each step is critical*. Some students may want to create their own process and, in your effort to be responsive to them, you may be tempted to allow them to lead. But doing the steps in this order is not to be negotiated. We do this because the Re-Set Process is a structured process that has an established agenda—it is not a place to escape to in order for a student to conduct his or her own agenda. Most importantly, by following the steps, we are laying down neural pathways that allow a student to self-calm. Practice makes permanent, so we want to be systematic in that practice—remember, we are developing the brain version of muscle memory! Later, when the student acquires regulation fluency, he or she can experiment with variations on the theme in his or her personal life. In fact, we want to have students become more flexible with how they regulate over time so they can be successful in a wide variety of settings. *The Re-Set Room Process, however, is happening during the acquisition phase of the behavior, not during the generalization phase, so the process must be followed without improvisation.*

How Long Should Each Step Take?

We have found that giving students a time frame is helpful to move them through the process. It is important, however, that the process be student-responsive. If a student needs a little more time at a certain step or steps, provide that. Typically, we suggest 2 minutes at each of step (Steps 0–3), with a check-in on what the student is noticing about his or her body and brain at the end of those 2 minutes (e.g., *What do you notice about your hands now? Are you ready for the next step?*). We have found that, because this process is so brain- and body-friendly, students rarely need more than 4 minutes (initial 2 minutes and a follow-up 2 minutes) at each step. Step 4 may take a longer time frame (perhaps 5 minutes or even more).

Where Should a Re-Set Room Be Located?

Most of the Re-Set Rooms we have designed have been a designated room, and this is the ideal setup. When there is a room created for this purpose, there can be permanent visual cues for both the student and the coach, such as signs for each step of the process. Materials can be located in each step's area for easy access. Lighting (low or natural, covered fluorescent lighting), wall color (calm, pleasant colors) and other environmental features (furnishings) can all be specifically selected to support the process. A student's privacy is protected. The room does not need to be a large one. Several of our schools reallocated book storage spaces or small offices for this purpose. In fact, sometimes small, cozy spaces help create calmness.

Sometimes, it is a challenge for schools to allocate a specific room for the process. We encourage schools that don't have a Re-Set Room to find a space that can be adapted to support all the steps of the process—even if it is not a single-purpose room. Some schools have found a space, such as a quiet area at the end of an infrequently used hallway, and some have created space within a room that has other purposes (e.g., a portion of a school counselor's office, a room also used as a sensory room). When these spaces are used, care has to be taken to import the qualities necessary for fidelity.

How to Implement With Fidelity

Re-Set Rooms need to provide specific aspects to facilitate the Re-Set Process:

- A reasonable amount of privacy for the process, so that the involved student feels both emotionally comfortable and focused on the process. (*Note*: Some rooms, such as family resource rooms, are not recommended because there is a lack of privacy in the rooms.)

- A method to mute some of the sounds of school life and to provide auditory privacy (e.g., white noise machine)

- Sufficient space for the physical movements of both the coach and the student as required by each of the steps

- Visual supports to assist the student with processing the steps

- Lower visual stimulation overall, so key information is accessible, and dysregulation is not increased

- Quick access to materials that are needed for each of the steps and a way to keep those materials secured when they are not in use

- A method to designate that space is currently being used as the Re-Set Room rather than how the space or room might otherwise be used if space serves dual purposes

- Access to coach-oriented materials, such as those needed for documentation

- A space devoid of interruption during the process

Notes From the Field

At my school, we were fortunate enough to have a specific room for the Re-Set Room, but I discovered a couple of things about the space that needed adjusting. I could not work with students with the door closed, but I was concerned about the lack of privacy when they were going through the steps. The team came up with the idea of using a beaded curtain on a pressure rod, which gave students some degree of privacy from peers. It worked perfectly. It was the right mix of openness and privacy, and it could be taken down at the end of the day, so that the door could be closed and materials kept secure.

However, with the door open and our location at a very busy corner, sometimes the noise bothered students as they were going through the steps. To address this, I used background sounds of nature, which blocked out other student voices and allowed the student who was going through the process to concentrate on what he or she was doing.

Building Assistant, Middle School

APPLYING STEPS IN THE RE-SET ROOM: REACTIVE USE

Step 0: Cocoon

Purpose

Physiologically   To allow a student who is in freeze mode to become more present by being in a place where he or she feels emotionally safe. To introduce weighted items in order to increase the calming chemical dopamine, which will expedite a sense of safety and calm.

Relationally   To allow the student to feel safe and in control before being asked to respond to a coach's directives involved in Step 1.

A Peek Inside
What the student may be experiencing that you may or may not be able to observe:

- An extreme need to see where others are. May seek a corner where he or she can see everything coming at him or her.

- Use of vision over hearing in order to take in information.

- Inability to access the brain's language centers in order to express self correctly. May answer, but the answer might not reflect the student's true feelings, understanding, or needs. May not be able to verbally respond at all.

- Body temperature may feel off—colder or hotter than usual.

Environmental Considerations   A highly dysregulated student may need some time before moving to the designated Re-Set Room so this step might happen in a variety of places in the school building. We have found that children who elope as part of their dysregulation often automatically seek a location in the school building where they can do this cocooning. This might be a place in the classroom where the student feels safe (e.g., under a desk, in a corner away from other students, turtling into his or her clothing) or somewhere in the school building (e.g., in a reading tent in the library, a restroom, a niche in a hallway, the counselor's waiting area). Instead of trying to force the move of a dysregulated student to a designated space, allowing time in his or her chosen cocoon spot often is the best choice.

For students who cocoon outside the designated Re-Set Room, consider providing a visual cue (e.g., a picture of the cocoon spot in the Re-Set Room) or an object that connects with the space (such as a small version of a weighted object) to help make the transition to the Re-Set Room an easier one.

When students learn through experience that the Re-Set Room is a safe place, we often see that they will seek it as their cocoon spot rather than eloping to non-designated locations. In addition, as we learn more about a student, we may be able to use the Re-Set Room proactively to avoid this intense need for cocooning.

Regardless of where Step 0 occurs, the process is the same. It should be noted that for some students, if he or she has some cocoon time in an alternative place, he or she may still need to resettle and have an additional cocoon time upon arrival in the Re-Set Room.

Coach's Role   This is the student's time to regain him- or herself with very little adult intervention. Table 6.1 provides additional guidance.

- Think zero—very, very little—adult language.

- Offer a time frame for check-in.

- Offer a calming object by placing it near the student or by offering it with a brief phrase (e.g., a stuffed toy, a heavy book with lots of visuals—not for reading but for thumbing through, a soft blanket, an item that is personal to them, such as an article of clothing).

- Stay in the vicinity but do not hover. Engage in an alternate task (e.g., reading some materials) that keeps you from watching the student directly, giving the student some emotional space.

Sounds Like   Here are some examples of how a coach can balance availability and reassurance with giving the student space during this step:

- *I will set the check-in clock for 2 minutes and see how you are when it rings.*

- *Take a couple of minutes. I will be right over there and will check in with you shortly.*

- *When you are ready or when this timer ends, join me.*

- *Checking in. How are your arms feeling? Ready to move to Step 1 or do you need a couple more minutes?*

Student's Role   Engage in quiet, self-soothing sounds such as singing or humming, or simply be quiet and use calming objects appropriately.

Types of Activities   Cocoon—and that is it!

Before We Knew   Historically, we often tried to move a student who was in this freeze mode. When we did this, we found that the student locked in or suddenly became much more agitated or aggressive. The image of a child under a desk, hanging on to the legs of a chair to keep themselves locked in, or a student hiding in a restroom, refusing to come out, are not pretty, but they are familiar to folks who have been in education for a while.

We tried to move students to alternate locations, not out of malice, but because we were concerned that the upset student posed potential harm to other students or, at the very least, would disrupt the learning process. Doing nothing felt like, well, doing nothing! We now know that our attempts to create safety probably contributed to the upset student feeling *less* safe, and even caused the rest of the class to be more disrupted. We now know that what prolongs freeze is our intrusion into it. We now know that the non-action that is giving a dysregulated

Table 6.1.   Step 0 in the Re-Set Room: Dos and don'ts

This table guides adult behavior for interacting with a student in the Re-Set Room at Step 0.

Dos	Don'ts
• Use a quiet, calm, even tone of voice • Say things in as few words as possible • Demonstrate caring, calm body language • Use belly breathing to keep yourself in a regulated state and to provide student with an appropriate model • Respond to other students' inquiries about what is going on with the student by saying, *We are fine. Thank you!*	• Hover, stare, use crossed arms or any other emotionally distancing body language • Use phrases that may have a punitive history for that student (e.g., *I am going to set the timer now*) • Talk about the student to other students, other than the short phrase provided in the Dos list

student the emotional and physical space he or she desperately needs is, in fact, doing something *very* important.

Common Questions

What Is the Time Frame for Cocoon?   We typically anticipate 2–5 minutes for this step. Check in after a brief time—1 or 2 minutes—to see whether the student is ready to move to Step 1. The check-in is so that the student does not simply shut down or go to sleep, which he or she may do if left for a longer period of time, particularly if he or she is in a freeze state.

What If the Student Is Still Making Noise and Disrupting Others?

- You certainly can gently remind the student: *This is your time, but it needs to be quiet time.* This should be done in a very quiet tone of voice—model your expectation. Keep the reminder very brief.

- You also can offer to the student to have his or her cocoon space in another location, where he or she can be louder if he or she wants to. We recommend that you provide a visual to help him or her process this offer.

- Consider backing off a little more. Sometimes, the noise is how the student's stress bubbles to the surface, and the closer the adult is, the more stress a student may feel.

- Consider checking in more. Sometimes, the noise is a student's way of bringing an adult closer, in essence, saying, *Do you still care about me?* Because this is the opposite of the intervention in the preceding list item, you may have to do a little detective work by watching how the student responds to your choice of approaching or distancing. Although verbalizing his or her preference may be difficult for a student to do when he or she is in freeze, you could also try gestures when asking, *Would you like to me to come closer or move farther away?*

- The rest of the class tends to follow the lead of the teacher or other key adults. If the adult looks worried and disrupted, other students will also experience this. If the adult focuses on the task and engages students in learning activities without looking distressed, students are better able to focus on learning.

Types of Materials

- Bean-bag chair
- Small pop-up tent
- Weighted blanket
- Weighted stuffed toys
- Weighted lap pads or weighted stuffed snakes
- Regular blanket or throw
- Books or reading materials with lots of pictures on age-appropriate topics (e.g., coffee table books). It is helpful if some of the books have some weight to them.
- The student's own clothing (e.g., sweatshirt, sweater) for turtling

A Reminder About Students Who Are Shut Down   There are times when a student needs to go to the Re-Set Room but is in a freeze state. Although we can physically reach the student, we cannot safely move him or her. Remember that freeze does not mean locked completely still and silent. That is freeze for some students, such as for the students who curl up in a tight ball and the only movement is from their breathing. Freeze can also be locked in a repetitive behavior (e.g., kicking at anything in proximity), being in the tight ball *and* crying, or being caught in a cycle of repetitive words (e.g., *I am not going anywhere, I am not going anywhere!, No! No! No!*). These times call for the mirroring/sensory focus strategy that was discussed in Chapter 3.

Step 1: Move Your Body

Purpose
Physiologically   The intent is to burn off stress chemicals (e.g., cortisol, adrenaline) and increase calming chemicals (e.g., dopamine) so that the student's body becomes calmer and the thinking regions of the brain become more accessible. It also provides a predictable structure that allows the student's brain to begin to calm.

Relationally   This begins the process of connecting the adult with the student through structured, simple, action-oriented verbal interaction. It provides the opportunity for the student to offer the coach to join them in the physical activity, and then engage in parallel activity—a start to attunement through *being with*.

A Peek Inside
What the student may be experiencing that you may or may not be able to observe:

- A very active body
- Use of vision over hearing in order to take in information
- Focus is more inward; there is a greater awareness of self over others; focus may be directed toward the movement
- Language that is functional but limited
- Body temperature that may feel off—colder or hotter than usual
- Inability to make big decisions but increasingly ready to make small, concrete decisions, such as which movement to do next

Environmental Considerations   Because the visual component of this step is so important and the body is still at a high activity level, methods of delineating the area for Step 1 is important. Use of visual cues (e.g., borders, signs, taped marks on floor) will help contain the activity, thereby assisting with regulation. For example, in one space, we had handprints on the wall to mark the place for wall push-ups. In another space. a student moved from one block to the next when changing physical activities, to better sense progress.

Coach's Role   The coach is offering structure, taking the lead while still being open to some student choice in the activity. Table 6.2 provides additional guidance.

1. Welcome student to Step 1, remind them of the purpose of the step (e.g., *Now is the time to move your body to get rid of stress, Let's move first to help our bodies begin to calm."*)

2. Designate the first movement and ask whether the student would like you to join (if appropriate to the type of activity). To enhance processing, use a visual that represents the activity, or offer an object that will be used in the activity.

3. Designate a number of repetitions or length of time for the first movement.

4. Count to keep the movement regular—if appropriate.

5. Set a visual timer—if appropriate.

6. At the conclusion of the first activity, offer the student a choice of the next activity—use visuals for choices.*

7. Check in with the student at the end of each activity to see how his or her body is feeling. The coach can do this by noticing things about the student (e.g., *I notice your arms are more relaxed.*) and/or the student may on their own describe a calmer state. If the student and coach do not see a status that is calm enough to move to the next step, offer additional activities.

8. When the student describes a calmer body or agrees that his or her body feels calmer in response to your observation, move to Step 2.

Sounds Like

- *I will set the check-in clock for 1 minute while you bike. When it rings, I will see how you are.*

- *Let's do 10 kettlebell lifts together—nice and slowly, so we can feel our arm muscles contract and stretch.*

- *What are you noticing about how your neck feels?*

- *What will work next for you?*

- *Notice your arms . . .*

Student's Role   The student's role is to:

- Engage in physical activities in a cohesive, patterned way.

- Reflect with the coach on the calmness of his or her body after each activity

Table 6.2.   Step 1 in the Re-Set Room: Dos and don'ts

This table guides adult behavior for interacting with a student in the Re-Set Room at Step 1.

Dos	Don'ts
• Use a quiet, calm, even tone of voice • Say things in as few words as possible; talk more than Step 0, but not much more • Demonstrate caring, calm body language • Join in movements if student would like • Count or do activity with student to set pace that is patterned and even	• Offer an activity to a student for which he or she does not have the physical skills to do successfully/ fluently; always default to a physically simple activity if the student's skill level is not known • Offer student an opportunity for choice and then decide on something different than what he or she picked • Use a tone reminiscent of *Drop and give me 20* when providing a number of repetitions • Join if student wants to do activity on own

Note: Some students settle better with an established routine than in being offered the opportunity to make the decision of which activity to do next. The safer default is to have a prescribed protocol the first few times the student comes to the space to regulate, after which you can try to offer choice. You will find the right balance for each child—a balance of safety that is created through predictability and routine, and safety that is created through choice. The key is to pay attention to what the student is telling you through his or her responses.

Types of Activities

Without Equipment

- Walking on a visual path to a prescribed count

- Marching to a count

- Wall push-ups regulated by using words *near* and *far* slowly and by counting

- Chair push-ups regulated by using words *up* and *down* slowly and by counting

- Floor push-ups regulated by using words *up* and *down* slowly or by counting slowly

- Jumping jacks to a count

- Arm circles to a count

- Helicopter to a count

- Up and down on balls of the feet to a count

- Big steps, alternating legs

- A stretch series that is always followed in the same sequence—using only positions that are on the feet and that are emotionally safe. We recommend avoiding downward positions because they might make students with trauma histories feel vulnerable.

- A rowing movement to a count

With Equipment

- Walking on a treadmill at an even pace

- Jumping on a trampoline to a count

With Materials

- Stretch bands pulled across the body one way, and then the other way, to make an *X*

- Small medicine ball (or other weighted item) passed from one side of the body to the other side or between the student and coach

- Kettlebells lifted to a count

- Stretch band while sitting on a chair—stretch with heels or with toes

Before We Knew   As we have noted, we once thought that students benefited from running out their rage or burning off excess energy. We took them to open places and let them run and run. When they came to us, breathless and sweaty, we thought, *They're ready to go back to class now!* And we took them back, expecting that all would be well. And it was. Initially. And then the problems came roaring back.

What we were doing was dealing with those energizing stress chemicals by expelling them from the student's body and brain through exercise, which was great, but we were only addressing half the issue. When that student was running wildly around the empty gymnasium, he or she was purging stress chemicals, but the student was simultaneously becoming more and more dysregulated. The student's system was still shaken up, but he or she became too tired to manifest it . . . at least for a little while. When the student got back to class, he or she would slowly revive, more dysregulated than before, and behavioral issues would reemerge.

We were absolutely right in trying to meet a student's needs—we solved part of the equation. Now, with the vast amounts of neuroscience information that is available to us, we know that we need to structure that movement, regulate it, pattern it, and then systematically modulate down from those bigger movements. We have found the other half of that equation we needed to solve.

Common Questions

What Is the Time Frame for These Gross Motor Activities?   We typically anticipate 2–3 minutes in total for this step. That said, it is key that the coach assesses the student and allows for more time, as necessary. It is important to remember that the goal is *not* to tire the student out, but to burn off some of the high levels of stress chemicals in the brain and body. The time frame does not need to be as long as it would be if our goal were to exhaust the student. In fact, it is counterproductive to exhaust the student because we do not want to send a really tired student back into the learning environment.

Can We Use Catharsis Practices Such As Punching a Pillow?   Before neuroscience enlightened us, we were taught that a good way to deal with stress was to get rid of it through alternate-target aggression or catharsis. We thought it was healthy to punch a pillow or throw something hard at a target. Unfortunately, many people still believe this catharsis approach is a good idea, and companies continue to market products that are designed to encourage the connection between *I feel bad/angry/stressed* with *I hit this.* Although a desk-side punching ball or a huge, soft, smashable delete key next to your computer keyboard may seem humorous when viewed in a gif, the reality is that this kind of practice is downright dangerous, particularly for a child's developing brain. As we noted earlier when we contrasted the Re-Set Room with a padded room, when a student responds to big, stressful feelings by practicing aggression toward *anything,* he or she is simply practicing aggression, wiring it into his or her brain so that it becomes the default response anytime the student experiences those overwhelming emotions (Bushman et al., 1999).

We do not ever want to teach a student to pair a feeling such as anger, frustration, loneliness, confusion, or grief with an act of aggression or we are dooming that student to be aggressive. Even some trauma-informed materials we have reviewed will make suggestions such as guiding the upset student to do wall push-ups by telling them to try to push the wall over—which pairs a feeling with a destructive behavior. Our words are powerful—they help make significant associations in the minds of the vulnerable students we teach. We need to use our words with great care and precision.

What If a Student Does Not Want to Do What I Want Him or Her to Do?   If a student resists the first activity you direct, it may be an indication that he or she needs more cocoon time, including possibly a mirroring activity. Do not immediately jump to that reasonable conclusion with your response, though. Offer the student another option in a thoughtful way (e.g., *Are you feeling like that will not work for you right now? Is there another one from our list that would work better for you today?*). This respects the student by conveying a belief that they are resisting not in order to be difficult, but because of a genuine need. It respects the student without relinquishing the structure of the process.

If a student continues to resist, you should gently notice that he or she does not seem ready for Step 1 (e.g., *Not being ready to do Step 1 is telling me that you need more time to feel safe and quiet. Let's go to Step 0 for a couple more minutes, and then I will check in again.*). Notice in the example that the language is *Let's go to Step 0,* and not *Let's go back to Step 0.* Needing to return to a previous step is not a failure, a falling backward. It is good if a student—and the adult, as a coach—can notice when the student needs something different. Going *back* rings of failure for many students, so it is best to avoid that word.

Think of alternatives that come easily to you, such as:

- *Step _____ seems like a match for you at this time.*

- *What is your body telling you that you need?*

- *Check yourself. Do you think your body is telling you that you need more time at Step _____?*

- *I have found that when I am stressed out and don't want to move, I usually just need a couple more quiet minutes.*

This type of language is applicable across all steps in the process. It is very valuable if you as the coach reflectively evaluate your own needs out loud (e.g., *When I was upset about something the other day, I was thinking my body was ready to use isometrics to help me calm, but then I realized it was really telling me I really needed to go for a walk.*) You are teaching ways to connect how a dysregulated body feels with methods of addressing the dysregulation.

If a student stays resistant despite these offerings (which has not happened much at all, in our experience), create a cocoon without asking the student to do anything. Stop using words and just give the student some quiet time before checking in with a phrase (e.g., *What can I do to help?, Can you show me what you need?*) or move to the mirroring process described in Chapter 3.

What If a Student Misuses Materials or Equipment?   If you have this concern, begin with an activity that requires no equipment or materials. You can then move to activities that require only equipment (e.g., a treadmill) and finally, move to ones that involve smaller materials (e.g., kettlebells).

If you start with a piece of equipment or materials and then have to redirect because of improper use of the equipment or materials, begin by modeling. If modeling does not bring about the desired behavioral change, shift activity to a different one that does not require any physical object. Just be sure to do this in a manner that does not seem punishing or shaming.

What If I Thought the Student Had a Physical Skill, but He or She Does Not?   A good way to prevent this from happening is by beginning with something simple and paying attention to the physical abilities of the student. Once a student is choosing between activities, limiting the choices to ones that you feel confident are within his or her physical skill set is helpful. Still, we guess incorrectly sometimes.

In one of our Re-Set Rooms, we had a first-grade student who appeared to be master of the traditional push-up and who loved to do them anytime he was allowed to do so in PE class. It seemed logical to allow this to be one of his choices for Step 1. However, as soon as the student began doing push-ups, he was falling over, becoming frustrated with himself for not being able to do them properly, and getting more out of control after only a couple attempts. How did this happen? Often a student may have a physical skill during his or her most regulated times, but when he or she is dysregulated, the skill disappears or becomes fragmented.

This is true not only for little kids. It is true also for adolescents and, frankly, for all of us. Think of the Olympic skater who has incredible jumping skills, but with the nerves of competition, cannot seem to land a clean jump for the life of them. So, it happens, and the trick is moving on without having the student feel like a failure. Here are some of your options:

- Simply change the activity, no explanation provided. *Now, let's try ___!* or *Time to pick your next activity!*

- To limit the number of dysregulated repetitions, offer the student a choice: *One or two more, your choice.*

- If you are doing the activity with the student, say that you yourself need to switch to something else—give the student an opportunity to be kind by switching with you.

What If the Student Wants Me to Join but I Am Not Physically Capable?   As a coach, we might not have the physical ability to do some activities, we might not be dressed for them, or the space might not allow for our safe movement. Explain your truth—whatever it is, in a way that is as appropriate and as short as possible—and thank the student for inviting you. You might offer to do a modified version, you might offer to do another activity using the same count while the student does his or her selected movement, or you might suggest that you can join the student in another activity. Some middle school students feel self-conscious doing gross motor activities if they feel that someone is staring at them, and that is why they want may want the coach to join in. When we do something beyond simply counting, this feeling is diminished.

What If the Student Does Not Want to Choose an Activity?   Some students do better in Step 1 with a prescribed set of activities. We found this to be particularly true for students with very complex lives. It is soothing to know that there is an established routine (another dopamine-inducer). Many athletes have a prescribed set of warm-up exercises that they do each and every time before they compete. Changing the athlete's warm-up would completely throw the athlete off his or her game. This may be true for some students—they are comforted by knowing what is coming next, what is expected of them. They are able to get in the zone, and this helps them move forward. Even students who like to have the opportunity to choose sometimes just want someone else to make the decision. For example, from personal experience, we are reminded, after a particularly crazy work week, of how nice it is to have someone else pick the restaurant or the movie. So, choice is *not* a requirement of this process. Choice is an option for the students who like to have that opportunity.

What If the Student Goes at a Pace That Does Not Match My Counting?   Sometimes, a student's dysregulation causes them to move erratically despite the pace our counting is intended to set for them. Using a metronome or a metronome app that eliminates our voice and human variability may help. You also may want to bear in mind that visual is a more important processing channel and make the counting more visual. This might be by joining them in an activity, moving your arms with each number said, or by using a ring of numbers and flipping them over with each count. Pausing and having the student attend to your counting is another option. When you do this, you are focusing the student's attention on what you (and they) need. The student might just need that simple cue in order to pay attention.

Certain activities by nature are slower-paced and may be easier to follow with a count. For example, switching from jumping jacks to kettlebell lifts might take care of the issue. If a student is pretty revved up, you might want to start counting faster to match the pace of the student, but still keeping it even and patterned. Then, you can methodically slow down—think modulation, not a big shift all at once. The student should be more capable of matching you as his or her body becomes calmer.

Types of Materials

- Treadmill
- Stationary bike
- Trampoline with a hold bar
- Stretch bands
- Medicine balls
- Kettlebells
- Stretch bands

- Visual cues

- Metronome or device with a metronome app

Step 2: Modulate Down

Purpose

Physiologically   After shedding high levels of stress chemicals, this step allows the student to settle even more, to continue to burn stress chemicals while introducing more calming chemicals into his or her body and brain. The intent is to modulate the student's movements, to bring those movements more under control. It is a time to ease down from fast movements to slower movements; from big movements to smaller movements; from more energetic movements to more controlled, precise ones; and to tune in to senses, including an awareness of one's breathing.

Relationally   At this step, we are continuing the process of connecting with the student as he or she slowly shifts from being fairly unfocused to being self-aware. During this step, we can call the student into awareness of his or her own body without being invasive.

A Peek Inside
What the student may be experiencing that you may or may not be able to observe:

- Body and breathing are settling down

- More awareness of self, of senses

- Language may still be simplified, not as present

Environmental Considerations   If a more controlled gross motor activity is one of the choices for this step, attention needs to be paid to providing sufficient space for the movement. Because these slower movements often do well with the coach doing them with the student, there needs to be enough space for both people. This does not mean that the area must be large, it just needs to allow for the movements being selected. It can occur in the same physical space as Step 1 but there should be some visual method of delineating the move to Step 2, even if it is just a poster and a change in direction the student is facing.

At this step, if the student is moving into activities that are fine motor in nature, having a desk or table for them to sit at makes sense because it is similar to the classroom setting. Having the adult sit across from them in a chair that is the same height subtly provides the adult with the opportunity to look at the same materials, to interact with the materials, to connect with the student through a physically closer shared space, and to communicate *with-it-ness.*

Coach's Role   The coach provides an overview of options, provides materials, and might do quiet, parallel activities with the student. The coach also should establish time frames for each activity, as appropriate, and check in on the student's calmness and focus. Table 6.3 provides additional guidance.

1. Welcome student to Step 2 and provide them with the option of continuing large movements or moving to smaller movements. If the student does not or cannot choose, begin with large movements, but move deliberately to controlled movements in activities that follow.

2. At the conclusion of the first activity, offer the student a choice of the next activity. Use visuals or actual items to demonstrate or represent the student's choices.

3. Suggest that the student might want to try some routines or tools that he or she could use later in class. Allow for experimentation with different fiddle objects and encourage breathing practices or other tuning into their senses practices.

4. Check in with the student at the end of each activity to see how the student's body is feeling, but now also ask about his or her breathing and the ability to focus. This can be done by the coach noticing things about the student (e.g., *I notice your arms are more relaxed; I see you are really considering different tools and using them well.*) and/or by the student describing a calmer, more focused state.

5. When the student describes a calmer body and more focused thinking or agrees that his or her body feels calmer and he or she is thinking more clearly, move to Step 3.

Sounds Like

*   *I will set the check-in clock for 2 minutes and will see how your thinking is doing when it rings.*

*   *Which one of these tools do you think might help you continue to calm down and get ready to focus?*

*   *I would like you to imagine with me. I am going to put a lemon in your hand, and you are going to very, very slowly squeeze all the juice out of the lemon. Next, let that lemon get bigger in your hand and push your hand open very slowly and then tip your hands forward so that lemon can drop to the floor.*

*   *Breathe in and hold it. 1 . . . 2 . . . 3 . . . 4 . . . 5 . . . 6. Now a long, slow breath out 1 . . . 2 . . . 3 . . . 4 . . . 5 . . . 6 . . . 7 . . . 8. What next?*

Student's Role

*   Engage in gross motor activities in a calmer, slower, more precise manner following the directives of the coach, shift to fine motor activities, and then shift to tuning-into-senses activity.

*   Reflect on the calmness of the body and ability to focus with adult after each activity

Types of Activities

Modulated Gross Motor

*   Movement routine

*   Slower or more precise versions of arm circles, toe touches, crossing body with stretch bands

*   Level balancing

*   Walking a balance beam line on floor

Fine Motor Activities

*   Celtic knot tracing

*   Glitter bottle observations

*   Marble maze movement

*   Coloring

*   Putty movement

*   Dry erase board—erase one line at a time

- Hook and loop strips—run two fingers along the two different kinds, smooth and hook, simultaneously

- Fidget twists

- Gel bead gloves

- Pipe cleaner fiddles

Tune In to Senses

- Breathing technique (e.g., elevator breath, hand breath)

- Tense and release exercise with story

- Chime listening

- Focus object

Table 6.3. Step 2 in the Re-Set Room: Dos and don'ts
This table guides adult behavior for interacting with a student in the Re-Set Room at Step 2.

Dos	Don'ts
• Use a more typical conversational level of voice, beginning this step with a quieter level and moving toward the more typical voice level	• Become louder, bigger in your own movements
• Talk, but keep it focused on task; allow silence	• Offer an activity to a student for which he or she does not have the fine motor skills to do
• Demonstrate caring, calm body language	• Offer student choice and then decide he or she should do something different than what he or she selected
• Use the word *tools* when referencing the materials for this step	• Talk about topics other than those related directly to activity or tool use
• Join in using a similar tool if student is using a quiet, more individual tool	• Join if student wants to do on own
• Provide direction in tool use, as necessary	

Before We Knew   We remember being trained that once a child was settled down—that is, no longer engaging in tantrum or aggressive behaviors—we could move on to problem-solving, which we did with positive intention. We often got the answers we were looking for, but then we found that despite the student *knowing what he or she should do*—and being able to tell us—he or she would engage in the same problematic behavior shortly thereafter. We affectionately (and somewhat graphically, sorry) call this binge-and-purge responding. Students reluctantly swallowed our words and then, after misbehavior and a brief calming down, threw them up at us, not digested at all. Those words had not had a chance to become part of who the students were, to help them become healthier, happier, more behaviorally successful kiddos. That meant that we were all doomed to go through the whole process over and over, which was, just like in our analogy, pretty unpleasant for everyone.

Why did these students not digest our incredible words of wisdom, which would have made their lives (and ours and countless others) so much easier? Perhaps we had provided them at the wrong time—when their bodies and brains were not prepared to make use of them. Our previous approach failed because we pushed the attempts at reasoning too early in the process. Perhaps, too, we had missed the opportunity to use more effective instructional practices, such as involving the students in the thinking process, rather than simply lecturing.

But, what about the times that we had instructed well, and the students had acquired the knowledge, but they just were not at fluency, so they still engaged in problematic behaviors? Why could they not problem-solve with us then, when they actually knew the right things to do? Our error was that we introduced problem-solving before its time, skipping this step and the next, asking their brains to do something they were not ready to do.

We now know that waiting until the cognitive centers of the brain are available will yield significantly better results *and* that we can actively support those centers coming online instead of simply waiting for them. We also know that this well-timed coaching in tandem with cohesive, effective proactive instruction grows children much more significantly.

Common Questions

What If the Student Misuses the Tool That He or She Selects?   To make this less likely, you should briefly model how to use any new tool. You could do this simultaneously, with both you and the child using the tool, or you can do it first, and then have child follow you—whichever seems a better fit for that specific student.

If a student misuses a tool after your demonstration, quietly and calmly intervene by using a cue phrase such as *pause, please*, and then demonstrate again. Avoid asking *why* questions or other questions that might be difficult to answer, or which might feel confrontational. Model and describe briefly what you are doing, and then say, *show me*, and pass the tool to the child.

Be open to tool use that is novel as long as it is not destructive or socially distancing if used that way in front of peers. We have learned a great deal from children who improvised with a tool to meet their needs.

What If the Student Does Not Want to Choose an Activity?   Just like in Step 1, some students do better with an orderly, prescribed series of activities. Again, choice is *not* a requirement for this step in the process—it is an option for children who like to have that opportunity.

Types of Materials

- Movement routine cards
- Breathing cue cards
- Tense and release cue cards/story to be read
- Chime
- Celtic knot tracing pattern
- Glitter bottles
- Marble mazes
- Coloring sheets or coloring in pairs activity
- Putty
- Pipe cleaners
- Dry erase board and markers
- Table or desk for a writing surface
- Two chairs, one for student, one for coach—same height

Step 3: Activate Thinking

Purpose

Physiologically   This step is designed to activate the cognitive portion of the brain, and to keep it activated through the use of tasks that are emotionally nonthreatening.

Relationally   In this step, the adult is to continue the process of connecting with the student as he or she slowly shifts from being inwardly focused to being outwardly focused. In this step, the *serve and return* of social interaction is begun in order to nurture further attunement and attachment. The step provides structured, shared interaction—deliberate, but not open-ended.

A Peek Inside
What the student may be experiencing that you may or may not be able to observe:

- Body and breathing are settled

- Awareness of outer world increases

- Language abilities begin to return

Environmental Considerations   At this step, students are moving into individual activities or student-coach interactive activities. The activities themselves are either a combination of fine motor activity and cognitive activity or are purely cognitive ones.

If space is limited, the table used for Step 2 could also be used for Step 3—if there is a clear way to show a shift from one step to another. This might be as simple as a taped line on the table and moving chairs to the other half of the table or turning a laminated card over from the number 2 to the number 3. Because this step is a powerful opportunity to practice attunement—serve and return—both chairs should be relatively the same height and positioned to allow easy eye contact.

Because the activities that are used need to be at each student's mastery level, this step tends to require the most materials. Organization is critical so that the coach can quickly access the needed items. Any downtime to look through materials can break the flow of the process and distract from connection.

Coach's Role   The first activity might be one where the student participates more on his or her own. Talking with the student about the activity is one way to build connection. The coach should be a bit more animated than in previous steps—making eye contact and showing focused interest. The coach offers choices such as: 1) choice of an activity the student does on own, with coach commenting; 2) choice of an activity that student does along *with* coach; or 3) choice of who goes first in a task that bounces between student and coach. Throughout this step, the coach should assess the student's responses and adjust task difficulty if necessary. Table 6.4 provides additional guidance.

1. Welcome student to Step 3 and provide him or her with the option of beginning with an activity that is more individual—a paper-and-pencil task—or a shared activity.

2. At the conclusion of the first activity, offer the student a choice of next activity.

3. Engage in one or two back-and-forth tasks.

4. Check in with student at the end of activities to see how his or her brain is feeling. This can be done by the coach noticing things about the student (e.g., *I notice you really were fast with those flashcards, your thinking is becoming stronger,* or *I am noticing your thinking is quicker.*) or by asking the student to evaluate his or her thinking.

5. When the student describes self as in a thinking state, congratulate them and move them to Step 4.

Sounds Like

- *Do you want to start with an activity on your own or do one with me?*

- *Would you like to start saying the ABCs or do you want me to start?*

- *What are you noticing about how you are thinking?*

- *I am seeing how much more quickly you are coming up with ideas for the categories.*

- *Ready to problem-solve now?*

Student's Role

- Choose tasks that are not too hard.

- Engage in cognitive activities with focus and light excitement.

Types of Activities

On-Own Tasks

- Trace letters

- Trace numbers

- Trace name

- Dot-to-dot paper

- Paper and pencil mazes

- *Circle all the _____ you can find* sheets

- Color-by-number paper

Interactive Tasks (Turn-Taking)

- Color naming

- Shape naming

- Whisper counting

- Skip counting with coach (e.g., 2s, 5s, 10s)

- Recite days of the week

- Recite months of the year

- Opposites: Adult offers a word, student gives opposite (and vice versa)

- Synonyms: Adult offers a word, student gives synonym (and vice versa)

- Rhyming: Adult offers a word, student gives a rhyming word (and vice versa)

- Flashcards: Math or high-frequency reading: words, letters, pictures-to-be-named

- Categories: Adult gives a category, student names an item (can be done in ABC order or just open category, back and forth)

- Simon Says (for very young children: Simply give a set of directions, model a behavior, and have student follow you

- Cooperative: Draw-a-monster

- Dice games: Roll dice and say the number; roll dice and add numbers together

Table 6.4. Step 3 in the Re-Set Room: Dos and don'ts

This table guides adult behavior for interacting with a student within the Re-Set Room at Step 3.

Dos	Don'ts
• Use a typical conversational level of voice; allow yourself to show animation as you interact; show genuine reactions to student's thoughts	• Become too loud, too big in movements; animation should not be overwhelming
• Encourage student to move from on-own task to interactive task	• Offer an activity to a student for which he or she does not have the cognitive skills to do
• Demonstrate caring, calm body language	• Talk about any topic other than the activity directly at hand
• Assess difficulty of task; adjust or shift task if student is manifesting frustration	• Allow the activity to go on more than a couple of minutes

Common Questions

What If the Student Wants to Work Independently   This is a pretty good sign that the student is not yet ready to do the serve and return that is essential before moving to problem-solving. Allow the student to engage in a more solitary activity. Move to engaging in the same activity with them in a parallel manner. After a couple minutes, offer the student choice among interactive tasks.

What If the Student Will Not Choose an Activity   At this point, if the child has progressed well through the steps, this should not be an issue. He or she should feel comfortable enough to make choices and not need the structure of the adult directing them. Being unwilling to choose an activity is a signal that the student might have miscued you as the coach, or even themselves, that he or she was ready to move on.

   Returning to Step 1 might feel like regressing no matter how careful you are with your language, but the student probably needs to do more gross motor activity and modulate down again. Rather than more obviously moving to Step 1, suggest an activity that you can do in a blended manner—mixing Step 1 with Step 3. An example would be saying ABCs while doing a slow helicopter move at the waist with each letter and then holding a stretch position while counting to 20 or reciting lyrics while stretching. After this, ask the student to choose the final Step 3 option.

Types of Materials

- Number, letters, name tracing sheets
- Dot-to-dot sheets
- Shapes of assorted colors
- Flashcards: math or high-frequency reading words, letters, or naming pictures
- Pencil and paper mazes
- *Circle all the _____ you can find* sheets
- Dice
- Writing implements
- Desk/table for work surface
- Two chairs of same height
- Paper
- Assorted writing tools

Step 4: Make a Plan

Purpose

Physiologically   At this step, the purpose is to support the student's engaged cognitive brain in thinking that is related to one or a combination of problem-solving, restoration, and positive practice. The primary intent is to prepare the student to go back to class and reconnect with learning activities and his or her classroom community.

Relationally   The purpose is to move from serve and return to a more in-depth level of interaction in which the coach provides guidance, active listening, effective questioning, and sometimes, challenges to the student's thinking. The coach is to convey value and caring and to encourage empathic thinking through conversation and role-play. In addition, the coach should affirm the innate goodness of the student and the student's sense of competency and value.

A Peek Inside

What the student may be experiencing that you may or may not be able to observe:

- Relief in moving forward with returning to the business of learning and possibly with making restitution

- Desire to be an active participant in the thinking process

- A slight increase in stress chemicals as a result of thinking about his or her behavior, but usually at a manageable level after having moved through prior steps

- A small amount of anxiety about returning to the classroom

Environmental Considerations   At this step, it is very important that the adult be in a side-by-side position with the student. The side-by-side positioning communicates that the two of you are looking at the problem together from a similar perspective, and it avoids appearing oppositional. Chairs of approximately the same height should be used, to communicate the collaborative nature of this step. A desk or table for writing and a little bit of open space for potential role-play both are recommended.

Coach's Role   The coach must use his or her judgment about how Step 4 should proceed based on knowing the student, knowing the student's plan—if there is one—and having some understanding of the situation that brought the student to the Re-Set Room. Table 6.5 provides further guidance.

1. Welcome the student to Step 4 and select the method of processing and moving forward. The coach has several options from which to select:

   A. *Future Orientation* (e.g., *What are you going to do when you go back to class?*). Younger children may do best if they simply go back to class and return to learning. Help the student identify two actions he or she will do when the student returns to class (e.g., *Walk straight to my seat, open my folder.*) and do a mini role-play of the actions. The coach may ask the student about one way the student can keep his or her body calm if he or she feels stressed. It is critical that the involved teachers understand that, in this case, re-engagement in learning is the act of restitution—it is how the student is being held accountable.

   B. *Small amount of processing*—as in the first option, but student is able to talk a bit about the incident. For students who can do a little processing, the emphasis should *not* be on what happened, but on a plan going forward. Language such as, *What was the big thing that happened? How are you going to fix it?* is simple and to the point. If anything is written down—make it the positive steps—reinforce them by using visuals. Ask the student what he or she notices about his or her body when he or she is getting stressed. Ask for a couple ways to calm down that were practiced in the Re-Set Room. (*Note*: If the student is given a calming object, this should be approved by the teacher before the student returns to the classroom.). Figure 6.1 is an example of a processing form that is typically used with younger students and Figure 6.2 is an example of one typically used with intermediate students.

C. *Problem-solving.* Appropriate for older students and some younger ones, actual problem-solving by walking the student through the difficulty and generating alternative ways to self-manage can also be an outcome of this process. The adult should provide more questions than answers to help students be actively engaged in thinking about solutions for themselves. Questions should be *How* and *What* questions rather than *Why*, and the student should not be bombarded with questions. The questions *What was the big thing that happened?* and *How are you going to fix it?*, along with *What can you notice about your body or thinking that tells you that you may need to regulate?* and *What is your plan for regulating?* are the key questions.

Problem-solving may lead to an act of restitution appropriate to the situation. Options may be combined or singular and might include:

- Repair: Returning to class and cleaning up a mess that was made. (*Note*: Cleaning up in tandem with the coach or another adult who is assisting or supporting prevents a sense of shaming that might re-escalate the student. It also may be appropriate for some of the mess to have been cleaned up without the student prior to his or her return to class.)

- Apology: Writing a note of apology or saying *I am sorry* through words or action. This needs to be used cautiously as forced apologies are often insincere. One way to increase sincerity is by supporting the student to designate a time frame in which he or she will make his or her apology (e.g., *Sometime before the end of the day . . .*). A slip of paper can remind the student of his or her apology and its time frames. Some students will want to make an apology when they re-enter the classroom. We should let them lead with that if they so desire.

- Restricted privilege agreement/re-earn trust: Codesigning a logical, temporary restriction of movement in the

Figure 6.1. This processing plan can be used with primary or elementary students as part of Step 4: Make a Plan.

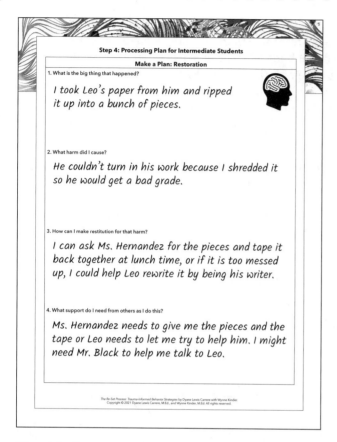

Step 4: Processing Plan for Intermediate Students

Make a Plan: Restoration

1. What is the big thing that happened?

I took Leo's paper from him and ripped it up into a bunch of pieces.

2. What harm did I cause?

He couldn't turn in his work because I shredded it so he would get a bad grade.

3. How can I make restitution for that harm?

I can ask Ms. Hernandez for the pieces and tape it back together at lunch time, or if it is too messed up, I could help Leo rewrite it by being his writer.

4. What support do I need from others as I do this?

Ms. Hernandez needs to give me the pieces and the tape or Leo needs to let me try to help him. I might need Mr. Black to help me talk to Leo.

Figure 6.2. This processing plan can be used with intermediate or middle school students as part of Step 4: Make a Plan.

school, access to a specific opportunity, or another freedom (e.g., not participating in kickball on the playground for the remainder of the week, no traveling alone in the hallway for the next 3 school days. After this conversation, the coach should complete a plan with the student—either written or as a picture, as appropriate to age and ability of the student. It is imperative that the coach do the writing if writing is a struggle for the student, so that the student's cognitive energy can be spent on thinking rather than writing. Then, the plan should be shared with the involved parties. The student should be positively acknowledged for engaging in this process of re-earning trust.

D. *Review of social script.* The student, with support from the adult as needed, reviews or writes a social script that helps them negotiate things better the next time a similar situation arises. This script should be part of ongoing social and emotional instruction for that student and, in most cases, should relate to regulation strategies.

E. *Review of goal-setting plan.* The student, with support from the adult, reviews his or her goal-setting plan, perhaps through a PATH process (O'Brien, Pearpoint, & Kahn, 2015), a Possible Selves process (Hock, Schumaker, & Deshler, 2003), or another goal-setting process.

F. *Review of contract/plan.* The student and coach review a contract that was cocreated by the student and his or her educators earlier. Discussion of how to stay calm and focused to be able to follow the plan also should occur. The tone of this discussion (like all options in this step) is not to be lecturing, but to encourage and remind the student of his or her capabilities and supports, and to invite his or her reflection.

2. Process with the student by using the selected technique. The coach should ask questions of the student rather than interjecting his or her opinion. At the completion of this process, prepare the student to return to class. Preparation should include a mindful check-in and a Scan the Class/Make a Re-Entry Plan (see Section II resources for details about these processes). The student needs to be able to return to the class and be welcomed back in a low-key manner—perhaps as low key as simply joining the activity at hand. Some students may need a signal from the classroom teacher that they are still welcome in the classroom (they may be anxious and be thinking, *The teacher hates me!* or have other such thoughts).

Research on the effectiveness of any time-away space indicates that the way a student is welcomed back into the class is pivotal to the entire process. An irritated or unresponsive teacher can, in the span of only a second or two, undo all that was accomplished by the Re-Set Space. Making sure that all receiving teachers are onboard with the thinking behind the approach is critical. The coach is to facilitate this reconnection, and that facilitation may take various forms. The options are:

- Encouragement only: The coach completes any established paperwork process and sends the student back to class with an encouraging word. It makes sense for the coach to check in on student later, if possible. Some schools find that a return pass facilitates this transition. The pass can have action steps or simply a statement on it, such as, *I am ready to learn.* This pass can provide a structure for reconnection, but students also must be taught how to handle the pass when the teacher is actively teaching and may not want to be interrupted. A coach also may help facilitate a re-entry for a student who needs to be assured that he or she is indeed welcome by collaborating with the teacher to identify a secret signal and pre-teaching that signal to the student.

- Return with student: The coach accompanies student back into the classroom. Sometimes, when teachers are not fully comfortable with a student returning, a coach can return with the student and remain with them for a short period as a way to transition back that may be more assuring to the involved teacher. In some situations, the student may want the coach near them; in others, the student may prefer that the coach be less obvious and simply be somewhere in the classroom. The teacher *must* be welcoming (regardless of internal hesitation) or the process will be defeated.

- Support through act of restitution: The coach may join the student in the act of restitution and may also encourage them during this time of heightened emotions. There are some circumstances where an act of restitution simply makes sense (e.g., picking up the contents of a desk that were emptied onto the floor during the escalation).

The restitution act could be part of the action steps in a written plan or part of a return pass. Even when restitution is required, the student should be welcomed back (e.g., a head nod, a thumbs-up, a small smile) and the act of restitution should be quietly but positively acknowledged (e.g., a thumbs-up after the student cleans up). Acts of restitutions are designed to be healing (to the damaged relationship) not shaming. All interactions should follow that purpose.

As we mentioned earlier, apologies, although acts of restitution, are more genuine if the responsible party makes that apology in an unforced context. Time is the friend of the unforced context. The coach can support an apology through rehearsal (role play) encouragement and setting up the context in which the apology will happen when the coach is no longer by the student's side. Although the coach may accompany the student to the classroom and do a brief reminder regarding the apology plan, the coach should *not* force an apology just because he or she is there to witness it. Facilitate the student picking a time frame during the remaining portion of the day (or for the following day if the event happens late in the school day) by when he or she will genuinely ask for forgiveness. Structure a way that the student can document the apology (e.g., an apology slip, a verbal report to the classroom teacher), if needed, for accountability purposes.

- Coach contacts teacher in advance of return to establish return timetable as immediate or slightly delayed. Finally, sometimes a teacher is just too escalated from the incident that led to the student going to the Re-Set Room to welcome the student back on the student's timetable. Having a student who has been highly disruptive, exhausting, and possibly very caustic show up again at one's door in short order can be overwhelming for some teachers.

In these cases, the coach can touch base with the teacher and offer the option of *Now* or *In 5 minutes, In 10 minutes*, and so forth. Although the teacher is professionally responsible to welcome the student back, this option recognizes how very emotionally challenging it can be to do so in certain situations. The delay option allows for the receiving adult to get his or her head around the student's return. It also may allow for the completion of processing with the rest of the class if that was occurring.

In the case of a delay, the student should be coached that even adults sometimes need to regulate, and that the call to the teacher is a reminder for that teacher to use his or her strategies to do so. During this additional wait time, the student should be allowed to engage in any of the activities in the Re-Set Room that he or she chooses.

Sounds Like

- *What was the big thing that happened? What are your thoughts about how to fix it?*

- *Let's review your social script for handling doing work that is hard.*

- *Name two things you can do to get back into learning.*

- *Imagine going back into class. What is your plan?*

- *Would you like me to help you clean up or do you want to do it on your own?*

Student's Role

- Engage in thinking process: Respond to coach's questions, offer ideas.

- Return to class and participate in learning activity immediately unless the plan guides otherwise.

Types of Activities

- *Social script review*: Review a student's social script, act out using the script as guideline

- *Goal-setting plan review*: Review contract, or other form of goal-setting, and elicit from the student one or two behaviors that he or she can show when he or she goes back to class that are in line with the student's goals. Model optimism. Avoid any focus on negative behaviors that resulted in the student needing to engage in the Re-Set Room.

- *Object processing* (for older students): If you need to process in more depth the behavior that occurred, consider introducing objects in order to process what happened and how to move forward. There is no need to use objects of any specific type or symbolism—whatever

Table 6.5. Step 4 in the Re-Set Room: Do's and don'ts

This table guides adult behavior for interacting with a student within the Re-Set Room at Step 4.

Dos	Don'ts
• Sit next to student, with materials between the two of you	• Be the one who is solving the problem
• Listen to the student, ask clarifying questions and keep your input as minimal as possible	• Accept a seriously flawed plan
• Demonstrate caring, calm body language	• Tell the student all the things that he or she should <u>NOT</u> do upon returning to class
• Encourage student to use a calming strategy if an increase in nervous behavior occurs during the problem-solving process	• Over-hover when returning with the student to the class
• Document decisions the student makes if appropriate	
• Envision a positive classroom outcome for the student (imagine so he or she can see it before it actually happens)	
• Provide a calming object that student returns to classroom with *if* receiving teacher agrees to it	

is convenient is fine because it is the process that is important, not the objects themselves. The objects allow the coach and the student to look at the problem situation side by side in order to solve it. It also allows the student to *stand outside of themselves* and view the situation more objectively.

- *Footprints-on-floor perspective-taking* (for older students): Have the student stand in his or her own footprints and talk about what he or she did. Stick with actions, not feelings. Research has shown that it is very difficult to actually feel what others feel from an activity such as this (Suttie, 2018). Do not try to get many details—get the general sense of what happened. Remember that the sequential part of the brain tends to go offline under stress, particularly in students with trauma histories, so accurate sequential telling is nearly impossible. Next, have the student stand in a different set of footprints (e.g., designated as teacher's, peer's, paraprofessional's) and then ask questions such as, *What do you think this person was thinking or was concerned about?* Now, have the student go back to his or her own footsteps and make a different choice of behavior. Then have him or her step again into the other person's footsteps and imagine how the person might react behaviorally (not emotionally) to this new behavior. Affirm the student's ability to follow through with this new behavior decision. This process may require some modeling and role-playing by the adult to increase the student's comfort with it.

- *Perspective-taking via 90-degree thinking* (for older students): Another option is to employ physical position as part of discussing events and options, again focusing on actions, not feelings and be aware sequencing may be a challenge.

First, have student describe a very simple series of events that lead to a negative consequence. This is done by walking in a single direction and taking a step with each step in the sequence. Do not try to gather a high level of detail—this may overwhelm the student and he or she may not be able to recall significant detail. Get the general gist of what happened. Stick with actions, not feelings.

The adult faces 90 degrees from the student's position and presents an alternative sequence of events that would lead to a better outcome—acknowledging that those choices may require more thinking and strength for the student to do.

The adult and the student brainstorm together a set of realistic, alternative steps that fall between the choices the student made and the adult-demonstrated choices. As these choices are discussed, they are walked out, as well. The adult and the student may create two of these routes between the 90 degrees—with the caveat that these routes must lead to reasonably effective endpoints. After this discussion, the student decides which route he or she feels confident that he or she can do. The adult writes down the steps and practices that option again with the student.

Before We Knew   When a child showed difficult behavior, our default was to remove the child and hope that the removal would *teach her or him a lesson*. We dreamed that the child would return to class ready to learn and sufficiently chastened to not repeat the behavior of concern. When we did talk with the child, we also may have fallen into the channeling-our-parents trap in which we lectured (shared our wisdom with the student while the child's brain remained under-stimulated or under-engaged). We tended to not invite students to think for themselves in any meaningful way. In doing so, we prevented students from experiencing the desire to make restitution. We also did not adequately prepare them to re-engage in learning.

Now, if we are completely candid, although the challenging students themselves may not have benefited from the removal, the rest of the class and the teacher may have. We do not want to lose sight of this fact as we move forward with a new concept. No doubt about it, the Re-Set Room provides a break for the teacher and the classmates of a student engaging in challenging behaviors, *however*, almost always it results in a much quicker return to class. This presents its own challenges that we must address but we assert that, ultimately, a quick and behaviorally successful return is better for *all* parties than a slower but behaviorally unchanged return. It is abundantly clear from research on exclusionary practices that not only do such practices not work, but they actually do harm (Skiba & Peterson, 2000). In 2015, to move forward the critical conversation about the problems of exclusionary practices, the American Federation of Teachers devoted its winter journal to articles that addressed best practices in behavior (American Federation of Teachers, 2015–2016). We can and must do better, and the Re-Set Process is one way to accomplish this.

Common Questions

What If the Student Wants the Coach to Do All the Talking/Thinking?   This is where you need to stay strong and express your belief in the student's ability to problem-solve. Provide the student with time to think. It is also where you want to ask questions rather than answer questions. If you believe the student to be truly stuck, you can offer some choices and prompt the student to think through those choices.

What If the Student Is Nervous About Returning to the Classroom?   It is not surprising that some children are afraid to return to a place where they may have done things that they regret, or things that they might not even remember. If the student expresses concern, you may ask the student what you can do to help him or her be more comfortable. If he or she has not openly expressed concern but you notice signs of anxiety, you may want to use the accompany-the-student method of return—your presence may be of comfort. Another option—if the classroom teacher is open to it—is to have the teacher briefly meet with the student just outside the classroom door while the coach steps into the class to be with the rest of the students. Clearly, the coach would need to know the students he or she is supporting and know the faculty in the building to make the best choice.

What If the Teacher Triggers the Student As Soon As the Student Returns to Class?   As much as we wish this were not true, this does sometime happen. The reality is that sometimes an exhausted teacher is almost as dysregulated as the student and is not in the emotional place to interact with the student. At that moment, the best thing to do is to protect the student from spiraling out of control again and to respectfully help him or her understand the behavior of the teacher (e.g., *"Mr. Smith is human, and it seems like he is still not himself. Let's just give him some more time. What activity would you like to do in our Re-Set Room?"*). For the future, talking with the teacher and asking what will help a return go better is recommended. You may end up implementing a different form of return as a result of that discussion. The other future strategy has to do with data. One reason we keep data is to know why things are not working. Sometimes, that data also happens to reveal an adult who is having trouble adhering to the process. In a building that has committed resources to a Re-Set Room, that reality becomes an administrative issue, one in which the administrator determines how best to support a staff member who is struggling with accepting his or her student's return.

How Might We Support Staff Through the Return?   With all things behavioral, it is best if we can set up systems proactively rather than reactively. That means being proactive with and supportive of the entire school staff.

In thinking proactively about the teacher's experience when he or she has a challenging student return to class in a relatively short time frame, the people who establish the Re-Set Room should:

- Be sure that all staff members have been sufficiently in-serviced on the purpose, methods, general design, and anticipated outcomes of the Re-Set Room. Provide proactive opportunities for staff to provide input into the logistics of the return process as much as possible. Some points of discussion might be:

    How do you want to be notified about a student returning to class?
    What kind of support would you like the coach to provide in terms of the return?
    What do you want the student to do with the pass when he or she returns to class?
    How do you want to be informed about any acts of restitution or any other disciplinary follow-up?

- Be sensitized to the fact that teachers who support students with pervasive trauma may be experiencing higher levels of stress, or they may be experiencing some vicarious trauma. Acknowledging this when sharing information about the Re-Set Room is critical.

- Seek feedback from teachers who have had students use the Re-Set Room. *How has it impacted the teacher's class functioning? How did the student return? Has it been helpful? Has it not seemed to make a difference? What kinds of differences has it made?*

- Share data about the Re-Set Room on a regular basis, including typical time frames, number of students served, number of student cases who use the system proactively, and its relationship to reactive use by the same students—recidivism rates, and feedback from teachers on impact.

- Remind staff that the Re-Set Room is not magical—it is only one piece of the school's behavioral, social, and emotional support efforts.

Types of Materials

- Writing implements

- Forms associated with various strategies

- Extra calming objects for student to take back to class

- Return passes, if being used

- Social script book

- Table and two chairs—same height

This chapter has demonstrated the application of the steps in the Re-Set Process to the reactive use of the Re-Set Room. Next, Chapter 7 discusses planning and implementation considerations for implementing any of the forms of the Re-Set Process.

Chapter 7

Re-Set Process
Planning and Implementation

We began our personal journey of applying trauma-informed neuroscience to the school setting by developing the Re-Set Room and its associated process. It was breathtaking how this simple-yet-precise structure affected the behavior of children at the elementary school and middle school levels. In the years since its first implementation, the process has evolved in subtle ways and developed new forms, but it has never strayed very far from its original construction. We are exceedingly grateful to our early implementers who took a leap of faith in embracing our ideas. These original implementers provided us with feedback and suggestions that refined the practices and helped us better understand how to provide staff development to support and expand the process.

We have learned the following information from implementation of the Re-Set Process in the field:

- Understanding the science and philosophy of the Re-Set Process Re-Set Room is critical for successful implementation.

- The process is appropriate for use with students in Grades K–8. (It may be appropriate for high school populations, but we have not guided implementation at that level at this point.)

- The process reduces the amount of time students are disconnected from learning either due to in-class disciplinary measures or suspension. It changes the experience of school for many children with trauma histories and for their educators.

GETTING STARTED

Whenever we work with educators on trauma-informed practices and introduce the concept of Re-Set, the question that we immediately hear is, *Where do we start?* The answer, like many things related to behavior (ours and our students'), is . . . it depends. What does it depend on? It depends on a whole host of factors, including:

Who in the building is committed to implementation

The school's general needs and the specific needs of its students

The other practices that already exist in the school

The resources—physical, financial, and personnel

The knowledge base of the staff regarding trauma

The commitment at the district level to support the school's efforts

These factors will lead to different decisions. First and foremost, the level of commitment drives the implementation structure. If you are an educator and you are the only one in your building who is committed to implementation, this process will be only for the group of students who you directly serve. You will develop the Re-Set Process in a unique way. If you are an administrator and there is broader commitment among your staff, the rollout of the process will affect a higher number of staff and students than if only one educator is implementing it. Rolling out the process will be done in a way that reflects your role, your vision, and the supports you have from your staff and from the school's central office. To address these significant differences, we will share implementation guidelines for these two different scenarios.

INDIVIDUAL IMPLEMENTATION

If you are a professional who would like to implement some type of Re-Set in your classroom in a building that is not involved in the Re-Set Process, you need to follow the same general format that a whole building would follow: Plan, Implement, Assess, and Revise. Along the way, you also will want to advocate for expansion beyond the walls of your classroom, so we will add Advocate to your process. We have seen educators make a difference with their students by using these practices on their own, but there are limits to an individual implementation. We really encourage you to find ways to not be an island in your efforts.

Plan

Consider how this practice will interact with other practices that are occurring in your building around supporting students who struggle. First, make sure it is clear in your head, and then come up with language that bridges your efforts with your school's so that you can speak about it clearly to students, families, your colleagues, and your administrator. For example, if your school uses a specific social and emotional curriculum, tie the purposes of Re-Set to one or more of that curriculum's goals.

Inform your administrator of both your rationale for implementing Re-Set and of your plan. When should you do this? We recommend that you develop enough of an outline so you can explain it clearly—the intent, the process, the resources you will use, and the way you will assess process effectiveness. Do not order or develop materials or talk to students and families before you run this preview version by your administration. When you have the administration's go-ahead, further develop your implementation plan and begin the process of acquiring materials and informing other key parties.

Start with Re-Set types that have variables you can control (Proactive Whole-Class Re-Set, Proactive Student-Choice Re-Set, Proactive Individual Re-Set). Establish a schedule for Proactive Re-Set Process for All. This is when you will teach the regulation strategies to all your students. Consider setting up regulation caddies in the classroom (see Chapter 9).

Make a list of materials that are essential and a list of materials it would be nice to have, but which are not essential. Establish your budget.

Assess your classroom layout. What is the best location for the Re-Set Space? Think about managing the care of the space—how will you keep the Re-Set Space in order? Materials cannot stray into or out of the space. How will you manage that?

Reflect deeply about the language you will use as appropriate for your students' age group. For example, with younger students, we often say, *Check in with how your body feels*, but because of the typical hyper-body-sensitivity of adolescents, we know that we cannot use that language for middle school students. Instead, we say, *Notice your neck. What do you sense?* Think carefully about your language. How will you cue a student to use a Re-Set Space in a way that is calm and positive? How will you talk about the states of regulation and dysregulation? So often, we get focused on gathering the materials related to a process that we forget that what we say and how we say it is just as important, or even more so. Write down the language you want to use. Develop posters that cue not only your students, but you (and any involved support persons) to use consistent language when referencing key concepts related to Re-Set.

Decide whether you want or need to inform families. Is this something you would like to share with families? How is it best explained? Is there a time when families will be in the school that you could model it for them? This is a good topic to discuss with your administrator, who may be able to provide guidance that falls in line with schoolwide communications with families.

Decide on data you will use to assess the impact of the Re-Set processes you are implementing. Do not make yourself crazy, but plan to collect enough data to inform yourself and your administrator. Data related to Proactive Re-Set Process for All might be something as simple as periodically timing how quickly all your students are able to make a transition. (*Note*: Systems that are more settled transition more smoothly.) You might note how many times you have to stop and restate a directive. Think of how you might take a snapshot of how the class is functioning. To evaluate the in-class Re-Set Space, you might want to have a simple sign-in to provide data regarding use. High use might actually be a good thing—it might indicate that students are choosing a positive alternative to disruptive behavior. A sign-in also can provide you with a pattern of need that may inform other decisions you make—such as when you might want to insert short movement breaks. Data might be in the form of a student survey on topics that your students may reflect on, such as focus, safety, comfort, and staying on task. You could administer the survey before implementation of the process, and also during implementation. Remember to keep any survey simple and quick—one or two questions. Surveys can be verbal or written and can be done with all students or with a number of randomly selected students. Be sure to collect related baseline data before beginning your Re-Set Process.

Get physically ready. Order materials, create visuals, and set your target date for implementation rollout.

Implement

Practice Re-Set for All with all your students. This provides students with the language they need when you implement other forms. It nests the Re-Set Space in a tone of positivity.

Teach your students how to *do* the Re-Set Space. Model, practice, and take questions. Teach students how to behave when someone is in the Re-Set Space. Teach students how to care for materials and how to report if there is a problem with the materials.

Maintain the space in good order. Keep materials that are needed inside the space and keep other materials out of the space. Check that items are working.

Celebrate successes with students—privately, if they are individual successes, and as a classroom if they are whole-group successes. Notice what students are doing well. Notice the changes students are making, and how the changes positively affect other things (e.g. *I have been noticing how quickly we are settling into our groups. I am wondering whether our Re-Set time is helping us do that? What do you think? I am thinking we are so much more focused that perhaps we can take 5 more minutes out at recess today to celebrate how quickly we are able to get to work!*).

Assess

Remember that when we are talking about behavior change in general, and particularly behavior for students who have had trauma, change often comes slowly and incrementally. Do not expect overnight changes or miracles. Instead, expect growth to come as growth does—over time. We remind ourselves to consider the law of the farm when designing for behavior change. We plant seeds, but we do not go to our fields a week later and expect to harvest. We must tend and wait. Give at least 6–8 weeks for your first big assessment of the process. This does not mean that you should not make minor revisions based on feedback. Using the farming analogy, maybe you need to water your seeds a little more than you originally anticipated because you notice the ground is very dry, but not because the seeds have not sprouted as quickly as you were hoping.

Review data.

Talk with your students about the process and how it is feeling to them.

Reflect on how you are feeling about how the class is using the process.

Revise

Decide on needed revisions, and then share anything that directly affects what is expected of students and what students may expect from the process, as appropriate. If specific materials have proven to be challenging to manage, explain that, and explain what students can find there instead. (e.g., *I noticed that the putty is getting kind of gross, and it is pretty expensive to buy. Instead of finding putty in our Re-Set Space, you will find more water bead gloves. Let me show you how to use them, and then let's practice and talk about how to care for them.*)

Make note of your revisions and cycle back to implementation.

Advocate

Share your successes with your colleagues and your administrators—using data as much as possible.

Find like-minded colleagues who may be willing to dive in with you, be your sounding board, brainstorm with you, and ultimately, co-advocate with you for expanded involvement by others.

ADMINISTRATION-SUPPORTED IMPLEMENTATION

Planning Considerations

Some forms of the proactive and reactive Re-Set Process require a broad group of school adults to be informed *and* engaged, which often is a big challenge in our schools. As you know, your faculty is juggling a whole host of demands related to initiatives, the instructional components of their classrooms, and the personalities and needs of their students. Getting a full staff of adults on the same page is a daunting and time-intensive task, made more difficult when a school is large. Where you start is based on where your building currently is in its practices and knowledge, and in its willingness to commit, even on pure logistics, such as what professional development time is available.

PAUSE AND CONSIDER: Barnett found in his review of 36 public programs that the impacts of empirically based early childhood programs were affected by the quality of implementation (Barnett, 1995). Also, Greenberg et al. (2005) stated that often, "within-school" initiatives are not implemented with the same quality as the program designers initially intended, resulting in poor outcomes. Therefore, it is imperative that schools begin to actively embrace implementation considerations when designing and evaluating initiatives. This will be more cost-effective overall and more efficient in promoting positive change (Fixsen et al., 2005).

What kind of professional development is essential as you design and implement the Re-Set Process approach? Training on the Re-Set Process should be related directly to the need-to-know status of the staff who are being trained. This often means that there are two kinds of professional development that happen in a building—the first is provided to those who are directly implementing Re-Set; the second type brings a general awareness to the entire school staff.

Individuals who are directly responsible for implementing any of the Re-Set forms should be engaged in targeted, carefully tailored training in every Re-Set form they are expected to implement. This professional development should provide ample opportunities for application questions, and for role-playing through the steps. These implementers also must have ongoing access to processing opportunities—their follow-up professional development should be a combination of review of core information and application discussions.

All other staff in the building should be engaged in professional development that provides an overview of the big picture—the purpose of Re-Set, the core steps, and their scientific rationale—prior to the start of any Re-Set Process. Often, it is helpful if staff understand what Re-Set is *not*—how it differs from other practices with which they are familiar (available in Chapter 3). Finally, if the broader staff have expectations related to Re-Set (e.g., how they will welcome a student back from the Re-Set Room), these must be clearly articulated and perhaps even reinforced with focused, written materials.

To increase fidelity and positive outcomes with implementation of the Re-Set Process, we offer two very different starting points for implementation based on our experiences in schools: 1) beginning with the Reactive Re-Set Room, and 2) beginning with implementation of proactive forms of the Re-Set Process. For both of those starting points, consideration will need to be given to the *scale* of the rollout. Is it done with a cohort of committed educators, or is it done schoolwide? Our personal preference is almost always to default to starting on a smaller scale if it increases the chances of solid implementation.

START POINT OPTION 1:
BEGINNING WITH MOST INTENSIVE–ADVANCED TIERS

Most schools, facing the realities of staff development time and the challenges of building staff cohesion, choose to begin their trauma-informed work with the most intense reactive strategy (Re-Set Room—Reactive Use of the Re-Set Room, Chapter 6). They build their system from there, usually instituting the Proactive Re-Set Room practice next. In contrast, most recommended approaches today, including the MTSS approach, support the opposite—starting with the least intensive supports, and then progressing to more intensive supports for students who do not respond. Why do some schools choose this more intensive strategy as a first approach? We have found that beginning there has offered several advantages.

First, the reactive approach requires fewer resources. Getting the Re-Set Room up and running requires a targeted, small number of people to be thoroughly trained in the methods. The rest of the staff need to be provided only with brief, awareness-level training and access to an established protocol. The contents of this book provide the necessary training material. A school may either have a point person read, study, and lead training or it can have a group of educators read the materials together.

In this smaller context, fidelity of implementation is more easily monitored, and progress is relatively easily charted and shared with key staff members, protecting student confidentiality, of course.

The next benefit is improved student outcomes, especially for students who desperately need something different than traditional school disciplinary practice. The downward spiral of behavior that had been associated with punitive approaches ends and reverses as students respond to this new relational and regulatory approach. Students experience success and are motivated to apply what they learn in other situations. We recommend that a school first target students who are struggling but are *not* the very most challenging students in the school. Why not the neediest, most behaviorally worrisome students? Our rationale is based on what we know about students who have deep-seated needs. Our most complex students are not quick to respond with noticeable behavior change. Their behaviors require both more time and a multifaceted plan—not just one intervention, regardless of how appropriate that intervention may be. When we start with students who definitely need the process but who are not heavily in need of other supports, we are able to see progress. Progress helps sustain the implementation energy for students who are not as quick to respond. In addition, as we are developing our fluency with the skills related to coaching in the Re-Set Room, we need to develop and practice our habits in slightly more favorable conditions, and then, when we are fluent, we should move to apply them to the neediest students in the school. A third benefit is improved staff buy-in. The process affects the whole school because it can serve students from different classes and different grades—it provides support to many teachers and students. When reactive measures successfully address the acting-out behaviors that disrupt learning and threaten the emotional and physical safety of students and staff, overall staff buy-in is enhanced. As a result, the staff are more open to hearing about related processes that require their greater engagement. In fact, some schools found that staff actively sought out information to extend this practice into their classrooms because of the behavior improvements that were witnessed.

We caution schools that start with reactive measures that although you may start here, you must not end here. It's true that the Re-Set Room helps many students with intense needs, but the more expansive out-at-sea strategies are critical to fully support all students. Section III addresses these more proactive strategies, which include building classroom culture and regulation skills. In an MTSS approach, those universal strategies would be Tier 1 in nature.

You may want to use the Option 1 approach if:

- Your staff have only an introductory understanding of trauma and its impact on students' brains and daily functioning.

- You have limited whole-staff professional development time to comprehensively teach new in-class practices but sufficient time to teach the purpose and methods related to the Re-Set Room (including guiding educators in how to handle the return of the student to the class after Re-Set).

- You have professional development time and funds for a small group of implementers who will directly support the process to be trained and to meet on a regular basis.

- You have a fair number of students who are being referred to the office or other out-of-class options for behaviors that are not seriously endangering.

- You have a high level of concern about your suspension rate.

Re-Set Room First: Whole-School Implementation

Plan **Establish your budget.** Plan for expenses associated with initial professional development and setup of the space, as well as for some ongoing expenses, such as replenishment of supplies and ongoing funds for team meetings, if needed.

Establish your implementation team. *Who should comprise the team?* Essential: school administrator, school counselor and/or school psychologist, *all* persons who are responsible for direct contact with students. Helpful: special education consultant, occupational therapist (OT), a representative from any on-site mental health provider.

With this team:

Determine how people resources will be deployed. Determine answers to the questions: *Who will cover room and when? What will these people's responsibilities be when the room is not being used? How will coverage happen if the designated person is unavailable (e.g., out sick, pulled for another meeting).* It should be noted that because the Re-Set Process is both effective and efficient, schools have found that eventually there is less staff time needed for this intervention compared to previous reactive interventions. The process does require some upfront time commitment. Early intervening and effective intervening with one student help reduce the amount of triggering of other students, which otherwise could consume more staff time.

As we have supported schools implementing this process, we have seen different ways of providing a coach for the room. Some buildings have a paraprofessional staff member serving full time in this coaching role (often doing clerical work when the room is not in use). Other buildings have several paraprofessionals who share the responsibility. Some schools have used professional staff members—such as the school counselor, special education consultant, school social worker, assistant principal, and other professional staff who do not have classroom responsibilities—to cover the room on a schedule or on an as-needed basis. Some have been able to tap into outside mental health resources for some of the coaching responsibilities. For ultimate consistency, our preference would be for a committed, well-trained individual, but we know this is not always fiscally possible. If multiple adults are the coaches for the room, it is critical that they are all trained and that they meet on a routine basis to discuss implementation. Written plans and notes support consistency across multiple adults.

Provide explicit professional development on the Re-Set Room including appropriate resource materials. Be sure to provide sufficient opportunity for questions. Assure this team that there will be ongoing opportunities for discussion and reflection.

Consider how this practice will interact with other practices that are occurring in your building to support students who struggle. Make sure the team is clear about how these all relate and that team members can articulate those ideas with the faculty at large.

Reflect deeply about the language that will be used as appropriate for the age group of students who will be supported. (*Note*: You may wish to select from suggestions provided in this book.) Be sure that the team is clear that language is to remain consistent across all implementers.

Determine the location of the Re-Set Room or Re-Set Space. Check that space follows the guidelines provided in this text. This may require some creative thinking. We have found ourselves helping move books out of storage rooms to create a space, ordering a privacy screen to use the space at the end of a hallway, and moving support services offices—after talking with staff—into a shared space in order to free a space. Every time we appropriated space, we have worked hard to make sure that the change does not create undue consternation, which could hinder the acceptance of the practice. This means that we tend to relationships as well as to logistics as we find space within a school.

Make a list of materials that are essential and a list of materials that would be nice to have but which are not essential. Establish priorities based on the big picture. Consider how some materials may be acquired at no cost. (We cannot tell you how many treadmills and bikes have been donated by teachers who were using them only for clothing racks because they were already walking more than 20,000 steps over the course of a typical school day!) Touch base with an OT, if your district has one—OTs are a good source of places to shop inexpensively for many of the materials that are used in the Re-Set Room.

Think about managing the care of the space. Determine who will be responsible for keeping materials in order on an ongoing basis.

Determine how students will be referred to the Re-Set Room. We recommend that students be referred in one of two ways: 1) as part of an action plan created for that student as a result of a team planning process, and 2) through an administrator or designee who determines that the room is an appropriate intervention in response to an educator request. Allowing classroom teachers or others to directly send students from the classroom or other school location to the room is highly likely to cause an overuse and overwhelm the room, rendering it ineffective.

Schedule staff development time for the entire staff. This should include initial information about trauma, the purpose and process of the room, and the process of referring a student to the room and responding to his or her return from it. Engaging the whole faculty in the conversation about return passes and other such processes increases buy-in. If your school is a PBIS school, integrate use of the Re-Set Room in your behavior flow chart so that staff know how it works in coordination with other school practices.

Decide how to inform families. Assure that families are informed about the process, whether through written materials, a video on the school web site, or a presentation at open house or parent-teacher meetings. Consider including key information about the process in the school's student handbook. One of the most powerful things we have done is to conduct sessions for families in which we walked them through the steps and helped them consider what a Re-Set might look like in their home.

Decide what data will be collected. In Chapter 3, we discussed specific data points that many schools collect using Excel spreadsheets. Your school may have unique data that you want to collect in addition to the more routine ones of date, student, grade level, arrival time, departure time, total time in room, proactive or reactive implementation, and notes.

In addition to determining what data should be collected and how, you should create a plan for sharing the data with team members and the staff at large.

Get physically ready. Order materials, create visuals, set your target date for implementation rollout. Some cautions about visuals from our experience in the field:

Make sure that visuals *either* reflect the whole student body (e.g., culture, age, gender) or are completely generic (e.g., an animal school mascot, a brain with feet). Also, do not let the desire to form an acronym cause you to distort the process or miss the purpose. Acronyms, although memorable, are nowhere near as important as adhering to the fidelity of the process and presenting it with clarity. Keeping it simple and straightforward is important.

Remember that students with trauma histories need spaces that are not overstimulating. Set up the room to be welcoming but not too visually busy. Think simpler. Keep extra materials in closed, opaque bins or closed away in a closet. Have only the posters on the wall that guide the steps. Keep furniture to a minimum as prescribed in the process. If possible, allow for natural light or lamps and cover harsh or flickering fluorescent lights. Avoid anything environmental that even subtly communicates that it is a padded space.

Implement **Use the room as the process delineates and *only* as it delineates.** It is very confusing to students if the room is used differently by different people or if it starts becoming a room for other disciplinary activities. Keep it clean and separate. We do not need to pre-teach the room to some students—we simply teach it through a student's first experience in the room. We also simply inform other students, if they ask, that the room is part of improving our school's focus on learning.

Maintain the space in good order. Remember that chaotic environments create dysregulation.

Celebrate successes with students and staff. Notice students' positive efforts and successes in re-regulating both at that moment and other times (quietly, privately) was redundant when that student is seen in the school. The team should share with their colleagues, both formally and informally, the positive outcomes of the room (while respecting student privacy, of course.

Process difficulties first within the team. Struggles related to the room should be processed by the team before they are shared with the whole staff. (*Note*: Not all struggles need to be aired to everyone . . . some things are solved within the team, such as frustrations with incomplete data documentation by implementers.)

Assess   **Review data.** Analyze both trend data (e.g., how the room is being used, when it is used) and individual student data on a regular basis. Decide whether other data points are needed. Discuss how complete the data is. (*Note*: Missing data is an issue in many places, and that leaves us handicapped when it comes to assessing both the room and the student.) Use data about an individual student in tandem with other assessments related to that student's behavioral progress.

Conduct monthly implementer meetings. Monthly meetings allow implementers to support one another in operationalizing the process with fidelity and are essential during the first year. It is important that these meetings follow a structure and touch on consistent points: 1) discuss implementation to maintain fidelity of practice, 2) examine new activities being considered for use, and 3) review data and discuss any new learnings from discussions with students and the staff at large. In these meetings, issues are resolved, and progress is celebrated. Decisions can be made based on what the data yields. An agenda shared before the meeting and follow-up notes from the meeting sent to all trained personnel are both highly recommended. Figure 7.1 shows a sample agenda for Re-Set Room meetings. A blank template is available for download within the online companion materials for this textbook.

Check in with staff at large. Ongoing conversation with the staff at large is an important part of assessment. What are their questions? What have they noticed? What are their recommendations? This process works best when the whole staff are engaged.

Revise   **Decide on needed revisions** based on data and on input from the staff at large.

Cycle back to implementation.

Expand   **Move to complementary forms in a systematic manner.** As soon as there is a sense that the reactive form of the Re-Set Room is operating smoothly, introduce the proactive form of the Room for students who have used it reactively. Over time and with ongoing opportunities for staff development, move toward less intense, more proactive forms of Re-Set.

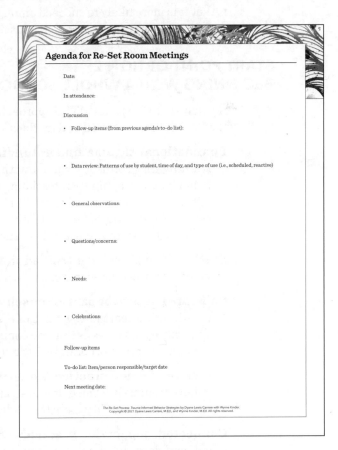

Agenda for Re-Set Room Meetings

Date:

In attendance:

Discussion

- Follow-up items (from previous agenda's to-do list):

- Data review: Patterns of use by student, time of day, and type of use (i.e., scheduled, reactive)

- General observations:

- Questions/concerns:

- Needs:

- Celebrations:

Follow-up items

To-do list: Item/person responsible/target date

Next meeting date:

Figure 7.1. Agenda for Re-Set Room meetings.

THOUGHTS ABOUT SCALE

You may want to do this on a smaller scale (i.e., with a cohort of educators who serve the *same* students and who are highly interested and committed to the process) instead of the whole school if:

- You lead a building that has a culture that leans toward skepticism unless the staff see it happening in their own community; you do not have a large proportion of staff buying in.

- You have limited funds or time for whole-school meetings/professional development but enough for this smaller group.

- You do not have a commitment of support from the central office unless you can first prove success with a smaller group of staff and students.

Re-Set Room First—Cohort Implementation

Cohort implementation is applying the same process as seen in the whole-school implementation on a smaller scale. The students who are referred come from and return to a smaller group of educators who are committed to the process. In this case, the team is whoever is directly involved in coaching, the referring teachers, and the administrator. Because it is a smaller pool of students, often the coaches may be pulled from other responsibilities (e.g., they may be the school psychologist or counselor or a special education consultant). This approach is a slower way to roll out the concept, and it presents both an opportunity and a drawback. The opportunity is that it is more likely to succeed among a small group of committed staff; the drawback is that the approach may not be as efficient as making a room available to the whole school.

START POINT OPTION 2:
BEGINNING WITH A WHOLE-SCHOOL APPROACH—TIER 1

If you want to follow an MTSS approach and begin with enrolling all the staff in implementing the Re-Set Process for all and in-class versions of Re-Set there are some key considerations:

Foundational trauma understandings are essential. All staff must have had trauma training that connects trauma with its psychological and physiological effect on student behavior and learning. Professional development also should include serious consideration of the importance of self-care. Staff need to understand that many trauma-informed practices fall under the concept of universal design—essential for some, valuable for many others, and do no harm for the rest of the students.

Staff need to have been trained in the proactive in-classroom processes and be provided with the related materials in order to implement.

Self-care needs to be part of the school culture. Because an educator's nervous system status directly affects the systems of his or her students, self-care skills are critical. Self-care as a priority also means that the community members care for each other, and that there are structures of support built into the school's practices, also known as Community Care.

Trauma-informed practice is one of the top five priorities of the school. Staff need to believe trauma-informed practices are an essential focus of the school community and worthy of ongoing staff development, fidelity checks, and data analysis.

Connected, supportive practices are in place. Other approaches within the school are compatible with trauma-informed practices.

In-Class Proactive Re-Set First—Whole Whole-School Implementation

Plan

Establish your budget. Plan for any expenses associated with initial professional development and materials that should be provided to all staff, including reference materials.

Conduct staff development on specific types of Re-Set. Determine which types of Re-Set educators are expected to implement. Provide ample opportunity for questions and materials development.

Provide time and guidance so that teachers can think about:

- The space they will use inside or just outside their rooms

- How they will manage the care of the space

- How they will teach the process to their students

- How they will direct students or allow students to opt into a type of Re-Set

- The language that will be used schoolwide

- Relevant data they may collect

Make a list of materials that teachers determine, chosen from the list of recommended materials related to the types of Re-Set, to be the materials they will need.

Decide how to share information about Re-Set with families. Determine whether it will be shared in the school's student handbook, on the school's web site, or at events scheduled with families.

Integrate the approaches with existing practices. If your school uses approaches such as PBIS, restorative practices, Responsive Classroom, or others, be sure to engage the staff in discussions related to integrating practices.

Decide on common points. Because students with trauma have smaller working memories, it is important to have consistency (sameness) across staff regarding language and many visuals. We also know that it is important to allow for educator individuality, because it is part of what connects students to the adults around them. To strike a balance between these two valuable concepts (sameness and individuality), determine as a group what should be the same (e.g., perhaps some certain charts of the steps) and where each adult can be creative. Keep the idea of balance in mind but perhaps with a tip toward sameness.

Get physically ready. Order materials, create visuals, set your target date for implementation rollout. Some cautions from our experience in the field regarding visuals:

Make sure that visuals *either* reflect the whole student body (e.g., culture, age, gender) or are completely generic (e.g., an animal school mascot, a brain with feet). Also, do not let the desire to form an acronym cause you to distort the process or miss the purpose. Acronyms, although memorable, are nowhere near as important as adhering to the fidelity of the process and presenting it with clarity. Keeping it simple and straightforward is important.

Also remember that students with trauma histories need spaces that are not overstimulating, so keep in-classroom Re-Set Spaces neurologically calming.

Implement   Implement practices within classrooms.

Provide schoolwide supports to those practices. If the Re-Set Process for all is an expectation of classroom teachers at the beginning of the day, make sure that announcements support—or at the very least, do not disrupt—the process by setting time frames.

Assure that support personnel are involved. Adults that do not have classrooms should interact with students by using the same language and approaches. These adults need to receive the same core information regarding trauma and the Re-Set Process so they can be consistent.

Celebrate successes with students. Notice students' positive efforts and the effect they have on how the classroom is functioning.

Assess   **Check in with staff routinely.** Ongoing conversation with the staff at large is an important part of assessment. *What are their questions? What have they noticed? What are their recommendations?*

Connect administrative observations with the implementation of Re-Set. Notice and reinforce, including in professional evaluations, the use of practices that are done with fidelity.

Revise   **Decide on needed revisions** based on data and input from staff.
Cycle back to implementation.

Expand   **Move to complementary forms in a systematic manner.** As educator comfort with some forms of Re-Set, offer additional staff development and or ideas for expansion.

THOUGHTS ABOUT SCALE

As is true for Option 1, you may want to do this on a smaller scale (i.e., with a cohort of educators who serve the same students and who are highly interested and committed to the process) rather than whole school if:

- You lead a building whose culture is to lean toward skepticism unless they see it happening within their own community; you do not have a large proportion of staff buying in.

- You do not have a commitment of support from central office unless you can first prove success with a smaller group of staff and students.

In-Class Proactive Re-Set First—Cohort Implementation

Proactive cohort implementation, just like reactive cohort implementation, is applying the same process as seen in the whole-school implementation, but on a smaller scale. When a cohort is comfortable with their skills, the administrator should provide opportunities for sharing with the whole faculty.

BIG-PICTURE SUPPORT (REGARDLESS OF START POINT OR SCOPE)

Schedule staff development early enough but not too early. Structure staff development to fit how and when the Re-Set Process is being rolled out in the building. Professional development needs to be done early enough so that those who are involved can think deeply about the process and then develop related materials, protocols, and language, but not so early that critical details are forgotten during implementation.

Recognize the need for all to mean all. *All* means the school secretary, the custodian, specialists, paraprofessionals, and cafeteria personnel—everyone who interacts with students. It also means that if the scope is a cohort, the non-implementing staff still need to have some level of staff development about trauma. Although these people may not directly support any form of the Re-Set Process, it is critical that they have staff development to learn about trauma-informed practices.

Schedule coordination time. Provide opportunities for ongoing checks for fidelity by scheduling coordination time for all parties involved in the process to meet. Schedule coordination time to discuss how it is going, share ideas, ask questions, review data, and work with written materials or a consultant who is well versed in the process. Depending on scope, this may be in faculty meetings, grade-level team meetings, or cohort-specific meetings.

Support struggling implementers. Provide individuals who struggle with implementation with necessary supports. Assume positive intent and take the same supportive approach with an adult who struggles that is recommended for students who struggle. Be present, listen, value their input, set reasonable expectations, identify how you will support him or her, set check-in points, goals, and timelines. Avoid shaming and blaming. Of course, after supports have been offered or provided and if no change has occurred, there may be appropriate actions if progress is not made or if behaviors are causing emotional harm to students.

Encourage peer supports. Consider using a peer coaching approach for implementation. Support peer-to-peer collaboration time and build in accountability measures as needed.

Get new staff in the loop quickly. Set up mentoring opportunities for adults who are new to the school and who may not have had the same staff development opportunities. Use technology to support catching up by creating videos that show implementation examples and offering a mini-course, perhaps on-line, that reflects information that was shared in staff development activities.

OTHER WAYS ADMINISTRATORS CAN SUPPORT IMPLEMENTATION OF THE RE-SET PROCESS

- Allow personnel and time resources to be used creatively for staff development, collaboration, and reflection among staff who are involved in implementation.

- Consider how you might support a book study or PLC by some members of your staff (guiding questions are provided in the on-line Study Guide).

- Model commitment to the process—especially when there are implementation dips.

- Notice staff who are appropriately implementing practices related to the Re-Set Process as part of evaluations.

- Support implementing educators in innovation within the structure of the framework.

- Collaborate with other leaders in the district to move toward consistent practice across the district.

> *Adopting new programs necessitates change. . . . People need to be ready for change and. . . . Creating optimal conditions for an intervention is crucial to its maintenance.*
>
> —Fixsen, 2005

MT. TOM'S—AN ANALOGY

In my town, there is an ice cream shop that makes dozens of different kinds of frozen concoctions. Some are dairy-free, some are sugar-free. There are sorbets and ice cream. You can have your favorite served in a sugar cone, cake cone, waffle cone, between two cookies, or in a dish. You can have a child size, regular, or large. Plain, rainbow sprinkles, or chocolate sprinkles. Servers patiently hand out samples, just to make sure something works for their customers. They have a suggestion box for flavors, which also serves as a staff compliment box. The result? Pretty much something for everyone.

Despite all those options, there are some things that are remarkably structured—certain processes that must be followed in a certain order, certain elements that must be present in some form. The shop opens at a designated time, products are kept in freezer chests, special flavors of the week are always listed on the dry erase board near the door, you can't scoop your own, they will not serve any of the options into your hands, and there is a line that you follow to place your order. I am guessing that some of those processes were the result of trial and error, and that the store has settled on the processes that it has because they worked well. I am also sure that there are guidelines that the store must follow, which it did not design (can you say Department of Health?), and which are based in the bigger picture of what is good for the welfare of all involved. I really like how some of the scoopers respond to the question, "What's a good flavor?" by asking a question in response, such as "Are you a sweet/salty combo person or a more of a straight sweet person?" The owner gets right in there as a scooper and models warmth. People come to the store for a treat, but they also come for community. Mt. Tom's is that kind of place. I think the owner of Mt. Tom's is part scientist, part organizer, part connector, part role model, and part artist. He's kinda amazing in that way.

Implementation of the Re-Set Process is sort of like that ice cream shop. There are structures, elements, and processes that are firmly established, but there also is a variety of options that allow Re-Set to fit the needs of the students it is supporting. We can help students find their way to what works for them by offering samples and by asking guiding questions. We are guided by big good-for-the-welfare-of-others knowledge. What works for students may not be the thing that works for us, but that is okay. Kids come to Re-Set for regulation; they love it for the relationships they discover.

The most successful implementers of Re-Set Process are definitely that magical mixture of scientist, organizer, connector, role model, and artist. And, oh my heavens, how I stand in awe of them.

Appendix A
Re-Set Activities Organized by Step

Here we describe the activities you may choose to use for each step in the Re-Set Process. The various proactive and reactive forms of Re-Set may use different activities for different steps. Implementers should refer to the specific guidelines provided for each form to determine appropriate activities. Finally, some activities may appear in more than one step because of their use in the different forms of the Re-Set Process.

When referring to body awareness and requesting or directing physical movement, it is critical to have a trauma-informed lens on what we say and how we say it—we must be careful of both our words and of our tone. Being invitational and offering choice when appropriate is an essential part of the Re-Set Process in all its forms. Terms like *notice*, *try*, and *maybe* all create a sense of choice.

You may have noticed that we describe some familiar movements by using unfamiliar terms. We have done this intentionally in order to avoid words that have the potential to trigger students with trauma-histories (e.g., lunge is described as a big step). Our recommendation would be for you to use these same alternative words. Likewise, we have intentionally selected specific movements and avoided others to keep students from feeling vulnerable. We do not have students bend over to touch their toes, for example; we do not have them lie on the floor. We keep them on their feet, doing movements that are emotionally safer.

We also have chosen to use mindfulness activities that allow for a sensory focus rather than quiet or internal thought activities. For students with trauma, time spent in quiet or an internal thought or activity may provide space for intense emotional memories associated with trauma—something we want to avoid in the context of school, with its primary responsibility to educate rather than to provide psychological counsel. The selection of specific movements (and avoidance of others), the avoidance of quiet time, and a focus on being still are three points where trauma-informed school mindfulness practice diverges from many other mindfulness practices.

The language "to a count" is meant to stand for the number of times you do something and the rhythm you do it to. Speed is indicated for each activity when necessary. The length of time for each activity or the number of repetitions is specified in the At-a-Glance documents in Chapters 4 and 5 and available online for download. Refer to these for additional detail.

Some activities listed for Step 2 and Step 3 refer you to the next appendix (Section II Resources Appendix B Scripts for Regulating Activities) where specific details and scripts are provided.

Activity Options for Step 1: Move Your Body

Arm circles (large)   Student stands, arms remain straight and rotate in circles with focus on synchronizing movement to a fairly fast count. Keep circling movements at a consistent pace and at an equal number for each side.

Big steps   Student steps out (a big step) using alternating legs, emphasizing a knee bend and even movement on both sides. Count at a slightly fast pace, but not so fast that precision of movement is compromised.

Bicycle (stationary)   Student bicycles legs at an even pace on a stationary bike.

Chair push-ups   While seated with hands on outside of thighs, student pushes body up (does not need to be lifting body off chair) to a count, relaxing arms and body between each push-up.

Dance (for example, short dance recordings or videos on GoNoodle)   Students engage in short dancing, either unstructured or structured. For Proactive Whole-Class Re-Set only.

Helicopter (fast)   Student stands with arms in T position, gently twists upper body, maintaining arms up at shoulder height, rotating torso quickly and precisely.

Hopping (both feet)   Student engages in rhythmic hopping in place to a count. It helps if there is a mark on the floor that keeps the student hopping in one spot. Be aware that this can be too challenging for many students.

Hopping (one foot)   Student engages in rhythmic hopping in place to a count. Alternate feet after a count of 10. It helps if there is a mark on the floor that keeps the student hopping in one spot. Be aware that this can be too challenging for many students.

Jumping Jacks   Student does Jumping Jacks using rhythmic arm and leg movement in one place to a count.

Jumping on trampoline   Student jumps on a small trampoline to a count, to the same height each time. It helps if trampoline has a bar, which controls height of jump and body movement.

Kettlebell lifting   Adult chooses a fitting weight (not too heavy) for student. Student lifts kettlebells to a count. Should require a little effort but not cause any straining. In situations where multiple students are involved, kettlebells can be cautiously passed between students, counting to assure pattern.

Line pattern on floor   Students walk following a line marked on the floor. Repeat the pattern multiple times. Steps should be even. Markings can help with that.

Marching in place   Student marches in place rhythmically, to a count, keeping movement even between both sides (same amount of lift on both sides).

Rowing movement   Student makes rowing movements (student grabs two imaginary oars out front, pulls oars toward body, and repeats) while sitting or standing, to a count.

Running in place   This is recommended only for the Proactive Whole-Class Re-Set, where students run in place next to their desks. Running in an even pattern and at an even pace is critical. It is difficult for a highly dysregulated children to run evenly enough to achieve regulation. This type of running may increase rather than decrease dysregulation.

Running on treadmill   Student runs at a reasonable pace (at their comfort level) on a treadmill.

Small medicine ball passes   Student passes medicine ball to the adult to a count. Medicine ball should be heavy enough to require effort but not so heavy to create strain. In situations where multiple students are involved, a ball can be passed among students counting to assure pattern.

Stair ascending/descending   Student walks up and down stairs at an even pace, either alternating feet (e.g., left foot first for Step 1, right foot first for Step 2) or repeating the same foot first (e.g., left foot first, then right for every step); method determined by student's skills level.

Stretch band stretches   Student stretches the band in an X pattern across the body or simply in a horizontal movement at chest or waist level. Evenness to movement is important. Stretching a band between the student and adult is another option, as long as the movements are rhythmic in nature.

Stretch bands on chairs   Adult places stretch band across the front of chair or desk. Student either places heels in front of it and pulls back to a count or puts toes behind it and pushes out to a count. The stretch band should <u>not</u> be kicked at to burn off energy.

Up and down on toes   Student lifts heels to go up on toes then eases back down from toes to a count. May stretch arms up for balance or keep arms lowered.

Walking   Student walks at an even pace, adult to walk by their side to set pace. May be done in hallway or in a limited defined space.

Walking on treadmill   Student walks on a treadmill which keeps a steady pace.

Wall push-ups   Student stands a short distance from wall, places palms of hands on wall just below shoulder height, bends elbows to get close to wall, then pushes body away from wall, repeats multiple times. Focus should be on the feelings in the muscles of the arms.

Weightlifting   Student lifts any items of even weight (water bottles, for example) above head, or in any movement pattern that is controlled, to a count. Can be passed back and forth between student and adult in a predictable, patterned movement.

Activity Options for Step 2: Modulate Down

Arm circles (large to small)   Student stands, holding arms out straight and then rotating arms in circles with focus on doing this to a count and keeping movements consistent between both arms, make circles slower and smaller as movements are continued.

Big balloon   *Specific guidance provided in Section II Resources Appendix B: Scripts for Regulating Activities.*

Big steps   Student steps out (a big step) alternating legs, emphasizing a knee bend and keeping movement even on both sides. Trace 8. Done to a count at a slower pace that really concentrates on precision of movement, achieving a deep knee bend and holding the position.

Bobblehead   *Specific guidance provided in Section II Resources Appendix B: Scripts for Regulating Activities.*

Breathing techniques   *Specific guidance provided in Section II Resources Appendix B: Scripts for Regulating Activities.*

Celtic knot tracing   Student follows a Celtic knot pattern repeatedly, using a chopstick or other non-writing pointer that glides over a laminated page, breathing naturally with pattern.

Chime listening   Adult rings a bell or a gentle chime (perhaps using a Tibetan singing bowl or bell chimes). Student(s) listen and raise their hands when they can no longer hear any sound. Repeat three times.

Coloring   Student colors or doodles on own with crayons or markers.

Coloring in pairs   Student colors one part of a page, adult or peer colors another.

Crescent arch   *Specific guidance provided in Section II Resources Appendix B: Scripts for Regulating Activities.*

Dry erase board   Adult provides a set of erasable lines on a dry board and student erases lines slowly one at a time until all are erased, using a small eraser or fingertip.

Fiddle object use   Adult reminds student of tool-not-toy status of fiddle object then models appropriate use. Student then uses the same material. If student misuses material in any way, adult asks student to pause and then provides an additional model. Adult may continue to use same type of material at same time to be an ongoing model for the student. *For more information about fiddle objects, refer to Section II Resources Appendix C: Fiddle Objects and Marble Maze Directions.*

Finding your center   *Specific guidance provided in Section II Resources Appendix B: Scripts for Regulating Activities.*

Focus object   Student looks at an object and shares descriptions. Adult may join in and do alternating to create a back-and-forth exchange on descriptions. May be done between students if as a whole-class or small-group activity.

Glitter bottle observations   Student gently shakes a glitter bottle, perhaps tracking a specific item in it or simply watching the glitter settle.

Head rolls   Student begins with head facing front and then rolls head in a total circle in a slow and controlled manner.

Helicopter (slow)   Student stands with arms stretched out in a T formation, elbows locked then rotates upper body at waist very slowly while maintaining arms at shoulder height.

Hook and loop strips   Student runs two fingers along the two different kinds of hook and loop tape strips (smooth and hook) simultaneously. Strips should be affixed to a surface, parallel to one another.

Imaginary weightlifting   Student pretends to lift weights, in slow-motion, controlled-fashion.

Isometrics   Student holds elbows out to side, pushes hands together with heels of hand in opposite directions. The push and release should occur in a rhythmic pattern with release being extended and focused.

Level balancing   Student is provided with a small builder's level that has 3 glass-bubble points and is guided through balancing process. *Specific guidance provided in Section II Resources Appendix B: Scripts for Regulating Activities.*

Marble maze movement   Student moves a marble within a fabric maze. *Directions for making marble mazes appear in Section II Resources Appendix C: Fiddle Objects and Marble Maze Directions.*

Mirror game   *Specific guidance provided in Section II Resources Appendix B: Scripts for Regulating Activities.*

Self-wrap   *Specific guidance provided in Section II Resources Appendix B: Scripts for Regulating Activities.*

Shoulder shrugs   Student raises shoulders up to their ears in a slow rhythm, tense and release, tense and release, with emphasis on the release and the associated feelings.

Squeeze and release   *Specific guidance provided in Section II Resources Appendix B: Scripts for Regulating Activities.*

Twist and turn   *Specific guidance provided in Section II Resources Appendix B: Scripts for Regulating Activities.*

Up and down on toes   Student lifts heels to go up on toes then eases back down from toes to a count. May stretch arms up as a balance or keep arms lowered. Pace is very slow.

Walk a balance beam line   Student walks, placing one foot in front of another on a line marked on floor, as if on a balance beam.

Activity Options for Step 3: Activate Thinking

Circle all the _____ you can find   Student completes a worksheet searching for an identified item (for example, circle all the verbs, circle all the capital letters, circle all the color words). Work needs to be at student's mastery level.

1-minute math paper   Student completes a work sheet of math problems at their mastery level for 1 minute. Emphasize quality over quantity or stress may increase.

Adjusted Simon Says (for young children)   Adult gives a simple set of directions to follow while modeling a behavior and requesting student(s) to follow. Increasing the pace of directions slowly, never going very fast. The usual *Oops, Simon didn't say . . .* component of the game is eliminated.

Alphabetical category sheet   Student completes a category sheet by naming items A–Z under categories (e.g., animals, people's names, foods). Good for older students.

Breathing techniques   *Specific guidance provided in Section II Resources Appendix B: Scripts for Regulating Activities.*

Categories   Adult gives student a category. Student names an item (can be done in ABC order or simply back and forth taking turns).

Celtic knot tracing   Student follows a Celtic knot pattern repeatedly, using a chopstick or other non-writing pointer that glides over a laminated page, breathing naturally with pattern.

Chime listening   Adult rings a bell or a gentle chime (perhaps using a Tibetan singing bowl or bell chimes). Student(s) listen and raise their hands when they can no longer hear any sound. Repeat three times.

Color naming   Student says color names on own or in a back and forth manner with adult or coach.

Coloring by number   Student completes coloring sheet that is more structured. Must color in areas as defined by numbers.

Cooperative draw a monster   *Specific guidance provided in Section II Resources Appendix B: Scripts for Regulating Activities.*

Count forward/backward   Student counts forward or backward on own or in a back and forth manner with the coach.

Dice games   Student rolls dice and might do things such as: name the number that comes up, add the value of the dice together, or tap the one that is larger. Task must be at mastery level.

Dot-to-Dot paper   Using a writing implement, student follows numbered dots to create a picture. Must be at mastery level.

Draw letters in the air   Write letters or words in the air with finger using large, controlled movements.

Fiddle object use   Adult reminds student of the tool-not-toy status of fiddle object, models appropriate use, asks student to use object, directs a student to pause if misusing material, and then re-models appropriate use. Adult may use same type of material at same time to be an ongoing model for the student. *For more information about fiddle objects, refer to Section II Resources Appendix C Fiddle Objects and Marble Maze Directions.*

Finding your center   *Specific guidance provided in Section II Resources Appendix B: Scripts for Regulating Activities.*

Flash cards   Student solves flash cards or names words as adult shows the card (math or high frequency reading words/letters/pictures-to-be-named). Speed is not emphasized.

Focus object   Student looks at an object and shares descriptions. Adult may join in and do alternating to create a back-and-forth exchange on descriptions.

Opposites   Adult offers a word, student gives opposite (or vice versa).

Paper and pencil mazes   Using a pencil, student follows a paper maze to the end; maze should be within skill range of student.

Recite days of the week   Student says days of week by self or alternating with coach or adult, repeat as necessary.

Recite months of the year   Student says months of year by self or alternating with coach or adult, repeat as necessary.

Rhyming   Adult offers a word; student gives a rhyming word (or vice versa).

Saying or lyric completion   Adult offers a saying or lyric very familiar to student and student completes it.

Shaded coloring   Adult has student color at various pressures (hard, normal, light) as coach calls out the different pressures randomly. As student warms up with the activity, coach should call the changes more quickly. Coloring should be done up and down across the paper, from top to bottom of a narrow sheet (about 1-inch wide; great use for scrap paper).

Shape naming   Student says different shape names by self or alternating with coach or adult, repeat as necessary.

Skip counting   Student counts by 2s, 5s, or 10s by self or alternating with coach or adult.

Squeeze and release   *Specific guidance provided in Section II Resources Appendix B: Scripts for Regulating Activities.*

Synonym sheets/antonym sheets   Student completes worksheets at their mastery level identifying synonyms or antonyms as designated.

Synonyms   Adult offers a word, student gives synonym (or vice versa).

Squeeze and release exercise with story   Adult reads script and student engages in activity alone or with the adult. *Specific guidance is provided in Section II Resources Appendix B: Scripts for Regulating Activities.*

Think-Pair-Share with simple question   Adult poses a question, students turn to a partner and share their responses with one another, then collect input from some or all pairs.

Trace letters/numbers/name   Student completes a worksheet by tracing letters, numbers, or their name given dashes or full, light models.

Whisper counting/whisper ABCs   Student whispers numbers or ABCs by memory or with visual prompt on own or alternating with coach or adult.

Activity Options for Step 4: Make a Plan

Mindful Check-In Script

1. First, notice your feet on the floor or seat in the chair, or both. What pressure or weight do you feel? Just notice the feeling of being on the floor or in a chair.

2. Now, focus on breath. Feel it in your body, your ribs, and even your belly. Maybe it is smooth, quick, short, or long. No matter, just notice.

3. Next, shoulders. Can they ease and go down? Hands get to rest, notice how that feels.

4. Attention goes to your jaw. Swallow, and notice whether your bottom teeth can drop to create space from the top teeth.

5. Check in on the rest of your body. If there is tightness or discomfort, just notice and settle a little more.

Mindful check-in complete: breath continues in and out, body settles, attention rests on yourself.

Simplified Mindful Check-In Script

1. Check in physically. Are you holding tension anywhere?

2. Take a moment and release that tension by stretching or changing your position.

Mindful check-in complete: breath continues in and out.

Scan the Class and Make a Re-entry Plan

Student (with or without coach or adult support) surveys the class and determines where they should be working (for example, in small group, in large group, at desk, any location in the room). Observes materials they need to use in the determined space or the materials they need to obtain in order to participate in the appropriate activity. Student then creates a mental or verbalized plan of what to get and where to go in order to begin being a learner. Where to go may include where to sit or stand within the group that is being joined.

For all other activity options, see the details provided in Chapter 6 under Step 4.

Appendix B
Scripts for Regulating Activities

The following scripts support many of the regulating activities that are used in the Re-Set Process.

Breathing Techniques

Elevator breath

Sit like a tall building—the kind that has an elevator.

Let your shoulders rest down. Your body is energized but calm.

Place hands palm to palm, flat, in front of your belly button.

Lift top hand (elevator) with an inhale to top of head (like saluting).

Exhale to float the elevator hand down to rest on the other hand.

Repeat 3 times. Switch hands, if you wish.

High-5 Breath

Start: Breathe in as you trace up to the top of your thumb.

Breathe out to slide down the other side.

Pointer: Breathe in and trace up to the top.

Slide down as you exhale.

Repeat with each finger, until you trace down the pinky to your wrist again.

Take your time and return in the opposite direction.

Trace the 8 With Breath

Sit comfortably. Shoulders rest down.

Use your pointer finger to slowly trace the track of the figure 8.

Begin at the top, breath in to fill with air. As your finger traces down, breathe out.

Once at the bottom, pause. Now breathe in to trace up to the top again.

Continue, exhale down, and inhale up.

Rainbow Breath

Sit tall and relaxed.

Arms hang down at your sides. Palms face forward with thumbs to the side.

Breathe in to reach wide and up.

Pause and rotate palms to face forward.

Breathe out to float arms wide and down.

Repeat 3 times. Try to slow your exhale each time.

Belly Breathing (https://www.youtube.com/watch?v=_mZbzDOpylA and https://www.youtube.com/watch?v=Xq3DwzX6MUw)

Put your hands gently on your belly. Allow your body to relax.

Breathe in through your nose, and then do a long, slow breath out through your mouth.

Feel your belly rise and fall.

Think . . . rise and fall, rise and fall.

Movement Exercises

Big Balloon Series

Use your imagination for this movement series. Sit or stand tall.

Balloon Around You

Pretend that you are inside a big balloon.

Press the walls of the balloon, in the front first. Breathe in to press, breathe out to release.

Inhale to press wide to the sides. Exhale to release (arms return to sides).

Press up breathing in, release down.

Try diagonal, one up and wide, the other presses down and wide. Inhale press.

Exhale, let go, and release.

Balloon Inside You

And now imagine that the balloon is inside of your body and that you are pressing on it.

A small balloon is inside your belly, hands rest there.

Breathe in as your belly balloon expands, hands can feel that.

Exhale as belly balloon deflates.

Then one hand above head and one hand near hip. Both hands face inward.

This bigger balloon is as tall as you are.

Hands can expand and imaginary balloon inflates.

Switch hands, upper and lower. Expand with inhale and deflate with exhale.

Finding Your Center: Tick-Tock-Tap

Sit tall. Rest hands on your lap.

Upper body straight, hinge at hips to tick-tock side to side.

A little at first, then try bigger leans as you go.

Slow the leans, then stop at center.

Now, tick-tock forward and back, small then bigger.

Slow it down. Stop at center.

Tap your feet on the floor. A few more times.

Stop. Then make sure they both feel heavy, resting flat.

Tap hands on legs, pause, and settle hands on your legs.

With your weight centered in your chair, hands rest, feet settle on the floor.

Be still, at center.

Bobblehead

Sit tall without leaning back. Shoulders rest down.

Lift and lower your chin as much or as little as you like.

Continue as fast or as slow as feels right, for you.

Tilt one ear down to your shoulder on one side. Return to center.

Then tilt the other ear toward the other shoulder.

Continue tilting side to side. Slowly and carefully.

Repeat a few times.

Crescent Arch

Sit like a mountain, tall and calm. Arms hang at your sides.

Rotate right hand out so thumb points to the side or back.

Inhale to raise your right arm wide and up. Exhale to soften but keep reaching up.

Inhale tall and then exhale to arch left as much as you are comfortable.

Smooth your breath. Stay for one more calm breath in and out.

Inhale to reach up again.

Rotate reaching hand—palm out—so you can exhale the arm wide then down slowly.

Rest for a breath or two.

Repeat on the left side, this time arch to the right.

Self-Wrap

Sit or stand tall like a strong yet calm mountain.

Arms open wide to breathe in.

Exhale as arms come forward and cross around front like a hug.

Next time, your arms go wide, look up a little.

Breathing out—arms cross in front while chin tucks and eyes gaze down.

Your back might round. Stay here, breathing for a moment or two.

Repeat for 3 more breaths.

Twist and Turn

Sit tall without leaning back.

Place your hands on the outside of your right leg.

Breathe in to sit a little taller.

Breathe out to rotate shoulders toward the right. This is a gentle twist.

Carefully, let your body twist and turn gently.

Breathe in.

Breathe out to turn a little more, if comfortable.

Breathe in to return to center, face forward. Notice how your body feels.

Repeat to the left.

Time to Rest

Rest back in your chair or on the floor.

Soften your muscles.

Eyes can close or stare softly at a spot.

Notice if you need to adjust or shift to feel more comfortable. Do that.

Once comfortable, your body will be still.

Rest comfortably for 3 easy, slow breaths.

Other Activities

Cooperative Draw a Monster

Adult tells student that together they will draw a picture of a funny monster.

Have student pick a crayon, then coach picks one.

Without starting, provide a model of how game will proceed so student understands process.

Hand a piece of paper to student and call out a part of the monster or face that child is to draw. It is more fun if you start with something unusual (e.g., instead of saying *Draw the shape of the head*, try something like *Draw the nose*).

Give the student just a few seconds and then call out *Pass*.

Student passes paper to coach and calls out a part of the monster for the coach to complete. After a few seconds, calls out *Pass* to coach.

Proceed back and forth until the monster is created.

Level Balancing

Adult provides student with a small builder's level that has three glass bubble points.

Student first tries to get the bubble in the center, with level being held horizontally.

Student then centers the bubble when the level is held vertically.

Student finally then centers the bubble, holding the level on the diagonal.

May repeat centering in reverse direction.

After student has had many experiences balancing the level, adult may guide the student to imagine doing the activity without actually using the level itself. Have student imagine each of the steps and centering the bubble in each of the three positions. Adult should explain that student can do this at his or her desk if he or she needs to find a way to increase his or her regulation.

Mirror game

Adult faces student (or students face students), standing or sitting.

One person in each pair will take the lead by using one hand to create a series of movements that their partner will copy. Leader is to move slowly enough that partner, looking in their eyes, can mirror the movement.

After a period of time, add a second hand into the movements or add head or shoulder or other types of movements, still moving slowly enough for partner to successfully mirror.

After a period of time (1 minute or so), switch and leader becomes follower and follower becomes leader. Go through same process.

Eventually, see if leadership can switch without any stated switch—mirroring one another and going back and forth.

Squeeze and Release

Imagine picking up a big lemon in each of your hands. Hold them there and feel their weight.

Now, begin to squeeze each lemon slowly, slowly, so the juice comes out of a tiny hole in it.

Squeeze until your fingertips are in the center of your palms.

Now, slowly, very slowly, feel those lemons beginning to come back to their original shape, pushing your hands slowly, slowly open.

Now they are back to the size they were before you squeezed them. Do they feel lighter?

Slowly, slowly allow them to roll to your fingertips and let them roll off your fingertips to the floor as you bend forward. Repeat, if desired.

Sample Self-Talk

I'm learning to stop and think before I touch or lean on people around me. When I'm calm, I remember to stop and think, and I enjoy being with my friends more. When I want to find my calm, I can do thumb push-ups, a breath in and long breath out, or chair push-ups.

If I'm still having trouble finding my calm, I can ask my teacher or another adult for help. I can show someone my *I need a little break* card, and they will help me find something to do that will help me find my calm.

Appendix C

Fiddle Objects and Marble Maze Directions

The following items are potential regulating tools that may be used as part of the Re-Set Process. These tools also should be considered for the regulating caddies described in Chapter 9.

Potential Fiddle Objects

- Marble mazes
- Pipe cleaners
- Balls that are sensory (have more activities associated with them than simply squeezing)
- Stretchy animals, rods, or shapes
- Paper clips
- Nut and bolt sets
- Hook and loop strips—two strips with different textures next to each other, adhered to a firm surface
- Thinking putty
- Small hair bands
- Rubber bracelets
- Water bead–filled non-latex culinary gloves
- Pencil boxes with fabric covers or faux fur covers
- Commercially made fiddle objects that require repeated movement interaction by a student, such as fidget pencil toppers and flip key rings but not spinner items.

Directions for Making Marble Mazes

Materials

- Acrylic felt (purchase felt that is in bolts, not pre-cut rectangles which tend to be thinner and less durable)
- Small marbles
- Thread
- Sewing machine
- Scissors

Directions

1. Cut two pieces of felt in required sizes (suggestions follow).
2. Sew three edges together about 1/4-inch in from the edge. Slip a *small* marble in before sealing the fourth edge. Be sure to double-stitch back and forth at all corners. Use very small stitches so that seams are stronger.
3. Sew channels—as per images below, usually about 1 inch in width. Move the marble out of the way as you create the channel. Again, backstitch several times where the channel connects with the seam and where the turn of the marble happens to prevent the maze from coming apart, because these are the pressure points.
4. Trim all thread ends. Trim felt if necessary.

Two-Channel Maze—Great for breathing practice, can be a silent fiddle object

2.75 inches by 5 inches, two 1-inch channels

Most popular: Single-Channel Maze—Good for keeping in a pocket, very discreet. Also imitates the feeling of popping plastic air bubbles if marble is moved between two thumbs.

2.25 inches by 1.5 inches, single channel

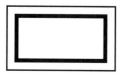

Five-Channel Maze, medium size

5 inches by 4.25 inches, five .75-inch channels (approximately)

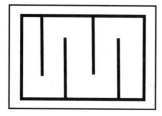

Trauma-Informed Behavior Practices

Section III addresses trauma-informed behavioral practices that support the Re-Set Process and that are appropriate for any trauma-informed school environment.

 Section III Online Companion Materials

Help Flip Sign (blank template of Figure 8.1)
Basic Regulation Plan (blank template of Figure 9.5)
Intermediate Regulation Plan (blank template, online only)
Advanced Regulation Plan (blank template, online only)
HELPS Self-Care Plan (Figure 11.1)
Section III Resources   Appendix A: Team Collaboration Survey
                    Appendix B: Seating Positions
                    Appendix C: Spotlight Strategies: Simple Ways to Create Predictability
                    Appendix D: Spotlight Strategies: Simple Ways to Protect Emotional Safety
                    Appendix E: Spotlight Strategies: Simple Ways for Nurturing Adult-to-Student Relationships
                    Appendix F: Spotlight Strategies: Simple Ways for Nurturing Student-to-Student Relationships
                    Appendix G: Cooperative Learning Structures
                    Appendix H: Modulation Exercises
                    Appendix I: Behavior Management Systems: Risk Assessment
                    Appendix J: Ticket and Pocket System
                    Appendix K: Playing Card Reinforcement System: Delivering Specific Positive Feedback to Students

Chapter 8

Classroom Culture

When you hear the words classroom management, what are the first couple of things that come to mind? Some people will immediately think about point systems, charts, reinforcements, and consequences, which is quite understandable because these often are labeled behavior management techniques. Although these techniques are *part* of classroom management, they are far from the whole of it.

Classroom management is a much larger entity than explicit behavior management techniques. It is comprised of the classroom's physical arrangement and materials, instructional practices, social structures, relationships, procedures, and routines. Together, these items reflect the culture of the classroom.

Although these cultural elements of classroom management typically are not labeled behavioral techniques, their effect on how students perform behaviorally is significant. In fact, the culture frequently is what dictates what kinds of behavioral techniques are selected for use for the other part of classroom management—furthering the techniques' influence on behavior.

Managing a class is a complex task that involves both off-stage and on-stage work (Danielson, 2007), relationship and structural skills, and short- and long-term considerations. It affects the feel of each lesson, each transition, each day, and each school year. It touches every single student in the classroom.

Research shows that the reach of effective classroom management is not even limited to the year that the student is in a specific classroom; its effect extends well into a child's future. Sheppard Kellam and his colleagues from Johns Hopkins University found that "highly aggressive six-year-old boys placed within well-managed first-grade classrooms run by effective teachers were *three times less likely* to be highly aggressive by the time they reached eighth grade than similarly aggressive boys who were placed in a chaotic class with ineffective teachers" (Garbarino, 1999, p. 66). This makes sense when we think about how the brain is shaped by experience, especially during certain critical periods.

As we consider classroom management for students of trauma, we will view these cultural elements through the concepts of predictability, emotional safety, and relationships. As you will notice, these three lenses are inextricably interwoven; it is difficult to pull one string without tugging on the other.

CREATING PREDICTABILITY

We know that children with trauma histories do best in environments that provide high amounts of predictability. In a life that has been characterized by chaos or one in which there has been a choiceless, chaotic event of significant proportions, predictability allows the child's hyper-alert neurological system to experience a big, satisfying *Ahhhhhh*. Adults who behave in predictable, consistent ways provide core stability. Beyond that, when a classroom's structures and procedures are clearly articulated and carefully taught,

Predictability and clarity of expectations are critical; consistency is essential. Children from chaotic backgrounds often have no idea how people can effectively work together, and inconsistency only promotes further confusion.

—Bessel van der Kolk (2014, p. 355)

students know both what to expect from the adults *and* what is expected of them as students. Experiencing a highly predictable life lays the foundation for being able to tolerate novelty (and even come to enjoy it at times!) which is a key life skill.

Notes From the Field

Rehearsing and reinforcing predictable routines helped to decrease, and in some cases, eliminate, explosive episodes in my students.

Also, during morning meeting, we would talk about and role play how to respond to potentially triggering situations so that students were practiced and prepared when a triggering situation arose.

Elementary Educator

Being a Predictable Adult

Being a predictable adult is no small feat when the students who you are supporting are highly unpredictable. It is all too easy to slip into following the students' chaos. Having clear expectations of how you will respond and having a compassionate understanding of what is driving students' chaotic behaviors help educators *stay in the trauma-informed lane*. Tools for being a more predictable adult include 1) procedures for handling behavior issues, 2) whole-class settling procedures (in which the adults should also participate), 3) having self-talk that allows us to stay on track, and 4) offering genuine apologies when we model dysregulated behaviors.

The procedures we have for handling behavioral issues help us respond appropriately and predictably to our students at the most difficult times. Having a set of steps to follow not only is calming for the student because they know what to expect, but it is calming for us to know what it is we expect of ourselves. When we have a procedure that provides a built-in break from a challenging student, there is an additional benefit. For such a break to work for a student of trauma, they need to know that the break is a time to regain self-control rather than a pushing away or punishment. The Re-Set Process (Chapters 3–7) was designed to meet the needs of both student and adult by nurturing self-control and reregulation in a relational context. The process returns a student to both learning and positive interactions.

But what happens when there is no built-in break? What if the overwhelm is related to multiple students who need to settle? How do we find a short amount of time to reestablish our footing in the life of a classroom, and how do we attend to the needs of the students who are dysregulated and engaging in difficult behaviors? Where are *those* minutes? One answer is to develop whole-class settling procedures and implementing them as part of the classroom schedule. It also means that we as the adults need to fully participate in the process *with* our students. The procedure could be a few gross motor movements followed by a stretch and then a breath in and a long breath out. Settling procedures do not need to be lengthy, and a simple 1-minute series of activities may be sufficient to change the emotional temperature of the room and help you to recenter so that you can act in a predictable, healthy manner.

Another way to increase our predictability is to have a set of things to say to ourselves when we are becoming stressed. This self-talk or inner voice grounds us in our principles and anchors us to who we want to be as an educator. Self-talk does not always have to be super serious. It may be humorous and provide us with respite through our inner smile.

One of our favorite exercises to do with adults is to give them time to identify the self-talk that will work for them when they are feeling their self-control slip. We ask, *What can you say to yourself about the student, about your circumstances that will let you listen to your better angels?* We hear responses ranging from humorous (e.g., *Only two more days until the weekend*) to humbling (e.g., *I may be this child's only caring adult today, What if this is how this student will always see me?*).

By the way, if you are a skeptic of the power of the inner voice, start out driving to one place and then intentionally think about another place and what you might do there. If you continue to think about the second place, odds are you will end up driving there. A study of mental imaging by Fontan and coworkers found that the act of visualizing impacts muscular abilities such as strength and power. This study reflects a large body of research that show that our minds have powerful influence over our physicality (Fontani et al., 2007).

Our thoughts also show on our faces. Knowing how students with trauma histories tend to be hypersensitive to what they see, think about how important it is for us as educators to control our facial expressions around students. Self-talk affects our facial expressions dramatically.

Did you know that when humans are severely stressed, a natural response is to smile? Sometimes, those smiles are interpreted as smirks because they come at a time when smiling is incongruous with the situation. This confuses students, and they may feel as if you are not taking them seriously, which may further escalate the situation. Likewise, if we say we are calm, but our faces show anger, students are more likely to believe the visual and be further triggered.

Being able to show a calm, neutral face—rather than a tense smile—is an important tool to have as an educator. What is the best way to practice that calm, neutral face? Find a partner to sit across from you. Think about something stressful that happens in your school setting. Ask your partner for feedback and together, work on creating and practicing your neutral or calm face. There are three important elements here: 1) we need another person—not a mirror—to give us feedback, 2) we need to be thinking about what stresses us, and 3) we need to practice.

Of course, we are human, and we will slip and respond out of emotion or exhaustion sometimes. Rather than beating ourselves up, we can use those times to identify our misstep and genuinely apologize, if it is appropriate. Part of us being predictable adults is that when we model dysregulation, when we make mistakes, we apologize and re-set.

You probably have experienced students who do not know how to handle being apologized to because it is not in their schema of how life goes. They may be confused by it and may need some time (or more experiences) to understand the genuineness of the apology. They may even perceive an apologizing adult to be weak, which may both embolden and frighten them, leading to more problematic behaviors. For supportive adults, the key to making an apology is to genuinely offer it without expectation of an acceptance or some other positive response. Voice the apology, and then move back into something else that is positive and predictable. What would that sound like? *Lynn, I am so sorry I raised my voice. I should have taken a moment to breathe first.* Breathe. *Now, what can I do to help you clean up? Would you like me to find the glue top? The scraps of paper can go right here in the center of the table.*

When the student has a sufficient amount of personal experience with genuine apologies, there will be a shift to understanding that this is how caring individuals interact with one another. Always though, we need to remember that in building trust, we are playing the long game.

Predictability Among Adults

When a school uses a PBIS approach, one of the marks of fidelity of implementation is the cohesiveness of practice among the adults. We do not have to be a PBIS school to value that kind of cohesiveness, though. When multiple adults interact with students, we create predictability through shared expectations and continual dialogue. The more adults reflect together on actual events that happen in the classroom or building and have time to think about the adult responses that occurred, the greater the opportunity for consensus about cohesive future responses. It is important to note that the need for consistency should not be focused solely on adult reactions, it should be a reflection on proactive adult behaviors as well. These reflections can be done very informally or through established meetings, depending on the number of adults involved, the relationships among the adults, and the disparity of practice.

Having clear expectations in the school and in the classroom is key. Clear expectations help us to be more consistent and set the stage for sameness of language among adults. When we consider how students of trauma struggle with receptive language and working memory, the importance of the consistency of our adult language becomes even more evident.

The other way we maintain predictability across students' experiences with adults is through authentic dialogue with one another. For some people, bringing up a point of potential conflict may be difficult to do informally—structuring that reflection into meetings may make the discussion more approachable. Just like we do when we conduct problem-solving meetings with students, we do not necessarily need to point out the person who is inconsistent. We can use polling methods, surveys, and other ways to get information more privately, and then share the trends or findings with the group at large.

During staff meetings, we can have checkpoints and reminders and create space for conversation around adult behavior. We can pose questions like, *How well are we redirecting without lecturing? What type of language we can use? What student behaviors are you experiencing that are leading to less-than-wonderful responses from us as adults? Is anyone finding it difficult to be out in the hall redirecting behavior? What are the main challenges? What strategies do we need?*

Of course, sometimes we may need to be more direct and address concerns through statements such as, *There have been several incidents of adults raising their voices at students in the past week. Let's brainstorm supports we need as a staff to remember how important it is to talk calmly to students. All of us agreed to be out in the halls monitoring students who are moving to lunch, but a couple of quick assessments reveal that only about half of us are doing that. What are your thoughts about this?* In Section III resources, we have included a Team Collaboration Survey that may help guide these conversations.

We also can articulate critical expectations of adults in writing so that everyone who needs to work together has common information. In our own work, when we have written behavior plans for students, the plans often articulate how adults are expected to consistently relate to that student—and that is perfectly okay. The intensity of student need can result in a formal—and sometimes legally binding—agreement about our adult behavior. When we recognize the merits of predictability and consistency for our students, it simply makes sense—for our students and for us—to align our adult behaviors accordingly.

One final thought as we seek to become a more unified community of practice: Whenever we come together to reflect on our practices, our focus should be growth-oriented. We need to demonstrate the same non-shaming compassion for each other as we do for our students. We should guide and support one another as we are developing our competencies regarding trauma-informed practices; it is a process not an event.

Environmental Predictability

WHO'S HERE BOARD CASE STUDY

I was contacted to help a church-run after-school program that served children, most of whom had significant trauma histories. The volunteers were caring and dedicated to the purpose of the program, but they were confused and frustrated by the behaviors being exhibited by some of the children.

We began by looking not for behavior management strategies for those specific challenging children, but for an understanding of the complexities of the lives of all the children in the program. I wrote on our whiteboard, "Understanding begets imagining, imagining begets answers," and we began to see through the students' eyes, to imagine what might help them feel safe and secure. I shared a quote from a woman, Mary Gonzalez, from John Calhoun's book, *Hope Matters*. "I'd comb their hair, and I'd tie their shoelaces. I think sometimes they'd untie their shoes just so they could be touched" (Calhoun, 2007, p. 67). We talked about behavior as bids for connection, for security, for knowns. We discussed how very little predictability characterized their young lives.

And that is how we came to focus first on creating predictability. Because the people working in these programs were mostly volunteers who approached child behavior in widely different ways, we found ourselves emphasizing environmental predictability. Our plan was that eventually, this environmental predictability would create more and more consistency among the involved adults.

Because of the nature of volunteer-based programs, one of the first things we did was create a Who's Here check-in board so that the children would know who they could expect to see that day as soon as they walked into the space. We took smiling pictures of all the volunteers and posted them on a bulletin board in the hallway where students entered. Each day, a bright frame was put around each of the pictures of the volunteers and staff who were there that day. The program leaders reported that they noticed how intently children were looking at the board and talking with each other about it; it was quickly very clear how important the board was to the children.

We encouraged them to use the Who's Here board for other related communications. They used it to communicate that volunteers, even though they were not there some weeks, had not simply disappeared from the program. It was shared with the students that as long as an adult's picture was on the board, they were planning on being there again. If a volunteer was on vacation or out with an illness, the board provided a way to talk about that.

The reality of the situation, however, was that many of the volunteers in the program were elderly, and some unpredictable changes happened. People became chronically ill and could not return, some moved away to be with family, and, on occasion, someone would pass away. The board then served as a way to begin the conversation about these changes, to encourage card-writing, to mourn, facilitated by clergy who were associated with the program.

The visual of the Who's Here board became an anchor for that particular program, and it has been shared with other faith-based after-school and Sunday school programs. It also prompted the use of other visuals in that program, ones that we find in many school classrooms. The use of supports such as a visual schedule, posted expectations, and defined personal spaces for coats and backpacks all established order and provided the foundation for positive adult–student interactions.

Physical organization and visual cues also support positive adult-to-student interactions. They become a foundation for Socratic language that encourages student thinking (e.g., instead of, *Why do you always throw your coat on the floor where people trip on it and it gets dirty?*, adults tried *Show me where your name sign is. What belongs there?*). In the Responsive Classroom model, we find excellent examples of trauma-informed teacher language, such as the Responsive Classroom 3 Rs: reminding (*Who can remind us . . . ?*), reinforcing (*I noticed . . .*), and redirecting (*Check yourself . . . what do you need to fix?*). These phrases serve as alternatives to the directing language or lecturing that can come too easily to overloaded, weary adults (Denton, 2013).

The use of small task cards at student cubbies or at other critical locations is another method for providing needed adult guidance in a way that encourages student responsibility and reduces adult nagging. The task cards can be a picture or a written checklist that supports a student following a procedure and, if laminated, can become a daily celebration of following a procedure as they check off each step along the way.

The other advantage of any visual support is that, although our words disappear into the air, a visual support remains constant. Students who struggle with focus because of trauma, depression, or fatigue might not take in or process verbal information, but they can continually, or as needed, access visual information. Just think about how important your own visual tools are to you, such as your calendars and your lists.

The student I was observing skipped up to her teacher and with a big smile said, "Thank you for my home spot, I love it!" And she promptly sat down on a carpet square in the midst of her peers.

I had to investigate the story behind this! The teacher shared that this student often was late in coming to the carpet and would become upset as she searched for a place to sit. Knowing this child's history of constant chaos, she felt that it would be helpful to give her a designated spot and assure her that it would always be there for her. She named it the child's home spot, and it significantly reduced behavioral issues during transition times.

As I witnessed, it also became a source of connection between this student and her teacher. This child, who frequently cried inconsolably, found joy in this predictability, and she declared it for all to see.

One of the easiest but highly effective things we can do is create a sense of predictability for our students through predictable places. That can mean a designated cubby, a mailbox for their papers, a chair pocket for their materials, an assigned seat, or a home spot.

Assigned seats may take away a choice that students might otherwise have, but the benefit is worth that sacrifice. How comforting it is for students to know when they walk into a classroom door where they will sit down and who will be around them. They do not have to experience the awkward search for a spot or the rejection of, *That seat is saved for someone else.* They do not have to think about who they want to sit near or try to assess the day's current social dynamics. When they walk by others, it is because they are going to where they are expected to be. When others walk by them, it is not because they are being rejected, but because they are going to where they are expected to be. They come in and sit down. A potentially difficult task is taken off the agenda for the day, for every day.

This does not mean that students need to stay in one spot all the time. Our girl with her beloved home spot sat in work groups at tables and got in line when called, flanked by different people at different times. There are times we can and should allow students to sit other places, to be surrounded by other people, but establishing an anchor spot is a critical emotional safety technique, particularly early in the day or early in the class period.

You know those students who seem to be doing pretty well when you are present but who fall apart should you get sick or attend a professional development activity? We *could* think of these children as taking advantage of the situation. But what if, instead, we saw their behavior through a regulation-issue lens? What if we let ourselves consider how connected a student may be to us and how destabilizing it may be when we are not there? What if *we* are the predictable element that helps them keep it together? Based on our hypothesis that this destabilizing issue may underlie some of the behaviors we were observing in children whose teachers were absent, we developed and began to experiment with While I Am Away cards.

Inspired by the children's book, *The Kissing Hand* (Penn, 1993), we created cards that were handed to children when their teacher or another significant adult was away. The front of the card had a picture of the adult, smiling, and a note that said something similar to, *I will miss you today, but I will be thinking of you. Can't wait to hear about good things that happened while I was away.* The instructions to the substitute were to give the card to the student with a smile, and to tell the student that his or her teacher or other adult wanted the student to have this while the adult was away. The substitute then instructed the student to write or draw one good thing that the student wanted to share with his or her teacher or other adult when the adult was back, and offered help if the student needed it. We laminated the cards to make them durable and reusable. Substitutes reported that the students held the cards tightly and looked at them often. The card was many things—a security item for the child, a conveyer of optimism, a method of associating the substitute with the trusted teacher or adult, a structure that allowed both for a positive initial interaction with the substitute and a positive interaction with the returning adult. We have since had teachers of older students do similar things with journals or emails, making the concept age-appropriate.

When we are aware of the great need for predictability, we also can rethink some of the things we do in the life of our schools because we see them through new eyes. We can begin to change how we deal with change. After paying attention to students' reactions when they entered school after a long weekend, we were prompted to reflect on *when* educators make changes in the classroom and building. As teachers, we personally used school breaks as a chance to create a fresh start in the classroom. After a long weekend or a longer break, students would come back to new seating or to an exciting new look to the classroom. It was logical to us—*new year, new routine!* We used a structure (the break from school) to change things up a bit. Well, at least, it seemed logical.

As we thought more about the importance of stability for students with trauma, and as we watched them return almost startled (instead of delighted) by the changes they saw, we found ourselves recommending to our colleagues to leave the old bulletin boards up, to keep the seats the same, to wait on rolling out any new system until after the first few days back. Then, the students could be systematically prepared for the change... or better yet, they could be engaged in the process of making the change. When teachers made this change in how they introduced change in their practice, students did better behaviorally.

This new strategy allowed students who may have had a less-than-predictable time away from school to come back to what gave them a sense of security and safety. They settled back in, and then had time to adjust to the upcoming change, which was shared with them before being implemented. This experience helped us remember that what we perceive as a small change can feel much more significant for students with trauma histories. And what we see as a positive change can be a disorienting loss of the treasured familiar for a student with trauma. A trauma-informed lens means that we pay attention to how changes affect our students and adjust accordingly.

We now call this our Monday Needs to Be the Same rule. If at all possible, do not make any big changes to the classroom, school, or routines on the first day back from a break, even just a weekend break. Have students come back to the known, and then prepare them for the change. Allowing students to participate in and help with the change (e.g., moving desks into a new group formation or clearing the bulletin board for the next display of student work) is a great way to help students process and prepare for change.

Ideas from this segment, and additional ideas, may be found on the Spotlight Strategies forms in Section III resources.

PROTECTING EMOTIONAL SAFETY

*A different day has come, though.
I flinch less and less when I am touched.
I don't always see gentleness as the
calm before the storm because, more
often than not, I can trust that no
storm is coming.*

—Roxane Gay (2017, p. 283)

Helping students of trauma feel emotionally safe enough to be academically, socially, and emotionally successful is a critical part of trauma-informed practices. Some of that emotional safety is directly related to how we construct and delineate the use of our physical environments. In our schools today, we are already highly attuned to making the physical environment *secure*: We lock our exterior doors, we have sign-in processes, we monitor hallways, we intervene in fights, we know who we can release students to, we have fire drills and weather drills. Security is about keeping students safe from real threats—the real tigers in our society.

Now, we can turn to thinking about how the physical environment and our interactions within that environment can contribute to emotional safety, particularly for students who have trauma histories. Because trauma is a visceral experience—because it is known in the bone—students with trauma histories may react to stimuli that would not be perceived by others as a threat—paper tigers. The students' hyper alert systems make them respond to common stimuli in uncommon ways. Their dysregulated neurological systems get tipped off-balance by something that might not even show up on our radars or the radars of other students.

When we understand that a number of our students have neurological systems that respond to some sensations and experiences as sharp-toothed and sinuously muscled as real tigers, we are better prepared to recognize the paper tigers that live in the innocent touch of a peer trying to gain a student's attention, the loud bell of a fire drill, a visually busy classroom, or the placement of a student's seat. We can consider what might be overloading to their systems, what might startle them, and how we can make environments emotionally safer. We can build in physical comfort and encourage comfort with taking risks. We can use the layout of the classroom, physical objects, classroom procedures, focused opportunities, and our teacher language to increase the sense of emotional safety and calm that is essential for learning.

Providing Comfort

BRADYN

Bradyn had his blanket with him almost all the time in Kindergarten. He put it on the table and leaned on it, wrapped it around his waist, made a headscarf with it, piled it on top of his head. None of his peers commented on it or complained about it. If he transitioned to a different table, he usually remembered it, but on the rare occasion that it was left behind, a peer would bring it to him. His classmates and his teacher understood that Bradyn needed that blanket.

That did not mean that there were no limits regarding the blanket. His teacher established procedures for its use, but they were limited to safety issues (e.g., it wasn't allowed to go with him into the bathroom, it could not be whipped around, it needed to stay in his personal space).

There was no direct attempt to wean Bradyn from his blanket, no behavior program established to end its use. Instead, his teacher allowed his growing sense of safety in the classroom to be what allowed him to let go of it. His ability to function without it waxed and waned, but that was understood as well.

When a child's neurological system is on edge, one of the simplest things we can do is provide that child with an item that is comforting. It may be a treasured item that travels from home to school and from school to home, or it may be something that simply stays in the classroom. Many educators worry about such an item being lost, so having a special place where it resides when not being held is a good idea. A treasured item should not be something of monetary value; rather, it is something that the student has positive associations with. We have developed treasure boxes where students can keep those sacred items and visit with them, either on a schedule or as needed depending on the individual situation. We also can allow sweatshirts or coats that provide a sense of safety. We understand that they will be set to the side when the student is emotionally able to do so.

Some schools are finding that periodic access to a comfort animal is helpful. We have supported schools that each have a service dog, designed just for that purpose, but we also have seen guinea pigs and rabbits fill that comforting role.

One behavior consultation led us to create a comfort item out of a pencil box. We observed a student who had a need to *pet* something, which often ended up being other students' hair or clothing and that set the stage for conflicts. As an alternative way for the child to be comforted, we provided a pencil box with a top covered with fake animal fur. The student would sit in circle or during any group time, holding the pencil box and pet it as needed. Child comforted, social issues resolved.

Meeting basic needs also is critical for helping students feel comfortable in the classroom. While this is true for all children, addressing these needs may be a more urgent issue for children of trauma. Access to water is a simple but critical strategy. Proactively, water is essential for effective brain functioning; we do not think as well when we are dehydrated. In addition, feeling thirsty causes us to kick into a more survival mode of functioning, which also runs counter to being able to think. Establishing a habit of getting a drink of water can calm a student who is mildly dysregulated, and it can help him or her think more clearly.

Reactively, offering a drink of water to an escalating student or a student in freeze can also help them re-regulate because the cool drink sparks a healthy feedback loop—a cooled down internal system makes the student feel calmer, and feeling calmer further cools his or her internal system. The offering itself is evidence of a caring connection, and the acceptance of the offer further affirms that connection.

Offering a student a cool paper towel when he or she is escalating is another water-related option that may break the cycle of behavior and change the physiological status of the student. This act, too, is a demonstration of kindness at a time when a student really may need that connection affirmed.

Having snacks available, just like making water available, helps prevent a child from shifting into that survival mode. Fortunately, many schools are structured with breakfasts and lunches, but augmentation may be necessary at other times. Offering food also has that relational component that makes it an even richer strategy; sharing food bonds people together.

Students who experience a great deal of stress may have a greater need to access the bathroom. When stressed, a child's system may be more sensitive or agitated by some of the biological sensations it is experiencing. We often see this request for the bathroom as a work-avoidance behavior (which it may sometimes be) but it may very well be related to a genuine, intense physiological cue. It is hard to feel comfortable and focus on learning when your body is sending that type of signal, especially if it has a sense of urgency to it. Consider how important it is to allow students who have been (or are) in an escalation cycle to go to the restroom if they request to do so. Oftentimes, this is when we find ourselves restricting movement, but addressing this need could help things de-escalate more rapidly.

We might not think of seating positions as related to a sense of emotional safety, but a body that is comfortable is calmer and is not sending distress signals to the brain. Allowing students to use a variety of seating positions that are nontraditional can facilitate an increase in focus. Physical therapists and occupational therapists have shared that certain positions are neurologically calming: Seating that provides pressure into the large joints (shoulder and hips) releases dopamine and calms the body. These positions would include kneeling, side-sitting and leaning on one arm, and squatting. Some seating positions help a student better control his or her body. Children often discover for themselves that locking their arms around their bent knees is helpful to keep their hands away from others or that locking their feet around the legs of the chair feels better. These positions also offer the advantage of pressure.

Standing as an alternative to sitting requires more strength and burns more stress chemicals, so it is a good option when appropriate. Standing and leaning on the work surface with locked elbows adds the calming pressure element to a standing position. We would recommend great caution in using some energy-burning alternatives that are recommended for students with attention deficit-hyperactivity disorder (ADHD). Yoga balls, T-stools, and wobble-stools burn energy but may increase dysregulation in children of trauma. Students of trauma struggle with knowing where their body is in space (due to an under-developed posterior-cingulate cortex), so seating that is unsteady may cause their focus to be drawn toward maintaining stability and away from learning.

Teachers who have offered their students a variety of options for sitting on the floor have found that instructional time has increased and behavioral issues have decreased. The often-used position of criss-cross applesauce does not create deep pressure that is neurologically calming. With this knowledge, teachers taught new options, provided visuals of the options, and then used the phrase, *Select your carpet position*. Specific seating options and their use are identified in Appendix B in Section III resources. We would also highly recommend resourcing occupational and physical therapists in discussions of calming seating positions and many other interventions.

Teacher Language

Language from Responsive Classroom forms the basis of our trauma-informed teacher language. The concepts of reminding (*Remind me, how should we touch people to get their attention?*), reinforcing (*I noticed that you helped Julie find her pencil. That was a kind thing to do.*) and redirecting (*This is the time to listen to others.*) show respect for the student and supports the development of a healthy internal voice (Denton, 2013). We would encourage anyone interested in reflecting on his or her teacher language to read Paula Denton's book, *The Power of Our Words*.

Some teacher language is particularly important to highlight when being trauma-informed.

Noticing   Noticing is a phenomenally powerful technique for children of trauma. *I noticed you have been sticking with your work more these days. I noticed you walked away from that situation. What have you noticed about how you are handling conflict these days?* When we notice, we are telling students we see them. When we notice small steps forward, we are telling students we believe in their ability to move forward, to become. When we invite them to notice, we affirm their abilities and encourage reflection.

We also can notice how hard things can be for students. *I noticed that you have looked pretty tired recently. I noticed you didn't get lunch today. I noticed you've been hanging back a bit.* These also communicate that you see the student and that you are open to helping. *I see you. I am here for you.*

When we notice, we also need to be responsive to what we see. This is where we can offer help and ask students for their ideas of how we can support them.

Pause   In classrooms and with children, there is a need to stop the action for a variety of reasons. Prior to our work in the field of trauma, the word freeze served that purpose for us but, given that some traumatized children have learned to freeze in order to survive difficult situations, it no longer makes sense to use that word in a trauma-informed context. It may feel frightening. The word pause stops the action without the burden of the association, and it connotes a sense of continuity. What came before will continue, in some way, afterward. The word pause is also used in mindfulness practices—it is a cue to focus, to pay attention, to settle.

Child's Name   Using a child's name to call attention for positive reasons is highly encouraged, while use of it for correction is discouraged. So many traumatized children bristle at their name because of its negative associations and we do not want to contribute to that. Learning to associate the calling of one's name with something pleasant helps a child respond, at a gut level, more positively. It starts the ball rolling in the right direction. How many times have you noticed that a child answers their name being called with, *I didn't do it!* or *What?*, or by a tortured facial expression? Turning that around improves social outcomes for students in not only their interactions with adults but also with their peers.

Time Language   Predictability is important, and time is an important element of prediction. When we use time-related language, we help children feel emotionally safer. Students with pervasive trauma may have less awareness of time and sequence due to a compromised dorsolateral prefrontal cortexes (van der Kolk, 2014). The more we can use time-related words, the more we exercise and strengthen that part of the brain which allows the world to become more predictable.

What do we mean by time-related language? We include specific time frames (e.g., *Talk with your partner for 1 minute. I will flip our sand timer.*) and broader concepts such as *beginning, middle, end* and *before, during, and after* and *first, next, last.* Supporting this language with visuals as often as possible is recommended.

Nebulous words such as *soon* and *later* often are frustrating for any child. Be aware that for students of trauma who struggle with time concepts and also with trust, these words can provoke strong negative responses. Using words that frame your intent more concretely (e.g., *After our special, When I finish with this group at 10:15*) may evoke a better response. As always, referencing visual supports helps support understanding.

Conducting Check-Ins

Check-ins build relationship and establish a structure for sharing. Check-ins are designed to be behavior-neutral connections with a student to see how they are doing. They should not be based on a student showing a difficult behavior or agitation but should occur unconditionally and periodically. Check-ins are brief and involve minimal language, but they allow us to demonstrate care and concern for a student and provide an opportunity to share a need with an adult. A quiet check-in by the classroom teacher may happen during transitions when other students will not notice the interaction. Some classroom teachers slip them in when talking to a student about individual workpieces or during some form of individual assessments. Each classroom may call for a unique approach to checking-in so that it can occur privately and with reasonable frequency.

Check-ins do not need to be the sole responsibility of the classroom teacher. School counselors, mentors, and administrators can also participate. *Just checking in to see how things are going* and *Wanted to stop by and see whether you needed anything* are the types of opening phrases we use when checking-in. Initially, a student may be hesitant to engage much in these check-ins, choosing to answer with an *I'm fine* type of response. Over time, these walls are likely to come down and more genuine responses may occur.

Controlling Stimulation

Children whose neurological systems have been wired under the conditions of high stress and trauma may be easily overstimulated and feel anxious if an environment is bombarding them with sensory input. Teachers can help by controlling stimulation.

Visual   Many teachers turn off artificial lights to avoid the overstimulation caused by the flickering of fluorescent bulbs. Others cover ceiling lights with fabric to cut down on their harshness. Many classrooms we walk into have lamps with low-wattage bulbs illuminating a reading corner, with the rest of the room lit by the natural light from the classroom windows.

Turning on lights can be startling to some students. We can avoid this overstimulation by instructing students to close their eyes as the shift to "on" is being made. This simple strategy makes a difference for many students and can be taught as part of the procedure if there is a student job of turning on the lights. Consider having students who are sensitive to changes in lighting be the ones who turn the lights off or on; active participation helps their systems to be more prepared for the change.

Teachers might also cover materials that are not being currently used and limit the number of things hanging from the ceilings and displayed on the walls. Closed, opaque, and labeled bins keep things accessible but less distracting. Many experienced teachers have found joy in simplifying. This does not mean that their classrooms are visual deserts, but rather, they are more curated with intention regarding what they post and display. *Hot tip*: One teacher told us that taking pictures of her classroom while students were working helped clarify for her which areas were too visually stimulating.

Of course, a certain amount of visual information must be on the walls of the classroom, in hallways, and in other common areas. Our goal should not be to create stark environments but to find a happy medium between bare and over-stimulating, between interesting and overwhelming.

Auditory   Sensory stimulation is more than just visual stimulation. Loud noises and loud voices are startling to traumatized systems. Consider placement of noisier gathering spots in relationship to other quieter spots to assure that those quieter spots are true refuges. In upper grades where the bodies are bigger (and often klutzier or noisier), it may be difficult to create quiet spaces, so an alternate strategy may be creating quieter times or resourcing other learning spots that provide quiet. We can also use rugs in classrooms to help absorb sound and provide headphones and earplugs (marked with student names and kept in appropriate bags or containers) to decrease overstimulation in environments such as the cafeteria or auditorium.

We cannot prevent all noises from happening—chairs tip over, doors get closed harder than intended, a student in the hallway may scream, fire alarms go off. A trauma-informed response to these things is to acknowledge that such things are startling and then provide some quick settling activity.

Notes From the Field

Over the years, I have noticed that my students have become more dysregulated in general. Recently, even things as simple as the trash truck making its rounds at the school created disruption in my class. Students would jump with the sounds and be out of their seats and looking out the windows. Even though the truck was there on a schedule, it still startled them every week.

I figured out that if I reminded my students on trash day that the garbage truck would be arriving soon, they were less agitated by the loud sounds. It was a little proactive thing, but it helped. It allowed my students to anticipate the bangs associated with the trash pick-up and gave the sounds meaning so they were less startling.

Intermediate School Teacher

Gaining Student Attention Without Causing Overstimulation

How do we gain student attention in a way that does not contribute to overstimulation? Flicking lights to gain student attention clearly is problematic if simply turning on lights creates dysregulation in some students. The intention behind this—not using a raised voice—may have been good, but finding gentler ways to call for attention, such as using a low-tone chime, can be just as effective, and without the negative effects. A strategy such as the adult raising their hand and students following along by raising theirs and becoming quiet may take more time, but the payoff of decreased startling is worth the few extra seconds. Turning off background music slowly (a fade-out), having two or three designated students walk around to whisper a specific attention direction, or a simple repeated movement sequence are all effective and non-startling strategies we have seen employed in classrooms.

Touch   Touch is another contribution to stimulation, and some of our students may hyper-react to appropriate or incidental touch because they are already so highly dysregulated. Others may hyper-react to touch, perceiving it to be aggressive in nature because of their personal history of touch being hurtful. Interventions to address these overreactions tend to fall into two broad categories: systematic desensitization to touch and reframing perceptions about touch.

To systematically desensitize students who hyper-react to touch, planned, systematic exposure to incidental touch during high-preference activities can be routinely scheduled into the school day. This can be accomplished through instructional games that require mild bumping into one another or highly interesting academic activities that require close proximity, such as experiments or certain types of cooperative activities. The rationale for doing these things during high-preference activities is that it is during these positive moments, when a student is *least* likely to react. Over time, students learn, at a subconscious level, that being touched is not hurtful, that it is okay. With each experience, their systems become more tolerant of touch.

We also can address touch at a conscious level by reframing perceptions about touch. When a student reacts to a touch, we can show mild concern (e.g., *Are you okay?*); ask the student to give a point value to the intensity of the touch, and reference how to react to that point value. We also can dive into intent. These types of conversations often involve personnel beyond a classroom teacher—individuals such as the school counselor or school psychologist. This cognitive approach is critical if a student experiences ongoing, significant triggering around touch.

The Big Picture of Sensory Input

We may wonder how these students ever make it in the world, bombarded with sensory input, if we have to construct our classrooms so carefully. It is the very fact that they *are* bombarded that makes our adjustments to our environment so important. Students who come in on overload do not need *more* stimulation—particularly if we hope that their thinking brain will be available to learn the valuable concepts and skills we are teaching them. As they grow and go out in the larger world, they will have more control over where they spend their time and they can avoid environments that overwhelm them. During their school years, they have no such control, and it becomes imperative that we give them calmer environments in which to learn both regulatory and academic skills.

Safe Physical Environments

Students who have experienced pervasive trauma often perceive physical spaces in very different ways than other students. Some may need to have their back literally against the wall, where they can see what is coming at them or, conversely, they may panic at the idea of being cornered or backed into a wall. Having peers on either side of them may be perceived to be as much of a corner as the actual physical corner of the room and, depending on their experiences and needs, this may be comforting or completely unnerving. They may seek out small spaces or darker spaces or less stimulating spaces in order to feel safe, or they may be extraordinarily frightened by them. The key, as one principal told us, is to be an observer, to notice how different experiences impact the individual student.

Noticing where students go when given a choice helps us decipher their safe spaces. We can also pay attention to where they go when they are escalated. We could conceptualize a student's safe space as where they do their best academic work. This might mean that they feel safest seated near the teacher or near the door or in the back where others are not looking at them. As a student becomes more self-aware, engaging them in identifying the types of spaces where they best focus on work allows them to make emotionally sound choices for themselves at the time and to self-advocate in the future.

Statistically, according to the National Child Traumatic Stress Network (n.d.), students with trauma are at greater risk of being the targets of physical or emotional bullying by their peers. How are we monitoring social interactions and intervening in problematic ones? Where in the school is bullying more likely to happen? What actions might be needed to decrease the issues in those areas? School safety research tells us that places with the most trash or graffiti are the ones that lack monitoring. A strategy for identifying these locations? Ask the school custodian.

Another method is to create a safety map with students. Provide students with a map of the classroom or school and ask them to identify places where they feel safe and unsafe physically and emotionally by using color-coded dots or by coloring certain areas according to a color-code system. This kind of activity should be done in private with a school counselor or school psychologist who is professionally prepared for any issues that may come to light. The value of the map is that it is a nonverbal sharing, which may be easier for students than a face-to-face discussion. Studying patterns that emerge by looking at safety maps from many students may provide insight into systemwide issues that can be addressed.

Safety is also about protecting students of trauma from making harmful social choices and, thereby, protecting other students from the impact of those choices. Students with trauma histories are at a higher risk for poor social interactions, including *being* the bully. They may be behaviorally provocative toward others because their systems are dysregulated or because they have not had the opportunity to develop pro-social skills (particularly if some of their closest role models have poor social interaction abilities). Monitoring these students more closely may be necessary at times to prevent them from engaging in problematic behaviors, while receiving instruction in those pro-social skills.

LIAM

Fourth-grader Liam had been engaging in seriously problematic behaviors in the boy's bathroom. Several boys independently reported that they had witnessed him engaging in several behaviors, including pushing peers while they were using the urinals and causing them to get urine on other surfaces and their clothing; threatening to take pictures of their private areas; and urinating in the sink.

It was decided by the school behavior team that it was best if Liam used the bathroom in the nurse's office until his provocative behaviors were addressed through other interventions. The team was aware that Liam had been a victim of child abuse and they struggled with this isolating response, but they also wanted to do their best to ensure the safety of their other students. They knew that the subtleties of implementation were going to be critical.

To make this an emotionally safe intervention for Liam, the school counselor met with him to explain the decision. The counselor invited Liam into a conversation about how much he wanted friends to hang out with, how he needed to gain some self-control skills so he could make and keep friends, and how, for now, the alternate bathroom was a safe spot where he would not be able to engage in behaviors that would make it less likely that others would want to be his friend.

The school reached out to Liam's private counselor to share their concerns and planned interventions and to coordinate their efforts. Other interventions included regulation skill instruction and other pro-social skills instruction. The alternate bathroom requirement was kept private from all other students.

Follow-up was focused on discussion regarding Liam's demonstration of self-regulating strategies, along with other pro-social skills. In collaboration with his teacher and the counselor, Liam determined when he felt he was ready to return to the hallway bathroom. When he returned, it was initially under carefully constructed conditions, and continued access was based on ongoing appropriate behavior.

Academic Safety

Academic safety is certainly related to effective instructional practice. Students with trauma histories do not need a different kind of instruction than other children; they simply need the instruction that research says makes a difference for all students (e.g., approaches such as active engagement and differentiated instruction). We do, however, want to address three concepts related to instruction that are particularly important—asking for help, handling mistakes, and holding high expectations.

Asking for Help   When a student already feels vulnerable, asking for help may be very difficult. Students of trauma benefit from classrooms where asking for help is part of the culture, is encouraged, and is taken seriously.

For dysregulated students, having to wait for help may be a challenge, even if they become comfortable with the act of asking. Raising one's hand and waiting for adult support is extremely hard for a student whose body is dysregulated and whose focus can shift easily. A two-sided help flip sign can be used to signal the need for help while supporting the student to move on to another approved activity until help is available—a blank template is available for download. The help flip sign, as pictured in Figure 8.1, has an added advantage of providing a visual cue to the student that help is coming.

When a teacher is working with one student and another one approaches for help, a simple shift from holding up a finger to indicate 1 minute (which can seem distancing to some students) to using the sign language sign for waiting can make a powerful difference. This active signing (waiting sign involves fluttering fingers) is a more inviting visual signal that communicates that the teacher is aware of them being there without shifting attention away from the first student.

The ask-three-then-me procedure (ask three of your peers before coming to the teacher) also is a helpful part of a trauma-informed classroom culture. Students' comfort with this may take some time and may be contingent upon them having securely attached relationships with at least some of their peers but it often is a way a student can get help more rapidly.

A second-grade teacher we consulted with was looking for ways to support a student who often would often struggle with independently completing academic tasks. The student's frustration would lead to off-task behavior, which the teacher found disruptive to the rest of the class. When the teacher asked the student why she would not raise her hand to indicate she needed help, the student admitted that she was embarrassed to do so.

The teacher began utilizing help cards with all the students in her class, as to not single out the student who they were primarily intended for. The cards looked like small speech bubbles with different messages. Green: *I'm good right now*; Yellow: *I may need help in a minute*; Red: *I'm stuck*; Blue: *I'm done*. Utilizing this system allowed the teacher to have a greater understanding of the supports needed by all the students in her class while addressing the need of the student who was often disruptive.

Handling Mistakes   For students who have experienced harsh punishments or who have had limited academic success, another critical emotional safety element is making mistakes an acceptable and expected part of the learning process. When educators model making a mistake, when they talk about and react to mistakes as learning opportunities, it is much easier for a student to take risks in learning. Explicit lessons in the value of making mistakes can be helpful, but it is really the day-to-day modeling that allows students with trauma to really believe that it is okay if they take reasonable risks and fail. Similarly, creating a culture in which not knowing is an acceptable part of being a human is valuable as well. We have found that saying, *We are not all-knowing but we all can be growing!* is a great way to communicate this to our students.

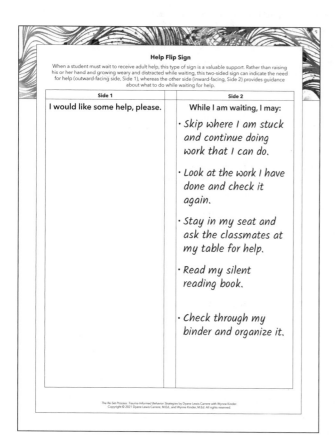

Figure 8.1.   An example of a help flip sign. A blank template is available for download.

Modeling not knowing and how to access resources, including other students, is another powerful opportunity to teach students these critical concepts.

A related consideration is allowing for passes or repeats when students are providing verbal information in an around-the-circle fashion. This allows a child to participate in some form (rather than shutting down) but respects the fact that they might not be able to generate an answer at the moment of demand. Phone-a-friend-type strategies are other great ways teachers have found to avoid putting a student on the spot and perhaps sparking a fight-or-flight moment.

Maintaining High Expectations

DANESHA

Danesha came to school late because her stepfather had shown up at the family home the night before—against a protection-from-abuse order. He had pushed his way in, and the family spent the evening trying to keep him, as Danesha reported to the school counselor, "calm and happy." One of her older siblings finally managed to make a call to the police, but the whole night was exceedingly turbulent. Danesha hadn't slept at all, first out of worry about what the stepfather would do, and then because of the intervention that followed.

She said none of this to her fifth-grade teacher. She walked into the room, her late slip in hand, and slumped in her desk. When her teacher asked her to get out her math book, she muttered and put her head down on her desk. Her teacher gave her a minute and then approached her again and posed several questions. She refused to respond and turned her head away from him. Her teacher paused and evaluated her behavior. Although Danesha had been disrespectful toward him at other times and she frequently delayed engaging in work, he felt that this time there was something else going on. He made the conscious decision to respond to her as a hurting child rather than as a disrespectful one. He called the school counselor, pulling the phone into the hallway where other students couldn't hear him, and reported what he was seeing. He asked the counselor to come to check in on her.

Danesha ran to the counselor as soon as she arrived. The two left and Danesha was gone for most of the morning, splitting the time between processing the events of the night before and sleeping on the counselor's bean bag.

When Danesha returned to class, she jumped into her work. Her teacher asked whether she would like to take a few moments to get caught up on what she missed in math, and Danesha asked to come back early from lunch to do that. Her teacher agreed, and she was back on track.

Many of us are familiar with the famous study by Rosenthal and Jacobsen (1968) known as *The Pygmalion Effect*, which showed that teacher expectations profoundly influenced student performance. We recently had a conversation with educators who, once exposed to a bit of information about trauma, began to drop their expectations of students. In exploring their thinking, their motivation was rooted in kindness—not wanting to create any more pain in children who were already hurting. It was clear that their trauma information had not sufficiently emphasized the healing and powerful role of high expectations, so we explored that topic with them. We shared that finding the balance between academically challenging a student and allowing them the time and space to deal with their internal emotional challenges requires really knowing a student.

What do high expectations do for a child of trauma? When we hold high expectations of students, we convey that we believe in their abilities. Of course, we scaffold in supports and give access to resources and materials to meet those expectations. When students then work hard and succeed at that work, they experience a release of dopamine, a happy, calming chemical that becomes associated with the effort of working—otherwise known as the joy of flow. A positive upward cycle is established, and over time, the student's self-image comes to include being a successful learner. In addition, when students engage with great focus in a "hard but do-able" task, the work itself is a buffer against becoming lost in thoughts related to their traumas. Work may become something that pushes thinking about their trauma experiences to the side for a while; it can provide a healthy break.

There are, however, times when we do need to modify our expectations, as our case study teacher did for a period of time. Danesha's teacher gave her the time and space to address her pressing needs, but then also moved her back into the respite of being a learner for the rest of the day. Because he knew her and understood her normal patterns of behaviors, he was better positioned to make a sound decision.

Validating Feelings

Another opportunity for creating emotional safety lies in how we treat students when they share their feelings. When we listen and give credence to a student's feelings, they are more likely to express those feelings to us openly; they learn that it is safe to do so. Psychotherapist Lena Aburdene Derhally (2016) writes in a *Washington Post* article, "Validation is the most important part of any safe relationship. Validation is saying *Your perspective is important to me and you make sense*" (para. 8). This approach to coaching *accepts feelings and limits behaviors*. Derhally sees, as many other therapists do, that boundaries and consequences can coexist with validation. In fact, students feel safer when they know where the boundaries are, even when they push against them. For children of trauma, who may have experienced wildly variable boundaries (e.g., in charge of a parent who has mental health issues one moment, then forced to comply with that same adult's every directive at another moment), having a clear sense of what is nonnegotiable is emotionally soothing.

Adults can accidentally make statements that invalidate a student's feelings and drive out connection. This happens for a variety of reasons: We channel phrases we have heard ourselves, our personal view on a situation is vastly different than the student's view, we have to spontaneously respond to multiple students experiencing big feelings, or we may be trying to help a student feel better. The problem is that at the core of invalidation is the denial of the student's feelings. As is true for many interactions with upset students, listening carefully and responding with less language is often best because it keeps us out of the hot water of invalidation. Some common invalidations and alternate responses are shown in Table 8.1.

You will notice that the intention of the validation statements is to acknowledge and accept the feeling, to offer "with-it-ness", and defer cognitive interaction to another time. We can also always limit behavior. *I see you feel strongly. Your feelings are important, and it is also important that we act in ways that keep all of us safe.* It is critical that a child of trauma learns that strong feelings and safety can coexist, even if his or her prior experiences may not have led him or her to believe in that possibility.

Navigating Quiet

Finally, although moments of quiet for many students are emotionally calming, for our students of trauma, it may well be the opposite. For some students, quiet invites the monsters of trauma into their heads. Did you or any of your teachers ever ask the class to put their heads down and just be quiet for a minute—not as a consequence, but as a way to help everyone transition from a more active time of the day? Perhaps the lights were even turned off. When we understand that this is tranquility for some and torture for others, we can find new ways to

Table 8.1. Examples of validating and invalidating statements

Reflect on the language that comes easily to you and, if you use that type of invalidation, consider a shift that may improve your communications with students.

Invalidating statement	Instead, consider . . . (validating statement)
Telling how to feel	
You should be happy. It easily could have been a lot worse than it is.	*That sounds _____ (frustrating, upsetting).*
Defending the opposition	
You know that she didn't mean it. I am sure her feelings were hurt, or she wouldn't have done that.	*You are feeling _____. Shoving someone is not acceptable in our class, though. Would you like to Re-Set here or elsewhere? I promise, when you are ready, we will talk about this.*
Denying significance/minimizing feelings	
You are making a big deal out of almost nothing. Just get over it.	*This feels big to you. Can I help in any way?*
Negating the feeling	
If you think about that, you'll have to admit it isn't the case.	*I can tell you're feeling a strong feeling about this.*
Philosophizing/offering clichés to console	
It will not be a big deal a week from now, I can assure you. Time heals all wounds. Things happen for a reason.	*I am here for you. I am sorry you are hurting.*
Defeating by reason/debating	
Let's stick to the facts. Let's make a list and see if that is actually accurate.	*Your feelings are valid and real, and pretty big right now. I couldn't think if I felt that way. Please take a minute to Re-Set, either here or in the Re-Set Space.*

invite in a quiet that leaves no space for the monsters of trauma. Quiet can take many forms: softly clapping a pattern with our hands, focusing on an object and listing its qualities, looking for a pattern in a piece of music or a work of art. These are all ways to use quiet in a trauma-informed manner.

Emotional safety weaves through everything we do with our students, as does the opportunity for feeling unsafe or vulnerable. Because of the unique experiences of children with trauma histories, we cannot always guess all that makes a child feel safe or less safe. We can, however, know the things that are highly likely to decrease safety, and then we can pay attention. In the simplest of language, we protect emotional safety when we take time to not just look at things, but to really see them; to not just hear things, but to genuinely listen to our students. Ideas from this segment and additional ones may be found on the Spotlight Strategies form in the Section III Resources.

NURTURING RELATIONSHIPS

We can think about nurturing relationships in schools in two ways. We can nurture the relationship between ourselves and our students, and we

I've come to a frightening conclusion. I am the decisive element in the classroom. It is my personal approach that creates the climate. It is my daily mood that makes the weather. As a teacher, I possess tremendous power to make a child's life miserable or joyous. I can be a tool of torture or an instrument of inspiration. I can humiliate or humor. Hurt or heal. In all situations, it is my response that decides whether a crisis will be escalated or de-escalated and a child humanized or dehumanized.

—Haim Ginott (1972, p. 13)

can nurture relationships among our students. Some of our students need our support more than others. Some do well with adult relationships but need more guidance with peer relationships or vice versa. Our students who have experienced pervasive trauma probably need our help with both. Class-wide time and effort spent on building relationship skills makes sense because every one of our students needs us to be in relationship with them, and all our students need some support in navigating the ever-changing, complex world of peer relationships.

Nurturing Adult-to-Student Relationships

We had knee-to-knee time every week, my students and me. It wasn't that long, only about 5 minutes with each of them individually, but it was the most fiercely protected time of the week. My class was all boys, middle-schoolers with emotional support needs. If you were to have passed by my class, you would have seen many who presented as angry and dominating, and a few who appeared anxious and withdrawn.

But all 14 of them treated the afternoon of knee-to-knee time with reverence. It was their time with me to use as they wished, and not one of them ever declined to participate. A student who had been struggling with being aggressive and disruptive all day would become quieter and more focused when the hour began. I could see their temporarily curbed restlessness just below the surface as they waited their turn.

I sat, away from the rest of the class, and they would come sit next to me or, if they preferred, across from me. There, our knees often touching, we bent our heads down and, close to one another, talked in almost a whisper.

Sometimes they came, fiddle object in hand, with a clear sense of what they wanted to share. Sometimes they came with questions about how I thought they were doing. Mostly, they came and talked about things that popped into their heads after I asked my opening question, "What would you like to share today?"

It was the time in the week that my learning curve was a fierce arc, when I learned about their lives, their pains, their perceptions, their dreams. I was naïve when I made the decision to do this with my class. I often felt I was not prepared for what I heard, so I mostly listened and sometimes quietly teared up. Often, it felt like my tears were the ones they themselves could not afford to shed; they consoled me, consoling themselves in the process. It will be okay. It will be okay.

I did the things that I could do, mostly changes I could make in my classroom. I sometimes found ways I could better advocate for them at the school level. I carried some things to my colleagues, the school counselor, or the school psychologist and passed them on for their expertise. I helped my students plan the tiny steps to their dreams, no matter how distant.

Mostly, I listened and tried my best to feel <u>with</u> them.

Although a positive relationship is not itself enough reason for change, the absence of such a relationship can sound the death knell to success.
—John Seita & Larry Brendtro (2005, p. 108)

Relationship is made in the simplest of gestures, and yet it is one of the most complex things we can ever navigate. We make our way to relationship step by step through those small gestures. You can be in relationship with a student without ever discussing his or her trauma. Connection is not based on knowing the whole of the student's story; it comes from what happens in the here-and-now between you and the child. It is about seeing the child holistically, even without knowing all the details of his or her life. If we want to be in relationship with a child, we must choose to be consciously open to the child, allowing them to reveal who they are, when and how they choose to do so.

Relational Listening

We nurture relationship when we listen carefully. What is relational listening? It is, as M. Scott Peck (2003) advises us, something that cannot be done while we do other things. We interviewed more than 100 teenagers. The two things we heard over and over about what they wanted from their educators were

- Pay full attention to me. If you cannot, I would rather wait to talk when you are able to give me your full attention.

- I do not always go to adults first for their opinions, but when I do, I really want you to help me. I want your opinion, but I also want you to listen completely first.

We asked the same group what irritated them the most, and they said it was

- When an educator corrected their grammar while they were sharing something important

- When an educator jumped to conclusions before they finished talking

- When their privacy was not respected (e.g., a teacher replied too loudly or shared private information with others)

These students told us that they can see distraction in our eyes, and they can tell whether we are faking at listening by nodding and echoing their words. They said they do really want to hear our advice, but only *after* we have really listened to them. All of this gives us potent information about what to do to relationally listen.

Students with trauma histories tend to be experts at detecting deception; establishing a relationship with them cannot be faked. Fake-it-till-you-make-it does not work. To be the most effective, we must embrace that new lens regarding behavior so that our actions are based on our *genuine* belief in the unconditional value and the great potential of the student.

If we can share our story with someone who responds with empathy and understanding, shame can't survive.

—Brené Brown (2012, p. 75)

Hearing With Your Other Senses

Students who struggle with trust often reach out to us in unusual ways. Are we tuned in to truly hearing these messages? We mentioned the use of bids earlier, and here is another opportunity to reflect on them. Think of the student who complains about being in your class or school and yet who often hangs out just outside the door at the end of the school day. What about students who say, *I don't care*, and act as if they are ignoring you? Consider the times a student asks repeatedly for directions—could that be a bid for connection? What if we reframed many of the behaviors that we think of as "annoying" as bids for connection? What if those are the only way a student is comfortable bringing us as educators closer to him or her? How do we respond to these in a way that does not reinforce the use of negative behavior as a social tool and yet is responsive to the child?

We can begin by routinely teaching socially appropriate ways to gain our attention and our interest. But . . . when negative bids do happen, what are our options? The key is to hear the intent and to respond by describing that intent. The more trauma-informed we become, the more fluent we become in the language of intent—we can translate our students' behaviors into the need that is being expressed. Table 8.2 shares some bids we have heard from

Table 8.2. Responding to student needs

Student language (bids)	Educator response (need-based)
I hate this work.	*It is hard. You sound like you would like some help.*
I need the directions again. I didn't hear them.	*I'm here, I'll make sure you understand them. Now, what do you remember of what I said?*
Everyone hates me.	*That is a terrible feeling, isn't it? (Pause)* *Let's talk about how to get you involved. Who would you like to play with at recess?*
(Head down on desk)	*It looks like you might be stuck. Let me help.*
(Walking out of class)	*Hey. It looks like you need a break. Stay close, please, and give me a minute to get everyone working on a problem. Then, we can talk about what you need.*

students and the needs-based responses their teachers used because they de-coded the message of the bid.

If these responses are judged by you or some of your colleagues as too nice or reinforcing, let us offer a bit more clarity. We certainly do not want students to speak rudely or to walk out of class in order to gain our attention. When a student bids for attention, they are almost always asking for something else—something they may not know how to express or may not be comfortable expressing. We should always ask ourselves, *Now that they have our attention, what are they needing us to do with or for them?* When we do this, we are able to respond to the underlying need, which is the first step toward meeting that need. After you have connected with the student by being responsive to his or her need, you can offer a better way to communicate the need in the future. *Tonya, next time you feel like walking out, could you give me some sort of signal, so I know you really need to talk? I can't always stop immediately but I promise I will find time for you as soon as possible if you use that signal. What might that signal be?* This is a place where the teaching of regulation skills, discussed in Chapter 9, comes into play.

The more we understand about trauma and student needs, the more we see that often, a student's words or actions that seem intended to push us away are actually the student's best attempt to pull us closer, to have us be present to support them.

> *Classroom management is not about having the right rules FOR kids . . . it's about having the right relationships WITH kids.*
>
> —Danny Steele (2017, para. 5)

Being Honest

We all have found ourselves having to say difficult, honest things to students—*Yes, I will have to tell someone that you said you are thinking of hurting yourself. This is not yet an area of strength for you. I can't fix this for you, we can only do this if you do it with me.* But our students, especially those who have not been able to trust adults, need to hear the truth from us. We do not need to be brutal about it, but we need to not sugar-coat it either, and we can always offer ways we can help. We can and should always leave the door open for hope.

Honesty is also about having our body language match what we are saying with our words. Are we congruent? Do we mean what we say? Will the student see that we mean our words completely or will they be confused?

Positioning

Students whose brains are on hyper-alert are more sensitive to physical positions. When we stand over them, it feels threatening. When we interact by being at the same physical level or even slightly below their level, the amygdala can relax, and we can connect better. This position also communicates that we trust them and that we are *really* present with them. Consider also how you approach a child. Fast is more frightening, slow is more calming, lots of motion is more alerting, and open-body posture and little movement are more settling.

Showing Respect

When we respect students and treat them as we wish to be treated, students are more likely to respect us. For some students of trauma, learning to respect us may be a long journey. Every time we show them respect, we are one step further down that path. Feeling respected is essential for developing a sense of empathy for others. In the book *Kids Who Outwit Adults*, an incarcerated young man, Marty, articulates this with aching precision, "It is not easy to feel somebody else's pain when your own pain has taught you not to feel anything. It is not easy to feel compassion for another when so few have felt it for you" (Seita & Brendtro, 2005, p. 26). It has to start with us, with our clearly evidenced compassion for our students.

Protecting Privacy

We protect relationships with our students when we are positive publicly and redirect privately. We also protect it when we deal with personal information privately and when we understand that the concept of what is personal should be defined rather broadly. We observed one educator loudly share to another educator how a student came to school without warm clothes, and we found ourselves cringing right along with the student. That was very personal, as are other topics such as grades, eating habits, relationships, personal habits, friendships, and more. How do we know what information belongs only in the private arena? A great test is imagining how we might feel if someone said the same type of thing in front of a group of our colleagues, some of whom we are close to and some of whom we are not. If it would not be comfortable for us, then we should keep it private for the student.

Here is the harder thing to get our heads around—for some students who are learning to trust, even positive things may need to be more private than public. Although we may think positive things will feel positive, that is not always the case. Pay attention to how a student responds to positive statements and adjust accordingly. For students who seem uncomfortable with positives, consider the power of little gestures.

Utilizing Little Gestures

A kind touch, a smile, a nod, the affectionate use of a name, greetings, farewells, and words of appreciation—*Thank you!*—all work to build connection. When we know little things about students and become familiar with their interests, we show we care. Sometimes, it is one grain of sand at a time, but these gestures accumulate and shape the relationship.

Have you ever had someone smile at you and it stays with you for the rest of the day? Or have someone pick up something you have dropped and hand it to you, and you feel your spirit lighten? Little kindnesses have the advantage of feeling more genuine; they fly under the defensive radar of the child of trauma. They do not trigger the *What do they want from me?* response.

All of these things may seem common, and perhaps they are what you seek to do every day for all your students. So, what do you do *differently* for students of trauma when it comes to building relationship? Trauma-informed relationship-building means doing common things with uncommon dedication. It also means persisting when you get no response, and even when you get a negative response. Persisting when challenging behavior is the lead story of every day's news. Persisting when many of your students struggle. Persisting when you are weary, when it would be so easy to just not do that little gesture but you summon the energy to do it anyway. Persisting because you know in your core that it is phenomenally important to be relentlessly kind.

It is worth repeating: *Trauma-informed relationship-building means doing common things with uncommon dedication.*

System-Level Supports for Adult-to-Student Relationships

At the school level, we can build structures that support relationships. We can have school counselors follow a cohort of students across their years at a particular school, we can loop from one grade to another, we can assign mentors or run advisory groups. Because it often takes longer for students of trauma to develop trusting relationships with adults, finding ways to create continuity of relationship across the years is extremely valuable.

Often though, we may not have the gift of years with students, so we need to look to other ways to develop relationship. Administrative support for structures such as Responsive Classroom's Morning Meeting or restorative practice's circles allows teachers to enter into more meaningful, holistic relationships with students. Honoring and encouraging activities that allow for ongoing relationship-building assures that students who move into classrooms at various point throughout the year have the same opportunity to connect as the students who began their school year in the classroom.

Principals also support connection when they get coverage for a class, so that the teacher who best knows the student can deal with a difficult situation with that student. Whether that difficulty is because of a student's challenging behavior or because he child is struggling with a personal situation, having a trusted adult involved generally makes the situation better, and it supports the adult-student relationship to become closer.

Nurturing Student-to-Student Relationships

Although building an adult-student relationship is challenging, you have control over one of the parties—yourself. As an adult, you are a (mostly) predictable responder.

As we move into developing positive student-to-student relationships, our influence is more tangential, and the variables increase exponentially. Although that may make it feel daunting, coaching relationships is an essential part of schools. As educators, we are a whole lot better at this than the general population. Still, we must continue to learn more about how to succeed in helping our students build connections with one another.

Modeling   One of our most powerful tools in this process of connecting students with students is the model we provide as we interact with our students. Time and again, we have been impressed by how students related to a peer who manifested severe behavior issues. *How can such young children be so wise? How can these usually prickly pre-adolescents be so tolerant?* we asked ourselves. Then we see their teachers and we know exactly how. We see respect and calm and tolerance in limit-setting, redirecting, intervening. We see positivity and high expectations and encouragement. And, we see these things demonstrated toward every student, even those presenting with the greatest difficulties.

We were once watching a teacher whose student was among the most unpredictably aggressive children we had witnessed, and that teacher's calm strength never broke in front of her students. There were times after incidents, in the privacy and safety of the principal's office, that that teacher shared how tired she was, how concerned she was that nothing seemed to be working but, in front of the students, no one ever would have known she held any doubts.

She embodied Ginott's (1972) notion that the teacher is the weather-maker in the classroom. As a result, the disruption and unsettling of her whole class was minimized, and her other students routinely showed kindness and connection to the aggressive student. *Were they sometimes afraid of their aggressive peer? Of course. Were the unexpected outbursts disruptive to their learning?* Absolutely. *Were other children set off by that one child?* Without a doubt. Nothing by itself solves everything, but some very intentional decisions can be powerful mitigating factors. This classroom was profoundly shaped by the teacher's lead and everyone was better for it.

> *The more healthy relationships a child has, the more likely he will be to recover from trauma and thrive. Relationships are the agents of change and the most powerful therapy is human love.*
>
> —Bruce Perry (Perry & Szalavitz 2006, p. 258)

Reinforcing Connections   Beyond this very important adult model, there certainly are more ways to nurture positive relationships among students. We can be cautious about how we use competition. We can consider how things like sharing can become a challenge and create distance between students rather than create connection. We can deliberately tune into existing relationship because, although peer relationships may be a struggle, most students will have some peers with whom they prefer to engage. We focus on and support these existing relationships by having the student complete a connections chart, guided by an adult. The approach is more likely to reveal true heart connections rather than a typical sociogram, which may document more transactional relationships.

Figure 8.2 provides guidance in how to complete a connection chart with a student. The adult should phrase the descriptor of each ring into age-appropriate and casual language.

Guidelines for Creating Student Connections Chart

The process for creating a student connections chart allows students to reflect on their social world and how it feels to them. An adult sits with the student, and together they reflect on the student's perceived connections. Some kids may like to draw the circles and write the names down themselves. Others may need more help. This is an opportunity to reinforce and potentially illuminate connections for both parties. Adults may incorporate this information into their work with students.

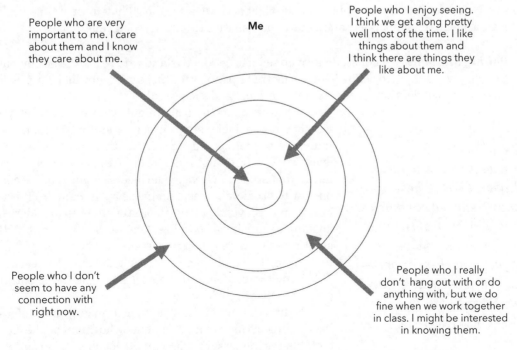

Figure 8.2. Circles of connection are a visual illustration of a student's perception of his or her social world.

Instead of having a prepared form, drawing the circles on a blank piece of paper with the student reinforces the relaxed, organic feeling that best serves the discussion. In identifying people, the adult should encourage the student to think about the student's peers and people who may be younger or older. Come back to this perhaps a couple of times in the year, using a different colored pencil or marker each time the chart is visited.

It is important that the adult who is guiding this process have a comfortable, warm relationship with the student. Because this requires individualized time with the student in a more private context, sometimes having an adult other than the student's teacher lead this discussion may make more sense—perhaps look to school counselors, psychologists, or other school-based mental health professionals for fulfilling this role.

Creating Opportunities   Structures such as community-building classroom meetings are obvious ways of developing relationships. Within those meetings, students can learn about each other and find common ground, practice social skills under the guidance of an adult, and bond through laughter, synchronicity of movement, and shared experience. The interactions tend to be brief and relatively low risk, such as a simple greeting or participating in a song together.

Certain cooperative learning structures (Johnson, Johnson, & Holubec, 2008) also facilitate brief interactions. For example, with an inside-outside circle, a group of students are arranged in two concentric circles. Pairs (one from each circle) ask and answer questions, and then the circle rotates to pair new partners. This practice allows students to have a short interaction with one other student, and then move on to other short interactions. The adult structures the responses, reducing the social demands, and yet giving lots of interactive experiences that lay the foundation for friendships. Similar structures include Slide-the-Line and Mix and Freeze, both of which allow for interactions that are brief and guided. Additional information regarding these structures can be found in the resources at the end of this section.

When using small groupings, partners tend to be socially less stressful than triads. Groups of four or five also tend to be easier than triads, in which it is extremely easy to leave one person out. Using cooperative groupings for the right activities, for the right length of time, and at the right time in the school year allows us to be sensitive to various social challenges.

Pairing Students   For students who seem to be social islands, there may be no obvious relationship with which to begin. When selecting a partner for these students, look for predictable positive responders and keep interactions short and successful.

No doctor can write a prescription for friendship and love: These are complex and hard-earned capacities. You don't need a history of trauma to feel self-conscious and even panicked at a party with strangers—but trauma can turn the whole world into a gathering of aliens.

—Bessel van der Kolk (2014, p. 79)

When students struggle mightily with relationship skills, we should consider using ourselves and other highly skilled individuals, such as older peers, as their partner when doing dyad work. Adults and older peers can respond more consistently to a student. (*Note*: Older peers might require coaching on how to predictably respond in the right manner.) It is important to move beyond partnering a student with an older child or an adult as quickly as possible. One teacher we knew faded the adult role this way: 1) starting as the child's partner; 2) moving to a triad: the child, another student, and the teacher; and 3) leaving the students to themselves as partners, with initial closer monitoring, of course.

To find the right initial partner from within the classroom itself, think of three to four students who might be the most predictable responders (or who can be coached to do so). Partner those students with children needing more support when dyads are required. When a relationship is working, it is tempting to let it continue, but care needs to be taken to rotate partners rather than have the student connect with only one supporter. This helps to not only prevent supporter burn-out but also builds a larger social circle for the student with a trauma history.

Recovering From Difficult Moments

When I was a parent of young children, I developed the ability to stay calm during all those falls and bumps that happen during the toddler years. My toddler would fall, and I would keep my voice even and compassionately check in with her, gently lifting her up and comforting her. My calmness did not escalate the situation, and it allowed me to assess just how serious the hurt was because I had not contributed to her upset.

As a grandparent of toddlers, I find myself gasping and rushing in to pick them up, my every sound and move expressing a panic that they then reflect back to me. I realize that I need to re-find my parent Zen or we all will experience unnecessary stress.

It is a reality that sometimes the acting-out behaviors shown by some students with trauma is unnerving to their peers, particularly when it becomes aggressive or verbally hurtful in nature. We need to first regulate ourselves before we can be of help to our students. Finding our teacher Zen is something many of us must do very deliberately. The first step is taking care of ourselves as a routine practice—well before the moments of increased stress in our classrooms. When we figure out how to control our own dysregulation, we can better assess how upset the other students are, and we do not stress-share with our students.

Beyond that initial teacher Zen skill, we need a plan that we mentally practice before a difficult moment occurs. Part of that plan is having a few go-to lines that signal to students your awareness of the situation, as well as a sense of calmness. For example, you might say *Check-in moment. Any supports needed?* or *Pause. I need everyone to take a seat,* or *Let's do a pause, friends,* or *Eyes here, please.* The line should be designed to pause the actions, to have all students pay attention to you, while it also creates a safer environment without showing any alarm. It may be a way to address a behavior of concern without pointing out a single student or small group of students.

After that initial response, *how* we talk about that behavior is so critical if we are to preserve a student's existing relationships and keep the door open for new ones. How do we talk to a student who is being verbally or physically aggressive in front of the other students? We need to talk calmly and minimally, if possible, targeting the positive behaviors we want to see rather than focusing on the problem behaviors (which would only serve to shine a light on them and cause more anxiety).

If the student leaves the room or is removed from the room, how should we conduct ourselves after that removal? We need to provide the right dose of concern and provide ways the other students can calm themselves and then get back to work. Although our gut might lead us to call the class into a circle and discuss what happened, the time right after an incident is not when students are most capable of generating great ideas. They also need to not be sitting; they need to move. Finding the right balance between some level of processing, addressing the issue, and returning to learning is a tricky undertaking—no one can hand you a precise answer. Our one caution is to not dwell on the event excessively, which can inadvertently cause even more stress to everyone.

It is difficult to give an actual script for such situations because of the unique nature of these incidents (e.g., student age, time of year, proportion of other students who struggle, students' relationship with the child who was aggressive). Consider the ideas that follow as models and not an end-all-and-be-all. You will need to shape your response so it fits you, the issue that occurs, and your students. The big *do not do* in processing is to not slip and share personal information about the student.

What follows is a process we have used for recovering from difficult moments. The process is similar to the one we shared at the end of Chapter 5, but it is slightly more condensed.

1. Talk about what everyone sees. *That was disruptive and upsetting, and I know there is a bit of mess in the room right now.*

2. Express words of caring about the aggressive student. *I am worried about Ben. People sometimes act that way when they are hurting.*

3. Move to teaching a quick coping strategy. *Okay, if you want to take a walking lap around the classroom or shake it off, this is your moment. If anyone wants to join me in picking up a couple things and returning them to their spots, that would be great.*

4. Encourage a return to thinking through a fun question or activity. *By the time you are back in your seat, come up with a number between 1 and 20.* The act of arousing their curiosity as they burn off their stress chemicals may help them return to their thinking brain.

5. Get them actively focused on a simple task. *Write your number down.* Wait, and then ask the students you notice who are most dysregulated by the event to collect the numbers.

6. Complete the activity. *Now, let's see what number was the one most frequently picked.*

Repeated incidents of the same nature from the same student can be dealt with more expeditiously. We can always do a quick, *Whew, tough moments there. We will get Ben back into the flow of things when he is back with us. Feel free to shake it off for a minute, then we will take up where we left off. I am trusting all of you to continue to be respectful, responsible, and safe students, even at these tough times.*

Another option for repeated behaviors is to let students know in advance that they have your permission to move their bodies for a minute or so after an incident to get back to calm while you do an academic activity that is low-intensity (e.g., *Okay, turn to a partner and remind each other what we were discussing.* Table 8.3 is a quick-reference of steps to follow in both novel and repeated situations.)

Proactively, if there has been a pattern of behavior, we can follow an incident with a reminder of what students are supposed to do when the problem is occurring. We can also provide positive feedback for how the students completed their jobs. *I noticed you all did your best to keep on working and let the adults handle things. Thank you.*

When we have institutionalized ways of discussing concerning behaviors and structures, such as in problem-solving meetings, this work may be easier because students will have learned to talk respectfully about challenges. We can use these meetings proactively to explore how to react, as well as ways to find an empathetic position. (*What should we do if . . . ,*

Table 8.3. Quick-reference steps: Recovering from a difficult moment

Novel experience	Repeated incidents
1. Identify what everyone has observed and the sense of dysregulation to be addressed.	1. Acknowledge dysregulation.
2. Express words of caring for a challenging student.	2. Shake it off.
3. Engage in a quick coping strategy.	3. Back to work.
4. Encourage a return to thinking.	4. Remind of expectations.
5. Get back to routine.	

How would you want to be treated on your worst day?) Then, we can use these suggestions to generate real solutions for the situation. (*What did you notice that helped the situation? How can we remember to do those things?*) In any of these situations, we need to show utmost care and concern for students who struggle while respecting their privacy. Talking about general situations proactively helps to set the stage for more successful reactive conversations. (e.g., *Remember when we made our list of what to do if someone is having a hard day? Let's check it and see how we did.*)

Finally, if you are a classroom teacher, remember to resource other professionals in the school whose training and career has prepared them for this kind of work. Trauma-informed educators know that this hard work is best done in collaboration with others.

Building Social Value

One of the struggles I had when working with students with emotional challenges was helping them become more genuinely connected and supportive of one another. I sought to build relationships among them through a variety of ways, but it was clear that some students were not connected with others.

We had a daily snack during which one of my students would have the job of passing out the napkins before I passed out the snacks. One day during snack time, I had an epiphany. Why not flip the jobs? What if I handed out the napkins—which quite frankly weren't a high-value item to elementary-age children—and their peers were the ones handing out the snack—the higher-value item? This required more organization on my part (purchase of small culinary gloves, portioning out snack into individual cups) but the results were well worth it. Students got to show graciousness to their peers as they handed out the snack, and the receivers got to show appreciation to their peer. Questions such as, "What is the snack today?" were answered with, "Check with Jaylen, he is snack-giver today."

My next step was to have two students dispense the snack as a team (one napkin-giver and one snack-giver), practicing cooperation and being seen as the snack team. Although this didn't change everything about their relationships, it did begin to connect my students better, and it opened the door for new relationships. Baby steps.

Children with trauma histories may be a bit pricklier with their peers, so they are at greater risk of being lonely. Educators can raise the value of a student by giving them high-value tasks (e.g., encourager during a group task, opportunity to call for a class mini-break, opportunity to be snack-giver). By pairing a student with a positive experience, that student has a positive association that may help him or her develop relationships with his or her peers.

Some educators have created a classroom book which is developed through the teacher working with each of the students to identify a strength or powerful interest unique to them. A document is created, in which students can look up who might have a certain type of knowledge or skill. Teachers can coach students who don't have strong peer connections to pick something that is a frequent need or something that is very interesting, that draws other children to them. This is like taking the "Ask three before me" structure to another level.

Other educators have used technology to connect students by having a classroom page, on which the teacher posts interests, pictures, and positive stories about their students, which generates interest in each other (e.g., *Zion has a new brother! Think about a question you can ask him about this! Did you know that Diedre and Yvonne both have pet snakes? Here are pictures they have drawn of them. See if you can discover who in this class has lived in a different country.*) A classroom page also can be used for reporting commonalities or positive statistics about the class (e.g., *Did you know that 100% of our class finds hibernation interesting? Check out this bar graph; what are you noticing about our class? I will be asking for your observations in our next community meeting!*).

Connecting Through Service

When you hear the word *service,* do canned food drives and clean-up projects come to mind? When we talk about creating opportunities for service in this context, we are talking about finding simple ways to help one another on a daily basis (e.g., *Cameron, can you please bring me that chair? Jazmin, could you go get Edward the microscope from the top shelf?*). Building positive interactions through small courtesies is a powerful strategy. Explicit instruction in handling courtesies and modeling kind asking and grateful receiving help launch this practice successfully. In a world that emphasizes independence, we build relationships by finding ways to practice the profound joy of interdependence.

At the elementary school level, we often have the foundation for this through class jobs. Pause at some point in the week to notice the helpfulness of the person doing their job (e.g., *How about if we take a minute, look at how all the scraps of paper have been picked up off the floor, and give a quick thank-you to Lonnie for helping our room stay so nice looking.*). One job can even be the job of noticing the hard work of others who are performing jobs!

At the middle school level, we find our moments for service in more spontaneous opportunities (e.g., *Mark, can you give us a beat as we review the vocabulary? Freida and Ana, while we are taking a quick break, can you two set up the desks for group work?*). With older students, it often is easier to find ways for students to be of service to us, but we also need to continue to find ways for our students to help one another.

Why is this idea of service so very important for children with trauma histories? It accomplishes many things through one strategy. The social value of a student who is doing a kindness and who is then thanked increases. Their name is being used in a positive way. It helps bond one student to another. (*Note*: Research shows that we like people who do favors for us, but we *really* like people for whom we do favors.) Perhaps, most importantly, it completes the circle of connection for the student with trauma.

What is the circle of connection? Children of trauma often are the recipients of caring and support—including from their peers. For any of us, care and support does feel good but, it also has a degree of vulnerability to it. When we are able to accept that care and support, it is a sign that we have come to trust the genuine intentions of the people who are giving it to us. Figure 8.3 reflects this type of social connection being made with a child with a trauma history. Being able to accept good intentions is foundational for developing authentic relationships.

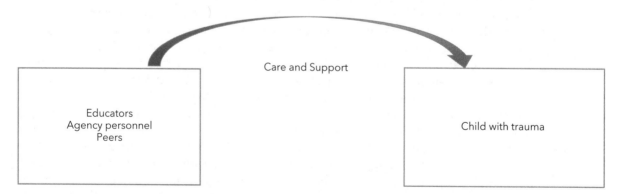

Figure 8.3. Circle of connection: the first half. There are two components of social connection. Being open to receiving care and support from others is one half of the circle. Children of trauma often receive care and support from others, including educators, peers, and agency personnel.

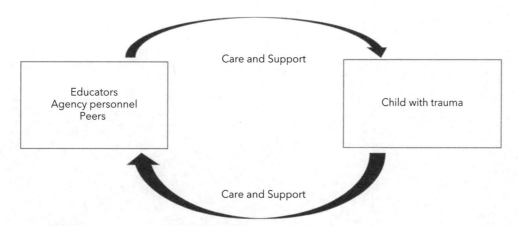

Figure 8.4. Circle of connection: completing the circle. Being able to provide care and support for others completes the circle of connection. In having the full circle, students can feel needed, valued, and capable.

However, when we are *only* the recipients of care and support, we are missing the other half of the circle of connection and the opportunities that come with that. When we create situations where students of trauma can be the givers of care and support to others (even in the smallest of ways) we allow them to experience being trusted by other people, to experience trustworthiness. Trustworthiness increases our sense of value and purpose in ways that being a recipient of good things never can. It completes our connection with others in our world, a full circle of connection as seen in Figure 8.4.

In the next chapter, we will learn more about teaching behavior regulation skills and how to integrate those opportunities across the whole of the school day.

Chapter 9

Building Regulation Skills

... it is only by being regulated that a child develops the ability to self-regulate.
—Stuart Shanker (2016, p. 183)

Finding opportunities and methods for teaching regulation and providing regulation skills practice throughout the school day is essential. We have found that if we teach regulation skills robustly, we are able to dial back the intensity of implementing other practices, such as structured feedback systems and individual behavior support plans. When universal practices are effective, the need for advanced-tier supports decreases. The regulation skills that are described in this chapter complement or support the efforts of the Re-Set Process. Regulation instruction also can be implemented at the school or classroom level in a less formal capacity.

Nurturing regulation skills benefits all students and can be addressed at the Tier 1/universal level in schools. Because dysregulation lies at the root of so many issues for children of trauma, regulation skills can and should be addressed at advanced levels and in more individualized supports.

REGULATION DEFINED

In Chapter 2, we conceptualized regulation as the ability to manage one's physical movement, attention, and emotions in order to function successfully in the greater social environment. When children are regulated, they are better able to learn, to interact well with peers, and to respond appropriately to adults.

Regulation is the path to focus and growth. That said, it is important to know that having a well-developed set of regulation skills does not mean getting to a specific single point. Rather, it is learning to regulate within a range between alertness and calmness that allows for the focus that is needed for a specific set of tasks or circumstances.

When a student is *not* regulated, the manifestations of the student's dysregulation can create a downward cycle that could dramatically shape his or her school experience and life, overall. We have seen dysregulated students accidentally hurt others and then be perceived as aggressive, particularly if they also struggle with other social skills. This perception, and the experience of *being in trouble,* begins to shape how the student sees adults and peers and, most importantly, him- or herself. Figure 9.1 shows the potential impact of unaddressed dysregulation. This downward cycle reveals the danger of unresolved regulation issues and their interaction with both intended and unintended consequences. The progression explains how some students get lost in school and are at higher risk for significant negative outcomes. Early intervening by explicitly teaching regulation can make an extraordinary difference in the quality of a child's life, in school and beyond by allowing a student to experience social success, build healthy relationships, and develop a positive sense of self.

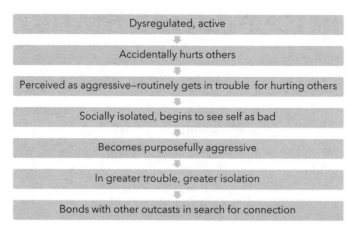

Figure 9.1. Potential life-long impact of dysregulation and traditional disciplinary reactions.

PAUSE AND CONSIDER: When dysregulation is not addressed, it can lead to disproportionate rates of suspension and expulsion—especially for students who typically are considered at-risk. Therefore, explicitly teaching regulation is a form of early intervention. Consider how your school can implement the regulation strategies that are described in this book to mitigate disciplinary challenges.

We know that pervasive trauma during childhood disrupts a child's ability to regulate in the moment and to build calming pathways for future moments. Because learning to regulate is a developmental task, when we say students are dysregulated, we are indicating that their regulation is out of sync with other children of their developmental age.

Children with significant trauma histories may experience difficulties with regulating down (settling) or regulating up (tuning in). We will first consider the need to regulate up. Initiating behavior, becoming alert and engaged, and then participating in activities or tasks can be challenging for some students. When dysregulation has left a student exhausted on the inside, shut down, or even frozen (a nervous system reaction), the regulation strategies we use might have a different tone and order than those we use when students need to settle their systems—as we indicated when discussing the variations of proactive and reactive Re-Set in Chapters 4 and 5.

Regulating up does not mean that we demand jumping jacks or dancing to a video—those strategies would not meet students where they are. Instead, we can invite small movements, maybe just toe wiggles for the count of 3. We also might try to engage the student through curiosity by asking questions like *How many times do you breathe out in 30 seconds?* and then offer, *I'll count mine, too.* We might then move to wiggling fingers for 10 seconds and then pause. We are guiding them to raise their energy step-by-step. Alertness and attention come back online and the nervous system links up with the surrounding circumstances and begins to feel matched rather than mismatched. The goal of regulation is not always to create calm; it can instead be about tuning in, initiating, and re-engaging with the environment.

From this point forward though, we will focus pointedly on the need to settle because it tends to present greater challenges in most school settings. When carryover stress (allostatic load) keeps a student's system on high alert, the student's energy spills over into everything he or she does. Dysregulated students will, more often than not, touch too hard, move too fast, talk too loudly, and shift activity too often.

It is important to recognize that dysregulation is a socially communicable phenomenon. Dysregulated people tend to set off other dysregulated people. With enough frequent and intense occurrences, there is the chance that even regulated children may become dysregulated. This is why we see dysregulation move through our classrooms and other school settings like the wave at a football game and why sometimes, we as adults can get caught up in it ourselves. It also is why deliberate structuring of whole-group regulation opportunities is so critical. Remember that although dysregulation is rooted in trauma, it also is caused by numerous other factors. Therefore, regulation practice is valuable to many, if not all, of our students.

In addition to often being in a high state of arousal, many students with trauma histories also struggle with moving smoothly and logically from one state of arousal and activity to another, a process that is known as state-shifting. The quick, profound shifts that were once self-protective in high-stress conditions become exhausting, distracting, and disruptive to healthy relationships. These shifts prevent the brain from being in a learning state much of the time as the student struggles with matching their arousal state to the current context. Both instruction in modulation and cognitively connecting behaviors with specific social contexts are essential for children to learn how to state-shift appropriately.

Do children with trauma ever learn to settle without our guidance? We will answer that question in a bit of a long way around. Think about a time when you experienced a rapid surge in stress energy. Maybe it was a close call when driving, perhaps it was a time you stepped off the curb only to see that you had failed to see a turning car, or maybe it was when you slipped going down an icy set of stairs. Remember that heart-pounding feeling, the whirring in your head that followed? Imagine that your body feels this way often, and without notice or cause. This prolonged discomfort will lead traumatized students to subconsciously search for ways to settle themselves. In the process, they may stumble onto healthy ways to settle, but they also may encounter unusual, age-inappropriate, or unhealthy ways of managing that feeling of discomfort. We see this in students who pluck out their hair strand by strand, ones who rub holes in their pants, and others who obsessively smoke marijuana—all in a desperate attempt to calm their bodies from the allostatic load they carry. In *Lost Boys*, a book focused on understanding boys with significant trauma histories, author James Garbarino (1999) shares the story of a 16-year-old boy who was stabbed in the chest. As the young man was relating the incident to his therapist, he claimed that he was not afraid of anything, and then he began to rock in his chair and suck his thumb. He may have been denying fear, but his body was reliving it and desperately attempting to cope with it.

Some students search for ways to settle but instead find ways to tire themselves out. They run around a room and bounce off walls until they can bounce no more. They are no longer active but, as we discuss in Chapter 6, they are in fact more dysregulated than before, which means that when the exhaustion abates, the chaos returns. Effective regulation guidance is how we help students become aware of their dysregulation and develop effective, healthy ways to bring their nervous systems to a state of calm. It affects the here and now as well as the future.

When we effectively support a student to regulate, we do several things:

1. We help settle their system so that they know what a settled system feels like. Think of a time you were developing a physical skill, such as flipping a pancake or shooting a free-throw. Remember when you finally got it down? You developed muscle memory for the task and could repeat that skill over and over with a high rate of accuracy. When you missed, you probably even realized that you were going to miss, well before you got the visual feedback of the pancake hitting the edge of the skillet or the basketball bouncing off the rim. Your mind registered early on that you were *off*. To know when you are *off your game* (dysregulated), you must know what it feels like to be *on your game* (regulated). Experiences of settling, time after time, develop pathways in the brain—what we equate to *muscle memory*. When students know what regulation feels like, their brains are learning to get to that state more quickly and easily.

2. We help students find a neurological state that results in them being more integrated into the *positive* interactions of the classroom. Being successful at sitting next to someone without annoying them, being able to offer a correct answer when your name is called and being able to play a game without losing your temper are all highly positive experiences. Those successes create a calming response. When students engage in a challenging but doable task and succeed, when they have positive social interactions, **dopamine** (the happy and calming chemical) is released into their brains. Their efforts are positively reinforced at both a social level and physiological level.

3. We affect all our students, because the more regulated students there are in the classroom, the more regulated the class is as a whole. The more regulated the class is as a whole, the more positive interactions occur, and the more learning opportunities are maximized.

Notes From the Field

Because the process of regulating is often nebulous, subjective, and difficult to quantify, I wanted to make it more concrete for the students I supported, and for myself. Steve Graner, program director of Bruce Perry's neurosequential model of education, taught me that we can quantify regulation through the use of pulse oximeters. We decided to utilize these pulse oximeters for heart rate monitoring in a middle school and high school alternative education program. We had students document their heart rates at the beginning of each day, which created a baseline rate for each student. Students would then check their heart rates at the time of a disciplinary referral or a request for a calming break (either by them or by an adult) and compare the result to their baseline. Students would then engage in regulating activities and recheck their heart rate. We found that linking heart rate tracking with body awareness exercises increased students' understanding of the power of regulation and allowed them to understand more fully what helped them regulate successfully.

Secondary Educator, Neurosequential Model in Education Trainer

ADULTS AS MODELS OF REGULATION

As educators, we are ongoing regulation models for our students. We have an impact on our students' regulation status through the processes of co-regulation (explained more below), voiced modeling, regulating experiences, and modulation opportunities. By seizing the mantle of lead regulator, we are positioned to be more deliberate in our efforts to support student regulation.

Co-Regulation

Co-regulation occurs when an adult provides an intentional model of a regulated state so that a child can regulate in tandem with them. Seeing an adult regulating helps set the child's status. Access to regulated adults and the resultant experience of co-regulation is pivotal to a child's success in learning how to regulate. Co-regulation helps a child to "understand, express, and modulate their thoughts, feelings, and behaviors" (Rosanbalm & Murray, 2017, p. 1). A co-regulating adult can provide three categories of support:

1. Development of a responsive, caring, and warm relationship.

2. Structuring the environment for physical and emotional safety.

3. Teaching regulation skills (Rosanbalm & Murray, 2017).

We addressed the first two categories in Chapter 8, so now we turn to the adult's role in the teaching of regulation skills. Before we discuss any formalized instruction of skills, we need to consider the teachers and adults themselves. Teaching regulation begins with who we are and what we bring to all interactions with our students. It is about our state of regulation when we greet children, when we deal with minor frustrations, and when we handle crises.

Dr. Nicholas Long, founder of the Life Space Crisis Intervention (LSCI) Institute, which focuses on strength-based approaches to working with children and youth, uses the analogy of a thermostat to suggest our role in supporting students' emotional and physical regulation. Dr. Long says that, as professionals working with traumatized youth, we need to be the thermostat that sets the temperature rather than the thermometer that merely reads it (Seita & Brendtro, 2005). Setting the temperature begins with reading and then managing our own temperature.

We need to consider these questions: What type of nervous system do we bring to our classrooms? How do we check ourselves? Are we open to feedback from our colleagues regarding our regulation status? How do others support us when we are not well-regulated?

Developing a trauma-informed lens is an essential element for arriving at and maintaining a regulated state. When we know that we should not take student behavior personally and when we attribute behavior to its complex roots instead of to the willfulness of the child or the fault of the family, we are better poised to handle the stresses that are associated with being an educator.

How much co-regulation a student needs from us at any given point depends on how regulated the student is. The more dysregulated the student, the more he or she needs us to be regulated. Of course, there is a challenge inherent in that because the more dysregulated a student is, the more likely we are to be fatigued and, therefore, not be our best-regulated self. And rarely is it only one student who needs us to be his or her co-regulator.

This means we must pay attention to self-care and never pass up the opportunity to engage in regulation activities *with* our students. We should not turn on a video and hustle around the classroom straightening up while the students engage in calming activities. We should breathe with them, move in a pattern with them, listen for the chime with them. This means we need to employ community—the community of students and our colleagues—in order to accomplish all that we need to do. We will discuss these strategies and more in Chapter 11.

Voiced Modeling

Engaging in the meta-cognition process of a think-aloud is a powerful way of illuminating for students the thinking that undergirds regulatory behaviors. *I need to focus before I start this next task, so I am going to take a few quiet breaths and then exhale slowly* connects the why with the how for the students. The added bonus? Modeling a healthy breathing technique provides the adult with an opportunity to self-settle.

We may be comfortable with using this think-aloud strategy when teaching math processes or when reflecting on a piece of writing, but educators have reported to us that it initially feels a little awkward to use this concept with behavioral instruction, that somehow talking about one's own behavior feels more personal. Selecting targeted times to talk about specific behaviors seems to help most people get over the implementation hump (e.g., *I will do a think-aloud right after the first transition of the morning.*).

Regulating Experiences

Consider that the underdeveloped neurological systems of children with pervasive trauma are quite similar to those of young infants whose neurological systems also not fully developed. What do we do with that potent piece of information?

Think of a newborn baby in the first 3 months after birth. The infant's neurological system is immature and extremely dysregulated. This is manifested by sensitivity to noise, easy startling and extreme reactions to being hungry or to needing a diaper change. Now, think about what loving parents do to help that infant remain calm and to reregulate when he or she is upset. We can use those same strategies when we support older children (even tweens and teens), though we need to adjust what we say and do to be developmentally appropriate.

Although science tells us what the human neurological system needs to be quieted and regulated, we also can determine those things for ourselves when we think about what we do for infants. We can see how effective it is to provide certain kinds of supports, we simply need to translate them as appropriate to our role and the child's age. Consider the chart in Figure 9.2. Think about the strategies that people use for settling newborns in relationship to the concepts of pattern and rhythm, pressure and weight, breath, sensory focus, and modulation.

Now, think about what you would *not do* when responding to a distressed infant. Would you even consider that raising your voice at a two-month-old would stop his or her crying? Would you pat an infant in an irregular pattern, stopping and starting erratically, and hope it would be effective in calming them? Would you expect the infant to calm down first before you would change an uncomfortable diaper?

Using our understanding of what calms an infant, we can figure out how to not increase dysregulation. Then, we can apply concepts related to increasing regulation (like breath and weight/pressure) in an age-appropriate way in the classroom.

Brous (2014) reports on research that shows that the five big concepts of breath, sensory focus, weighted pressure, pattern/rhythm, and modulation connect with strategies that have proven to be successful in regulating students with trauma. Researchers in this area support activities such as singing, drumming, walking, trampoline jumping, and other movements that can be integrated into the school setting.

If, when we see behavior issues, we first think *dysregulation*, what might we do? The chart in Table 9.1 helps us consider the developmentally appropriate methods for addressing school-age children's regulation needs in a way that mirrors what we do naturally when responding to infants. One goal of a trauma-informed school is to develop natural default responses to the regulation needs of its students.

One of our favorite calming strategies that was used by a primary teacher was Grandmom's rocking chair. This teacher had a rocker that she had adapted by making a pillow

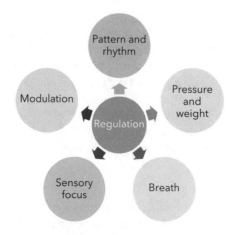

Figure 9.2. Regulation web.

Table 9.1.   Applying infant regulation strategies to school-age children

Strategies for infants	Strategies for school-age children
Check the water before we put them in the bath	Establish a calm climate—classroom or student experience—before you introduce the student who has serious dysregulation issues into it
Rock them	Have students engage in a repetitive, calming movement—rocking, cycling, wall push-ups
Hold them against our chests	Allow students to access a comforting sweatshirt, offer a weighted blanket
Pat them on the back to a rhythm	Drum with them, give a patterned reassuring pat, share a clapping pattern
Play quiet music	Play quiet music Allow headphones, to lessen auditory stimulation
Be attuned to their needs and respond promptly	Be attuned to their needs and respond promptly Teach them how to request support
Keep the lights low	Keep the lights low
Hold them securely as we pass them to others	Take time for transitions, provide warnings, and make sure they are comfortable with who you hand them off to next during the school day
Play nature sounds	Play nature sounds
Swaddle them	Allow clothing that is comforting, allow access to closed spaces that are comforting, have bean-bag seating available

that looked, sort of, like her Grandmom's face. The teacher attached the pillow to the chair where most children's heads would snuggle just under the chin. She made the seat cushion very deep and cozy like Grandmom's lap and made soft arms that could be pulled around anyone who was seated in the chair. The teacher told her students that when she was a little girl and would get frustrated, sad, or angry, she knew she could climb into her grandmother's lap and Grandmom would rock her until she was calm. She shared that she loved it so much that she wanted to bring that feeling to her class, so she made the rocker to be a little like her Grandmom. She told her students that when they were hurt or angry or just did not know what they were feeling, they could go sit in Grandmom's lap and rock. They could pull her arms around them if they wanted. They could sit still or rock, whichever felt good to them. Children could elect to go for some Grandmom time whenever they needed it. Children who were engaging in problematic behaviors were asked with great sincerity, "Do you need some time rocking with Grandmom?" Instead of being scolded or punished, the students were comforted.

What is the parallel for a middle schooler? Perhaps a bean-bag chair, a set of headphones with calming music, and a weighted blanket at Step 0 in the Re-Set Room. What is the parallel for you?

Most often, regulating experiences do not require lengthy periods of time. More frequent, brief opportunities are preferred over less frequent and longer options. Think of a plane that is heading to a destination—we want frequent corrections to the course rather than one major correction after it has been off-course for a prolonged period of time. Shorter more frequent opportunities for course-correction prevent problems and also allow students to avoid the experience of being dysregulated for longer periods of time. When we course-correct frequently, the body experiences a greater length of time within reasonable proximity to calm. This becomes, over time, the student's *new normal*.

Modulation

Not only do many students need support in finding a regulation status that allows them to function optimally, they need to learn the skill of smoothly shifting from one state to another—modulation. In our classrooms and other school environments, we can create conditions that invite the practice of modulation. We can think of modulation in a variety of ways; it is the journey between fast and slow, between loud and quiet, between large and small, between quick thinking and contemplation, and between open-ended activity and focused or predetermined activity. When we support students through a modulated process, not only do we avoid startling their neurological systems, but we simultaneously teach their brains and bodies how to modulate.

Think about a scenario in which students are to come in from lunch, sit down, get out their materials, and listen to information that is presented by the teacher. Students with regulated systems are able to quickly state-shift to match the demand because they have started from a comparatively calmer state and their body knows how to rapidly settle down. Students with dysregulated systems are more likely to come in, try to sit down, and then be up on their feet, wandering around, talking to peers, asking to go to the bathroom, and doing other things that may be considered disruptive.

Instead, what if students came in to the classroom and the expectation was for them to do a minute of partner talk on a posted topic while still on their feet, and then shift to writing down their ideas, either while standing or sitting (their choice), then taking their seat and doing a whole-group, 30-second breathing exercise before the teacher would begin to present information. This modulated approach is much more likely to result in academic engagement, and it helps the dysregulated student learn how a settling process feels. This experience is so important for children with trauma histories, but it also can be incredibly effective for all students during rapid-growth developmental phases.

There are myriad opportunities to structure modulation in the classroom. Quick sketching versus careful drawing, playing an instrument loudly and then quietly, doing a rough first draft versus carefully writing and editing a piece, talking in a whisper and then projecting to give an answer are all examples of modulation opportunities we provide.

Modulation experiences are not only the purview of the classroom. Some schools with whom we have worked have built modulation into schoolwide routines, such as when students are lining up from recess (e.g., a series of calmer and calmer movement routines while in line and before entering the building), when entering the building at the beginning of the day (e.g., playing faster music at the beginning of the transition, and then moving to slower-pace music as the time to be in class approaches), and when settling into an assembly (e.g., conducting a call and response that becomes quieter and quieter).

Some of these experiences are ones that students can simply *feel*, but other times, we want to explicitly raise a student's awareness of when he or she needs to modulate and what methods he or she may use.

WHOLE-CLASS REGULATION OPPORTUNITIES

Because regulation is a skill that all students need, guiding whole-class activities is an efficient and effective way to have students practice the skill.

Mindfulness

Mindful practices and mindful movement have become well-known calming and regulating whole-group activities. As long as the practices and movements being used are trauma-informed, these mindfulness-based lessons and breaks can be universal and enjoyable. It is important to recognize that trauma may change how a student reacts to mindfulness opportunities. Stillness, a heightened awareness of self, balancing, focusing on or adjusting breathing, and trying to rest while in a group of peers can all be potentially unsettling or even triggering for some students. Any educator leading these practices must be tuned into this possibility.

Before implementing any mindfulness practice, educators first need to become experienced with the practices, which will allow for proper modeling and smooth guidance. They need to be comfortable in any practice they lead. If they experience discomfort when engaging in a practice, they need to stop. They may set it aside to practice more personally until their comfort level shifts, or they may set it aside completely. The same is true when working with students. It is important that the leader take time to notice students' responses and cues of discomfort and adjust accordingly. Comfort and safety *always* come first. Mindfulness is not about pushing limits, breaking boundaries, or getting out of a comfort zone, either for the adults *or* for the students.

In rolling out mindfulness, educators should concentrate first on activities that are the safer defaults. Remember in Chapter 8, our warning about quiet often being a trigger for some students with trauma? Avoid completely quiet activities. Consider movements through a lens of vulnerability and pick positions and exercises that are emotionally safer. Avoid being on the floor or any bending over positions—keep students at their seats, on their feet and upright, and always offer choice.

In addition, you can always privately poll your students to see whether there are any movements or activities that make them feel uncomfortable or unsafe. We have used small slips of paper on which a student can circle a face from a choice of three (happy, okay, uncomfortable) and turn them in for a private, anonymous review of certain movements or activities.

As you work with students—whether whole-class or small-group—consider developing a mindfulness wheel of activities that take less than 2 minutes to complete. Figure 9.3 is an example of this kind of wheel. Remember as you implement that it is more important to have a small assortment of options instead of a huge array. As adults, we may get bored with the routine, but we need to remember that a traumatized brain is more likely to be comforted by the routine of completing many small familiar activities frequently. Just like a young child whose brain is developing connections craves the same bedtime story night after night after night, a child whose brain is in need of settling longs for familiarity and repetition of activities. Using a spinner also can help build students' resiliency by gently creating tolerance of the unknown. The spinner creates a small unknown (*Which activity will we do?*) in the context of more knowns (all the activities are familiar).

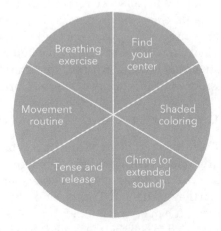

Figure 9.3. Mindfulness wheel.

Music

We can strategically use music to settle or energize students. Eric Jensen (n.d.), in his article *The Perfect Music for Brain-Based Learning*, makes the following associations between beats per minute and a calm-energized balance.

35–50 beats per minute: Significantly calming

55–70 beats per minute :   Seatwork

70–100 beats per minute: Energizing

100–160 beats per minute: Highly revved up

Most researchers concur that 60 beats per minute music is ideal for creating a sense of calm focus, and that music without lyrics is best.

One school where we consulted used energizing music to move their students into the building when the doors opened and then shifted to 60 beats per minute as students settled into their classrooms—a morning modulation experience for everyone in the building.

Regulation Tool Caddies

Supplying a collection of regulating tools that are available to everyone in the classroom has proven to be a very effective practice. In the schools in which we work, one of the first advocates for the use of the regulation tools caddy across a building was a speech and language pathologist who was a member of her school's PBIS team. She had seen the way that regulation tools made a difference for the students she saw for therapy—those with trauma, with selective mutism, and those identified as having autism. As she participated in the school's advanced tiers meetings, it became clear to her that there were many students (not on her caseload) who would likely benefit from regulation opportunities. In response to what she saw as a need throughout the school building, she spearheaded the systemic change that was the implementation of regulation caddies in all classrooms and in other adult-led spaces in the school (e.g., school office, therapist's rooms).

PAUSE AND CONSIDER: Who in your building, other than classroom teachers and administrators, may provide leadership in trauma-informed practices? Are you inviting them into this critical discussion?

This early implementer originally called these calming caddies. Later, we began to refer to them as regulation caddies because we realized that many of the tools could also help students who needed to regulate *up*. The process is simple—any student who feels like he or she needs a tool to regulate—either *up* or *down*—can quietly go to the caddy and borrow a tool. The tool supports the student's involvement in learning and is not intended to cause a break from learning. When the student is finished with the tool, the student returns the tool to the caddy. Of course, every classroom will develop its own procedures for using these materials and ways to maintain them.

Here are some of the tools we have seen included in these caddies.

Marble Mazes   These allow students to move a marble in a fabric maze or in a single channel. Two-channel marble mazes are good for both moving the marble and cueing breathing to a breath in and a long breath out. Older students like very small, single channel versions that can be discretely used when they need them. This is one of the most popular tools from both student and teacher perspectives. It can be small and is a quiet, soothing fidget. We have made larger ones for students who tended to rub their legs when anxious, so providing a few different sizes in the caddy is a good idea. Directions for making marble mazes are included in the Section II Resources.

Water Bead Gloves   Made by putting non-toxic water beads in a non-latex culinary glove (size small, good-quality) with a tablespoon of extra water and then tied-off, these are very soothing tools. It is better to not fill to a point of tension—the gloves are more sensory when the beads can move around a bit. Establish procedures for using the gloves or students may be tempted to squeeze and break the beads. Gloves usually will last at least 1–2 months. One student shared that he liked these especially during tests because he felt like someone was holding his hand when he was nervous.

Pipe Cleaners   We have found that students will choose one or two pipe cleaners to wrap around their fingers, around each other, or around a pencil. Some will run them between two fingers. Just like all the tools, we establish procedures for handling them before introducing them in the caddy.

Large Screw and Nut   We start with industrial size screws and nuts, and then glue a second nut to the bottom of the screw so that the nut that is being moved never falls off. The downside to this tool is that when it is dropped, it does make a loud noise. It is such a popular item, however, that we feel it is worth including.

Breathing Cue Cards   A ring of laminated cards that have directions for different kinds of breathing exercises helps students remember how to engage in effective options. Some students like to move through all the different kinds of breathing exercises, in which case, the flip ring becomes a process rather than a set of choices.

Small Movement Cue Cards   Like breathing cue cards, these movement cards on a ring can provide either choices for regulating or a movement sequence for regulating, depending on how a child chooses to use them. When introducing these cards and their contents, you can offer the two ways to use the flip ring.

Small Squishy, Sensory Balls   We greatly prefer these types of balls over stress balls. Squeezing is an activating behavior, not a calming one, and because the majority of students who access the tool caddy require calming, we want tools that are designed to do that. Sensory balls tend to invite many movements other than squeezing—avoiding the activating issue. A bonus is that these sensory balls tend to not roll away when dropped, unlike many types of stress balls.

Thinking Putty   Although very popular, we are not as fond of this option because it tends to get dirty, and it ends up places where it should not. Still, some educators and children like it, so we include it here for your consideration.

Glitter Jars   Again, these are not something we prefer to see in caddies. But some people have found them to be useful, so we include them in this list. Although we love these for use in the Re-Set Process when a student is already away from involvement in learning, we try to have tools in the caddy that allow a child to still be connected to the learning activity. We have found that students tend to get lost in watching the glitter jars, so we would not recommend protracted use. Perhaps a solution would be to have students learn that the glitter jar is a 1-minute activity and provide a 1-minute timer to go with the jar when it is in the caddy.

Commercially Available Fidgets   There are lots of items on the market that are great fiddles, but others—like some of the spinners—do not match the purposes of the caddy. If the fidget requires some movement or finger manipulation, is durable, can be washed, is not easy to eat, does not require intense focus, and is quiet, it probably is worth trying out in your caddy.

Notes From the Field

I offer pipe cleaners as a fidget. They work, and they are inexpensive. Some students I give pipe cleaners to wrap and unwrap them around their pencil or finger. One kindergartner who frequently came into my office dysregulated would use her pipe cleaner, and it helped her to not escalate, as she had previously done. The pipe cleaner also served as a transition object as she would fidget with it and then move into doing her schoolwork. By the time she was done with the schoolwork and ready to return to class, she would just leave the pipe cleaner on the desk, forgetting the value it held minutes before. I also keep nuts and bolts at the ready for students to fiddle with by winding the nut up and down the bolt.

Elementary Special Education Support Teacher

If a classroom has both a regulation caddy and a separate Re-Set Space, it is important to keep caddy materials in the caddy and Re-Set materials in the Re-Set Space—even if it means duplicating materials. This is critical so that students who use the Re-Set Space always have all the necessary tools available to them in that space.

The caddy becomes more effective when used throughout the school building, and when it contains the same regulating items in every location including special area classrooms, the cafeteria, the library, and offices. This allows a dysregulated student who is meeting with the principal, the school counselor, or another support adult to easily access familiar tools— regardless of where the student is at the time.

Notes From the Field

Calming caddies have been a game changer in my school's classrooms. Initially, teachers were hesitant to offer them because of fear that children would misuse them or just play, even when there didn't appear to be a need. However, when introduced, taught, and utilized appropriately, calming caddies are providing opportunities for students to get a needed break without leaving the classroom. Before we used caddies in the classroom, students were being excused from the class, walking to my office, using the tools for 5 minutes, engaging in some kind of conversation with me, and then returning to class. This process was taking at least 10 minutes. Although that does not sound like a lot, 10 minutes multiple times a day—or even 10 minutes in a week—adds up to a lot of missed instructional time. Now, students can remain in the classroom, absorb what the teacher is saying, and self-regulate at the same time. I have noticed a huge reduction in time spent out of the classroom and in my office. Teachers who are using calming caddies as intended are pleased with the effect they are having on individual student behavior, which, of course, affects the entire classroom.

Elementary School Counselor

Modulation Exercises

Modulation exercises can be integrated into the movement that happens routinely in the classroom. We can help students become aware of the different intensities of movement, voices, and thinking through our use of language (e.g., *Let's move back to our tables in slow-motion.*). This can also be built into instructional practice (e.g., *We are going to jot down two quick thoughts following this next passage.* Frequent, short opportunities to experience modulated movement is invaluable (e.g., *We are going to teach our bodies how to rev up and calm down smoothly. Run in place. Slow down to jog. Now, slow-motion jog. Now come to a stop and focus on your breathing, being sure to let out a slow, long breath.*).

These are some activities to specifically practice modulation with the whole class:

- Shaded coloring

- Reverse bowling

- Mirror me

- Modulated exercise sequence

- Make a monster

- Zoom

Descriptors of these activities can be found in the resources in Sections II and III. Opportunities to embed these modulation activities and others include community-building meetings, indoor recess, and brain breaks.

Guided Transitions

Transition cues that guide student state-shifting also can be valuable practices. When we provide a time frame for a transition, and perhaps even some intermediate steps along the way, we teach students how to state-shift from one level of activity to another.

Example A

1. *Time to wrap up your group work. In the next minute, please bring your voice levels down from conversation level to whisper level as you put materials away.*

2. *Now, please bring your voice levels down from whisper to voices off as you do your silent assessment—thumbs up, sideways, or down—of how group work went today.*

3. *Now, 1 minute to gather your personal materials and return to your seat, voices off.*

Example B

1. *We will be heading to lunch in 3 minutes.*

2. *Please put your materials away quickly. I will give you the signal when to move. You have 30 seconds. Voices are off.*

3. *Now walking, Group 1 get in line. Voice level 1 once you are in line, voices off until you are there. Group 2 . . . and so on.*

Notice that, in these examples, students are being guided both in changing their speed in doing a task and also in the level of voice to use. This guidance eases students from one step to the next. For classes that do not require the same depth of coaching, using more global transition signals makes sense (e.g., *You have 5 minutes to wrap things up and get back to your seat, ready for math.*). This guidance allows students to pace themselves. If there is a great deal of rushing at the end, that informs the teacher that students may need more guided practice related to transitioning.

SMALL-GROUP OPPORTUNITIES

Some students require extra doses of regulation practice, and schools have found creative ways to meet these needs. The small-group structure allows one adult to support several students at a time while still providing more guidance than in a whole-class opportunity.

Group Walk and Move

For students who need regulation practice as well as a movement break from the classroom, having an adult pick up students from classes and go on a walk together is a good use of people resources. The walk to gather the students is part of the movement opportunity (tip: begin at the class of the student with the greatest need so that student gets a larger dose of walking). When the whole group is assembled and has done a bit more walking, the group may go through a series of movements that are designed to address regulation. The session can wrap up with sharing an activity or two that can be done in the students' seats upon the return to class.

Schools have scheduled group walks in the morning and afternoon when students tend to be most dysregulated (often following a period of focused instruction). It may not be the absolute ideal time for every individual student in the group, but at least every student can anticipate the opportunity to regulate and know they will have access to it in the not-too-distant future.

Movement Sequence Activity

Several schools we support have their school counselor or another support person running a movement sequence group, with a focus on regulation activities. Because these groups are scheduled, they do not necessarily address issues that are emerging in the classroom, but the groups help build skills to help prevent future issues. These groups act as a bonus dose of practice that may help students develop regulation habits more quickly.

Notes From the Field

I have always been a proponent of having students move. During my guidance classes, I have the kids sing and dance. I also have several yoga groups a year to teach students self-regulation. Then, I heard about the research on how important movement is for de-escalation and self-regulation, especially for children who appear angry. When I realized how important it was to get students to move and how movement rids the body of chemicals like adrenaline and cortisol that could hurt the body over time, I started to use movement more and more. To be honest, the norm was—when a student was fighting or angry—to have the student sit in a time-out and then try to get them to discuss his or her anger. That never seemed to work, and now I understand why.

Now, we have students jump on a trampoline, ride a bike, do yoga, do a wellness walk (several movements in a row down the hallway), or just take a walk when they need to de-escalate or self-regulate. In short, it is working!! Students are learning what to do when they are angry. They calm down quickly and effectively.

Elementary School Counselor

Hallway Movement Paths   Recently, movement/sensory paths with the purpose of burning off students' excess energy have become very popular in schools. A path made with large floor stickers provides visual guidance that cue movements (e.g., hopping like a toad, crawling from one step to another, spinning, hopscotching), to help fidgety students calm down. For students without trauma, these paths may help support positive behavior. For students who are dysregulated, these paths may successfully burn off stress chemicals, introduce more oxygen into the bloodstream, stretch muscles, and get the heart pumping, but they may only *partially* succeed in addressing those students' overall needs. With minor adjustments, the paths can meet all of the preceding needs, and also help with regulation.

We recommend that schools who want a path to serve movement *and* regulation needs consider the items that follow. Be sure that physical movements are within students' mastery level. For example, if students fall over while toad-hopping, they are becoming dysregulated—partially or totally erasing the gains made by having a movement opportunity. Ensure that activities follow a pattern or have several repetitions of the same movement. Have the path provide modulation by guiding students from bigger, more active movements to smaller, more controlled movement—just as we do in the Re-Set Room. Think of the steps as falling into three categories, and then moving from Category 1 to Category 2 to Category 3 systematically.

Category 1   Bigger, faster, more energetic activity—all gross motor activities. Some options might be jumping jacks, hopping, fast arm circles, jogging in place, wall push-ups, helicopter twists. These activities burn off stress chemicals and provide lots of movement. Some even introduce dopamine—the calming chemical.

Category 2   Slower, more controlled gross motor activities such as big steps, slower arm circles, gentle helicopter twists, and walk the balance beam (a line on the floor). With this approach, we are systematically settling down student systems a bit—still burning off stress chemicals while modulating down and introducing more dopamine. Some of these activities contain a little bit more cognitive engagement, which helps prepare students for a smooth return to class.

Category 3   Breathing activities: Emphasize the long breath out; perhaps use visual cues, such as breathing in and out while tracing a shape in the air with a finger. Encourage students to hold certain stretched positions for a count of 10. These activities settle the system through breathing and controlled motor movement.

INDIVIDUALIZED OPPORTUNITIES

Although regulation experiences often are beneficial for the entire class, we can certainly provide additional ones to individual students as needed.

Notes From the Field

A second-grade student was having difficulty remaining on-task during partner reading and while completing lengthy weekly vocabulary quizzes. To allow the student more frequent opportunities to engage in gross motor activities, the teacher put a sticky note on every 2–3 pages. The notes indicated that the student could choose a movement activity from a set of cards at that time. Options for movement included wall push-ups, jumping jacks, a walk to the water fountain, and the mountain climber exercise.

In addition, small visuals were placed at the bottom of every other page on his vocabulary quizzes. Like notes, the visuals indicated to the student that he was allowed to choose a break card to engage in gross motor activities.

Elementary Intervention Specialist

Not every student who needs more movement opportunities requires direct coaching or instruction. For these students, developing procedures that govern how students access those additional opportunities can take many forms. The sticky-note break strategy combined with a set of appropriate movements, as described in the preceding Notes From the Field, is one such procedure that is highly responsive to a student's needs.

Other teachers have working-regulating cards on students' desks. Students leave the cards on the working side while engaging in work, and then, when they feel themselves becoming dysregulated, turn the card over to the regulating or break side. The student then goes somewhere within the classroom or just outside the classroom door and moves in a prescribed manner. The sequence and number in each activity can be guided by cards on the wall or in a flip book that hangs on a hook in the designated area. This strategy is a way to guide access to a classroom's proactive form of the Re-Set Process.

Flip books can be designed to guide students during these individual regulation activities. The book would have pages of different colors for different activities. Students can be taught that they do two activities from each color and then return to work. We encourage the use of colors other than red, yellow, and green—those three colors are emotionally loaded for some students, particularly when they are presented as a group. Using shades of the same color works well, or random assorted colors based on what is available in your school's storeroom as long as you avoid the stop light color combination.

Some students need a reminder of their regulation options to be located at their desk. A regulation card taped onto the desk that the student can mark each time he or she uses a specific exercise can be both a reminder and a way to collect data on strategies being used. For students who need a more portable option, a laminated regulation bookmark can serve the same purposes. In-seat activity options might include:

- Use specific tools, such as those recommended for self-regulation caddies.

- Stretch band across the front of chair legs or desk legs: Student puts heel in front of band and bends knees to pull back *or* places toes in back of band and stretches legs to push forward. Student is not to kick at the band or this tool will be dysregulating.

- Chair push-ups: Student places palms on seat of chair while seated and pushes up to lift body just off seat. Alternative: Student may simply lift his or her body weight slightly, and not actually off the chair.

- Hand isometrics: Student sits upright in chair, grasps his or her hands together in front of chest, and firmly presses them together, breathing naturally throughout the exercise. Hold for 10 seconds and then relax for 15 seconds.

- Progressive muscle tightening and release: Student tightens his or her hands and then releases them, then tightens his or her arms and then releases them, then the legs, and then the feet. Focus should be on the feeling of release and allowing muscles to return to a relaxed state before moving to the next tensing activity.

Notes From the Field

A strategy I have that works well for students is a box that has brain break–like activities. I call it the *When you're stuck, call a tow truck* box. It works well when kids will not talk to you. The activities are meant to distract the brain and help it move over the speed bump. The worksheets include simple math fact sheets, hidden-picture searches, and a technique I borrowed from a colleague, in which the student writes his or her name by using his or her non-dominant hand. It occupies the student's brain and serves as an override at the moment. I generated a worksheet that provides the student with 10 lines to write his or her name on. The student usually does not make it past three before he or she starts talking to me.

Elementary Special Educational Support Teacher

REGULATION PLANS

We can be regulation models and we can provide modulation experiences and regulation guidance, but, as we discussed in Chapter 2, it is essential that we bring students into the process of their own healing. Part of that healing is developing their own regulation plans. We need to be in partnership with them by listening to their perceptions of their world and by allowing them to explore which specific strategies work best for them. These plans are designed to guide students' thinking and their responses much like a set of directions that appear at the top of a form guide our written responses to be completed. It is a cognitive tool that, if used routinely, can develop a student's internal regulation script.

Any regulation plan must fit the developmental needs of the involved student. We offer three different versions of regulation plans for students—basic, intermediate, and advanced. We typically use basic with primary school-age students, intermediate with students in grades 4–6, and advanced with students in grades 6–8. These are general guidelines; any version can be used for any students of any age, as long as it matches the students' cognitive development and abilities. The components of each version are identified in Figure 9.4.

In the basic option, students are coached to check in on the state of their bodies and minds and then select a regulating strategy or tool from a toolbox that has been developed with them.

In the intermediate option, students check in on their bodies and minds, select a strategy or tool, and then reflect on its effectiveness in regulating them, so that their regulation status matches the context in which they are functioning. This reflection may be simply paying attention to the response, documenting their response and discussing it with an adult, or simply by reflecting with an adult periodically on the tools that they are noticing to be most effective for themselves, with the end goal of supporting the student to be more strategic in his or her use of strategies and tools.

In the advanced option, students are encouraged to think, in advance, of what situations or specific stimuli may cause them to become dysregulated.

Developing the Regulation Plan

To develop the *check* phase of regulation, we ask the student to notice his or her own signals that indicate that he or she is dysregulated, and that a regulation strategy is needed. These signals may be ones they notice about how their body is feeling or moving (e.g., *My legs feel jumpy., I pick at my skin., I feel tight.*) or they may be related to the thoughts that are in their

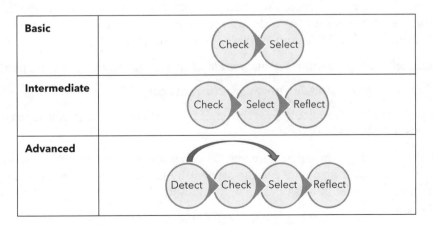

Figure 9.4. Steps for basic, intermediate, and advanced regulation plans.

head (e.g., *I am going to freak out., I am done., I can't hear anything.* We believe very strongly that the words that describe those signals need to be in the student's authentic voice as much as possible. We use their slang language, such as, *I gotta jet,* so that when the student sees it, it truly reflects what is going on in his or her head. Of course, some students' inner voice may be completely inappropriate. We would not condone writing, *Oh #$@&%*!,* even if a student might say that in his or her head. We would, instead, write, *I feel like cursing* or *I am cursing in my head.* Other than this type of exception, we recommend using exactly how a child phrases his or her thoughts or the way the child describe how his or her body feels.

Some students may be able to identify these signals on their own, but for many students, this noticing begins when an adult identifies specific behaviors that he or she perceives to be indicators of dysregulation for that student. This can be done gently by using noticing language (e.g., *I notice your hands curl into fists. What do you notice about your hands?)*

To develop the Select phase, we consider with the student a variety of strategies or tools that are effective in helping the student regulate. We should have the student practice with several and then choose the ones that he or she wants to begin with to create his or her toolbox. These are then written in the Select section of the plan.

Reflect is part of only the intermediate and advanced versions of regulation plans. Reflect remains blank until the plan is actually implemented and students can think about what tools were most effective for them.

In the advanced version, we also add Detect. In Detect, we guide students to identify situations that seem to trigger their dysregulation. These conditions are then listed in the Detect column. The purpose of Detect is to empower the student to avoid moving toward dysregulation by predicting stressful situations and engaging with a tool or process from his or her Select column just before or during the early portion of those conditions. With students, we call this *shortcutting your reaction* because engaging in Detect should allow the student to jump over Check—and what tween or teen does not love a shortcut?

Implementing the Plan

In the Check phase of the plan, students are cued to notice their signs of dysregulation. For example: *Max, I notice that you are in and out of your seat a lot.* (Adult points to that behavior on the chart.) *Did you notice that, too? I am thinking that means you need to use your toolbox.*

Over time, with practice, the verbal prompt should be both delayed and reduced, giving the student time and cognitive space to take more responsibility for recognizing the indicators of his or her dysregulation. The adult prompts should become simpler as the student becomes more self-aware—with the ultimate goal being that Max catches himself early and without needing a prompt. Here is an example of decreasing prompts:

Max, what are you noticing about your level of activity right now? (Adult points to chart.)

Max, check yourself. (Adult's eye gazes toward chart.)

Max, check in. (Max should be at the point that he knows to check the chart or has internalized his list of dysregulation cues.)

Select should be similarly referenced by using the level of support or cueing that the student needs. The adult also may cue the student by handing them a regulation tool or by providing a quick model of a regulation activity. With Select, it is about getting down to the work of regulation.

Reflect may initially be done with an adult or by the student on his or her own, and then later with an adult or completely on the student's own—depending on the situation. Typically, an on-their-own reflection occurs after a student has had many previous experiences reflecting *with* an adult and is being moved toward independence—and eventually engaging in the regulating process without needing to reference a written plan. Reflection should result in a notation about how a strategy worked for the student. Although Reflect does not appear in the basic version, adults certainly can reflect verbally with the student if conditions allow (e.g., *How did using that marble maze work for you?*)

For the advanced version, Detect may initially be prompted by the adult (e.g., a whispered, *We are going to switch to small-group work. What should you consider doing?* Again, any prompts should be faded out to move the student toward independence. To provide a discreet visual cue, at times we have created a bookmark that is aligned with the student's regulation plan—one side lists the Detect items and the other lists the Select content.

Sample Plans

Figure 9.5 shows an example of a basic plan, Figure 9.6 provides an intermediate sample and Figure 9.7 is an example of an advanced plan.

Who should be involved in developing a regulation plan? The student and one of his or her caring adults (e.g., a teacher, the school counselor, a mentor, a school psychologist, or a Re-Set coach).

The plans may be formal or informal depending on the student and the situation. Plans may be done with students who are struggling but are not identified as needing an individual education program (IEP), or they could be done with students who have IEPs. One school we worked with decided to shift their detention practice from sitting quietly and working, to an instructional detention, where the involved teacher coached students in developing their plans for regulating. In a Re-Set Rooms, the coach may use Step 4 as an opportunity to develop a regulation plan.

Assessment of the Plan

Assessing regulation plans is about checking in to see whether the tools that are being used are effective for the student. This is done through ongoing, periodic discussions between the caring adult and the student. Adjustments are made as needed (e.g., the student may need to add a new tool to their toolbox). If the student's use of the plan and its associated tools is tied to an IEP goal, additional assessment may be connected to it (e.g., documentation of uses of the plan or its tools, data regarding behavior issues).

Figure 9.5. Example of a basic regulation plan.

Check When I notice . . .	Select I will pick one . . .	Reflect How did this strategy work for me?
My stomach starts to hurt. I am thinking, I need to get out of here. I am saying things that are disrespectful. I am growling. I am not listening. I am worried I might lose control. I am working hard to stay calm.	I can take my break card and go rest at the nurse's office. I can get a drink of water. I can ask to go to the sensory area with an adult. I can silently read a book to myself. I can ask an adult for help. I can quietly tell an adult how I am feeling.	Getting a drink of water helps me feel calmer lots of times. I like walking to the water fountain and taking a break from the work. I still felt like running after a drink one time. Mr. Taylor had to find me in the bathroom to remind me about my break card. I will try to remember that I have it. Mr. Taylor said he will hang it near the water fountain so I will have it right there.

Figure 9.6. Example of an intermediate regulation plan.

Detect (What situations tend to lead to dysregulation for me?)	Check (What are my thoughts and body reactions?)	Select (What might I be able to do to regulate?)	Reflect (How did this strategy work for me?)
Tasks that are difficult for me to do—especially in front of others. Work on stuff I don't think I ever will need to know.	My thoughts: I will never be able to do it. This is ridiculous. I gotta get out of here. She just hates me. Body: I feel sweaty. My leg is jumping.	Do some progressive tighten-and-release exercises, starting with my legs. Do a long breath out, to count of 10. Give a signal to my teacher that I would like to pass.	With an adult, reflect on the tool I used and how it worked. I am finding that it takes me about 3 long breaths to calm down most of the time. It really helps if I do that before I even look at the work I am supposed to be doing if it is writing stuff—once I look at, it I start feeling angry. The tighten-and-release thing works better for when I am working in a group—the breath thing might look weird.

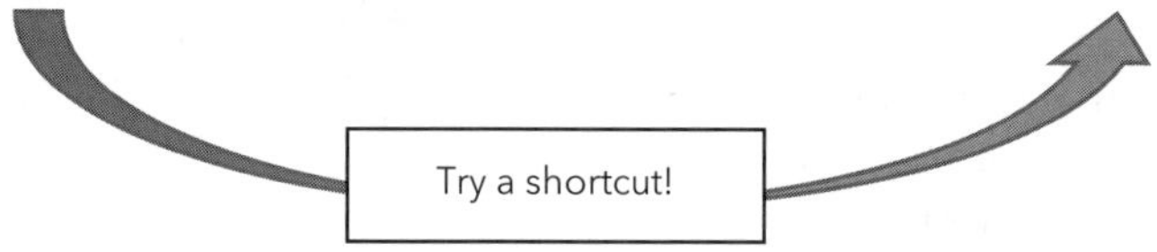

Try a shortcut!

Figure 9.7. Example of an advanced regulation plan.

CLOSING THOUGHTS

So, how does this broad concept of building regulation skills fit in with the Re-Set concepts shared in Section II? Re-Set processes are designed to teach students how to regulate but educators do not need to look only to formal forms of the Re-Set Process to provide this critical instruction. Re-Set as a process—and the more global approach to teaching regulation—should share tools and language so they are seamless in their support of students. This is where Re-Set moves beyond only being a specific set of steps to being a part of the culture of the classroom.

In the next chapter, we will continue thinking about school culture, specifically in the ways that it is communicated through how educators provide behavioral feedback to students.

Chapter 10

Providing Behavior Feedback

Don't judge each day by the harvest you reap, but by the seeds you plant.

—Robert Louis Stevenson (2013)

The Re-Set Process is one tool among many behavior tools that an effective, trauma-informed educator may employ. Without being nested in broader trauma-informed approaches, however, the Re-Set Process will not be as effective. We do not have to be perfect in our efforts, but we need to be committed to continual growth that reflects intentional and thoughtful movement toward being consistently predictable, safe, and nurturing.

We have already discussed many ways we attend to those needs in Chapters 8 and 9, and now we turn to more deeply examine the important role of behavior feedback in creating a culture of caring and support.

ETHAN

Ethan considered himself a very positive teacher, until he had a colleague collect data on his positive-to-negative verbalization ratio. As part of the peer coaching model his school followed, he had been the one who asked his colleague to collect this data, but that didn't make it any more palatable when it came back with a ratio of 1:2 positive versus negative verbal interactions with students—for every positive verbal interactions with a student, he had two negative interactions. After the initial shock passed, Ethan focused on finding a strategy for flipping the ratio around. He was determined to align his behavior with his beliefs.

The strategy Ethan chose was one he had heard about from one of his former principals. He placed green dots around the room and whenever one of those dots came into view, he looked around and found a student to recognize for positive efforts. Three months later, when his peer-coach returned to collect data, Ethan had flipped his ratio significantly—now it was 4:1 in favor of positives! Ethan's reflection on the new data? Even though he always loved teaching, he was enjoying his classroom even more and was sure that his students did, too. He reported that although the strategy he selected was very contrived, it changed the habit of what he noticed about his students.

When we last spoke, Ethan was considering adapting the green dot strategy so that his students could use the dots to remind them to say nice things to each other, and also to recognize internally their own positive efforts.

BEHAVIORAL FEEDBACK

In schools, we are comfortable giving our students feedback about their academic behaviors. We know that, without feedback, academic growth would happen only in fits and starts and, certainly, not in any reasonable time frame. We clearly understand that feedback on academic behaviors is essential to develop a robust skill set and we would never consider withholding positive feedback and allowing students to flounder. Nor would we use shaming or negative feedback in order to develop students' academic skills. We need to apply these same approaches when we provide behavioral feedback.

Think for a minute about all the ways you give behavioral feedback. What kind of feedback do you use and in what circumstances? Is it positive or negative? Specific or general? When? How often? In front of whom? Using what method—verbal, gestural, facial expression, written? In what proportions of positive to negative? If we think of feedback as seeds we are planting for an eventual harvest, we know we need to consider many elements—the types of seeds we are sowing, the preparation we have done, and the timing of the process.

Good feedback is timely, specific, and invites the student into the process. It also needs to happen within the critically important context of relationship. The foundation for providing feedback for *all* students is relationship. A study cited in Peter DeWitt's 2016 Education Week blog, *Relationships: The Yin to Feedback's Yang*, discovered that adding one sentence— *I am giving you this feedback because I believe in you*—to the end of critical diagnostic feedback to students had a significant impact. The study found that the group of students who heard the added sentence demonstrated higher achievement in the following year than the group who got the same type of feedback without that sentence.

Students are not the only ones who need feedback to occur within relationship; this connection is seen well into adulthood. Myriad business leadership articles on feedback also tout the importance of relationship first. Conley (2017), in the article *Leading with Trust*, suggests that giving feedback is "a moment of trust—an opportunity to either build or erode trust in the relationship" (para. 1). Like location is in real estate, in schools, almost everything comes down to relationship, relationship, relationship, and this is even more true for students of trauma.

Behavioral feedback also is essential in establishing social boundaries that keep students physically and emotionally safer. James Garbarino (1999) speaks to the importance of this when he writes, "Without adequate adult buffering and limit setting, the moral behavior of children is left in the hands of children themselves, where their own feelings and thoughts are the last line of defense" (p. 142). Students with trauma histories may have experienced unhealthy or inconsistent boundaries and their way forward lies in healthy role models and targeted feedback regarding boundary-related behaviors. Good feedback not only provides the guidance of what to do and what not to do in a current situation, good feedback also teaches how to figure out where the edges of a new setting are; good feedback teaches *how to think* in novel situations.

TRAUMA-INFORMED FEEDBACK

Our challenge is that students who have experienced pervasive trauma often react to both positive and negative feedback a bit differently than many of our other students. It is why the methods we have found to be effective with other students may be less productive when dealing with students of trauma. We will explore these differences before discussing specific feedback methods.

We each construct our own reality by interpreting the external world on the basis of our unique experiences with it and our beliefs about those experiences.
—Raymond J. Wlodkowski (2008, p. 8)

Students who have a limited sense of competency, who have experienced failure after failure in their lives become "positive feedback resistant." It is likely that their life experience has been marked by a disproportionate number of negative events—both big and small. It also is highly probable that they have internalized that they, like their experiences, are *bad* and therefore are not deserving of *good* things, including your positive feedback. Positive feedback does not fit with how they see themselves.

A student with a history of trauma may struggle with positive feedback on either an academic effort or a behavioral decision. *Can I do this again? Are they just saying this to manipulate me? I got lucky this time. They are in a good mood today. Oh no, I will never be able to do this another time!* These messages in their head are likely to externalize the success—not attribute it to their own efforts—or these thoughts might send them into panic or fear that they could never perform that way again. For some older students who have crafted a reputation as a tough kid, typical positive feedback in front of peers challenges that reputation, making them retreat further from a positive identity in order to maintain the only identity they have any confidence in . . . *I am tough, I don't care.*

To wrap our heads—and hearts—around these students' realities, we have come up with the analogy that these children are like parched earth. If we rain on them hard with big positive recognition, it will just run off as sure as torrential rain runs off dry, cracked soil, with relatively little of the water absorbed. If we instead take a gentle spring rain approach and provide many, little, frequent recognitions, there is a greater chance that those supportive messages will slowly soak in and, over time, actually change the soil—that is, change the child's sense of self toward one of greater positivity and being worthy.

For students with trauma histories, any corrective feedback may feel like a big negative instead of caring guidance. They may experience corrective feedback as a message that they are worthless, incapable, confirming how they already feel about themselves and how they believe the world sees them. As such, it does not create much momentum to change because there is no dissonance between how they see themselves (unsuccessful, bad) and how they perceive the message of the negative feedback (unsuccessful, bad). It all fits. If the negative experience does anything for students with trauma, it only further distances them from the belief that they can do better. They give up hope, and they often articulate that ultimate cover story of *I don't care.*

Despite these challenges, we need to be able to give our students both affirmative feedback and corrective feedback in ways that are useful in creating behavior change. Feedback in the context of a positive relationship is certainly more palatable for everyone, especially students with trauma histories. In relationships, affirmative feedback is perceived as more genuine and deserved; corrective feedback is less likely to be perceived as all-defining and overwhelming. Nurturing relationship is essential but, while connection grows, there are some ways we can deliberately approach behavior that supports our students and may even contribute to growth in our relationship with them.

POSITIVE FEEDBACK

There are several components of trauma-informed positive feedback.

Low-Key and Private

Educators know that the approach *praise in public, correct in private* has been found to be effective for many students. However, until confidence is built *and* until trust is established between the adult and the student and also between the student and his or her peers, even positive feedback needs to be low-key or perhaps even private, depending on the student. This is the gentle rain from our previous analogy.

We make feedback more private by using non-verbal signals like a thumbs-up or by jotting a few words on a sticky note. We can whisper or simply tap the edge of the desk as a secret signal that they are doing well. This is not the specific feedback that is ideal but, as relationship grows, feedback can become more specific and public—particularly positive feedback. A word of caution though—sometimes this ability to accept feedback in a more public manner will ebb and flow with the current status of a child's life. Be prepared to shift your methods as needed.

Highly Genuine and Positive

Students with trauma are highly sensitized to anything that feels disingenuous. Find something in a student's set of behaviors that you can authentically notice. With students who present many challenging behaviors, finding a genuine, positive behavior to notice may take some focused thinking. This is another place where relationship comes into play.

See the light in others and treat them as if that is all you can see.

—Dr. Wayne Dyer (2005, p. 170)

As you form relationship with a challenging student, your view of them changes and their strengths become more illuminated, their efforts more visible, their positive moments more expansive. Honestly, sometimes the first step is believing that you will see something before you actually see it. We are the adults; it is our responsibility for the change to begin with us. Believing in order to see is one way we may spark that change.

Frequent Opportunities

The key to *changing the parched land* is offering small positive feedback at a high rate. Although the general rule regarding feedback is to make it specific, during the *gentle spring rain* phase of feedback, interspersing that specific verbal feedback with gestures of approval and other short, positive modes of non-specific feedback may be needed in order to achieve the necessary high frequency. The key is to carefully maintain some specific feedback—perhaps through notes or private interactions. During this spring rain period of intervention, our intention is to help the student become accustomed to positive feedback, to develop trust in us and what we say. There will be a time when the number of feedback events can be reduced and the quality of feedback can be enhanced but, initially, our goal is acceptance of any form of positive feedback.

CORRECTIVE FEEDBACK

No child wants to be corrected publicly, least of all a student who may feel like an outcast already. Sometimes this means the feedback is not as timely as we would like it to be but, in this case, finding the right moment for feedback is more important than being prompt with it. An example of this is when we do not address the head down, mumbling of a student during whole-class instruction and instead, we shift the group to a partner-sharing activity and quietly approach the student—a delay, but one that allows for a higher degree of privacy.

Quick Redirects for Small Behaviors

Traditionally, when students misbehaved in small ways, we used the strategy of planned ignoring. But when we ignore the behaviors of students with trauma, it may feel to them as though we are ignoring them, which creates a breach in relationship. Also, thinking back to Chapter 2, if we ignore a minor behavior, we may be giving the student no other option than to *push the chaos button*, which assures that he or she will be seen.

Tagging Behavior

Instead of big redirects, *tag* the behavior but do not stay around for a debate. What is a tag? A tag is a short, low-key verbalization or gesture that indicates the behavior is not acceptable. Tagging is effective because we get-in-and-get-out, avoiding the opportunity for a power struggle to begin. Tagging also allows the adult to pay low-level attention to negative behavior, while paying more attention to positive behaviors. It shows that you *do* see the student, while communicating that you will pay only a minor amount of attention to negative behavior. The key to tagging is to be very focused on finding an appropriate behavior to notice after the tag and to be committed to unconditional, caring contact, such as offering help.

Checking In

An alternative to tagging is checking in. Checking in means responding to negative behavior with a question of concern, such as, *Are you okay?* or *Can I help with something?* or *Hey, do you need something?* These questions show concern for the student and interrupt the problem behavior without giving it a great deal of attention. They also are offers of connection; they communicate that you care and are poised to help. The key is to make sure that the question is delivered with genuine concern. In order to do this, we have to shift our thinking from thoughts such as, *This kid is being annoying again* to *This kid is in need of me again* and then offer help.

Request-Thank You-Pivot-and-Return

A third strategy that is particularly effective for students who are passive in their behavior is a request-thank you-pivot-and-return strategy. This strategy has several steps and quite a few subtleties, but with a little practice, it can be done quickly and smoothly. Table 10.1 describes each step of this strategy and the corresponding intention as part of the overall approach of engaging the student. When students are disengaged from the learning process or from relationship with the educator, this strategy allows the adult to show positive expectations while providing the student with physical and emotional space.

Separate Behavior From the Person

When a teacher needs to talk about a serious behavior that requires a longer, more intense interaction, it is vital to simultaneously speak of the student's goodness and strengths and, thereby, provide the student with a sense of hope. Sometimes this may require digging into your stores of positivity, but it is critical. It might sound like this: *I heard about the fight. That is not you. I have seen what efforts you have been making, and I know you are better than this. We will get beyond this; I will be here for you.*

Invite Self-Assessment

Asking students of trauma to reflect on their successes and their struggles is a difficult but essential part of the behavior guidance process. When asking for self-assessment, it is important to give the student time to respond rather than ask for an immediate response. For young students, Kindergarten through 4th grade, the focus should be only on the successes. This can be accomplished by keeping a simple success journal—a bulleted list of short, positive items of any sort—or through graphing the students' positive behaviors.

For older students, Grades 5–8, the foundation for all reflective questioning is a conversation that establishes their thoughts about who they are, who they want to be, and who they fear being, which then becomes the picture against which they can assess their behavioral choices. Seita and Brendtro (2005) describe the practices of youth work pioneer Anton Makarenko, who made planning for the future a central teaching objective. He structured this planning by having short-term, mid-term, and long-term goals, along with an anticipated joy for each day.

Self-assessment that is grounded in a student's personal goals has context that is meaningful for the student. Students' behavior, therefore, is not just about the here and now, but about building toward an outcome they desire. There have been several processes developed

Table 10.1.   Request, thank you, pivot, and return strategy

Adult behavior	Intention
1. Approach the student and greet him or her warmly while offering eye contact.	• Connection • Unconditional positive regard
2. Look at—and possibly touch—the learning material and give a simple, clear directive. Give the student a choice, if possible. *Pick a problem to start and I will come back and check in shortly.*	• Direct attention to the learning activity rather than looking at the student, which could trigger a power struggle—look where you want the student to look. • Choice provides opportunity for control. • Check-in reinforces connection and creates a sense of accountability.
3. Immediately say "Thank you" and pivot away from student. *Thank you!*	• Hearing the phrase *Thank you!* causes the student's brain to think that it has already started the task, and it models kindness. • Pivot shows positive expectation that student will follow through and avoids slipping into a power struggle.
4. Genuinely attend to another student.	• Time is provided for the student to follow your directive.
5A. Option 1: Student has *engaged* in the task and the answer is *correct*. Approach using friendly body language; look at the student's work, acknowledge that it is done correctly. Give a positive gesture and move to another student. Check in again shortly to see if student continues to understand the work. *You're rolling along.*	• Returning to the student with a positive is socially reinforcing. • Low-key reaction to the student's correct response avoids overwhelming the student. • Moving on to others gives the student a chance to maintain momentum on his or her own without feeling monitored. • Checking back in keeps the connection going.
5B. Option 2: Student has *engaged* in the task, but the answer is *incorrect*. Approach using friendly body language, look at work, comment on work behavior and offer help using *we* language. *You are getting to it. Good. Let's look at this together.*	• Returning to the student with a positive sets a collaborative tone. • Looking at the work cues the student and avoids the eye contact that could lead to a power struggle. • Affirming effort keeps things positive. • Offering help is what the student needs—*we* or *together* language connotes collaboration and equal footing—teacher and student are on the same side.
5C. Option 3: Student has *not engaged* in the task. Approach using friendly body language, then look at the work and warmly say something such as: *Looks like you are waiting for me. I'm here to help. Sorry it took me a few minutes to get back to you.* *Thanks for waiting. Okay, where do you want us to get started?*	• Returning to the student with a positive sets a collaborative tone. • Looking at work cues the student and avoids the eye contact that could lead to a power struggle. • Offering help is a gentler redirect than talking about not engaging in work, and it conveys that you do not believe that the student's intent is to be defiant. • Saying *Sorry* or *Thanks* offers grace to the student. *Note:* This option is effective only if the educator genuinely understands that the student has a greater need rather than seeing him or her as being defiant or willful.

that help students to consider their future and allow it to inform their present decisions. Connecting with their goals, reflecting on their supports, considering their barriers, and establishing short-term steps all help a student to construct his or her behavior in alignment with his or her hopes and vision. This type of approach is highly recommended for middle-school students as it brings their voice forward and is a way to value what they value for themselves.

This future-oriented conversation might be structured through a PATH process (O'Brien et al., 2015) or through a Possible Selves process (Oyserman, Bybee, Terry, & Hart-Johnson, 2004). The book *Possible Selves: Nurturing Student Motivation* (Hock et al., 2003) provides specific guidance.

Helping a student find the words to express how he or she feels about his or her future may take time, especially when a student is going through a personal transformation. This is why we should introduce this reflective practice, and then provide time for the student's sincere consideration instead of making an immediate request for disclosure. Oftentimes, we have provided the student with an outline of future-oriented questions a week in advance of our first meeting so that he or she has time to reflect before coming to the table.

When students wrestle with who they are, when they see their behavior in the context of who they want to be, when they are coached to understand that they are powerful entities in determining their life's direction, there can be real growth. We have used stories told by other students with similar struggles to serve as inspiration points for the students with whom we work. It is important to find these role models in the student's community as much as possible, but we may also find some role models in literature, such as Anne Frank (non-fiction) and Frodo in *Lord of the Rings* (fiction).

Since trauma sidelines the self-sensing parts of the brain, it is understandable how hard the task of self-assessment might be. Exercising those areas may take some deliberate work, but doing so can lead to better judgment, stronger impulse control and a sense of positive agency in the world. When we offer time in the Re-Set Room to decide how to make restitution, when we encourage reflection on behavior through literature conversations, when we provide supports for reflective thought, when we convey a belief in our students, when we give them the gift of time, we allow them to find themselves and their unique strengths.

TRAUMA-INFORMED FORMAL FEEDBACK SYSTEMS

A formal system is not always an essential part of behavior guidance but, when one is used, it needs to be considered as part of the behavioral feedback experienced by students. It must follow trauma-guidelines if it is to do more good than harm.

Classroom Systems

ALYSSA

Alyssa had been teaching first grade for 10 years when I met her for the first time. She was one of those teachers who was captivating to watch because she connected with the wondrous and magical part of being a young child. Her classroom was inviting, the materials were organized, and her schedule fit the developmental needs of her students. She checked in with each child as he or she entered the class, her smile and hug at the ready. She was an engaging instructor who made learning exciting, and she paid attention to when students needed additional supports.

Despite all this, this particular year Alyssa was frustrated. Her student population seemed to be getting more and more needy, or as she put it, "I feel like the mental health needs of my students are exploding." Until this school year, Alyssa had not used a formal feedback system, preferring to use social reinforcement by noticing students who were doing well with a smile, a thumbs-up, or specific positive feedback. When the entire class worked well together, they celebrated with an impromptu happy dance or by patting each other on the back or by having an extra 5 minutes at recess.

For the past several years, Alyssa felt like this approach was no longer working, so she began to use individual behavior charts with the students who had the greatest behavioral needs. She continued to use her less formal approach, as well. This year, she was exhausted from juggling so many individual charts, so she turned to some colleagues and the Internet for advice.

Alyssa decided that a formal classroom management system was the way to go. One approach that showed up consistently and prominently online was the clip-up, clip-down traffic-light system. Alyssa asked her peers what they knew about it, and she found that several of them used a version of this system. Alyssa liked the simplicity of the system, but she wanted it to be more fun for her young students, so she decided to go with a version that had animals. Giraffe at the top, bear in the middle, and alligator at the bottom—5 animals in all, so plenty of steps along the way. All students started as bears—warm and fuzzy teddy bears—and would then move up or down depending on their behavior. Alyssa decided that she would give her students two warnings before they would clip down, following the three-strikes approach she saw in other systems.

She created the visual scale, wrote her students' names on the clothespins, and introduced it to her class with great optimism. A couple of weeks later she contacted me to come in to see if I had ideas of how to adjust it. She felt that, although the system was working for many of her students, for quite a few students, it seemed to be making things worse.

I entered the class 15 minutes into the school day. In the middle of the floor was one of her students, sprawled out and making scissor-like movements with his arms as he cried in a tormented voice, "I am not an alligator, I am not an alligator!!"—while snapping at his peers' legs with his arm-alligator jaws.

Historically, formal classroom feedback systems have been given insufficient attention in many teacher preparation programs. Pre-service teachers report that they gained most of their understandings about classroom systems through their cooperating teachers during fieldwork. Like Alyssa, teachers in the field, both new and experienced, turn to each other and to the Internet for ways to address classroom behaviors that fall outside the norm. Some rely on their own experiences as students themselves and implement the same systems their own teachers used. Yet others have access to support personnel or formal teaming structures to help them design their systems. Unfortunately, much of the information that is out there in our field is woefully outdated, and many recommended systems have their roots in the 1970s. They may appear current, but the updates are only in the style of visuals used and the addition of some high-tech features. We can debate whether these systems were ever good for children, but it is clear that these systems do not match the needs of many students in our classrooms today, especially those with trauma histories.

When we examine a formal feedback system to see if it is likely to support students with trauma, we use the concept of *level of risk*. Higher risk means that the system has a greater chance of *not* working for the students who have intense behavioral concerns—although it may work for many of the student's peers who have lower levels of behavior. Lower risk means that the system is more likely to work for students who have intense behavioral concerns and for the rest of the class.

Alyssa found a system that we would consider higher risk for students with high stress or trauma. The clip-up/clip-down chart may have worked for students who did not need a system to support their positive behaviors, but it failed miserably for the students who were struggling with their behaviors, as was the case with the boy who rightly declared that he was not an alligator. The clip system does not stand alone; other systems have just as many unfortunate consequences. We will use it, however, to illuminate the concerns of many of these types of systems.

High-Risk System Features

We will describe several features of high-risk systems and explain why they are especially triggering for students with trauma histories.

Problem Behaviors Addressed in a Public Manner   With a clip-up/clip-down chart, clipping down often results in a *walk of shame*. The student is humiliated walking to the chart in front of peers to clip down the clothespin. The student may feel labeled by his or her clip. In our example case, the student felt defined as being on alligator. Because visuals are so powerful, this is branding the child in a highly memorable way. Struggling students already are more likely to have negative self-images. Declaring their negative behavior for all to see only hardwires that self-perception more. Think of that boy crying *"I am not an alligator!"* while acting like one. How long before he decides to embrace alligator behavior as who he is in his core? (By the way, we know that Alyssa had no such intention when she implemented this system.) Trying to make the clip system less painful, some teachers avoid the student's embarrassing walk of shame by having the teacher clip the student down. Still, the labeling persists in a very public manner.

Names Posted Publicly: Comparison Is Easy   The clip-up/clip-down chart is an example of a system that posts publicly, allowing for student-to-student comparison. We have witnessed volunteers coming into classrooms, checking the chart, and then making comments such as, *Well, I see someone is off to a rough start! Should be an interesting day.* We have overheard students saying that they would not play with other students because they were on red or another low-spot designation on the chart. We have seen students staring at their clip low on the chart, unable to engage in academic activity. Again, teachers have sought to reduce the public nature of the chart by making it smaller or placing it in less public places in the room, but it has a psychological draw that pulls students' attention.

Equal or More Emphasis on Negative Behaviors   Social scientists know that what we pay attention to, we get more of. Theoretically, positive behaviors can get as much attention as negative behaviors with a clip-up/clip-down chart. Realistically, that is unlikely to happen for several reasons. First, the warnings often associated with clipping down are public negative feedback, even though they do not result in an actual movement of the clip down. (*Note*: We are *not* suggesting that an improvement to the system would be to eliminate the warnings—that would not be an appropriate fix.) Second, it is human nature to notice negative behavior more than positive behavior (Marano, 2003). When we have taken behavioral data in classrooms that use these charts, we have found that there is little relationship between the exhibition of positive behaviors and when students move up on the chart. Students may exhibit positive behaviors for an extended period and not be moved up, but only a few exhibitions of negative behaviors result in a clip-down.

Our personal data and our research on the topic indicate that these systems are more of a bias-confirmation system than an accurate behavior data system. Students with chronic negative behaviors are monitored and responded to via the chart more frequently than students who misbehave infrequently and yet demonstrate the same negative behavior. This is just because of human nature and the fact that most classrooms have at least 25 students exhibiting positive or negative behaviors every single second of a full day *and* the adult who is monitoring these behaviors also is teaching. Although this multitasking affects any system a teacher might use, this particular system and ones like it tend to exaggerate the effect. Finally, we have witnessed much more student reaction to a peer being clipped-down than with other systems—probably due to the shaming nature of the chart.

Set Endpoint (You Win or Lose)   Some teachers operationalize their clip-up/clip-down system so that students can move up and down on the chart multiple times throughout the day; others say once you are clipped-down there is no moving up. Typically, however, the end of the day finds the students at a given point that is often reported to the family. For students who struggle with their positive behavior *endurance*, this system dooms them to ongoing failure because the likelihood of them ending up clipped down as the day progresses increases. They may have done well for large segments of the day then, toward the end of the day when fatigued by the hard work of holding it together, do less well and it is that clipped down status that is declared—to the student and often to home.

We observed one primary school that had all their students color in where they were on the chart on a note that went home to parents every single school day. The explanation was that this supported school-home communications (which on its own is a valuable thing just not with this particular use). Students on red spent the last minutes at school crying or putting on their emotional armor for heading home. If we paused and really thought about what this does to children and families, would anyone continue to do it? And when we understand the reality that how children feel when they leave school is carried back in the next day, is it not understandable that children living with this kind of system would come back to school defeated right from the beginning of the day? Stepping into those students' shoes, we imagine how we would feel if, at the end of a really hard workday, we got rated based on our worst moments and then we were forced to take that rating home to our spouses so they could show their incredible disappointment in us. We imagine we would be taking a new job in short order.

The clip-up/clip-down system probably is one of the highest risk systems being used in classes today. It also is one of the most prevalent systems that appears when one searches for *classroom behavior system* on myriad teacher-oriented web sites. These types of systems are based on the belief that the fear of the negative will motivate students to behave well, but this is a flawed understanding of student behavior, particularly in the context of trauma. Fortunately, the more schools become trauma-informed, the more educators turn away from these systems and look to other ways to guide student behavior.

Do you use a management system? If so, are any of the following statements true for you?

- There are times I hesitate to use my system with certain students because I know it will cause a problem.

- I need to find another individual system because my classroom system is not working for some of my students.

- I find I constantly need to make changes to my system—including my backup reinforcers—to keep my students interested in it.

- My heart just is not in this system, but I feel I should do it because other teachers in my school use it.

- I cannot keep up with this system—financially or with the work involved.

If any of these are true, you may want to consider using the self-assessment tool provided in the Section III resources and review a few low-risk systems that are included there.

What Makes a Classroom System Trauma-Informed or Lower Risk?

As displayed in Figure 10.1, students with trauma histories require systems that:

- Build confidence in their ability to be successful students with positive behaviors.

- Enhance their relationship and connection with the adults in the school setting.

- Support a positive sense of community with peers.

Systems that do this have the following qualities:

- Problem behaviors are addressed as privately as possible and are not given more *heft* than positive behaviors.

- Student progress is displayed privately so that comparison between students is not possible.

Figure 10.1. Relationships to consider when designing a classroom behavior system.

- Focus is on noticing positive behaviors.

- Cumulative tokens have a variety of exchange opportunities or a continuum of backup rein-forcers (e.g., points can be turned in for items of different values, or students can earn points over time and turn them in when they reach a designated level, regardless of the time frame.)

Positive Behaviors Have More Heft   The evidence for focusing on the positive is over-whelming. Whether you examine Fredrickson and Losada's (2005) research on flourishing, Gottman's marriage and divorce research (Benson, 2017; Lisitsa, 2013), or business performance research, the message is the same. Human beings do best and their relationships are enhanced when there is a significantly higher ratio of positive to negative interactions in their lives. *Harvard Business Review* found that when evaluating praise-to-criticism ratios, high-performing teams tended to function with a 5.6:1 ratio (almost 6:1), medium performing teams 1.9:1 (almost 2:1) and low-performing teams related at a ratio of .36:1 (1:3) (Zenger & Folkman, 2013).

In the school setting, the ratio that is recommended is 5:1 (Flora, 2000) and that magic number has become the standard for schools following the PBIS model. As children's lives are characterized by greater difficulty, this ratio becomes the minimum number rather than the recommended average.

When we focus on reinforcing the positives, we contribute to the *5* of that equation. The classroom system that is used is one source of positives, but it is not the only one. Some other ways to contribute include smiles, physical proximity with open, caring body language, positive gestures, opportunities for sharing, giving a student a responsibility, thanking a student for helping, greeting the student by name and myriad other ways of recognizing students. The more we focus on positives, the more we help students to flourish, to take on challenges and bounce back from adversity.

Negative interactions contribute to the *1* of that ratio. These include frustrated facial expressions directed at the student, criticism, reprimands, distancing body language, and other methods of communicating disapproval to the student. When a management system documents negative behaviors or rates behavior as positive or negative, it is contributing to the negative side of the equation.

If the 5:1 minimum ratio seems impossible to achieve—especially given that there may be 25 or more students with whom you are working at any given moment—we must consider what that might look like in practice. For the whole class, a single positive morning greeting may provide *everyone* with at least four—your smile, your greeting itself, your warm physical proximity to students as they enter, taking their papers as they hand them to you. The *Thank you, friends!* as they take their seats—tick, another one and you are already up to five before the pledge or before you start the lesson and that is for *every* student in your class. (*Note*: Although we may not use a thank-you for some students because it subtly communicates that they are engaging in a behavior to please us rather than based on an internal sense of doing the right thing, it is often very important for children of trauma. Using a thank-you provides a critical model of positive social interactions. The experience of receiving a courtesy also is important, especially if the student does not experience this routinely).

Remember, too, that your system and you are not the only source of positives and negatives that contribute to the ratio. A teacher who leads a positive classroom culture is likely to nurture student behavior that is positive with one another and create opportunities for students to provide positive feedback to one another.

If you are wondering about the student who needs even more and whose behavior tends to invite more negatives from others almost from the moment they enter the classroom? Here are a few strategies:

- Noticing them frequently—even if it is just by a smile and a head nod.

- Try a 20-second intervention of flooding with positives. Approach with warm body language, smile, greet with name, check in (*How are you doing today?*), listen respectfully to the response, offer help or provide some sort of affirmation, use a positive touch if appropriate, give a token for being ready to go.

- Use preprinted or pre-written notes—drop one on a student's desk or hand one to student.

- Encourage students to self-check by providing them with a structure for giving themselves positive feedback for tasks they do. We have created a laminated entry checklist for some students that hangs on their coat hook. They get to check off everything they have done and then turn it into the teacher.

- Do not go it alone—think about the whole community and how it may create a positive atmosphere by joining with other adults to provide extra support for your needier students. One elementary school stationed all staff without classrooms in the hallways to be greeters so that as their students came into the school in the morning, students were smiled at, verbally greeted, hugged or high-fived by at least three different adults before they reached their classroom door.

The easiest way for a system to support this critical ratio is to only chart positive behaviors. By not charting negative behaviors and by providing more private redirects, negative behaviors have less power—in the classroom and in the student's head. We also avoid the branding of a student and the resulting isolation.

It may be necessary to count problematic behavior for documentation purposes, but we can use different systems for different intentions. When we stop using our feedback systems for documentation purposes, we are freed from focusing our efforts on the negative and can use that found energy to reinforce positive behaviors.

Do we need to address problem behaviors? Of course! Do we need to document each one? Perhaps not. Often, in our effort to document the negative, those behaviors are given way more heft than the positive, in both the student's mind and in our minds. We have seen countless charts of smiley faces, straight faces, and frowny faces operationalized that way. A student may have demonstrated a high number of positive behaviors, but the one negative behavior results in a straight or frowny face—emotionally negating all those many positive efforts. It is not proportional; it is not data-accurate.

As educators, when we do these things, we certainly are not trying to heap hurt upon students, but because we want the student to change his or her behavior, we are seduced into talking about the negative behavior more and having it documented somewhere on a chart. This is what we mean by heft. When we want or need to document a student's problem behaviors, we feel compelled to note that in the system we are using—even when it is not designed to collect data accurately.

One of the best things we can do for students and ourselves is separate our feedback to students from documentation of behaviors. If we really need documentation, we should use highly accurate periodic probes done by people other than the teacher combined with teacher-friendly ways to document that are *not* shared with the student. When we have done this, we get more accurate counts to examine and we also get a general sense of the whole. We have seen teachers do the smiley-straight-frown face charts and never show them to the students—we use that global and very, very soft data to look at trends, a more appropriate use for the level of accuracy found in that type of documentation. Based on those trends, we may have someone collect more specific data or we design supports to meet the student's needs.

Progress Is Private   When we eliminate explicit comparison, we nurture and preserve relationships—ours with the student and the student with other students. When we allow students to understand their progress against their own baseline, they may see themselves as powerful entities, opening the door to change. When we have private conversations, we can talk about effort and growth. We can be both honest and encouraging.

Comparison motivates only someone who believes they have a good chance of coming out on top or in reasonable proximity to the top. Otherwise, comparison is dangerously unmotivating. When we have charts that compare one student to another, we set ourselves and our students up for frustration and failure. Students who lack confidence in their performance are often negatively impacted by these systems in subtle ways. For students with trauma histories, comparison to their peers is suffocating—it steals all the air in the room. Struggling kids protect their dignity in a wide variety of ways—non-attendance, sleeping in class, going to the nurse's office, staying forever in the bathroom, complaining about their teacher being unfair, being defiant, sabotaging their peers, and saying *I don't care!*—perhaps with some embellishments. When we instead shun comparison and focus on the individual's progress, we support forward momentum and we support the student leaning into possibility.

Continuum of Backup Reinforcers   Although there is a great deal of controversy regarding extrinsic versus intrinsic reinforcement, we can agree that positive reinforcement of some sort is important for children's social and emotional growth. How we provide that reinforcement may be different for different circumstances and in different school cultures.

Classrooms that use these more extrinsic systems should find ways to connect artificial, contrived reinforcement with the intrinsic value of behaving. We make extrinsic systems more intrinsic when we provide:

- Specific acknowledgment of behavior, along with directly connecting behavior to intrinsic benefits for that individual and others

- Opportunities for self-reflection about positive behavior choices

- Highly variable systems—mixing intrinsic feedback with extrinsic feedback

- More social reinforcers, opportunities, than tangible reinforcers (e.g., trinkets, food)

For classrooms that use a formal feedback system, in addition to operationalizing these practices, we recommend the following:

- If you want to have all students turn in their points for backup reinforcers all at the same time (e.g., turn them in on Wednesday afternoon), we recommend these practices, also:

  - Offer items of widely different values beginning with very low cost items so that all students can access backup reinforcement if they want.

  - Allow students to spend the amount they want and to save as they would like—this builds delayed gratification skills.

- If you can, allow students to spend points when they want to, or across several different designated turn-in opportunities. This allows students who have difficulty with waiting to obtain their backup reinforcement more quickly, while simultaneously allowing students who have the emotional ability to wait practice delay of gratification.

Other Forms of Feedback   Feedback beyond the system itself must continue to exist. Teachers report that sometimes, small, playful *noticings* are the most valued form of feedback. Some of the strategies we have collected for younger students are:

- Drawing a heart with your finger on the palm of a student's hand

- Using a wand and tapping a student gently on the head

- Dropping a small square of paper with a thumbs up drawing on the student's desk

- Using a finger to make an exclamation point on a student's back

For older students:

- Dropping a small square of paper with a thumbs-up or other positive icon on their desk

- Doing a fist bump with fireworks

- Simple smiles and nods

- Postcard sent home to student

Individual Formal Feedback Systems

Individual formal feedback systems such as behavior charts sometimes are considered synonymous with the term *behavior support plan*. We conceptualize behavior plans much more comprehensively, and we do not believe that behavior charts are a requirement of individualized plan design. However, they are a potential piece of the puzzle when it comes to supporting students with more complex needs, so we include them here.

When developing lower risk systems for individual students, our guidelines are the same as with class systems. By bearing in mind the three goals of any trauma-informed system, we are able to build a solid trauma-informed Individual Formal Feedback System as part of a student's behavior support plan. Again, those guidelines displayed in Figure 10.2 are:

- Build their confidence in his or her ability to be successful students with positive behaviors

- Enhance his or her relationship and connection with the adults in the school setting

- Support a positive sense of community with peers

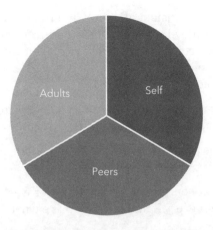

Figure 10.2. Relationships to consider when designing individual formal feedback systems.

Building Confidence: Emphasize Positives   Just as with a whole-class system, individual systems need to emphasize a student's positive behaviors. No one does better by feeling worse about who they are.

Building Confidence: Reinforce Successive Approximations   Some students need a radically different starting line in the life of the classroom and they need to have many mini-finish lines along the way to the ultimate finish line. We build their confidence by meeting them where they are and building success step-by-step. Sometimes this means that we need to task analyze a goal, sometimes it means that we need to pay careful attention to how we scaffold for success. We may need to solicit the eye of others—the student, their family members, and other educators—to identify strengths that we can then notice. Success begets success and starting small gets us in that positive upward spiral.

Building Confidence: Student Goal-Setting   Some students need to be directly involved in a formal, individualized contract process for their behavior to improve. They need to experience choices in the contract, and they need expectations laid out in a clear, predictable manner. Contracts should delineate expectations for students *and* staff and should provide a bonus for superior performance. Before the plan begins, there should be a plan for weaning the student off the plan. The tone of the contract discussion and implementation is critical—it needs to be upbeat, collaborative, and goal-focused. It also needs to engage the students and their supporters in discussion regarding intrinsic outcomes of student growth.

Building Confidence: Reinforcers   What is reinforcing for one student may be of little or no value to others. Having the student provide input into the reinforcers is essential.

    We are well advised on the topic of selecting what we use as reinforcers by L. Tobin (1991), who says:

> When working with discouraged children, I make two lists. One itemizes activities which they enjoy. I use this list for contingencies and rewards. The other shows what they value most in life, the things that make their day worthwhile. This list I *never* make contingent. (p. 47)

Using activity reinforcers rather than tangible ones is preferred because they not only may reinforce, they may also build connections. In addition, when developing a list of activity or opportunity reinforcers, consider allowing the student access to a treasured opportunity *non-contingently*, and then allowing the student access to an *additional* amount of that same activity through an established contingency. These two points of access should remain separate—and never withdraw the non-contingent access if the other is not earned. Some examples of this non-contingent with contingent pairing are:

- Ten minutes of non-contingent time on a computer for educational games, then 5 minutes more for every X number of points earned

- One day a week, be a peer buddy for a younger student, then add more peer buddy days for every X number of points earned

- Ten minutes of non-contingent library time per week, then 10 extra minutes library time with a classmate for every X number of points earned.

The unconditional opportunities communicate to students that their interests are valued and that they can be trusted to engage in certain activities. These opportunities also serve as a reinforcement sampling, so that students get a taste of what is possible when they strive to meet a behavioral goal or contract.

The schedule of when students have access to their backup reinforcement is just as critical as what that backup reinforcer is. Students with trauma histories typically require more frequent access to reinforcement including both access to the system's tokens and access to the backup reinforcer. Over time, we can build tolerance for waiting but that needs to occur incrementally and systematically.

Maintaining Connection With Adults

When we emphasize systems that are focused on delivering positives and when we keep an eye on the positive-negative ratio, we make it more likely that our presence is a present. We do not want the act of us approaching a student to become one that is associated with a problem. The one challenge to this is when we are trying to keep corrective feedback private, which often necessitates closer proximity. This may require that we consciously approach a student for both neutral reasons and positive reasons at a high frequency to serve as counterweight to when we must approach them for corrective reasons. We also need to make sure that we approach the student for many reasons other than to provide feedback through the behavior system.

Any time there is a formal feedback system for a student, we need to be verbally interacting with that student about a specific behavior instead of just, *You earned a point*. To move toward more intrinsic reinforcement, we should use Socratic language as much as possible so that the student is an engaged partner in reflecting on his or her behaviors. This type of reflection can be for both successes and struggles. We should use care to *not* say, *We are giving you points*. Instead, use language similar to, *Tell me why you think you earned these points during Math. I will give you my thoughts afterward* or *Tell me what you noticed about your self-control during recess. What tool did you use?* or *Check yourself. Are you following the expectations for in-seat work? What can you do to fix that?* The emphasis should be on the student's behavior rather than being intensely focused on the points.

Maintaining a Positive Community With Peers

Individual system feedback should respect the social and emotional needs of the student, which means that discretion is important. This discretion should be related to all elements of a comprehensive behavior plan but particularly with behavior charts. Most students are self-conscious about having a behavior chart so interactions related to it should be handled very carefully.

As students move into middle school, this is even more critical. We have observed students dashing out of class after having a very successful day just so that they were not seen having a behavior chart checked. For them, appearances were more important than any points and the associated rewards. Of course, ideally, feedback should be occurring throughout class time. Keeping feedback timely, quiet, specific, and quick is best when at all possible.

If there is a whole-class system, making bridges between it and the student's individual plan supports discretion and it also helps maintain teacher sanity. Juggling multiple systems, especially at the middle school level where students change classes is a big challenge. The goal is to always keep a system as simple as possible without losing its impact.

There are occasional situations where giving a peer a supporting role as a part of a plan may help a student to be more successful. When a student we know struggled with cursing when his stress increased, the student identified a peer who could help him see the downward spiral coming and cue him to pause and regulate. The key to this working was that the student both wanted peer help and he was the one who selected the peer supporter, who was a real friend.

If a fiddle object is an important component to a student's behavior plan (e.g., it is a replacement for more challenging behavior), consider protecting the student's status with peers by offering a basket or bin of fiddle objects for all students to access (see Chapter 8). One teacher we know also accessed the basket themselves, modeling the fiddle object use, and genuinely settling their own dysregulation.

MISCELLANEOUS BEHAVIOR STRATEGIES TO AVOID (AND WHAT TO DO INSTEAD)

Although the following strategies *might* be effective for a high percentage of students, they tend to create more issues with students with trauma histories. We recommend either not using them or proceeding with great care and attention to the effect they have on all students. It is important to be aware that often students with trauma histories are the canaries in the coal mines; they may react most drastically to some strategies, but other students may also be negatively affected while not being as demonstrative about it.

Heads Down and Quiet

As mentioned before, demanding students to put their heads down and be quiet has been used as a redirection method for a rambunctious group of students for a long time. We have found that the procedure tends not to be as effective for students with trauma because:

- Although the lights being turned off may help reduce stimuli, which could be calming, having them turned off in the context of someone being in trouble may trigger students.

- Being quiet may work for students who have positive things to think about, but it can overwhelm students who have many negative things to ponder. (Remember, quiet invites the monsters of trauma...)

- Sitting still does not burn off stress chemicals, so dysregulated students are not really settling or resting.

Instead, Try These

A movement-based or focus-based activity as a better alternative. For older students who may feel self-conscious with a movement activity, consider a simple focusing activity such as picking an object from a basket and thinking of five ways to describe it or by allowing them to pick a way to stretch at their desk. We can make these feel more procedural by framing them with time (*We will stretch for the next 30 seconds. And ready, go!*) or by using visual cues (a large picture card to indicate the activity or a countdown timer) or by having a short series of actions to do. Using these kinds of activities at natural breaks in instruction lets them not become something that occurs in response to the class or any individual getting out of control. Instead, it allows us to settle our students and settle ourselves in a more proactive and non-triggering manner. Remember that, if there is some resistance during early implementation, it will decrease as the practice becomes more familiar and routine.

Response Cost Systems

Systems in which students lose points, dollars, or tokens based on inappropriate behavior may seem logical on the surface. However, because negative behaviors tend to be more quickly and easily noticed by adults, the system is slanted toward noticing negativity, and a student's successful efforts can disappear in a moment. Such a system also is likely to cause a break in relationship between the student and the adult, *and* it harms motivation. The only condition in which motivation may be enhanced by failure is if the individual holds a very strong sense of agency and has the tools and experiences to bounce back from the failure. That does not describe many students of trauma nor other students who struggle behaviorally and, quite frankly, not many other children as they go through various developmental stages.

We have seen such systems operationalized where students not only end up back at zero—but move into owing points, dollars, or tokens. For students who struggle greatly with their behavior, having a bank account that is in the red—has a negative balance—is super defeating rather than motivating. As students move into negative numbers, the desire to show any positive behaviors is completely extinguished. To continue our bank analogy, they declare bankruptcy. Students who declare behavioral bankruptcy are going to find more accessible ways to feel okay, and rarely is that a good story for them, the involved adults, or their peers.

Instead, Try This

Try a system that recognizes positives via the system and handles the negatives outside the system with redirects and logical consequences. We have said this before but it cannot be emphasized enough, we do not need to use a student's standing in a data system to justify to them, to ourselves and to others that they need to be held accountable via a logical consequence. If a behavior is such that it requires a logical consequence, we simply implement the consequence, explaining it in a direct way to the student. The key, of course, is to make sure that it is a logical consequence and not simply a punishment.

Logical consequences are

- Directly related to the behavior of concern

- Designed to guide student in fixing his or her mistakes

- Designed to help a student take responsibility for his or her actions

- To prevent a behavior from occurring in the future because a new way has been learned

Punishment is:

- Not necessarily directly related to the behavior of concern

- Designed to have a student feel bad about his or her behavior—relies on shaming

- Meant to show a student who is in charge or in control and who has the most power

- Designed to stop a behavior from occurring in the future out of fear of the consequence that will follow (which may lead to more sophisticated hiding of the misbehavior)

Group Contingency With Response Cost

One of the worst things we can do to a struggling student is to have him or her be the cause of failure for the student's entire peer group. Group contingency systems, where the class as a whole, can lose a point based on the behavior of a single student, was based on the concept that peers would support or pressure each other to behave in a certain manner. On its face, this may seem to make sense—students are peer-centric, right? The simple truth is that many things that seemingly make sense of the surface fall apart completely upon closer examination.

Imagine, if you will, that you are a student who has high levels of stress or a student with pervasive trauma. Relationships are already hard. Feeling good about yourself is a daily battle. Being able to trust adults goes against much of your experience. Then, imagine that you impulsively call out in class and your call-out causes a strike or a lost point that prevents the entire class from getting the 5 minutes of social time they were anticipating at the end of the period. Stand in those shoes for a minute.

Once this has happened, will your peers exert a stronger influence on your future behavior or are you more likely to distance yourself from them and them from you? Will you find yourself more trusting or less trusting of the teacher who announced the lost point, which, in essence, is announcing how you ruined things for everyone?

Instead, Try This

Try a type of whole-class feedback system in which every student contributes to a reinforcer for the class as a whole—a collective positive system. This type of class system builds relationship among students through acknowledging positive effort. It is a collaborative effort toward a single goal. When we keep such a system cumulative without a specific end date, we maintain its positivity. Whether it is a pom-pom jar or earning the letters in *Ten Minutes Social Time,* it celebrates the efforts of all.

Many times, we have found ourselves recommending this type of classroom system instead of an individual behavior system for struggling students. This is a particularly good move if there are several students in the classroom who need extra feedback. Here is how it works. Catch your most difficult students doing the right thing at a high rate and use the whole-classroom reward (collective) system to acknowledge them. You give them high rates of concrete acknowledgment that helps them know the expectations you have for them and that builds their relationship with peers. The jar fills, the class celebrates.

This system does not have the inflation problem that happens when we use systems that give points to individuals which may result in high levels of points for our most challenging students (in order to encourage them) and lower levels for those students who behave all the time. Those kinds of systems do not feel right to many of the students who were able to behave well most of the time—setting up the possibility of resentment among peers.

The questions we hear most related to collective systems are, *What about the student who isn't contributing to the class system? How can that student misbehave and still get a reward?* Our response is twofold: reinforcer sampling and relationship-building.

Reinforcer sampling: When students who struggle get to experience the joy of an activity, it provides motivation toward that activity. In this case, they are more likely to contribute to the collective system if they get to enjoy the benefits of it. Think about a student who must sit out of a group activity because he or she did not earn enough points to participate. Can you hear the student's inner voice now? *I don't care, It's not that much fun anyway,* or *Only the nerds like that.* Contrast this with a student who gets to participate and who has a good time. The student's inner voice is going to be very different: *This is fun, I want to do it again,* or *I wonder whether we can get lots of pom-poms faster and do this again. I can make this break happen.* If we are in a cynical state of mind, we might imagine their inner voice saying *Ha-HA! I did nothin' but misbehave and here I am having a grand time!* Our response to that is . . .

Relationship-building: People bond through laughter, smiles, and shared experience. For those kids who "get a free ride to Funland" thanks to their classmates, they get to experience fun *with* others, something that probably is not a large part of their life experience. Research shows that we become better regulated/calmer when we laugh and smile. We become more attached to people and feel more accountable to others when we have shared experiences. When students are outcasts, they cast out others, and we lose our ability to influence them. When students are members of a community, they are more influenced by others, and their goodness has the opportunity to shine.

SUMMARY

As we have learned more about the origins of behavior at a neurological level, as we have more students with greater needs in our classes and as we shift our focus from quick fixes to lasting growth, we realize that it is essential to examine our previous practices with a new set of lenses. Sometimes, using those new lenses will be freeing—*I always felt that wasn't the right way to handle that situation!*—and sometimes it will be frustrating—*But that system has worked for me for a long time!* Those of you who have experienced getting a new pair of glasses know that when those new lenses cause a headache, you have to hang in there—it always takes a bit of time to adjust to a new prescription but then things become much clearer than before.

Remember that all of this is part of what builds the culture: The nest that is a trauma-informed approach to behavior. These strategies and practices are the twigs, strings, grass, and feathers that together form the nest that is a safe place for a children of trauma—a place in which they grow and from which they can take to the wing.

In our final chapter, we turn to you, the nest builders. How can you stay strong for this work?

Chapter 11

Educator Self-Care

Happy new school year! Summer is waning and we begin to make that mad dash to the first day of school, with every effort focused on what we will do for our students this new school year. We clean, cut, laminate, make lists, and revise those lists. We arrange the furniture that was pushed against the wall when our floors were waxed over the summer. We read, research, plan, organize, and prioritize, all while envisioning the students we will have—how will they fit in, feel inspired, and be comfortable in this new space? With me? If we know the students, we may wonder—how will they be this year? What changes can I expect?

We are not even officially back, but we are back.

In the opening days of the year, we meet as colleagues to collaborate, determine schedules, discuss students. There is never enough time during those precious hours before the students arrive. We sit in professional development sessions and our brains are already buzzing with thoughts as we try to incorporate new information.

And then, the student school year opens. We are optimistic. Everything feels fresh . . . those shiny floors, our organized materials . . . ahhhhh. We begin to attach to the students who are in our care. We lead with our hearts and want so much to make it all work for each and every student who is ours. We dip into our own pockets to fill in the empty spaces on the snack shelves, in the supply closets, and in the classroom library.

We have energy, stamina, and a clear vision. We arrive early and stay late. Daily, we pack tote bags or rolling briefcases with planning books, our laptop, professional reading, and paperwork. An evening on the couch awaits, during which we will pull out those materials and prepare for the next day and whatever it brings. The work lurks there as we attend to our home life and all that it might entail—making dinner, doing dishes, helping with kids' homework, starting a load of laundry, caring for an older parent, mowing the lawn. It starts out well enough—some evenings we may even carve out some time for a trip to the gym, a walk, or streaming a movie. It is early September, we just might be okay.

This chapter harkens back to quote from Jack Kornfield (1994) that we included in the opening pages of the book: "If your compassion does not include yourself, it is incomplete" (p. 28). Educators are notoriously bad at prioritizing themselves, and this is particularly true when the work is with children who have experienced trauma. Never forget that when we are supporting students with trauma histories, self-care is not selfish—it is essential. Before you can do anything else that is trauma-informed, you need to take reasonable care of yourself. In the nonstop action of schools, it is easy to lose track of that.

I began the year with a solid self-care solution in place, a sickness-prevention routine. It developed naturally over the summer. Wake early, drink a cup of coffee, do a mindful practice, and get outside for a brisk walk. It was my time, my self-care routine. It fit my work life and home life.

I was able to be faithful to it for the first few weeks, but meetings piled on and so did planning and grading. My morning turned into worktime; my evening was increasingly packed. By the end of September, I only walked two times a week. Coffee was never in jeopardy, but everything else was. A personal, digital health monitor would have loved how I counted being on my feet all day as weight-bearing, cardio workout.

By October's end, nothing strictly for myself could be wedged into my long school days. Weekends were for sleeping in and planning lessons. I sprinted to get through parent-teacher conferences and report cards. The fatigue was setting in, but the first break was still days of hard work away.

I just kept going and going, faster and faster, with more and more stuffed in. I felt like I was pedaling just to stay upright—much the way we ride two-wheel bikes—just keep moving and you stay balanced. No stopping or pausing or even slowing down. Just make it to Thanksgiving break—when I can really rest.

But as in years before, my immune system that had held me together until then crashed. The pause came too late and illness caught up with me.

Educators speak of holiday sickness but we always hope it misses us. All too often, an educator's body has a plan that is different from the one in our head. It seizes control, guaranteeing that we will rest, lay low, and be forced to renew. It comes in the form of a cold, the flu, a migraine, or utter exhaustion. We held it together for as long as we could, but there are limits to what our immune systems can do. So our body stepped up and shouted, *Enough! Time to take care of yourself!*

SELF-CARE DEFINED

What is self-care? Psychologist Raphailia Michael (2018) defines it as "any activity that we do deliberately in order to take care of our mental, emotional, and physical health" (para. 3). Self-care begins with creating a reasonable in-our-head-plan that cares for us proactively—well before our body-plan needs to jump in reactively. It means designating time and honoring it. We use the word *reasonable* deliberately because if we create a pie-in-the-sky plan, it is more likely to be completely abandoned than a practical one.

Self-care requires that we know which techniques are effective in coping with the inevitable stresses of our lives and which techniques do not work or are even counterproductive. This is another rip-tide moment where what we may do *by instinct*—or by the popular culture we absorb into our thinking—may be exactly the *wrong* thing to do.

WHY FOCUS ON SELF-CARE AND STRESS REDUCTION

Why is it so very important to find healthy ways to deal with our stress before it forms a storm of toxicity? In addition to a plethora of mental health issues, PennState Hershey at Milton S. Hershey Medical Center (n.d.) has aligned stress with the following physical health issues, and more:

Heart disease

Susceptibility to infections

Asthma

Gastrointestinal problems

Weight gain

Headaches

Sleep

Fertility

Higher rates of miscarriage

Aggravation of arthritis/joint pain

Aggravation of diabetes

Aggravation of skin disorders

If taking care of yourself is not motivation enough, remember that stress infects others. Your stress impacts the lives of the people with whom you work and people you love. In the school, your stress impacts how your students are able to function.

Certainly, being able to appropriately manage your own stress does not guarantee your students will function without issues, but it dramatically increases the chance that they will function better because you attended to self-care.

COMPONENTS OF SELF-CARE

To make a personal commitment to self-care, think about how you would answer this question: *What can I do for myself without fail?* Start small and expand from there.

Having a solid plan HELPS . . .:

Health: What one thing will you do that has a direct impact on your physical health?

Everyday Joy: What things will you commit to doing that bring you joy (an inner smile or an all-out laugh at least once per day)?

Loved Ones: What will you do to care for your personal relationships?

Pause: What will you routinely do that lets your mind and body rest and renew?

Sleep: What time will you go bed routinely, and how will you improve the quality of your sleep? (*Note*: Your brain will thank you.)

Figure 11.1 provides a format for such a plan. Although the plan you develop is personal (which is why it has a date line but not a name line), some people find that having an encouragement partner helps them stay on target. With self-care, it is up to you to do what fits you best—both the plan and who you do or do not share it with. The HELPS format is deliberately designed to create balance across many domains of self-care and is also intentionally simple. Keep it available as a reminder of your commitment to yourself.

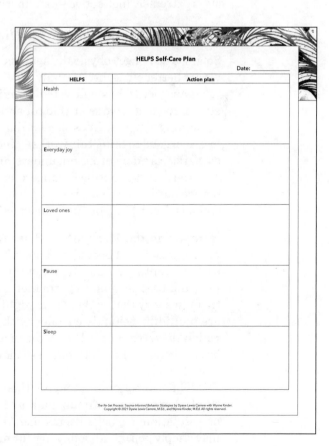

Figure 11.1 A guiding form for comprehensive self-care.

INEFFECTIVE METHODS FOR HANDLING STRESS

Catharsis: Hit Something, You Will Feel Better

In Chapter 6, when talking about students, we discussed the problems with pairing aggression, *any* aggression, with feelings of stress or frustration. Adults' brains and behavioral functioning is also compromised when we link aggression with emotion. Even if our aggression is targeted toward inanimate objects where it causes no outward harm, it is doing inward harm because it is teaching our brain to respond to our feelings by acting out aggressively.

Brad Bushman, Roy Baumeister, and Angela Stack (1999), in their studies of catharsis messages (i.e., vent or punch it out)—and aggression, identify three major findings:

1. Being exposed to catharsis messages makes it more likely that one will engage in an aggressive act in an effort to reduce stress.

2. A person who uses a catharsis approach is more likely to a continue to engage in personal aggression even *after* engaging in hitting an alternative target, such as a punching bag.

3. That elevated state of aggression was transferred to people other than the ones who had angered them in the first place.

In short, simply believing in a catharsis approach increases aggression. Using a catharsis approach makes us more aggressive instead of relieving our aggression, and it increases indiscriminate aggression instead of reducing it! Clearly, we need to get the message out that catharsis is extremely ineffective—for our students and for us.

Venting: Get It Off Your Chest, You Will Feel Better

So, if we do not get physically aggressive, and we instead verbally vent about our frustrations, we are better off, right? Actually, no!

Our society has cultivated a similar fallacy about the power of venting as a way to destress. You may have seen a blog or article titles online that reflect this cultural myth—perhaps something along the lines of *Why You Should Vent!* or *Vent and Relieve Your Stress*. Although it may feel good to *think* this works, science tells us this simply is *not* true; venting, like physical catharsis, is a dangerous misunderstanding.

Here is why venting is dangerous. When we vent, we may get a frustration out in the open, but we hardwire the aggravation into our brain and pull it into the core of our body. We also spread it like a toxin out into our social world.

Hardwiring the Thought   The more we practice a thought or collection of thoughts, the more hardwired it becomes. Remember the idea of mental muscle memory that we discussed earlier? Venting creates that mental muscle memory for negativity because venting is practice, and practice makes permanent. We are giving life to the negative thoughts, animating them in a way that makes them highly memorable. They are easily retrievable because they are multidimensional—encoded with rich and interesting words, with the social context in which they were shared, with the visual cues associated with them, and often accompanied by movement (our arms, our re-enactments, our facial expressions) in a highly memorable story format.

This collection of thoughts then becomes highly available and starts to shape how we think about certain stimuli, making it easier and easier for us to perceive a person, a setting, or a situation in a negative manner. Research also shows that once a thought is hardwired, it may simply pop up randomly in your mind without provocation—leading to an overall negative mindset (Stillman, 2016).

Damaging the Body   Negative thoughts also activate your body's protective response system. Your blood pressure rises and stress chemicals flood your brain, which prevents sophisticated cognitive thought. Your brain cues the release of stress chemicals into your body, potentially harming your immune system and affecting areas of health like weight, sleep, digestion, and more.

Infecting the Community   Venting also spreads negativity. Just as a smile is contagious, so is a negative attitude. When we vent, we infect others with our negative thoughts, changing how their brains and bodies are functioning. We either convert optimists or we drive them away by our venting and leave ourselves surrounded by others who are burdened with negative thoughts. We then add their stress to our own, driving us farther and farther away from our healthy center.

Practice the Pause

SELF-CARE IN ACTION CASE STUDY

Many times during the day we have seen self-care in action—whether observing teachers in the faculty room, administrators walking through a sea of middle school energy in a hallway, or school counselors leading a group of second-graders at the end of a busy week. Educators pause, notice what they themselves need, and take action—they stretch, lean, fold, and twist. They crack their knuckles, squeeze the knots out of their shoulders, circle their heads, reach up, bend back, fold all of the way forward—possibly pretending to tie a shoelace. They might then end with a sigh and a quiet moment.

And the first step in that process? The pause. They are able to notice what they need; they take a quick personal assessment. Then they silently move, led by what their bodies inspire them to do. Twisting the core of the body allows for a gentle wringing out of stress, both physical and emotional. So might pressing fingers or gently cracking knuckles. Allowing a full, eyes-closed, arms-stretched yawn re-sets the nervous system and cools the brain. Who knew? Their bodies did.

These are small, invaluable opportunities for creating positive outcomes for ourselves. We can directly teach, model, and encourage this kind of self-care by integrating mindful practices into our own busy days. Self-informed practices lie at the very foundation of trauma-informed ones. When educators get overwhelmed in the bustling energy of the classroom or in an interaction with students, they should call for a pause to create a personal moment, a chance to regulate, and provide the opportunity for the involved children as well.

A second-grade teacher in one of our local districts likes to say, "I need a moment," and then she walks over to the window. She stands tall, drops her shoulders, and does her own elevator breath (moving with breath). When students observe their teacher noticing what she needs and utilizing her own practice, students come to respect her need to settle, and at times will even ask, expressing care, "Ms. Waverly, do you need an elevator breath?"

Integrating and modeling self-care within our busy school days becomes a valuable classroom tool as well. Invite students into your elevator breath. Ring a gentle bell—we suggest a chime, real or digital—and listen for the sound to fade. Press play on a video that guides everyone to dance, stretch, wiggle, sing, balance, and then settle. Lead the group in your favorite energy-to-focus pair of activities. Allow yourself to fully engage. Give yourself over to the practice—confidence and authenticity will inspire your students to engage.

Because trauma-informed teaching requires educators to respond to their students carefully and thoughtfully rather than to react impulsively, the pause lies at the core of self-care success. Pause is something that should be built into your stressful workday—not just after you have left work. Pause is early intervening in your own care.

In our classrooms, in every reaction or response, our intuition, thinking, and behavior are directly affected by our own history, stress, and dysregulation. Mindfulness—paying attention on purpose, non-judgmentally and with compassion—and other contemplative practices train our attention, enhance our self-awareness, and increase resilience. Finding a mindful practice that will nurture you in your own life will fortify the responsive presence you need to create healthy interactions within the school day and beyond.

For so many, when mindfulness is mentioned as a practice, the picture that comes to mind is of complete stillness—a seated statue of silence. Few can imagine themselves or any child participating in this stance, let alone sustaining it as a repeated practice. Rest assured—neither can we. Instead, think simply, How do you clear your head? How do you release tension in your body? Think about small ways you accomplish those things. Now, think about a new strategy or two you could use. As you answer these two questions, you are beginning to build the pause of your self-care plan.

Build Self-Care Into the School Day

WYNNE'S SELF-CARE PRACTICE

My personal practice of paying attention and becoming more present (with compassion and without judgment) has long been combined with movement, in some form. I walk and hike. I do a flow version of yoga (in a chair or on the floor). I also dance in my kitchen. For me and many others I encounter, movement and mindfulness naturally enhance each other.

When I decided to leave my classroom and join other teachers to create a mindful program for schools, that program emerged (in 2001) where mindfulness and movement meet. People want, like, and need to move. We can encourage everyone to move, to create balance, to regulate, to energize, and to calm. Our teacher and classroom sessions are never motionless.

We tap, flap, glide, circle, open, close, twist, reach, fold, extend, cross, stand, sing, dance, drum, and balance. Then we sit, settle, discuss, listen, rest, and reflect. We begin with larger movements and move toward smaller movements. Our practices may vary as we find the ones that most engage, reach, and inspire our students and their teachers to feel safe enough to join in.

Remember that not only do you need to take care of yourself, but you also are a powerful model for the students in your care. We referenced this concept briefly early in the book, but we turn to it with more intention now. *Should the cabin pressure or air quality change during flight—masks will drop down from the ceiling. Place the mask over your own mouth and breathe calmly before trying to assist others with theirs.* For you as an educator, this sounds like, *Should the classroom/school pressure, volume, or energy get too high for your nervous system, take a moment to restore your sense of control, alertness, and care before trying to assist, guide, or teach your students or others.*

We educators must be reminded, supported, and encouraged to take the time we need, to build in the breaks that help us refresh and rejuvenate. When we do that, we offer the best of ourselves—as the compassionate professionals we are.

Proven supports are within our reach although sometimes we need to advocate for them. Well-crafted professional development can guide us to commit to our own wellness. Resources that are grounded in scientific research and years of experience bolsters our efforts to take care of ourselves. *We teach who we are*, and we need to hear and feel that often. The nervous systems that educators bring into the worlds of their students have far greater impact than we sometimes are willing to admit.

In addition to modeling that comes from us noticing and attending to our own regulation needs, most current social and emotional instructional programs encourage modeling regulation strategies to students. We should seize upon these moments to not only model but to fully engage ourselves in the opportunity. And, just as we remind our students, we should regulate early and often. It is best to not wait until you are gasping for air before putting that pause-mask over your mouth. And, remember that our students with trauma-histories increase our need for a pause. If we do not tune into it for ourselves, their challenging behavior will remind us of both their need and ours at a time that will be harder to focus on anything but their need.

What are the opportunities for regulation that *begin with your needs* that you can share with the students with whom you work? What are the opportunities that *begin with student needs* that you can join in as part of your self-care?

Know Your Limits

DYANE'S MENTOR'S WISDOM

I was a second-year teacher in a school where we served students who, for the most part, were returning to public education from youth incarceration or from long-term hospitalization. I found myself crying at the end of too many days, overwhelmed by the pain of these children, by all that they needed, by how inept I felt trying to meet those needs. My mentor found me one day and gave me a gift I have carried with me ever since. What was that gift?

He said something like this: The trick to being an effective teacher of students from difficult circumstances is wanting to be God . . . but knowing absolutely that you are not. Come in every day and do the work to the very best of your ability. Then, go home and really be home. Then, come back and really be back.

His words valued my moral imperatives but also connected me to my self-care responsibilities, and they have been a touchstone throughout my career.

Part of not getting to the point where our compassion overwhelms us is setting boundaries. This is particularly hard when we are aware that everyone around us is feeling overwhelmed by the same high level of need in the building. We do need to be team players, but we also must find a way to balance the needs of the team with our personal needs. Being honest is critical and, ultimately, more appreciated than half-hearted follow-through or continual cancellations.

Saying *no* is a very difficult thing for a caring person to say, but it is an essential skill for self-care. Now, if you find yourself saying no to just about everything, that is an indicator that you may be heading toward burnout. But, if you just need to set *some* boundaries of how much you take on, you will want to find language to say no in a way that is comfortable for you, and which fits your personality and style. Here are some ways to think about establishing and communicating your boundaries:

Plan your allocation of time: *I am honored that you want me to sit on that committee, but right now I cannot take on one more after-school commitment. Please feel free to ask me again next year if you need someone then.*

Know the amount of emotional space you have: *I just can't take on mentoring another student this year. I have the time, but I don't have the emotional space for doing that. If there is something less intense that I can do to help support our mentoring efforts, I would be happy to do that. Perhaps I can help organize the end-of-year event.*

Agree, with limits: *I would be happy to do this for the current marking period but then I will need to tap out.*

Offer to try something out but do not make an unconditional promise: *I'm not sure if I have the energy to be fully committed to that, but if you're okay with it, I will try it for a few weeks. Please just know that I will reassess at that point, and I can't promise I will continue.*

Be honest about your skills: *I just don't feel that is an area of strength for me, and I can't promise that I can get myself up to speed on it right now with other things I am juggling.*

It may feel uncomfortable to say we cannot do something, or to say that we cannot do something well. When you feel that feeling, consider the words of Brené Brown (2010): "Imperfections are not inadequacies; they are reminders that we're all in this together" (p. 61). This work of supporting children with trauma histories must be a collective effort.

How do you allocate your time? Do you make sure that you consider not only your personal, role-specific demands, but also the demands of the wider group (e.g., grade-level teams, committees) and spontaneous demands (e.g., a colleague asking for help)? How do you say no to requests? How do you say yes? How do you make those decisions?

Recognize Signs of Compassion Fatigue

You might walk into the faculty room, lunch in hand, ready to join the chatty group at the big table, like you so often do. Join the energy, the familiar stories, the connection. While heating up your leftovers, you observe the first-year teacher on his own at the side table. He has laid out the pieces of his well-wrapped lunch, but he pauses–possibly considering dessert first–looking a little dazed, unable to choose, reluctant to commit. The microwave beeps and it's your turn to choose–boisterous crowd or lone freshman? After first imagining that he wants his alone time, a quick memory of your first year flashes through your mind, so you head to his table.

His reporting of constant struggles, sense of overwhelm, and lack of hope in being able to get it right all resonate. "I hear you" you say. You feel that you should stop there. Being present, listening, and holding back on advice feels right.

Then he opens the door, that door for you to step through and share your wisdom, "What helped you? How did you get through? What was different back then?" he asks.

Your typical professional responses might have included references to the hurdles that all new teachers have to jump or the harsh learning curve of the first three years. You might have offered the consolation that, if he cares enough about the kids, he'll find his way. You might have been inclined to remind him to make the most of mentors and instructional guidelines.

But instead, you pivot to asking him questions, slowly and listening carefully to his responses. Are you making sure you refresh on weekends? Do you have healthy strategies for handling the stress? How do you de-stress over the course of the school day? Do you have a go-to person in school?

You question and then listen, holding your advice to yourself. You know your questions provide the guidance he needs. You glance at your watch. As always, lunch is over in a flash. "Thanks for joining me," he says.

You smile. "My pleasure, really," you say, and then you begin the long walk back to your classroom, the questions you asked him swirling in your head, awaiting your answers.

Sometimes we know exactly what we need to do to take care of ourselves, but we push it away. We give advice but do not heed it ourselves. We tell ourselves we will do better tomorrow or next week or the next month after. After . . . after . . . after. . . .

We need to find ways to not push off self-care, to not dismiss its importance. Just like our immune system gives out, so can our heart. Compassion fatigue is a thing. We got into this work to care for others, and the minute we think about our own needs, we feel a sense of guilt and quickly do an about-face and tune into their needs. We need to remember that if we do this continually, we *will* burn out.

Dare to be self-aware. Dare to take that pause. Dare to be authentic in front of your students and your fellow educators. We are not suggesting that you fall apart in front of a group of sixth-graders or sob at a faculty meeting. Those are perhaps authentic, but they are things that happen when we have allowed ourselves to push off self-care for far too long. We are talking about saying to a colleague, *I really can't process that right now. Let me get back to you tomorrow morning after I have regrouped,* or *I appreciate your consultation and value your input, but I don't understand that particular strategy. Can you show me what you mean?* or *I need a moment, kiddos. Let's all take some breaths and exhale slowly a few times.*

On your low days, ask for help early. Do not wait to do this until you feel like you have one nerve left and the people around you are jumping on it. Notice that your energy is low, your focus is wandering, or your body is tense. Engage in a pause, maybe several. And if you find yourself still feeling those things, ask for help.

When we ask early enough, that help does not require schedule changes or huge commitments by others. If you are a teacher, it might just be asking a partner teacher to have your class join their community-building meeting so you can have 15 minutes to regain yourself, to make a phone call to handle something that is causing stress, or to take a couple of laps around the building. If you are a school counselor, it may be having your lunch group first eat lunch in the cafeteria and then meet with you for 10 minutes rather than being with you the whole lunch period. If you are an administrator, it may be closing your door and being available only in the case of a crisis for a short period of time.

Dragging yourself into work may mean your body shows up, but it also is a pretty good indicator that your heart will not. Students will notice, and students with trauma histories will become dysregulated with you. Of course, there are days that we all must push ourselves to find the energy to face the challenges of the day or to leave behind our home life. We are not talking about that push-over-the-hump feeling that subsides once we arrive and begin to engage; we are talking about knowing in your bones you are not okay. One way we know this is that short pauses and even longer ones are not sufficient. We then need to recognize that we may need more time and more help. We may need a day; we may need to access a counselor or other support service.

What does burnout look like for you? Resentment, tears, emotional shut-down? Now, mentally back up to before that burnout point. What are your indicators that you need a bit of support? Who are your supporters? What can you ask of them?

Believe in Your Efforts

Self-care also includes being aware that what you do makes a difference in this world. This may be one of the most challenging self-care reflections for educators who support children with trauma histories. You sow the seeds, you water the soil, but you rarely are there to see more than just the first signs of greening on the landscape of these children's lives. The delay in seeing results is the very nature of this work. We all need affirmation to continue to do hard work. Where might we find it in this trauma-informed work we are doing?

See the Little Things Finding joy in small emotional progress provides sustaining energy. Notice those tiny steps, even if it requires putting a microscope on the behavior. Does this student now look at you when you greet him or her, even if he or she does not yet answer? Does this student now have other students ask him or her to be a partner when children are directed to turn and talk? Does this student now call out in class on-topic rather than off-topic? Does this student walk down the hall with more open, present body language?

Sometimes we need another person's perspective to see these changes. That is a support that we can provide to our colleagues and that they can provide to us. When a student smiled when told, despite the late start, that the class would have their time with the school counselor, that teacher shared that with the school counselor, who would not have known it otherwise. Shine a light on these moments. There is a bonus effect to this progress-sharing. Just as venting can release a toxin into the school community, sharing successes releases hope and positivity . . . for the educators and the students.

Keep a Success File Keep notes and print emails that remind you of the value of your work and the successes you have had. Ours include notes from colleagues, families, and administrators. There are a lot of items from students—drawings, photos they gave us, examples of student work that represented real growth after a long journey. Maintain that file in the drawer you can most easily access and pull it out after a hard day or week.

Be Aware of the Research Research that came from the Kauai Longitudinal Study and confirmed by many other longitudinal studies that followed gives us reason for great optimism. Werner's Kauai study (Werner & Smith, 1992) found that one out of three children who had a significantly stressful childhood were doing well by young adulthood, and that the majority of the remaining two-thirds of the children were doing well by the age of 40. This success was attributed to a constellation of factors, including supportive relationships with teachers, a sense of autonomy, inner direction, and reasoning ability. We matter and what we teach matters. A meta-analysis of more than 200 studies found that participation in evidence-based social-emotional learning resulted in gains in social skills, behavior, attitudes, and also in academic achievement (Durlak, Weissberg, Dymnicki, Taylor, & Schellinger, 2011). Who we are in relationship to children with trauma histories and what we do during our time with them makes a difference—and it is borne out in study after study.

Join With Others in the Work Trauma requires us as supporters to be collaborative and steadfast in our approaches. These students do best when how we support them across the school and across the years is cohesive and intentional. When our efforts are organized and comprehensive, they have a synergistic impact.

How will you look for those small signs of impact? What are the success stories that carry you through the tough times? What research do you need to share that is related to the importance and impact of this work? Who are your potential partners in supporting your work?

SELF-CARE AS A COMMUNITY VALUE

As you transform yourself, also consider how you can influence the transformation of the staff in your building toward being a community-care environment. When self-care occurs in the context of community care, where colleagues look out for one another and where systems and structures provide necessary supports, it is enriched and multiplied. An example of community care is: Schoolwide self-care breaks (think about scheduled announcements, such as a self-regulation activity scheduled after the pledge) which expands the opportunity for the whole community to pause and regulate. Sharing links to educator-friendly apps, buddy systems for frequent check-ins, book study groups, and brief practices during faculty meetings also are examples of community-care.

Research supports this move toward educator self-care and community care. Kamenetz (2016) reports on a study of the Cultivating Awareness and Resilience in Education (CARE) program, which found that when teachers were involved in a self-care program throughout the school year, not only did they report feeling better and less judgmental, but their classrooms were rated more positively and students were more engaged. In addition, the most vulnerable students in these classes showed an appreciable difference in their reading scores (Kamenetz, 2016).

CLOSING THOUGHT

Your work with children with trauma histories reminds us of a piece of literature, *The Man Who Planted Trees*. Author Jean Giono (1985) writes the story of a man who plants the seeds of trees in a desolate valley over many years. Toward the end of the book, the narrator returns to the valley and witnesses the fruits of this man's labor.

Creation seemed to come about in a sort of chain reaction. He did not worry about it; he was determinedly pursuing his task in all its simplicity; but as we went back toward the village, I saw water flowing in brooks that had been dry since the memory of man.

—Jean Giono (1985, p. 21)

Because you are an educator who chooses to nurture children with trauma histories and you *determinedly pursue your task*, the landscapes of these children's lives *will* change. They may change well after the timeframe of your shared experiences, but because those children had you and your colleagues in their lives, they will change. Knowing this in your depths is part of affirming your worth and should encourage you to take care of the valuable resource that is uniquely you.

Appendix A
Team Collaboration Survey

When seeking to increase predictability among adults, some educators find that this survey enhances authentic dialogue about the team's functioning. This survey could be used with any team whose goal is to support successful student behavior.

Team Collaboration Survey
Reflect on how you and those you work with on your team function when seeking to support students with challenging behaviors, using this scale: 1 = rarely, 2 = sometimes, 3 = frequently

_____ I understand the goals/expectations regarding the work we are doing.

_____ We have been provided both with information and resources to support the expectations of this work.

_____ I have opportunities to ask questions in a way that I am comfortable.

_____ My ideas are listened to by my colleagues.

_____ I feel that we can disagree with each other in a respectful way.

_____ I believe that we tackle difficult topics as well as easier ones.

_____ I see data related to the work we are doing and have an opportunity to discuss it with my colleagues.

_____ I participate in the group's conversations about our work.

_____ I believe that we share roles and responsibilities in order to get the work done.

_____ I believe that we set deadlines for the work that requires them.

_____ I believe that we are clear about who is responsible for what tasks.

_____ I support decisions, even if I don't personally agree with them.

_____ Others support the team decisions, even if they don't personally agree with them.

_____ I share our successes with my colleagues.

_____ As a group, we celebrate our successes together.

_____ I believe that we are student-focused and involve students as appropriate.

_____ I see evidence that our group values self-care in balance with responsibility.

Appendix B
Seating Positions

Seating Positions on the Floor

Long sit: Legs stretched out in front, back supported against wall or other firm surface, arms balancing on side or in lap

Side sit: Legs bent or folded to one side, leaning on one arm

Squat: Legs squatting, with arms wrapped around knees for stability

Pretzel: Legs folded in pretzel position

Half mountain: One leg stretched out in front, one leg bent at the knee, arms either wrapped around bent knee for stability or palms placed on the floor

Full mountain: Both legs bent at the knee, arms either wrapped around knees for stability or palms on the floor

Kneel 1: Sitting on heels (kneeling with seat resting on lower legs and heels)

Kneel 2: Standing on knees (kneeling on shins, legs and body straight up from knees)

Stand: Student standing

Lean and read or Lean and listen: Standing and leaning on hands with elbows locked, hands on table or another surface

Seating Positions in a Chair

Half kneel/Half stand: Chair turned backward and supported against a table or other surface, kneeling on one knee, standing with the other leg

Pretzel in a chair: Seated forward in chair with legs pulled up or folded underneath in a pretzel position

Wrapped feet: Seated forward in chair with feet wrapped around legs of chair or desk

Backward sit: Seated backward in chair with chair supported against a surface, arms resting on chair back

Appendix C

Spotlight Strategies: Simple Ways to Create Predictability

This exercise is a personal reflection opportunity to support your thinking about strategies that create predictability in the classroom. What do you have in place? What might you want to consider in the future? What can you address immediately? The exercise also might generate conversation across teams (grade-level or schoolwide) and/or help select valuable practices across classrooms.

Strategies to enhance predictability	I do!	Maybe?	To do!
Teach all procedures in the first weeks of school			
Employ a student ambassador to orient students who move into the school partway through the year (provide supporting materials for the ambassador).			
Use assigned seats, names on desks and/or tables as appropriate.			
Establish locations for homework and other materials.			
Post signs that indicate the number of people allowed per center/area.			
Use charts that indicate center tasks (order of task and/or persons in group).			
Define communal property clearly.			
Create a "Who is here?" chart to identify adults who are working in a room.			
Designate and maintain bulletin boards for selected purposes; post information about key routines so that students know where to look for specific kinds of information.			
Provide classroom calendars; send calendars out weekly or monthly.			
Post visual schedules.			

Strategies to enhance predictability	I do!	Maybe?	To do!
Use a visual that alerts students in advance to significant changes happening that day.			
Use chore charts.			
Provide countdown timers and auditory cues for student reference during transitions.			
Make sand timers available for certain activities.			
Designate a home spot on carpet for students who need consistency.			
Assign cubbies/lockers and have defined procedures for accessing them.			
Post signs that define certain procedures (e.g., morning routine: hang up coat and backpack, put homework into bin, find seat on carpet).			
Provide "While I am away" cards in your folder for substitute teachers for students who need extra support.			
Identify time frames for work before having students begin (e.g., "We will work for the next 15 minutes on _____.").			
Share a syllabus that has specific dates and/or time frames.			
Give long-term project plans, with suggested time frames for segments of the project; check in with students at key points in the timeline.			
Preestablish work groups and the tasks and/or roles within those work groups.			
Establish a format for binders; provide a set of guidelines and conduct periodic reorganizing checks.			
Support anticipation (e.g., "Tomorrow we will be going to assembly. What do you think might be different about our day because of that?").			

Appendix D

Spotlight Strategies: Simple Ways to Protect Emotional Safety

This exercise is a personal reflection opportunity to support your thinking about strategies that protect emotional safety in the classroom. What do you have in place? What might you want to consider in the future? What can you address immediately? The exercise also might generate conversation across teams (grade-level or schoolwide) and/or help select valuable practices across classrooms.

Strategies to protect emotional safety	I do!	Maybe?	To do!
Use natural light or soft sources of light, when possible; dim artificial lights and cover overhead fluorescent lights with fabric.			
Reduce visual clutter (e.g., reduce items on walls, shelves, and floor, and/or cover materials that currently are not being used).			
Establish and use cue colors to help visually organize specific kinds of materials (e.g., all vocabulary supports are backed with green paper, all math supports are backed with purple).			
Provide quiet areas away from noisier areas and create a place where students may retreat if they are overstimulated.			
Provide headphones and earplugs.			
Offer designated office space (separate space is designated by a board or screen) or a study carrel.			
Bring in nature, such as plants or fish.			
Use white noise/quiet nature sounds.			

Strategies to protect emotional safety	I do!	Maybe?	To do!
Engage students in keeping the classroom orderly and clean.			
Stay attuned to meeting basic needs of water, food and access to bathrooms.			
Allow student to pick a home spot (i.e., a place that is his or hers for specific instructional purposes).			
Allow for a variety of seating options.			
Allow student to identify a safe spot (e.g., a place—may be outside the classroom—that the student agrees to go to when feeling overwhelmed that is known to all educators who work with that student).			
Support a student in completing a safety map.			
Treat mistakes as learning opportunities.			
Model not knowing and accessing resources for help.			
Hold high expectations *and* understand pressing needs.			
Build community throughout the year, paying special attention to times when new students join the class.			

Strategies to protect emotional safety	I do!	Maybe?	To do!
Physically adjust your body to your students' levels (i.e., conveys that you are listening).			
Allow for comfort items and provide procedures for using them.			
Have a comfort pet in the class or school.			
Make a treasure box.			
Allow for passes and repeats (i.e., student can elect to not answer a question).			
Create a conflict resolution process and teach it to all students; use it only when there is a balance in power between students (use other processes for conflicts where power is disproportionate).			
Reflect on the importance of respecting diversity among students.			
Use help flip signs.			
Conduct check-ins with students or establish secret signal that student can give to request a check-in.			
Avoid total quiet; tune in to senses instead.			

Appendix E

Spotlight Strategies: Simple Ways for Nurturing Adult-to-Student Relationships

This exercise is a personal reflection opportunity to support your thinking about strategies that nurture adult-to-student relationships in the classroom. What do you have in place? What might you want to consider in the future? What can you address immediately? The exercise also might generate conversation across teams (grade-level or schoolwide) and/or help select valuable practices across classrooms.

Strategies to nurture adult-to-student relationships	I do!	Maybe?	To do!
Greet students—at the beginning of day, beginning of class.			
Use student's name in a positive manner.			
Smile and be tuned in to own facial expressions.			
Use appropriate touch (e.g., high-five, handshake, hug).			
Know the whole child; communicate that knowledge in natural ways.			
Collaborate with student to find solutions to challenges.			
Avoid making assumptions, investigate gently.			
Ask with kindness. Model social graces such as please, thank you, and excuse me.			
Respond to problem behavior in a firm, friendly manner.			
Be empathetic; listen, then listen some more.			

Strategies to nurture adult-to-student relationships	I do!	Maybe?	To do!
Create advisory groups in which students work with one adult over several years.			
Value and address individual needs (e.g., provide support for organizing notebook; provide a treasure box, snack, or comfort items/clothing).			
Schedule periodic, individual check-ins.			
Conduct community-building activities throughout the year.			
Physically adjust yourself to your students' levels (conveys that you are listening).			
Journal back and forth with students.			
Write mini-notes of encouragement and affirmation.			
Share appropriate information about yourself through pictures in your classroom; share your interests as appropriate.			
Notice students unconditionally (e.g., "So happy to see you here!").			
Use nonverbal ways of connecting (e.g., nodding, winking, thumbs up).			
Attach a *We missed you!* or *Class isn't the same without you* note to any papers a student must complete after an absence.			
Send an email or note to a student who moves away (e.g., use the new school's system or a family address).			

Appendix F

Spotlight Strategies: Simple Ways for Nurturing Student-to-Student Relationships

This exercise is a personal reflection opportunity to support your thinking about strategies that nurture student-to-student relationships in the classroom. What do you have in place? What might you want to consider in the future? What can you address immediately? The exercise also might generate conversation across teams (grade-level or schoolwide) and/or help select valuable practices across classrooms.

Strategies to nurture student to student relationships	I do!	Maybe?	To do!
Do *Get to Know You* activities at the beginning of each year and routinely throughout the school year.			
Pre-teach and practice cooperative learning skills before students engage in activities that use cooperative structures for academic purposes (i.e., fun activities that require interdependence); provide the opportunity to reflect upon the skills that were used.			
Use cooperative structures with caution and monitor for inclusiveness; adjust as necessary.			
Create a classroom search document—a reference chart that lists some areas of specialty and who has that knowledge; be sure that all students are represented.			
Rotate students in a supportive peer role (everyone gets a chance and a break).			
Allow students to be of service to one another through class jobs, the cooperative approach, "ask three before me," and through assigning organizational buddies who use checklists to help each other.			

Strategies to nurture student to student relationships	I do!	Maybe?	To do!
Use competition with caution. Lean toward competition that progresses the group toward an endpoint rather than against each other; use the concept of increasing personal best, whether as a class or as individuals.			
If setting goals for class (e.g., percentage of students who turn in homework), avoid targeting a percentage that may set up the most vulnerable students to be the ones who might be considered to have ruined it for the rest.			
Use language that values students.			
Correct students who engage in problematic behavior privately.			
Use peer interviews for reviewing content, then have class share their findings.			
Give students high-value tasks (e.g., opportunity to decide how long to work on a task, opportunity to choose odds or evens for homework, opportunity to hand out snack).			
Find common points and unique features among students and celebrate them on bulletin boards by creating a variety of charts (e.g., bar graphs, pie charts, webs).			
Engage in sharing activities with caution. Allow students to use their imagination when sharing rather than using actual items (see Appendix G: "I have in my hand" activity for details).			
Provide a farewell packet for students who are moving away.			

Appendix G
Cooperative Learning Structures

The following cooperative learning structures facilitate brief interactions among students, which is socially less challenging in the early stages of building relationships.

Inside-Outside Circle Format

Purposes

To gather information in a low-threat manner.

To guide students through exchanging ideas or information with a variety of partners.

To structure serve-and-return exchanges between students.

Preparation

Identify a topic that has several related logical questions.

Implementation

1. Divide class into halves.
2. Send one half to an area in the class to form a circle. This circle should be made by having the members face out.
3. Send the second half to find a partner who is standing in the circle and stand facing that partner.
4. Ask a question and delineate who should answer first (the student inside the circle or the student outside the circle). Have both students answer the same question.
5. Rotate circles by calling for either the outside or the inside to rotate a certain number of people to their left or right (e.g., *Inside circle, rotate left two people. Greet your new partner and be ready for your question.*) Pose a question (same or a new one) and have the new partners talk.
6. Continue switching until all the questions have been posed. (*Note*: Switch the rotating method to keep in interesting.)

Slide the Line Interview Format

Purposes

To create conversations between students through a quick exchanges of ideas—perhaps in preparation for independent work, such as a writing piece.

To guide students through exchanging ideas or information with a variety of partners.

To structure serve-and-return exchanges between students.

Preparation

Decide on a set of questions on a topic that ask for opinions, and for which there is likely to be a continuum of opinions.

Implementation

1. State the question and the far endpoint opinions related to the question. Ask students to move to take a place in the line that reflects their opinion on the matter.

2. Divide the line into halves and create partners by sliding one half to face the other half—so the endpoint people are lined up with the very middle people.

3. Have students talk for 2 minutes with each other about their opinion. Structure this exchange, if you wish. Have one line "slide" to create new partners.

4. Ask another related question, and repeat the process.

5. Do for four or five related questions, so students will have exchanged ideas with four or five peers before beginning their independent work.

Melt-n-Freeze Partners

Purposes

To create conversations between students (through a quick exchanges of ideas) perhaps as a review of a lesson or unit. It also could be used to generate ideas for writing or to gather background knowledge of the group before beginning a unit.

To guide students through exchanging ideas or information with a variety of partners.

To structure serve-and-return exchanges between students.

Preparation

Option 1: Decide on a set of questions on a topic that you will pose verbally. It is best if the questions have more than one correct answer. If the questions also could generate a bit more conversation than the answer, that would be a bonus. I like to have the question visually displayed, along with asking it verbally.

Option 2: Give students a set of questions cards. It is best if the questions have more than one correct answer. If the questions also could generate a bit more conversation than the answer, that would be a bonus. This option may be better for many students, in that it provides a visual they carry with them.

Process

1. State the question, then ring a bell or call out, *Melt*. Reference either a large visual version of the question or the students' question cards.

2. Students begin to move around the room until you ring the bell again or call out, *Freeze*.

3. Students turn to someone near them and give their answer to the question, and then listen to their partner's answer. If your grouping is an odd number of students, allow for pairs *or* triads, or join in freeze and melting yourself.

4. When the bell rings or *Melt* is called, students begin to move around again until you ring the bell or call *Freeze* again. You can re-pose the question or ask a new one or move students to the next one on their card, if using cards. Students respond to the question, taking turns.

5. Repeat, as you wish. It is nice to have at least four partnerings.

6. Conclude by gathering the group together and asking for the responses they heard to the questions. To make it emotionally safer, remind students that they are just to share what they heard; they do not need to identify a partner who shared the response.

Group Sharing Alternative

Children's imaginations and desires are big, but for some children, their opportunities are small. As an alternative to show-and-tell activities that can leave some children feeling less-than, or which can court students into creating a story—which sometimes is called out as a lie—try this *I Have in My Hand* activity. It is a simple strategy that can help build positive relationships among students rather than setting up competition.

I Have in My Hand Activity   In this activity, you instruct students that the point of this sharing activity is to use their imaginations. Give them a general topic, such as animals, places, or toys, or a ticket to go to _____. Coach students to not always go for the biggest imaginary thing, but to choose a creative one—modeling this is a good idea. As students go around the circle, have them hold out their hand, palm open to the ceiling, and share, beginning with, *I have in my hand . . .*, and then add their imagination. *A pony with a braided mane! A rare leopard that is so black, you can barely see its spots! A crab that is so little, it is smaller than my pinky fingernail! A puppy that already knows how to shake paws! A ticket to fly anywhere in the world!* Encourage peers to imagine with them, to look at the item, and imagine seeing it and reacting to it—*oooo* at the pony, big eyes at the leopard, squint to see the crab, *awwww* at the puppy. Allow for repeats and passes.

Next, pull a designated number of names from a name jar and have those children hold their invisible object up and say again what they have in their hand—repeating what they said earlier. Then, have them ask, *Any comments or questions?* to structure sharing more about their item. Typically, we recommend three comments or questions.

For older students, consider categories that may tie in with the content being taught, such as, *I will help save the planet using . . . an endangered species animal*, or *a mineral*, or _____ *from the Revolutionary War*, or _____ *from the Amazon Basin.* You also can provide older students with silly options, such as *a sundae with . . .* , or *a pair of shoes that can . . .* , or *a newly discovered dinosaur that has a . . . .*

Appendix H
Modulation Exercises

We can provide opportunities for students to practice modulation in a playful way that helps them feel the concept of smoothly moving from one intensity to another. These activities provide those experiences; some are appropriate both for group and individual practice, and others appropriate for either group or individual work.

Shaded Coloring

1. Give students a crayon and a 2 inch–wide strip of paper (this is a great use for scrap paper).
2. Model and then direct students to color in a tight, continuous zig-zag in the middle of the strip.
3. Model light pressure coloring, medium pressure coloring, and hard pressure coloring.
4. Have students practice these three different coloring pressures.
5. Next, randomly call out different pressures: light, medium, or hard. Students zig-zag at that pressure until a different pressure is called out.
6. Connect this concept with social skills or other touch-related skills. (For example, when you touch someone's shoulder to get their attention, use a medium touch. When we are doing high-fives, use a light touch. When we are rolling clay out to make snakes for our bowls, you will want to use a harder touch. If it is too hard and you are flattening your snake, use a medium touch.)

Reverse Bowling

This requires space in a hallway, in PE class, or on playground.

It is called Reverse Bowling because the point is to touch the pins but not knock them out of place.

1. Arrange large plastic bowling pins or milk cartons or some other set of pins that similarly could be knocked over or moved out of place.
2. Mark several lines in increasing distance from the pins.
3. Using a plastic ball, have students begin at the line farthest from the pins and try to roll the ball so that it touches the pins but moves as few as possible (hence the name, reverse).
4. After a few rolls from the most distant line, students should step to the next closer line and see if they can roll it to touch but not move or knock over the pins. As they move closer, they need to use a lighter and lighter and slower and slower roll of the ball.
5. Connect this concept with social skills or other movement-related skills. The language of "slow your roll" connects nicely with this.

Modulated Exercise Sequence

Pick an exercise from the Re-Set steps list, such as arm circles. Guide students through variations, changing size, speed, and direction (e.g., large circles fast, large circles slow, large circles becoming smaller and smaller until the only thing circling is your pointer-finger making tiny, tiny circles; now, really big slow circles again, now big circles going backward).

Make a Monster/Face

1. Break students into small groups of 4–5 students.
2. Have each group sit fairly close to each other in a circle or line.

3. Tell them that, together, they will be making a picture of something. Each one of them will get a crayon, marker, or pencil.

4. Hand a piece of paper to the first student and then call out a part of the monster or face that the student is to draw. It is more fun if you start with something unusual. (e.g., instead of saying *Draw the shape of the head,* try something such as, *Draw the nose.*) Give the student just a few seconds, and then call out *Pass.*

5. The student passes the paper to the next student in line, who is given another part of the face or monster to draw, also in a few seconds. The process continues through the line or circle of students.

6. When the drawing reaches the end of the line, it can pass back in reverse with the same quick call-and-draw process. If the kids are in a circle, it can just continue around the circle.

7. When sufficient parts have been called out, each group shares their picture with the other groups. You may post them in the classroom, if you wish, because they tend to evoke smiles and remind students of their connections with classmates.

Zoom (very popular with middle school students as well as elementary)

Zoom is a circle game that encourages laughter. It also fosters communication skills (eye contact, listening, and turn-taking). Zoom also can be used to practice modulation in speed, as it does in this version.

1. One person begins by saying *Zoom* and turning their head quickly toward the person seated next to them. The person on that side meets their eyes and then passes the *Zoom* to the next person until everyone has passed the *Zoom* around the circle.

2. Next, introduce the concept of slow-motion zoom. In this zoom, the zoom is to a three count. Practice this around the circle.

3. Next, confirm that the speed typically used is regular speed. Practice that again.

4. Finally, introduce the idea of warp speed—the zoom is passed as quickly as possible. Practice this around the circle.

5. The adult then calls different speeds and students pass the zoom at the called speed until a new speed is called.

6. You may want to introduce an *Eek.* When a person says *Eek,* the direction of the zoom changes. Every person in the group should have only one *Eek.* We call this an *on your honor* rule . . . everyone should do their best to only use one *Eek.*

Zoom also can be used to teach modulation of voice levels, as in the example that follows.

Voice Level Activity

Voice Level 0: Voices are off.

Voice Level 1: Voice can be heard at elbow distance. (Visual: hold your fists together at center of chest and extend elbows out to the side—this is elbow distance.)

Voice Level 2: Voice can be heard at arm distance. (Visual: Stretch out arms straight.)

Voice Level 3: Voice can be heard across the room. (Visual: Point to the wall of the classroom.)

Voice Level 4: Outside/cheer voice. (Visual: *Raise the roof* motion, which indicates that it can be heard beyond the walls of the classroom.)

For voice levels, the teacher is the caller—he or she calls out the voice level, and the group must adjust their voice to that level as they say *Zoom* (just as the teacher called speeds of Zoom in the earlier version). Hold off on *Eeks* as the group learns to modulate. After a while, adding in the *Eek* creates a new challenge because it must also be at the correct voice level. Even though there are five levels presented (0-4), some adults may wish to have students practice only Levels 0–3, because Level 4 is an outside/cheer voice.

Appendix I

Behavior Management Systems: Risk Assessment

When we examine a formal feedback system to see whether it is likely to support students with trauma, we use the concept of *level of risk*. Higher risk means that the system has a greater chance of *not* working for the students who have intense behavioral concerns—although it may work for many of their peers, who have lower levels of behavior concerns. Lower risk means that the system is more likely to work for the students with intense behavioral concerns *and* the rest of the class. This tool is designed to help educators assess systems in terms of risk.

Risk is higher   **Risk is lower**

$\longleftarrow$ ————————————————————————— $\longrightarrow$

Negative behaviors addressed publicly   Negative behaviors addressed privately

$\longleftarrow$ ————————————————————————— $\longrightarrow$

System displays student progress,   System displays student progress
so comparison is easy   privately/comparison is difficult

$\longleftarrow$ ————————————————————————— $\longrightarrow$

System is focused on consequences for   System is focused on reinforcing
negative behaviors   positive behaviors

$\longleftarrow$ ————————————————————————— $\longrightarrow$

Single cut-point/make goal or don't; there is   Cumulative tokens or continuum
a set number (#) of tokens in set time   of backup reinforcers

Appendix J
Ticket and Pocket System

This is a behavior management system that is lower-risk and offers an alternative to many higher-risk systems. It provides immediate feedback through a ticket or pretend dollar which can be collected and turned in for "back-up reinforcers" (actual items or opportunities that the student desires from an offered assortment). It is appropriate for elementary-level classrooms.

What It Is

Students earn tickets or pretend dollars for a variety of appropriate behaviors (e.g., getting materials out promptly, helping a peer, completing a task, using manners, getting in line as soon as called). Tickets or dollars should be given out frequently but intermittently.

Materials

Pocket chart with student names; fake dollars or tickets; backup reinforcer book that defines reinforcers and associated prices.

Target Group

Can be done with any elementary age group. The language that is used and the backup reinforcers will need to change to make it age-appropriate. The whole class, groups of students, or individuals may be reinforced for performing well.

Process

1. Hang the pocket chart, develop the list of reinforcers and costs in a book (or two), print the dollars or tickets. Be sure to have a wide range of prices for the various backup reinforcers so that children who currently need more immediate reinforcement can access those, and students who can delay gratification can wait and save for more expensive items or opportunities. Backup reinforcers should be focused on opportunities over tangibles. Engaging students in the development of the reinforcer list should be considered.

2. Explain the system to the students—how they are to handle dollars when they receive them, how and when to turn them in.

3. Distribute dollars or tickets randomly, but with specific feedback about behaviors.

4. Students place dollars into their assigned pocket and then, at designated times, turn some or all in for the desired backup reinforcer and save any unused dollars. Students also may choose to not spend at a given designated time, and instead save for future exchanges.

Examples of Backup Reinforcer

Note: Not all are age-appropriate for all groups.

Change seat with another student

Homework pass

Snuggle buddy (stuffed toy)

Honor seat

Rolly chair

Shoes off while in class

Teaching assistant for 30 minutes

Lunch with teacher

First in lunch line

First in class line

Trinket

Use a colored pen

Use special art materials

Chew gum

Wear a hat

Wear slippers while in class

Tech time

Sit with a buddy

Special note home

Call home

Mystery motivator (e.g., can be a random draw from items written on slips of papers or, if you want to use technology, consider creating a page of QR codes [quick response codes] that can be scanned to reveal a surprise item)

Grab bag

Crown or tiara

Sound effects person for a story

One of the most fun ones we have seen for younger children is call Trade a Name. Students get to pick a name tag that is a super-hero, movie character, person being discussed in learning content, a tongue twister, or another source of interest from an assortment of name tags provided by the teacher. For a determined amount of time (often simply the next school day), the student wears the name tag and is called by that name, so the teacher might say, *Superman, what answer did you get for number 4?* or *Nefertiti, could you get us started with our line?* or *PeterPiperPickedaPeckofPickledPeppers, could you tell us the name of this shape?* This is not only a joy for the student who has the novel name, it brings a bit more joy to the entire classroom.

Appendix K

Playing Card Reinforcement System: Delivering Specific Positive Feedback to Students

This is a behavior management system that is lower-risk and offers an alternative to many higher-risk systems that are used in classrooms today.

What It Is

This system is designed to make it easy for the classroom teacher or support personnel—consultants, paraprofessionals—to provide specific positive feedback and reinforcement for appropriate behaviors in whole-classroom or small-group contexts.

Materials

Three or four decks of playing cards, initialed on back or with unique back designs (to prevent infiltration of non-teacher cards, which could happen with older students).

Target Group

Can be done with elementary or middle school students. The language that is used and the backup reinforcers will need to change to make it age-appropriate.

Process

1. As students are engaging in appropriate behavior—social, emotional, or academic—drop a card on their work surface or hand a card to them—depending on context—accompanied by specific, brief, positive feedback. Examples are: *You came right to group. You kept working until you got it. That was kind to help Jose with the door. You used your words to express your feelings—excellent! Thank you for that thoughtful contribution. You got out your materials, awesome! You are really staying focused. You kept persisting until you figured that out. You were in your seat on time. Excellent answer! You have your eyes on me, your body is quiet. Thank you for raising your hand. You followed my directions promptly.*

2. Periodically, take the cards that you have left in your deck and split them, showing a card. Then ask one of the following questions, depending on your intention/situation/number of cards you have given out to students: *Anyone have a _____ of _____ (number and suit)? Show me.* Or, *Anyone have a _____ (number or suit)? Show me.* Or, *Anyone have a black card? Show me.* Or, *Anyone have a face card? Show me.*

3. After you assess how many students have that card, you can determine the backup reinforcer you will offer. If there are multiple students, pick a reinforcer that is appropriate for multiples; if single, pick one that is good for an individual. The key is to *not* announce the backup reinforcer until you see how many matching cards are out there. Ideas for reinforcement for these two scenarios (multiples and single) follow.

4. Then, you can either leave those cards out in circulation or collect all cards and begin again. Cards can be collected and reinforcers provided in the way that best fits the classroom and your student population. Some teachers collect after each segment of the class or after each class in middle school, and others run a longer time frame. In terms of reinforcers, using a combination of scheduled deck splits—the end of the designated time period—and intermittent or surprise ones keeps interest and engagement higher. This is one of those systems that can be

used intermittently or with greater and lesser intensity based on your assessment of what your students need on a particular day.

Really Making It Work

The key to this system is that you are handing out many cards but doing so intermittently. You do not have to pick one or two behaviors that you are looking for; rather, you are reinforcing a wide array of behaviors that lead to student focus and learning. This allows you to individualize in the whole-class system because you can look for different behaviors in different students. It allows the student who behaves all the time and the student who behaves on a more inconsistent basis to both be noticed for their positive efforts. It sends the message that we are all in this together.

It also is important that you don't just make it rain cards without the specific feedback, and that you pause to access backup reinforcements frequently, even if it is just for the people with the matching cards to take a bow or get to do something at the smart board, for example. Make it fun, build a community, connect with your students through the system, because that is what will bring it to life and what will make it the most effective. Don't forget to acknowledge the fact that cards are out there, even if there were not a lot of matches; be sure to acknowledge that the cards represent classroom success.

Getting Started

Several teachers have shared that it is easier to teach this system to students by using it first in small-group contexts, and then expanding it to other instructional structures. Others have jumped right into whole-group use with it (after teaching how it works and the procedures for handling the cards; for example, *They stay on the right-hand corner of your desk until we check for matches*).

Small-Group Options

Do not hesitate to use cards during small-group time that are collected at the end of that group time. This can be a great strategy when students are working with paraprofessionals or adult volunteers as part of a center rotation. Matching and reinforcement is done *only* within the context of that small group, so it could include things like getting to pick who reads first, what practice materials are used, and other specific, small group–relevant reinforcers.

System Limits

Because this system is designed to be very easy and as natural as possible, it does not have any documentation component, so there is no data generated by the system itself. To judge its effectiveness, other measures would need to be used. The focus of this system is to get a great deal of specific, positive feedback out into the classroom and thereby increase students' appropriate behavior and engagement. Time-on-task measures, disruption counts, progress in instruction all are ways to assess the effectiveness of this system (if you have taken a baseline prior to implementation).

Examples of Backup Reinforcers

Note: Not all are appropriate for all ages.

Multiple Students Have Designated Card

A matching group of students can:

- Stand up and say *Yee-haw!* and swing a pretend rope—or another vocalization or movement that you designate and that your students would love. You can add a phrase to the *Yee-haw,* something relevant to your goal (e.g., *We are learning amazing stuff today!*).

- Dance around their chairs for 30 seconds.
- Earn a minute to chill for the whole class based on the number of matching cards in the entire group (e.g., two matching equals 2 minutes).
- Leave the classroom first when classes change.
- Line up first for recess.
- Play an academic game.
- Work on the computers.
- Go to lunch first.
- Play air guitar during transition music.
- Get special writing materials.
- Pick materials (e.g., ball, rope) first for recess.
- Receive a Doing Great! slip to take home (you will have to explain this system to your families of course!).

Individual Student Has a Designated Card

The individual may:
- Pick the next activity.
- Line up first at the next transition.
- Pick odds or evens in math problems.
- Choose how long the group will read.
- Get to pass or be first (their choice) in the next activity.
- Write with a special pencil or paper.
- Pass out materials.
- Get to stop a minute early and chill.
- Be timekeeper.
- Move to a seat of honor until the next card is pulled.
- Add a picture to a *happy* bulletin board.
- Receive a little treat.
- Pick background music for work time.
- Get to do a special task (e.g., run an errand, feed the class pet, be the sound effects guy).
- Wear a crown or another fun accessory until the next card is pulled or for the remainder of the school day.
- Get to pull a slip of paper with reinforcer written on it from a bin or fishbowl (or scan a bar code that designates the reinforcer to be received).

Other Variations on the Theme

Individual System

- Can use only with an individual or can use in tandem with the whole-class system and simply interact with the individual by using their cards in a special way.
- Works across multiple teachers who work as a team or who simply have the same student.

1. Give out cards to students based on their targeted individual behavior, being sure to do so with specific, positive feedback.

2. Process follows the same split-and-check system—at the schedule (time and frequency) that works best for that individual student.

3. Before starting the system, create a star card or chart that has a series of stars. Intermittently, include stars of different colors—each color represents a different set of back-up reinforcers. Each time you do a split and check and there is a match, a star is crossed off and the student may pick a back-up reinforcer from the associated set of reinforcers.

4. To build delay, some stars may be steps along the way and not be directly linked to a reinforcer—for example, purple stars are along the way stars and get a student closer to the blue star that is linked to a reinforcer.

5. Just as with the whole-class system, the adult can make matches more or less likely depending on the type of match (exact, suit, color, number) that is called. Knowing the student's unique needs and current situation is key to the adult being able to adapt this system to meet those needs.

To add more interest, the colored star cards could be covered with a sticky note and revealed when they are reached, *or* all the stars could be covered by sticky notes and the mystery is even greater—*When will a card come up? What color will it be?* By being playful with it, the actual process of revealing may become reinforcing. Because students may be able to memorize star charts, the adult may want to have several versions laminated and ready to go. Again, whenever there is not a match and a star is not crossed off, it is important to acknowledge the success demonstrated by the acquisition of the cards and to celebrate that.

Classwide Use With Star Chart

When using this as a whole-class system and pulling cards for matching for a wide assortment of reinforcement opportunities as previously presented, you also can pull cards for a match to progress on a classroom star chart.

The teacher can announce, *This is for our star chart, does anyone have the four of hearts?* Or, *This is for our classroom star chart, do we have at least five diamonds out there?* The same star chart as was described in the individual star chart could be used. Some teachers have found that covering all of the stars makes the anticipation even more fun.

References

Ackerman, C. (2019, December 7). Learned helplessness: Seligman's theory of depression (+ cure). *Positive Psychology*. Retrieved from https://positivepsychologyprogram.com/learned-helplessness-seligman-theory-depression-cure/

American Federation of Teachers. (2015–2016). Seeding change in school discipline: The move from zero tolerance to support. *American Educator, 39*(4).

Barnett, W. (1995). Long-term effects of early childhood programs on cognitive and school outcomes. *The Future of Children, 5*(3), 25–50. doi:10.2307/1602366.

Benson, K. (2017, October 4). *The magic relationship ratio, according to science.* The Gottman Institute. Retrieved from https://www.gottman.com/blog/the-magic-relationship-ratio-according-science/

Blow, C. (2015). *Fire shut up in my bones.* Boston, MA: Mariner Books.

Brendtro, L., Brokenleg, M., & Van Bockern, S. (2009). *Reclaiming youth at risk: Our hope for the future, revised.* Bloomington, IN: Solution Tree.

Bronson, P., & Merryman, A. (2009). *NurtureShock: New thinking about children.* New York, NY: Twelve, Hachette Book Group.

Brous, K. (2014, April 11). *Perry: Rhythm regulates the brain* [Web log post]. Attachment Disorder Healing. Retrieved from https://attachmentdisorderhealing.com/developmental-trauma-3/

Brown, B. (2010). *The gifts of imperfection: Let go of who you think you're supposed to be and embrace who you are.* Center City, MN: Hazelden Publishing.

Brown, B. (2012). *Daring greatly: How the courage to be vulnerable transforms the way we live, love, parent, and lead.* New York, NY: Avery Publishing.

Burke Harris, N. (2015). *How childhood trauma affects health across a lifetime* [Video]. TEDMED. Retrieved from https://www.tedmed.com/talks/show?id=293066

Bushman, B. J., Baumeister, R. F., & Stack, A. D. (1999). Catharsis, aggression, and persuasive influence: Self-fulfilling or self-defeating prophecies? *Journal of Personality and Social Psychology, 76*(3), 367–376. doi:10.1037//0022-3514.76.3.367

Calhoun, J. (2007). *Hope matters: The untold story of how faith works in America.* Savage, MD: Bartleby Press.

Center for Responsive Schools. (2019). *Responsive classroom.* Retrieved from https://www.responsiveclassroom.org/

Charney, R. S. (1992). *Teaching children to care: Management in the responsive classroom.* Turner Falls, MA: Center for Responsive Schools.

Clifford, A. M., & Garn, S. (2015). Center for Restorative Process. Retrieved from http://www.centerforrestorativeprocess.com/

Conley, R. (2017, January 8). *How to give feedback that builds trust in a relationship* [Web log post]. Leading with Trust. Retrieved from https://leadingwithtrust.com/2017/01/08/how-to-give-feedback-that-builds-trust-in-a-relationship/

Danielson, C. (2007). *Enhancing professional practice: A handbook for teaching.* Alexandria, VA: ASCD.

Denton, P. (2013). *The power of our words: Teacher language that helps children learn* (2nd ed.). Turners Falls, MA: Center for Responsive Schools.

Derhally, L. (2016, March 23). How (and why) to create emotional safety for our kids. On Parenting. *The Washington Post.* Retrieved from https://www.washingtonpost.com/news/parenting/wp/2016/03/23/how-and-why-to-create-emotional-safety-for-our-kids/?noredirect=on&utm_term=.da90a9c34b4d

DeWitt, P. (2016, October 19). Relationships: The yin to feedback's yang. *Education Week.* Retrieved from https://blogs.edweek.org/edweek/finding_common_ground/2016/10/relationships_the_yin_to_feedbacks_yang.html

Durlak, J. A., Weissberg, R. P., Dymnicki, A. B., Taylor, R. D., & Schellinger, K. (2011). The impact of enhancing students' social and emotional learning: A meta-analysis of school-based universal interventions. *Child Development, 82*, 405–432.

Dyer, W. W. (2005). *The power of intention.* Carlsbad, CA: Hay House Inc.

Evers, T. (2016). Using positive behavioral interventions and supports (PBIS) to help schools become more trauma-sensitive. Wisconsin Department of Public Instruction. Retrieved from https://dpi.wi.gov/sspw/mental-health/trauma/pbis

Felitti, V. J., Anda, R. F., Nordenberg, D., Williamson, D. F., Spitz, A. M., Edwards, V., . . . Marks, J. S. (1998, May 1). Relationship of childhood abuse and household dysfunction to many of the leading causes of death in adults: The Adverse Childhood Experiences (ACE) study. *American Journal of Preventive Medicine, 14*(4), 245–258. doi:10.1016/S0749-3797(98)00017-8

Fixsen, D. L., Naoom, S. F., Blase, K. A., Friedman, R. M., & Wallace, F. (2005). *Implementation research: A synthesis of the literature*. Tampa, FL: University of South Florida, Louis de la Parte Florida Mental Health Institute, National Implementation Research Network.

Flora, S. R. (2000). Praise's magic reinforcement ratio: Five to one gets the job done. *The Behavior Analyst Today, 1*(4), 64–69. doi:10.1037/h0099898

Fontani, G., Migliorini, S., Benocci, R., Facchini, A., Casini, M., & Corradeschi, F. (2007). Effect of mental imagery on the development of skilled motor actions. *Perceptual and Motor Skills*. 105(3 Pt 1), 803–826. doi:10.2466/pms.105.3.803-826

Fredrickson, B. L., & Losada, M. F. (2005, October). Positive affect and the complex dynamics of human flourishing. *American Psychologist, 60*(7), 678–686.

Garbarino, J. (1999). *Lost boys: Why our sons turn violent and how we can save them*. New York, NY: The Free Press.

Gay, R. (2017). *Hunger: A memoir of (my) body*. New York, NY: Harper.

Ginott, H. (1972). *Between teacher and child: A book for parents and teachers*. New York, NY: Avon Books.

Ginsburg, K. R., & Kinsman, S. B. (Eds.). (2014). *Reaching teens: Strength-based communication strategies to build resilience and support healthy adolescent development*. Itasca, IL: American Academy of Pediatrics.

Giono, J. (1985). *The man who planted trees: A story by Jean Giono*. White River Junction, VT: Chelsea Green Publishing Company.

Goleman, D. (2005). *Emotional intelligence: Why it can matter more than IQ*. New York, NY: Bantam Books.

GoNoodle, Inc. (2019, August 12). GoNoodle. Retrieved from https://www.gonoodle.com/

Golden, A. (1999). *Memoirs of a geisha: A novel*. New York, NY: Vintage Books.

Greenberg, M. T., Domitrovich, C. E., Graczyk, P. A., & Zins, J. E. (2005). *The Study of Implementation in School-Based Preventive Interventions: Theory, Research and Practice*. Rockville, MD: U.S. Department of Health and Human Services.

Greene, R. (2008). *Lost at school: Why our kids with behavioral challenges are falling through the cracks and how we can help them*. New York, NY: Scribner.

Hall, S. (2009, April 9). CU study: Poverty can physically impair brain, reducing children's ability to learn. *Cornell Chronicle*. Retrieved from http://news.cornell.edu/stories/2009/04/poverty-changes-brain-reduces-childrens-learning

Harrell, S. K. (n.d.) S. K. Harrell Webpage. Retrieved from https://www.kelleyharrell.com/

Hock, M. F., Schumaker, J. B., & Deshler, D. D. (2003). *Possible selves: Nurturing student motivation*. Lawrence, KS: Edge Enterprises.

Horner, R. (2011). Positive Behavior Intervention and Supports. Session presented at the meeting of Pennsylvania Implementers' Forum, Hershey, PA.

Horner, R. (2015). Refining PBIS. Session presented at the meeting of Pennsylvania Implementers' Forum Hershey, PA.

Jensen, E. (n.d.). The perfect music for brain-based learning [Web log post]. Retrieved from http://www.jensenlearning.com/news/the-perfect-music-for-brain-based-learning/brain-based-learning

Johnson, D. W., Johnson, R. T., & Holubec, E. J. (2008). *Cooperation in the classroom* (Rev. ed.). Minneapolis, MN: Interaction Book Company.

Kamenetz, A. (2016, August 19). When teachers take a breath, students can bloom. NPREd: How Learning Happens. Retrieved from https://www.npr.org/sections/ed/2016/08/19/488866975/when-teachers-take-a-breath-students-can-bloom

Kooman, M., & Dimond, C. (2011). Lost in the waves [Recorded by Kooman + Dimond]. On *Out of our heads* [Audio]. Retrieved from https://koomandimond.wordpress.com/2011/08/14/lyrics-lost-in-the-waves/

Kornfield, J. (1994). *Buddha's little instruction book*. New York, NY: Bantam Books.

Lisitsa, E. (2013, April 26). *The four horsemen: The antidotes* [Web log post]. Retrieved from https://www.gottman.com/blog/the-four-horsemen-the-antidotes/

Lupien, S. J., McEwen, B. S., Gunnar, M. R., & Heim, C. (2009). Effects of stress throughout the lifespan on the brain, behaviour and cognition. *Nature Reviews Neuroscience, 10*(6), 434–445. doi:10.1038/nrn2639

Marano, H. E. (2003, June 20). Our brain's negative bias: Why our brains are more highly attuned to negative news. *Psychology Today*. Retrieved from https://www.psychologytoday.com/us/articles/200306/our-brains-negative-bias

Maslow, A. H. (1943). A theory of human motivation. *Psychological Review, 50*(4), 370–396. doi:10.1037/h0054346

Mcclelland, M. M., Ponitz, C. E., Messersmith, E. E., & Tominey, S. L. (2010). *The handbook of life-span development* (Vol. 1). Hoboken, NJ: John Wiley & Sons.

Metro-Goldwyn-Mayer. (Producer). (1939). *The wizard of Oz*. Hollywood, CA: Metro-Goldwyn-Mayer.

Michael, R. (2018, July 8). What self-care is—and what it isn't. [Web log post]. Retrieved from https://psychcentral.com/blog/what-self-care-is-and-what-it-isnt-2/

National Child Traumatic Stress Network. (n.d.) *Bullying effects*. Retrieved February 12, 2019, from https://www.nctsn.org/what-is-child-trauma/trauma-types/bullying/effects

National Sleep Foundation. (n.d.). *Napping*. Retrieved from https://www.sleepfoundation.org/articles/napping

National Sleep Foundation. (n.d.). *Trauma and sleep*. Retrieved from https://www.sleepfoundation.org/articles/trauma-and-sleep

National Technical Assistance Center on Positive Behavioral Interventions and Supports (PBIS). (2019). Positive Behavioral Interventions & Supports. Retrieved from http://www.pbis.org

O'Brien, J., Pearpoint, J. C., & Kahn, L. D. (2015). *The PATH and maps handbook*. Toronto, Canada: Inclusion Press.

O'Neil, J. (2004, November 16). Vital signs: Reactions: Your posture, a telltale fright sign. *The New York Times*, p. F6.

O'Neill, R. E., Horner, R. H., Albin, R. W., Storey, K., & Sprague, J. R. (1996). *Functional assessment and program development for problem behavior: A practical handbook* (2nd ed.). Belmont, CA: Wadsworth Publishing.

Oyserman, D., Bybee, D., Terry, K., & Hart-Johnson, T. (2004, April). Possible selves as roadmaps. *Journal of Research in Personality, 38*(2), 130–149. doi:10.1016/S0092-6566(03)00057-6

Palmer, P. (1997). *The courage to teach: Exploring the inner landscape of a teacher's life*. Hoboken, NJ: John Wiley & Sons.

Peck, M. S. (2003). *The road less traveled, timeless edition: A new psychology of love, traditional values and spiritual growth*. New York, NY: Touchstone.

Penn, A. (1993). *The kissing hand*. Washington, DC: Child Welfare League of America.

Perry, B. (2005). Maltreatment and the developing child: How early childhood experience shapes child and culture. In the Inaugural Margaret McCain lecture, *McCain lecture series*. Lecture conducted at The Centre for Children and Families in the Justice System, London, ON. Retrieved from https://childtrauma.org/wp-content/uploads/2013/11/McCainLecture_Perry.pdf

Perry, B. (2014, April 23). *Early childhood brain development* [Video]. Lecture presented at the Columbus Metropolitan Club, Columbus, OH. Retrieved from https://www.youtube.com/watch?v=DXdBFFph2QQ&list=PlxILd8__iAa506h_fLKZwLVbKykZu_neV&index=2

Perry, B. D. (2018). Regulate-relate-reason. Retrieved from https://www.bdperry.com/post/regulate-relate-reason

Perry, B. D. (2019). *Sequential Organization of the Brain from Neurosequential Model of Therapeutics Phase I Certification Materials*. Houston, TX: The Neurosequential Network.

Perry, B., & Szalavitz, M. (2006). *The boy who was raised as a dog*. New York, NY: Basic Books.

Purvis, K. B., Cross, D. R., & Lyons Sunshine, W. (2007). *The connected child*. New York, NY: McGraw-Hill Education.

Responsive Classroom. (n.d.) *Responsive classroom and PBIS: Can schools use them together?* [Pamphlet]. Turner's Falls, MA: Center for Responsive Classrooms, Inc. Retrieved from http://bit.ly/rcwhitepaper3

Rogers, F. (2003). *The world according to Mister Rogers: Important things to remember*. New York, NY: Hachette Books.

Rosanbalm, K. D., & Murray, D. W. (2017). *Caregiver co-regulation across development: A practice brief* (OPRE Brief #2017-80). Washington, DC: Office of Planning, Research, and Evaluation, Administration for Children and Families, US. Department of Health and Human Services.

Rosenthal, R., & Jacobson, L. (1968). *Pygmalion in the classroom: Teacher expectation and pupils' intellectual development*. New York, NY: Holt, Rinehart and Winston.

Seita, J. R., & Brendtro, L. K. (2005). *Kids who outwit adults*. Bloomington, IN: Solution Tree.

Sesame Street (2012). Common and Colbie Caillat – "Belly Breathe" with Elmo. Retrieved from https://www.youtube.com/watch?v=_mZbzDOpylA

Sesame Street (2020). Learn to Belly Breathe with Rosita – #CaringForEachOther. Retrieved from https://www.youtube.com/watch?v=Xq3DwzX6MUw

Shanker, S. (2016). *Self-reg: How to help your child (and you) break the stress cycle and successfully engage with life*. London, England: Penguin Press.

Siegel, D. J. (2012). *The developing mind: How relationships and the brain interact to shape who we are* (2nd ed.). New York, NY: The Guildford Press

Skiba, R., & Peterson, R. (2000). School discipline at a crossroads: From zero tolerance to early response. *Exceptional Children, 66*(3), 335–346.

Steele, D. (2017, June 15). *What great teachers know about kids* [Web log post]. Steele Thoughts. Retrieved from http://www.steelethoughts.com/2017/06/what-great-teachers-know-about-kids.html

Stevenson, R. L. (2013). *Robert Louis Stevenson's admiral guinea: Don't judge each day by the harvest you reap but by the seeds that you plant*. Exton, England: RHE Media Limited.

Stillman, J. (2016, February 29). *Complaining is terrible for you, according to science*. Inc. Retrieved from https://www.inc.com/jessica-stillman/complaining-rewires-your-brain-for-negativity-science-says.html

Stolorow, R. D. (2012, September 10). Never again!: A dramatic vignette shows how trauma alters our experience of time [Web log post]. *Psychology Today*. Retrieved from https://www.psychologytoday.com/us/blog/feeling-relating-existing/201209/never-again

Stosny, S. (2011, October 28). *Self-regulation: To feel better, focus on what is most important* [Web log post]. Psychology Today. Retrieved from https://www.psychologytoday.com/us/blog/anger-in-the-age-entitlement/201110/self-regulation

Stress: In-depth report. (n.d.). PennState Hershey, Milton S. Hershey Medical Center. Retrieved from http://pennstatehershey.adam.com/content.aspx?productId=10&pid=10&gid=000031

Student, Family, and Community Support. (n.d.). *What are restorative practices?* San Francisco United School District. Retrieved from https://www.healthiersf.org/RestorativePractices/WhatIsRP/

Substance Abuse and Mental Health Services Administration (SAMHSA). (2017). Understanding child trauma. Retrieved from https://www.samhsa.gov/child-trauma/understanding-child-trauma

Supin, J. (2016, November). The long shadow: Bruce Perry on the lingering effects of childhood trauma. *The Sun Magazine, 491*. Retrieved from https://www.thesunmagazine.org/issues/491/the-long-shadow

Suttie, J. (2018, May 22). How putting yourself in someone else's shoes may backfire. *Greater Good Magazine*. Retrieved from https://greatergood.berkeley.edu/article/item/how_putting_yourself_in_someone_elses_shoes_may_backfire

Sylwester, R. (1995). *A celebration of neurons: An educator's guide to the human brain*. Alexandria, VA: ASCD.

Tamietto, M., Castelli, L., Vighetti, S., Perozzo, P., Geminiani G., Weiskrantz L., & de Gelder, B. (2009). Unseen facial and bodily expressions trigger fast emotional reactions. *Proceedings of the National Academy of the Sciences of the United States of America (PNAS), 106*(42), 17661–17666. doi:10.1073/pnas.0908994106

theRSAorg. (2013, December 10). Brené Brown on empathy [Video]. Retrieved from www.youtube.com/watch?v=1Evwgu369Jw

Tobin, L. (1991). *What do you do with a child like this? Inside the lives of troubled children*. Duluth, MN: Whole Person Associates.

University of California, San Francisco. (2018, March 7). Birth of new neurons in the human hippocampus ends in childhood: Adult 'neurogenesis,' observed in other species, appears not to occur in humans. *ScienceDaily*. Retrieved from https://www.sciencedaily.com/releases/2018/03/180307141356.htm

van der Kolk, B. (2014). *The body keeps the score: Brain, mind, and body in the healing of trauma*. New York, NY: Penguin Group.

Vedantam, S. (2018, September 21). *Radio replay: Eyes wide open* [Audio podcast]. NPR. Retrieved from https://www.npr.org/2018/09/20/650114225/radio-replay-eyes-wide-open

Werner, E. E., & Smith, R. S. (1992). *Overcoming the odds: High risk children from birth to adulthood*. New York, NY: Cornell University Press.

Williams, K., & Lewin, S. (2014, December 10). Early childhood self-regulation through music [Web log post]. The Early Childhood Researcher. Retrieved from https://theearlychildhoodresearcher.wordpress.com/2014/12/10/early-childhood-self-regulation-through-music/

Wlodkowski, R. (2008). *Enhancing adult motivation to learn: A comprehensive guide for teaching adults* (3rd ed.). San Francisco, CA: Jossey-Bass.

Yun, K., Watanabe, K., & Shimojo, S. (2012). Interpersonal body and neural synchronization as a marker of implicit social interaction. *Scientific Reports, 2*(1). doi:10.1038/srep00959

Zenger, J., & Folkman, J. (2013, March 15). The ideal praise-to-criticism ratio. *Harvard Business Review*. Retrieved from https://hbr.org/2013/03/the-ideal-praise-to-criticism

Index

Note: Tables and figures are indicated by *f* and *t*, respectively.